RACING LIFE OF LORD GEORGE CAVENDISH BENTINCK, AND OTHER REMINISCENCES

RACING LIFE OF LORD GEORGE CAVENDISH BENTINCK, AND OTHER REMINISCENCES

John Kent

A General Books LLC Publication.

CONTENTS

1

SECTION 1

RACING LIFE
   LOED GEOEGE CAVENDISH BENTINCK.
   CHAPTER I.
Bikth, Parentage, And Early Years.

Lord William George Frederick Cavendish Bentinck, more generally known as Lord George Bentinck, was born on the 27th of February 1802, and was the third son of the fourth Duke of Portland, and of his wife Henrietta, the eldest daughter and coheiress of General John Scott, of Balcomie, in Fife, who had three daughters, distinguished from each other as " the rich Miss Scott," " the witty Miss Scott," and "the pretty Miss Scott." The f rich Miss Scott" married the Marquis of Titchfield, afterwards fourth Duke of Portland ; the " witty Miss Scott" married the Right Honourable George Canning, M.P. ; and the " pretty MissScott" married the Honourable F. Stewart, afterwards Earl of Moray.

The " rich Miss Scott," afterwards Duchess of Portland and mother of Lord George Bentinck, was an exceedingly kind and charitable lady, always ready to supply necessaries and comforts to the poor, especially when sick or in distress. Her sympathy was as unbounded as her disposition was generous. She took the liveliest interest in everything connected with the management of her husband's household and estates, and was an excellent woman of business. As her Grace declined in years she became very retiring in her habits, shunning the company of strangers as much as possible. Indeed during the last years of her life, which ended in May 1844, she was often unseen by the guests whom the Duke, her husband, entertained at Welbeck Abbey for many days.

A few reminiscences of Lord George Bentinck may not be uninteresting to those of a later generation who have heard of his Lordship's distinguished life and strongly marked character; for, with the exception of the Right Hon. B. Disraeli's political biography of his Lordship, no other memorial work has ever been attempted. I am therefore induced, through the repeated solicitations of friends, to commit to paper a few recollections of my noble master, whom I had the opportunity of knowing thoroughly from

i l/' JllAA. X-44– C.. .

A LABOUR OF LOVE. 3

long acquaintance with his character, disposition, and habits. It is a duty of which I have long desired to acquit myself, but which other avocations have led me to defer until, at my comparatively advanced age, I feel hardly competent to do justice to the many great qualities and exceptional merits which made Lord George Bentinck the most remarkable man that I ever knew. To me, however, it will be a labour of love to put down what I remember of my dear and honoured master, who was pleased to repose in my father and myself a confidence, and to admit us to an intimacy, which were, to say the least, unusual when our relative stations in life are borne in mind. Nor, in association with Lord George Bentinck, ought I to omit to mention, in the most respectful, loving, and grateful terms, the name of Lord George's confederate and valued friend, the fifth Duke of Richmond, who was my father's and my own master long before Lord George joined the Goodwood stable, and long after he left it. His Grace was one of those high-minded, large-hearted, and happily constituted noblemen whom to know was to love; and I verily believe that never before did it fall to the lot of any trainer to serve two such masters. In the reports occasionally given of them in newspapers and magazines, which have from time to time come under my eye, there is so much inaccuracy, and in the case of Lord George Bentinck often so much injustice, that I feel itincumbent upon me to tell to the best of my ability the story of his racing life as I knew and saw it from day to day. Having known the Turf and all its prominent patrons more or less intimately for nearly sixty years, I can conscientiously aver that the century which is now so near its end has produced but one Lord George Bentinck. To this conviction I hope to gain the assent of those of my readers who have the patience to read this book from its first page to its last, and to forgive its many imperfections and shortcomings.

At an early age it was thought desirable that Lord George, after leaving Eton, should have some profession, and he entered the army, by joining the 9th Lancers, and eventually attained the rank of Major in the 2d Life Guards; but as a military career offered him little prospect of profit or promotion, and as he was far from being insensible to the attractions of London society, he retired from the army in 1827.

The celebrated George Canning, who had married the sister of Lord George's mother, found in his Lordship one of the best and most energetic of private secretaries ; for he had all the qualities, such as sagacity, grace of manner, knowledge of human nature, method in business, shrewdness in negotiation, and skill and indefatigability in conducting epistolary correspondence, which such an office is generally supposed to require. At the same time, it presented to his Lordship one of the

Mrs. SCOTT AND HER ELDEST DAUGHTER (AKT. 15),

WHO AKTgRWARUS MAKRlEf) THE FOURTH DUKK OK PORTLAND.

M.P. FOR LYNN REGIS.

most favourable opportunities that could possibly arise for entering upon a public career.

In 1826 Lord George succeeded his brother, the Marquis of Titchfield, as member for Lynn Regis, which constituency he continued to represent for rather more than twenty years.1 On the accession of Lord Grey's Administration in 1830, Lord George was a general but independent supporter of the Government. In May 1832, when William IV. refused to make new peers, and Lord Grey tendered his resignation to the King, Lord George Bentinck gave a stronger proof than ever of his complete independence of the Whig party, by refusing to vote for Lord Ebrington's famous motion of unabated confidence in Ministers, which, being carried by a large majority, put an end to the Duke of Wellington's attempt at the formation of an Administration, and dictated terms of submission to the King and House of Lords.

On the retirement of Lord Stanley, Sir James Graham, the Duke of Richmond, and Lord Ripon, from Lord Grey's Government in May 1834, Lord George seceded from the Whig ranks. On the accession of Sir Robert Peel to office in December 1834, and upon the opening of Parliament in 1835, Lord George was extremely active in forming the party which was afterwards nicknamed by Mr O'Connell " the Derby Dilly," and for a period ofeleven years Lord George remained a steady supporter of Sir Robert Peel.

1 Parts of this and the following pages are taken from the ' Annual Register.'

As a frequenter of Newmarket, Lord George was constantly at work " whipping " up the sporting members; and once, on the approach of a close division, he showed his zeal by bringing up in his private carriage a country gentleman of very eccentric habits and manners, who, absurdly enough, repaid Lord George's kindness in submitting to his tedious companionship during a journey of sixty miles, by voting against the party to which Lord George belonged.

During the first four years of Sir Robert Peel's Administration Lord George Bentinck was never absent from his post. Awake or asleep, there he invariably sat, from the meeting of the House until its rising, generally occupying the same seat on the back benches on the Ministerial side.

At this time Lord George was very eager in his pursuit of the chase, and kept a stud of hunters in the neighbourhood of Andover for the purpose of hunting with Mr Assheton Smith's celebrated pack of fox-hounds. His Lordship was a very hard rider, and his custom was, after a prolonged debate in the House, to rise at six next morning, to start *off* from the London terminus of the South- Western Railway by the seven o'clock train, have a long day's hunting, and return by the same route to take his seat once more in the House of Commons. He was in the habit of wearing a

"PINK IN PARLIAMENT. 7

light - coloured zephyr paletot above his scarlet coat, and, fully accoutred in leathers and top-boots, he would enter the House, and sit out another long debate. Many a joke was indulged in by his brother members on seeing the red collar of his hunting-coat peeping out from under his surtout; and he was perhaps the only member ever seen of late years in the House of Commons in " pink." Often on these occasions has Sir Thomas Fremantle, then Secretary to the Treasury and Whip to the Conservative party, been heard to remark to some official members, " How I wish you gentlemen would take example from George Bentinck ! Look at him; his attendance is worth all yours put together, as he is independent of us, whereas you are office - holders." Constantly would his Lordship give his official friends a good scolding when he caught them coming in late for a division.

It is not my business, nor indeed do I possess the ability, to comment with dis- crimination upon Lord George's political career from the day when he first entered Parliament in 1826, as member for King's Lynn, until the sadly memorable 21st of September 1848, when he was found dead outside the deer-park at Welbeck Abbey. I must, however, claim the privilege of an old and attached servant to bear my humble testimony to the qualifications possessed by my noble master, which, despite the opin- ion of Mr Greville to the contrary, would in my judgment have made him a great success in public life. Mr Greville says that " Lord George never was, and never would have been, anything like a statesman." With all deference to Mr Greville, I cannot but think that Lord George had one gift which few statesmen possessla determination never to speak upon any subject until he had mastered its every detail. I never saw or heard of his equal in industry, perseverance, and powers of long - sustained application. Like all of his race, he became sleepy after eating heartily, and it was his practice not to touch food, after partaking of a very moderate breakfast at half-past eight o'clock in the morning, until he left the House of Commons at night. It was then his habit to dine at White's Club, in St James's Street, at a very late hour, varying between 11 P.m. and 2 A.m. I have heard that the cook at White's Club gave warning to throw up his engagement l a very lucrative one, as I believe he was in receipt of $500 a-year l on account of the late hours at which Lord George dined. To show Lord George's indomitable energy, I remember that after his lamented death, Gardner, his valet, told me that his Lordship's positive orders were that, however sound asleep, he was to be called at half-past seven A.m., although he often did not get to bed until four or even half- past four in the morning.

Furthermore, I find the following passage in Mr

LORD GEORGES STATESMANSHIP.

Greville's ' Diary,' written three years after Lord George's death :l

"November 24, 1851.lYesterday morning Disraeli called on me to speak about his work, ' The Life of Lord George Bentinck,' which he is just going to bring out. I find that he means to confine it to his hero's political career, and to keep clear of racing, and of his antecedent life. He seems to have formed a very just conception of him, having, however, seen the best of him, and therefore taking a more favourable view

of his character than I, who knew him longer and better, could do. I asked Disraeli, ' Supposing George Bentinck had lived, what he thought he would have done, and how he would have succeeded as a Minister and leader of a Government in the House of Commons ?' He said he would have failed. There were defects in his education and want of flexibility in his character. In his speaking there were physical defects he never could have got over. Disraeli added, what is very true, that he had not a particle of conceit; he was very obstinate, but had no vanity."

I must venture to demur to the truth of this prophecy, although emanating from such high authorities as Mr Disraeli and Mr Greville, by repeating what I have myself heard from equally high authorities. I have been told that the lateDuke of Richmond, the late Earls of Derby and Strafford, General Peel, and Colonel Anson stated repeatedly that never yet was there a parliamentary speaker who improved so much in two years as Lord George Bentinck did. I think the following passage, to which a friend has kindly called my attention, is more just to Lord George's character, foresight, and ability as a statesman, than it was possible for Mr Greville to be. It appeared in ' The Life of the Prince Consort,' by Sir Theodore Martin, and ran as follows :|

" On February 4, 1847, Lord George Bentinck, who had expressed himself, during the debate on the Queen's Speech, as dissatisfied with the Ministerial measures for the relief of Ireland, brought forward a very carefully devised and comprehensive scheme of permanent relief in the shape of advances to the extent of sixteen millions, to be made by the Government for the construction of railways in Ireland. Powers for construction of these railways had been already granted, and the Government advances were to come in supplement of eight millions to be provided by the companies authorised to construct them, but which they were unable to raise in the prostrate condition of the country. The scheme was enforced with all that minute accuracy of statistical detail and careful anticipation of practical difficulties which distinguished its author. Much might

INSTANCE OF HIS FORESIGHT. 11

have been done had labour been directed to such works of permanent utility as railways from the futile operations to which it had been applied under the Government grants of the previous session. A large portion of the public money, instead of being absolutely wasted, would have created a permanent source of national wealth, and developed the resources of the country many years in advance of what was otherwise possible."

My only remark upon this passage is, that Mr Balfour, the late Chief Secretary for Ireland, and leader of the House of Commons, is, I believe, engaged in giving effect to Lord George's well-considered proposals delivered nearly half a century since. I base my own confident convictions that Lord George Bentinck, had he been spared, would have played a very distinguished part in public life, upon one fact aloneI never knew him to fail in anything to which he gave his serious attention and which he took in hand in earnest. Whether he would have remained in Parliament after the final defeat of Protection I will not venture to say ; and my reason for entertaining doubts on the subject will be found in the account, subsequently given, of my last interview with his Lordship.

I cannot conclude this chapter without adding a few particulars about Lord George Bentinck's father, the fourth Duke of Portland, who was wellknown to my father and to my father's contemporaries. His Grace possessed so many admirable qualities, both as a landlord and as a patron of the Turf, that I deem it my duty to rescue some of them from oblivion; and all the more so because the influence of great territorial magnates is passing away in this countrylnot, as I venture humbly to believe, for our country's good. It will perhaps be remembered by some of my readers that in one of his letters to ' The Times,' Admiral Rons remarked that during his long experience of the Turf he had known but two menlthe fourth Duke of Portland and the fifth Earl of Glasgowlwho raced from pure disinterested love of sport, and without harbouring a single mercenary thought in their breasts. From what I have heard, there never yet was a supporter of horse-racing who took more pleasure than did the fourth Duke of Portland in breeding, rearing, and racing his own thoroughbred stock. For that purpose he kept a few well-selected brood mares at Welbeck Abbey, where he caused their produce to be broken as yearlings, and to be exercised and trained as two- year-olds until the Doncaster September meeting was over. At the end of September his Grace engaged some four or five good jockeys to come to Welbeck in order to try his two-year-olds, the best and most promising of which he sent to Newmarket to be trained by Richard Prince. His Grace deemed it to be a matter of prime import- f'

. I I I ' I !

; . 1.1 . (! !! :.'-,-', t, ; . . .,

lo i v i.:- i .-'-.. ' .- : '. i' v, ;,'.-:i i

! ' -i ' !, -J" -! . ! ' ; .J

A

FOURTH DUKE OF PORTLAND. 13

ance that his young colts and fillies should be made very tractable and quiet, and for this purpose he insisted that they should be familiarised with, and accustomed to, every object and every sound that was likely to render them nervous and timid.l The number of horses kept in training by his Grace was always limited, as in the course of some years he did not annually start more than three or four animals. One good horse, Tiresias by Soothsayer, he was so fortunate as to breed, and with him won the Derby in 1819, beating Mr Crock- ford's Sultan and Lord Rous's Euphrates (both good horses) and twelve other starters. Tiresias was a sound and powerful horse, and won nine times as a three-year-old, and five times as a four-year-old, over all distances. Next year he was put to the stud, where he proved a most unsuccessful stallion. So infatuated, however, was his princely owner about him, that, in spite

Un his 'Silk and Scarlet' Mr Henry Dixon ("The Druid") remarks : " Like all Lord Fitzvvilliam's horses when Scaife trained them, Mulatto was very badly broken. Clift, the jockey, used to say of him, and in fact of every one of them, 'Here's a pretty brute! I never get on one on 'em but I've a good chance of breaking my neck ; no mouth, no nothing. I've all to make.' Welbeck, on the contrary, was quite as remarkable for the height to which it carried its breaking. The fourth Duke of Portland used to say that a horse should never go on to a race-course till it could face anything. Hence, in order to complete their education they were marched over and over again past a drum and fife band, with a flag flying, in the park ; and so many screws of powder were let off in the corn-bin that at last they would hardly lift their heads out of the manger for a pistol report.' 1

of continued disappointments, he insisted upon persevering with him, in the confident belief that . one day he would become the sire of a great horse. Although a good honest runner himself, Tiresias was the son of Soothsayer, whose progeny were for the most part big and good looking, but very uncertain customers. In short, Tiresias proved to be as great a failure at the stud as Bay Middleton was, so long as he remained the property of Lord George Bentinck. At last, his Grace resolved to have recourse to better sires than the Derby winner of 1819, and in 1838 his bay colt Boeotian, by Taurus, won eight races, including the Column and Newmarket Stakes, and the St James's Palace Stakes at Ascot.

Never yet was there a more enthusiastic lover of Newmarket Heath, a large portion of which he owned, than Lord George Bentinck's father. His Grace was never absent from a Newmarket race meeting until old age prevented his attending ; and the training-gallops and race-course at " the little town in Cambridgeshire " were constantly receiving his attention, which involved the outlay of considerable sums of money. At the beginning of this century a large portion of what was called "the new ground" on either side of "the Flat" was covered with furze-bushes, which his Grace caused to be stubbed up and cleared away. The land was then ploughed and sown with cole-seed or rape, which was fed off with sheep and then"a Morta' Good Old Chap." 15

laid down in grass. His Grace next proceeded to purchase some land which lay contiguous to the above-mentioned " new ground," so as to prevent its ever falling into the hands of some purchaser who might not be favourably disposed towards the Turf. Since that time the land in question has been known as " the Portland farm," and portions of it have been added to the Heath. He also built the Portland Stand, at the end of the Beacon course, where the Criterion and Cambridgeshire courses finished.

I remember a characteristic story which was told not long after his Grace made the purchase to which I have just alluded. In riding for the first time over the ground, he encountered a shepherd, from whom he inquired " whether he knew where the land lay which the Duke of Portland had just bought ? " The shepherd pointed to the spot on which they were standing, exclaiming, " This be part of it." As they proceeded over the property the shepherd, little knowing to whom he was speaking, volunteered the remark, " I be moighty glad t' Duke of Portland 'ave bought this 'ere farm, because he be a morta' good old chap."

" And what makes you consider him ' a morta' good old chap' ? " inquired the Duke, smiling.

" Because he's good to 's poor, and finds work for a lot o' we," replied the unconscious guide.

During the intervals between the various racemeetings the Duke almost always remained at Newmarket, and busied himself in effecting alterations and improvements upon the Heath. For this purpose he employed many hands, and rode about among them inspecting the work, and encouraging them here and there by a few words of praise. A groom led the Duke's black cob about the Heath as he walked among the labourers, and in this way many hours of each day were spent. His Grace was always an excellent pedestrian, and I have known him walk home two or three miles in heavy rain, followed by his groom leading the well-known black cob.

During the races the Duke had a waggon fitted up as a movable stand, and supplied with every convenience. After he had seen the competing horses saddled at the Ditch stables, he would get into his waggon, which was drawn up near the Bushes, and would watch through a powerful telescope the running of the horses in the race. As they drew near to his " coign of vantage," he would announce in a loud voice what their relative positions were, and their respective chances of winning. Although his Grace never betted a shilling, and indeed held the practice in utter detestation, I have never known any one who took such keen interest in racing as he did. He had an eye, and an exceedingly discriminating one too, for the riding of each jockey, as I have often had an opportunity of remarking when he permitted

THE DUKE'S IMPROVEMENTS. 17

me to occupy a place in his covered waggon. His Grace's long and powerful telescope is now in my possession, as he gave it to Lord George Bentinck when advancing age prevented him attending the Newmarket meeting any more, and Lord George gave it to me when he sold his stud in 1846.

Although his Grace never took a very active part in political life, there were few noblemen who devoted themselves more energetically to improving their estates than he did. Being the most practical of men, he was well aware that a thorough and exhaustive drainage of land was needed to bring his Welbeck estates into a condition to produce abundant crops. With this end in view he drained thousands of acres, many of them at the cost of $100 per acre.

I cannot give a better illustration of the magnitude of his Grace's expenditure upon his property than by quoting the following passage from the last edition of Mr John Murray's ' Handbook to Nottinghamshire.' The writer says :l

" At two and a half miles from Mansfield a road leads by Clipstone and Edwinstowe to Ollerton, seven miles distant from Mansfield. Clipstone is an estate belonging to the Duke of Portland, and the road to it runs by the side of a canal of irrigation, formed by the fourth Duke at an expense of $80,000, and called 'The Duke's Flood-Dyke.' By it the stream of the river Mann, augmented

by the sewage and washings of the town of Mansfield, is distributed by minor cuts, tiled drains, and sluice-gates along the slopes below it, converting the previously barren valley, whose sides were a rabbit-warren overgrown with heath and gorse, and its bottom a swamp, producing hassocks and rushes, into a most productive tract of meadow and pasture land, yielding three crops of grass annually. The river is diverted near the" vale- head, and led along the hillside ; and the bottom has been drained. The canal extends to near Ollerton, and the latter portion of it is applied to the lands of Earl Manvers.

" These famous meadows have been often quoted, together with those near Edinburgh, in sanitary and agricultural discussions. The canal - water, after depositing all its more valuable ingredients upon the land, runs off through the bottom of the valley in a stream as clear as crystal and full of trout, though angling is forbidden. The domain of Clipstone exhibits a fine specimen of good farming, and is well worth a visit from all interested in agricultural improvements."

One of his Grace's favourite undertakings was to transplant large oak-trees by the aid of very powerful machinery ; and so successfully was this effected, that many of these trees are now great ornaments of the park at Welbeck. Clad in appropriate costumelthat is to say, in a rough

THE DUKE'S KINDNESS. 19

coat and long waterproof boots reaching up to his hips I the Duke personally superintended the draining operations of his labourers, and would not permit the tiles to be laid until he was satisfied that there was sufficient fall to carry off the water.

Lord George Bentinck, as was natural, took great interest in all his father's proceedings at Welbeck, and often remarked to me, when engaged in grubbing up trees on the Goodwood estate in order to make gallops for his race-horses, that his father, if they had belonged to him, would have transplanted them with his powerful engines.

In every relation of life the fourth Duke of Portland was one of the kindest and most considerate of men. When any matter was referred to him, he never came to a decision without the fullest and most patient inquiry. I remember hearing that on one occasion the house-steward at Welbeck suggested to his Grace the propriety of making a reduction in the wages of the household servants. "By all means," replied the Duke, "if you deem it advisable; but in that case it is of course to be understood that I begin with you !" I need hardly add that nothing further was heard of the house-steward's suggestion, or of another in which he represented that it was a piece of unheard-of extravagance and luxury for the servants to have fires in their bedrooms. "You may stopthe practice if you like," said the Duke, " but not until you first set the example yourself."

It was the Duke's invariable habit to sit down to dinner exactly at 6.30 P.m., and such was his punctuality that nothing would induce him to wait for any guest, however distinguished, who might be staying at Welbeck. The same rigorous punctuality was observed by him in every other transaction, but I cannot say that it was inherited by Lord George Bentinck, to whose nature it was foreign. Such was his Grace's consideration for others, that, upon hearing that one of his tenants had given notice to leave his farm, he sent for the man and inquired why he had taken this step ? "Because, your Grace," he replied, "I have not enough money to cultivate my farm properly." " What do you intend doing ?" was the next question. " I thought of taking a small dairy- farm, your Grace." " Would you not prefer remaining in your own house, to which you are accustomed," was the kind inquiry made by the Duke, " and carrying on the farm for me, if I paid you for doing so?" "I should, indeed, prefer that, your Grace." An arrangement was accordingly made to that effect, and two or three years later the Duke inquired from his agent in what condition this particular farm was, and whether it yielded a profit ? Reassured on this point, his Grace sent for the tenant, and observed to him, " If you are able to make this farm pay when

THE DUKE'S PEDESTRIAN POWEBS. 21

cultivating it for me, could you not do the same for yourself? " On receiving an affirmative reply, the Duke inquired how much capital the farmer needed for his purpose, and advanced the sum at once, with the happiest results.

I have already said that his Grace was an excellent pedestrian, and delighted in walking. In one of the letters written by Lord George Bentinck to Mr Croker in 1846, his Lordship remarks that he " believes his father, then eighty years old, was still equal to a ten-mile walk." I remember being at Harcourt House, Cavendish Square, on one occasion, when his Grace announced his intention of walking to some place a long way off. To this his two daughters, Lady Charlotte Bentinck, afterwards Viscountess Ossington, and Lady Lucy, now the Dowager Lady Howard de Walden, vehemently objected, and begged their father to order his carriage to the door. His Grace scornfully repudiated the idea that the distance was too long for him to accomplish on foot, and offered there and then to run either of the young ladies round the garden behind Harcourt House. The challenge was accepted by Lady Charlotte, and after an exciting race she won, as it were, cleverly by a head, to her own great delight.

There is not one member of this noble family to whom I do not personally owe a deep debt of gratitude. Hearing of my only son's dangerous illness in 1887, Lady Ossington (who has since passed away, followed by the blessings and grateful thanks of all who knew her) provided him with all the comforts and necessaries that he required, and showed the greatest sympathy with my wife and me. On my son's decease in December 1887, at the age of twenty-four years, her Ladyship caused a beautiful gravestone to be erected to his memory, bearing the following words at the end of the inscription: " This stone was erected by Viscountess Ossington, in consideration of services faithfully rendered to her father, his Grace the fourth Duke of Portland, and to her brother, the Right Honourable Lord George Cavendish Bentinck, M.P."

Nor should I omit to mention that the spirit of kindness, sympathy, and generosity which has always distinguished this noble house, has descended in full measure to the sixth Duke of Portland, who is now the head of this ancient and illustrious family. From his Grace, and from the Duchess, I have received so many favours and such unbounded kindness, not only in my own home but also at Welbeck Abbey, that I dare not trust myself to attempt to enumerate them here. I am persuaded from my own experience that their Graces have hearts as kind and warm as that which induced the fourth Duke of Portland to make provision for the poor tramps who shambled along the road in front of one of the lodges on the edge

n Pc

THE DUKE'S CHARITY. 23

of the park at Welbeck. At this lodge his Grace stationed a porter whose business it was to give relief to every indigent applicant for itla pint of beer and half a loaf of bread for a man, and half a pint of beer and the same quantity of bread for a woman. To children a slice of cake and a little wine-and-water were in each case dispensed. At Harcourt House, in London, his Grace's charities were absolutely boundless. I have often been present when Mrs Jones, the housekeeper, received letters from Welbeck, written by the fourth Duke and by his Duchess, giving instructions for the distribution of clothing, food, coals, and money among the poor inhabitants of his Grace's London property.

The Duke died at Welbeck on the 27th March 1854, at the advanced age of eighty-five years. His last words, addressed to his regular medical attendant, were these : " Dr Ward, in a few minutes the poorest labourer who worked on my estate, and has gone before me, will be my equal in eveiy respect." Throughout his protracted life his Grace was in the enjoyment of perfect health, the result of abundant exercise and of many hours passed every day in the open air without regard to the weather. The Duke preferred walking to riding; but when he rode, it was invariably on a stout trotting cob, which nothing could ever induce him to urge into a canter or gallop. In thebelief that Lord George Bentinck derived many of his most valuable and characteristic attributes from his father, I hope that what I have now written about the latter will not be considered inappropriate by those who take the trouble to read it.

2

SECTION 2

CHAPTER II.

NEWHARKJET AT THE BEGINNING OF THE CENTURY.

A Few words explaining how I came to be a trainer of race-horses may perhaps be not unacceptable to those of my readers in whom a taste for the past predominates over (what is far more usual) a taste only for the present. It would by many be deemed a sufficient reason for me to say that I was born at Newmarket, and that my father and grandfather had lived there for more than sixty years before I came into existence. My grandfather was a builder by profession, and constructed a considerable number of the principal houses and other buildings, including stables, in what has long been erroneously called, " The famous little town in Cambridgeshire " I erroneously, because only half of it is in Cambridgeshire, the other half being, as every one knows, in Suffolk. Among the buildings for which my grandfather was responsible may be included " The Rooms," of which a Mr Parrs, who also kept a school, was for a longtime lessee and manager. In addition to " The Rooms," my grandfather also built what is now called the " Rutland Anns Hotel," on the site occupied by which another inn (of far inferior size and pretensions, and called " The Ram ") formerly stood. I have often been told by my old friend Mr J. F. Clark, the ex-racing judge, that viewed as an edifice, the Rutland Arms is well calculated to confer credit upon its builder, as the brickwork is a very excellent specimen of neatness and stability. Mr J. F. Clark's authority on everything connected with Newmarket has long been acknowledged to be quite unexceptionable; and the fact that, in addition to being a racing judge, he has for many years followed the profession of an architect, lends additional weight to his opinion on such a subject. Previous to the erection of the Rutland Arms, which was commenced a few months after the battle of Waterloo, the Ram Inn, its predecessor, took its name from an incident connected with the strange, eventful history of the eccentric Earl of Orford, about whom so many queer tales were told. It is well known that on one occasion Lord Orford drove his favourite team, consisting of four stags, from Houghton Hall, his country seat in Norfolk (after which, by the way, the Houghton meeting is called), into Newmarket, a distance of about twenty-nine miles. When he was approaching his destination, the Essex Hounds chanced to cross the road along

THE EAM INN. 27

which he had passed just before, and catching up the burning scent of the four stags, they immediately gave chase. As they drew near to the vehicle, their loud notes, or what fox-hunters call " their music," alarmed the stags, which galloped at full speed into the little town, and dashed into the wide-open portals of the inn which stood on the site subsequently occupied by The Ram. The doors were immediately closed, and the lives of the stags saved from their eager pursuers. This occurrence happened about the middle of last century, and was the cause of the name, " Ram Inn," being bestowed upon this noted hostelry and posting- house. In 1775, it was kept by a Mr Barber, who hailed from the Bull Inn at Barton Mills|the last stage on approaching Newmarket from the Suffolk side, and close to which Sir Charles Bunbury's seat, Barton Park, was situated. Many famous race - horses were bred there *by* the Baronet in question, who lived to be the senior member of the Jockey Club, and Father of the British Turf. Sir Charles Bunbury, who was an excellent sportsman, died in 1820, and owned in his time some famous horses, such as Bellario, Eleanor (winner of the Derby and Oaks), and Smolensko, the winner of the Two Thousand, the Newmarket stakes, and Derby. I have often heard Admiral Rous recount that the first race for the Two Thousand ever seen by him was that won by Smolensko, in 1813. It is a thrice - told tale that, after the Derby, SirCharles gave Goodisson three ten-pound notes for winning the three races; remarking to him that he could not afford more because Brograve, a celebrated bookmaker of that day, had committed suicide, from inability to meet his Derby losses, including a large sum due to Sir Charles.

Mr Barber was succeeded, in 1778, by Mr Daniel Potter, who reigned for many years, and did not die until 1813, after which date his widow continued the hotel until 1828, when Mr Ratcliffe took it. It was in the hands of Mr Daniel Potter and his widow for thirty-five years. Mr Potter was an extremely stout man, and in his day there resided at Newmarket a man of the name of Robert Bones, who was very tall, and as thin as a rail. These two notabilities were talking together at the entrance to the Rutland Arms, immediately opposite to the shop of Mr Rogers, the stationer and printer, who was also a clever sketcher. With a few skilful touches of his pencil, Mr Rogers took the portraits of these two eccentric individuals, and a few hours afterwards placed the sketch in his shop - window, with the words " Flesh and Bones" inscribed beneath. I remember hearing my father say that for a short time this caricature afforded intense amusement to passers-by.

My grandfather resided in a house, which he built for himself, on Mill Hill, Newmarket. Close to his house stood the residence and stables of

NEWMARKET WORTHIES. 29

" old Mr Prince." After my grandfather's death, his house was occupied for many years by James Robinson, and then by Frank Butler, two of the very finest jockeys that I ever saw. The workshops and business premises occupied by my grandfather were, on his decease, taken by Mr John Clark, the father of the present much-respected ex-judge. They remained in the hands of the elder Mr Clark and his sons for many years. It is not generally known that, despite my lifelong connection with Newmarket and Goodwood, my great - grandfather was a native of Wantage, in Berkshire, where some of the best training-grounds for race - horses that England contains may not improbably have given him a taste for racing. Anyhow, it is certain that his son, my grandfather, took up his abode at Newmarket, and was greatly interested in racing for many years. I find that " Mr Kent of Newmarket, Cambridgeshire," Avas a subscriber to the 'Racing Calendar' in 1775, and has continued, with slight intermission, since. It will thus be seen that the surname by which I am known was borne by people associated more or less with horse-racing for a hundred and seventeen years. In my father's lifetime, no less than in my own, a vast number of changes have occurred in the noble sport, which is now more popular than ever among Englishmen, and, I must add, among Englishwomen; nor can I be blind to the fact that to the influence of the latter such " drawingroom meetings" as Kempton Park and Sandown Park are undoubtedly due. Some of these changes are, of course, unpalatable to an old man like myself, especially those identified with the short courses, which are now all the vogue. Upon this oft-debated subject I have no intention of entering with wearisome iteration at the present moment.

As I have previously stated, my grandfather lived in a house built by himself on Mill Hill. This house was within a few feet of that occupied by the grandfather of Mr Richard Prince. The latter trained for the fourth Duke of Portland, and for many other distinguished noblemen, and was one of the most upright men of his class that Newmarket ever contained. " Old Mr Prince " and his wife took a great liking to my father when he was a little child, and insisted upon having him over to their house as often as possible. In fact, he was adopted at a very early age by her and her husband, despite their own large family. Mr Prince himself was of Irish extraction, and was buried by torchlight, which at the time made a great sensation at Newmarket. My father was carried when a child to see this funeral by S. Wright, my grandfather's foreman, who, to distinguish him from another man of the same name, was called " slab Wright," being a bricklayer by trade. Mr Prince was succeeded by his son, whose mother kept house for him until his own death. All this time my father continued to reside under her kindly roof,

RICHARD PRINCE. 31

and upon her death she confided him to her son, and gave him a beautiful cane as a " souvenir " of herself. The cane in question has a fine ivory knob, and was preserved by my father with the greatest care, and on his death was bequeathed by him to me. It is now in my possession; and whenever I look upon it, my thoughts fly back to many precious memories of the past, which would otherwise escape my attention. I have ventured to reproduce some of them here.

The younger Prince, to whom my father was intrusted by Mrs Prince, his mother, had the kind heart of an Irishman, and was exceedingly good to the boy under his charge, sending him to school, and treating him in every respect as well as his own sons. As my father was a light-weight, and a good natural horseman, he was selected by Mr Prince to ride in many of the stable trials, and soon gained some reputation for his skill in managing dangerous and difficult horses. On one occasion a horse trained by Mr Prince, and looked after by my father, who invariably rode him at exercise, was sent to Black Hambleton, in Yorkshire, to be trained for some North Country engagement. Mr Prince could not spare my father, and consequently the horse, on arriving at his destination, soon became so riotous and violent that none of the Yorkshire boys could master or control him. Accordingly, my father was despatched to Black Hambleton to ride the horse back to Newmarket, which he effected, after encountering all sorts of difficulties and dangers, as the roads were very bad, and skirted by open ditches, into some of which the refractory animal would leap, seriously jeopardising his own limbs and life, and also those of my father. During the first four or five days he had, as may be imagined, a very uncomfortable time of it; but after that the horse acknowledged his own defeat, on finding that he had a horseman on his back whom he could neither frighten nor unship.

At school my father was a great friend of Frank Baker, a fellow-pupil and contemporary, who subsequently trained for George, Prince of Wales, afterwards George IV., and was an intelligent and well-informed man, devoting many hours daily to study, by which means he amassed a great stock of general information apart from horse-racing. Baker was a very steady and economical trainer, and also a great favourite with the boys and employees in his stable. For the Prince he was very successful, and by care, hard work, and thrift acquired a small competency. His house and premises adjoined those of James Edwards, who trained for Lord Jersey, Sir John Shelley, and many other notable patrons of the Turf. Baker owned the house in which he lived, and in it he passed his declining years, altogether secluded from company. At school the friendship between my father and Baker was very great, and it continued until my father left Newmarket in 1823, to Mr Prince's Stable. 33
accept the position of private trainer to the fifth Duke of Richmond, at Goodwood.

Mr Prince soon adopted the habit of intrusting the entire management of his stable and paddocks to my father, who took the greatest interest in his work, and was always a very conscientious and faithful servant to his employers. He was constantly sent away from Newmarket in charge of horses which had to run for provincial engagements far away from headquarters. Among the distinguished patrons of the Turf for whom Mr Prince then trained were included Lord Foley, the Right Honble. Charles James Fox, Sir Frank Standish, Sir Sitwell Sitwell, and many lesser luminaries. Lord Foley and Mr Fox were racing confederates, and their success during the early years of their connection with Mr Prince's stable was phenomenally great. It was a very heavy betting- stable about that time, and in the opinion of many observant judges the first impulse towards reckless speculation was administered to the Turf by Lord Foley, who in the end was so hard hit by gambling that his noble estate, Witley Court in Worcestershire, had to be sold for nearly a million sterling to the grandfather of the present Lord Dudley. While the success of these two confederates was at its height, their horses were always great favourites, a fact which led, in one instance, to that well-known and most disgraceful transaction with which Dan Dawson (an ill-omened name)

became notoriously identified. My father used to relate that in the Newmarket Spring Meetings of 1811 some horses in Mr Prince's stable were very heavily engaged, some of them in races upon which the betting was pretty sure to be heavy. A design was therefore formed by some unprincipled scoundrels, who hired Dawson and another tout to administer poison to those of Mr Prince's horses which were daily out at exercise and doing strong work. With this flagitious purpose in view, arrangements were made by Dawson and his accomplice to put arsenic into the drinking-troughs close to what is still called " Well Gap," half-way down " The Ditch." These troughs were Mr Prince's private property, and were covered over with wooden coverings, which were carefully locked up at both ends. It was at that time the custom for trainers to water their horses after doing a strong gallop, especially if the morning was hot. Every trainer, therefore, had his own troughs, which were scattered about at various places to suit their owners' convenience. As arsenic, unless chemically prepared, will not mix with water, Dan Dawson took into his confidence an old chemist named Cecil Bishop, and consulted him as to the best way of rendering arsenic soluble in water. Although Dawson was one of those " ne'er-do-weels" who pass their lives in the useless and disreputable occupation of watching horses, he had received a good education, and

POISONING RACE-HORSES. 35

might have turned his hand to better things. Apparently his object was not to kill the horses which drank at the poisoned trough, but to incapacitate them from winning a race for several days after. In some mysterious way a warning was conveyed to Mr Prince, cautioning him against watering his horses at a particular trough. For a time he acted upon this advice, and Dan Dawson, who for obvious reasons carefully abstained from being seen near the trough, came to the conclusion that Cecil Bishop had made a mistake, and that enough arsenic had not been mixed with the water, seeing that Mr Prince's horses continued to go in their usual form. He proceeded, therefore, in the middle of the night to inject a stronger dose of arsenic through a tube which he inserted under the lid. This tube was stuck into the neck of a bottle full of a strong solution of arsenic. It was subsequently discovered that one quart of the water thus impregnated by this unprincipled scoundrel was more than sufficient to kill the strongest horse.

One morning Mr Prince's horses were out as usual for exercise, and when they had finished their gallops the weather suddenly became very hot and sultry. Mr Prince remarked to my father, who was riding by his side, " This rumour about the troughs being poisoned seems to me ' gammon,' as I have heard nothing about it for a long time." My father replied, " Nevertheless, were I you, Ishould pull out the plugs at the bottom of the troughs, and let the water run off; after which I should fill the troughs again with fresh water brought from the well." "Oh," exclaimed Mr Prince, " that will take too long; there is no danger; so let the horses drink their fill, and I will be responsible for all risks." When the horses were brought to the troughs, their natural powers of scent led them at once to suspect that all was not right. Some of them began to snort, and refused to touch the water at any price; but others drank a little, and were hardly able to get home, in consequence of the violent griping which immediately overtook them. On the return of these latter to the stable, my father, who was a capital "vet," although all his knowledge had been acquired by rule of thumb, administered a strong dose of castor-oil to Coelebs and Reveller, two horses belonging to Sir Sitwell Sitwell. Spaniard, Pirouette, and The Dandy, which belonged to Sir Frank Standish, were usually attended, like all his other horses, by a Dr Bowles, of Cambridge, who was a certified physician for human beings, and also very clever in treating quadrupeds. At that time the veterinary art was at a very low ebb, as any one may see if he cares to exhume such books as ' Taplin's Stable Directory' and ' Lawrence On the Horse.' In this instance the delay which necessarily elapsed before Dr Bowles arrived from Cam-

RACE-HORSES POISONED. 37

bridge proved fatal. The three above - named horses belonging to Sir Frank Standish died in great agony; indeed I have often heard my father say that he had never seen a poor animal endure anything like the sufferings sustained by Spaniard, before death brought him merciful relief. He and his two stable companions were buried in the gravel-pit near "The Severals," opposite to the house in which John Robinson lived during his declining years. Thanks to the dose of castor-oil administered by my father to Ccelebs and Reveller, both recovered, and ran in many races, the latter winning nine times during the following year. Their recovery was attributed by the ignorant to the effects of some vinegar administered to them by a man calling himself a veterinary surgeon; but, in reality, they were saved by my father's prompt action in drenching them without a moment's delay with castor-oil.

It was upon Wednesday, May 1, 1811, that the horses drank poison at the troughs, and next day a notice in very big letters was posted all over the town. It ran as follows:|

"newmarket, *May* 2, 1811.

" TIHEEEAS several race-horses, under the care of Mr ' Richard Prince, training groom, that drank out of a trough on the Heath near the ' Well Gap' on Wednesday morning, were soon after taken ill, one of which is since dead, and many remain in a dangerous state;

"And it having been found, on investigation, that a preparation of arsenic had been infused in the water of two other troughs on the Heath, where the racers usually drink:

" This is to give notice that Whoever will discover the person, or persons, who put the arsenic or other poison into any of the aforesaid troughs, so that he, she, or they may be brought to Justice, shall, upon conviction, receive

A REWARD OF

FIVE HUNDRED GUINEAS.

" And furthermore, Whoever shall discover any person, or persons, who instigated or abetted the above offenders, or shall reveal any circumstances which may lead to the apprehension and conviction of any of the parties concerned in this nefarious transaction, shall be liberally rewarded by

applying to
MR WEATHERBY
AT NEWMARKET."

A few days later the other three horses died, and the excitement became intense. Suspicion ultimately settled upon Dan Dawson, who for some weeks previously had lodged at the "Five Bells," kept by Mrs Tilbrook, on the opposite side of the Mill Hill to that on which Mr Prince's house stood. Dawson had often been seen by my father walking across the Mill Hill towards Mr Prince's house, with his head down and a muffler round the lower part of his face, as though he desired to escape observation or recognition. On many occasions my father remarked to Mr Prince, as he pointed out Dan Dawson to him, " I cannot imagine who that fellow is; he comes

CAPTURE OF DAN DAWSON. 39

across the hill almost every morning, and passes our house about the time when the horses go out to exercise, at a very early hour. He carries his head as though he were ashamed to have his face seen."

As soon as the horses were taken ill, Dan Dawson left the " Five Bells." The First Spring Meeting of 1811 was then near its close, and several months were yet to elapse before the suspected culprit was arrested at Cambridge, on August 12, 1812. Into the details of his trial and death sentence I shall not enter, beyond saying that it seems incredible in these days that a man should be hanged for such an offence. One justification of the sentence being carried out in its full severity was said to be, that although horses were the only sufferers, it was obvious that human beings might with equal facility have been poisoned, because in the summer months the lads on the backs of the horses frequently drank at the same troughs. Mrs Tilbrook of the " Five Bells," being, like most of her sex, of an inquisitive disposition, had examined Dan Dawson's luggage, which he kept under his bed at her house. She soon discovered a bottle marked " poison" in one of his trunks ; and in the neck of this bottle there was a flaw which made it easy of identification. The bottle was afterwards found in Dan Dawson's possession, and was shown to Mrs Tilbrook, who stated, " If it be the same bottle I found under hisbed, there is a ' delve' in it into which I can put my thumb." This evidence led to Dawson's conviction and public execution at Cambridge, in presence of from twelve to fifteen thousand persons.

If I am censured by some impatient readers for entering at this length into a transaction with which many are familiar, I can but plead that the details given are generally inaccurate, and that my father was intimately connected with the discovery of this dastardly crime, and was never tired, in my youth, of talking about it. I remember that it was his habit to impress upon me most forcibly, what I afterwards learned from my own experience, that it was impossible to exercise too much vigilance as to the water supplied to horses away from home. This caution was not forgotten by me when I had Surplice at Epsom, just before the Derby of 1848.

I remarked at the beginning of this chapter that it would have been enough for me to state that I was the son of a trainer, and born at Newmarket, in explanation of the fact that I myself followed my father's profession. This, however, was not my father's desire. He would infinitely have preferred that I should have studied chemistry at the laboratory of a relative of his and mine, at Stratford, in Essex. The firm in question was that of Messrs Howard, Gibson, & Kent. I was placed under their care for a short time ; but soon after, my father became a widower, and

- i /I U

FRANK BAKER. 41

was constantly absent *from,* home at the race meetings where his horses had engagements. He found it necessary, therefore, to call in my assistance to do what I could towards managing the vast stud under his care; and most assiduous he was in teaching me the art of training race-horses. He carefully explained to me the various systems of training adopted by different professors of that art. As regards Mr Prince, my father regarded him as too severe with horses of delicate constitutions ; whereas Mr Boyce, though a most careful and honest man, seemed to my father to be occasionally too indulgent in dealing with some of his horses. When my father left Mr Prince's stable, and transferred himself as head-lad to that of Mr R. D. Boyce, he remained with the latter for many years. At last, in 1823, he was recommended to the fifth Duke of Richmond, by the Earl of Stradbroke, as fit to take command of the large Goodwood stable. He remained at Goodwood until his death in 1869, when he was eighty-six years old. The Duke of Richmond kindly permitted him to occupy until his death the house and garden at Goodwood, in both of which he took the greatest delight.

Mr Baker, who, as I have said, trained for the Prince Regent, continued to be very intimate with my father from their school-days downwards until my father left Newmarket for good. Their tastes and habits were singularly harmonious, and nothingpleased them more than to dabble in *quasi-scientific* studies. During their youth this country was continually at war with France, and a semaphore, or signal-post, was erected on the top of the Bury Hill, the highest elevation in the neighbourhood of Newmarket. They were never tired of watching the signals conveyed from Yarmouth by this semaphore to the Admiralty in London, and back thence to the sea-coast. With a curiosity which was natural under the circumstances, they endeavoured, by constant observation, to read the messages which passed backwards and forwards, and thus to acquaint themselves with the tidings received from the seat of war on the Continent. In those primitive days newspapers were not received in country places for many days after the arrival of a report which told of the loss or gain of a great battle. Everything connected with the Avar percolated through the Admiralty, to which the commanders of the different vessels engaged as carriers of news naturally sent their reports, by semaphore or by road. After many weeks of close watching, my father and Mr Baker got to understand the working of the semaphore sufficiently to write some of the messages down on paper. Unfortunately one day they dropped a paper on which they had written one of these messages. It was picked up on the Bury Hill, and carried by its finder to Mr Hylet, who was the official in charge of the semaphore, and was therefore deemed likely

READING THE SEMAPHORE. 43

to take interest in a paper which was supposed to be his property. Naturally Mr Hylet was greatly surprised at the accuracy with which the message had been spelt out, and at the intelligent comprehension of the principle on which the semaphore was worked displayed by the document. It was therefore forwarded to the Head Office in London, and a complete change in signalling was immediately adopted.

The two students were at first very much puzzled by the new signals, but were not long in discovering their meaning. The first message which they were able to read correctly after this occurrence, conveyed the following words: "A complete revolution in Holland"! Their persistency in observing and deciphering the signals was another instance of the truth of Lord George Bentinck's remark, to which I have so often heard him give utterance, that "you can accomplish anything if you will only try hard enough " ! I doubt whether in those ignorant days there was any other watcher of the signals exchanged from semaphore to semaphore, all over these islands, who succeeded in accomplishing a similar feat. The two allies began by mastering the shutter system of signalling, and thereby forced the Government to substitute for it the workable arms which are still employed on board H.M.'s ships of war for the same purpose.

Let me turn to another field of observation widely different from that to which I have justalluded. I have often heard my father relate some of the practical jokes indulged in at Newmarket in his youth, and which were much more frequent than in this prosaic age. I call it prosaic; for the undoubted effect of all our modern inventions and discoveries I like the railway, the telegraph wire, the telephone, and the electric light I is to extinguish the individuality and quench the imagination of men, women, and children. It was far otherwise in the England of my youth. There was then residing at Newmarket a Mr Thomas Bryant, who Avas greatly addicted to jokes of this kind. When, for instance, William Arnull, the well - known jockey, was sent for on one occasion to the north to ride some trials for the Hon. Edward Petre, who was a very liberal gentleman, he returned very much richer than he was when he started. Among the presents which, in addition to money, Mr Petre promised to send to " old Bill Arnull," was included a big hamper of wine. On his return home, Bill could not help boasting to some of his friends about the hamper that was coming. Mi- Bryant, hearing the news, thought it an excellent opportunity to play off an amusing joke at Bill Arnull's expense. Accordingly he made overtures to a dwarf, called " Little Peter," who was then well known at Newmarket, requesting that he would allow himself to be packed into a hamper, which was to be despatched to Bill Arnull's house.

BILL AENULL. 45

The latter's engagements and occupations in riding trials on the Heath were carefully ascertained beforehand by this inveterate practical joker, and the hamper containing "Little Peter" was conveyed in a luggage van to the jockey's residence. Mrs Arnull, who expected to receive, as per promise, a hamper of wine, directed that the new arrival should be put into the cellar. When Arnull got home his wife told him the gleeful tidings that Mr Petre's hamper had arrived, and was in the cellar. " I will go and see it directly," quoth the exultant jockey ; and down he went, followed by a little pet dog, who was his constant companion. Scarcely had the faithful quadruped got into the cellar before he became greatly excited, and barked furiously, running backwards and forwards round the hamper. Thereupon old Bill exclaimed, " Drat it, there must be a mouse inside !" As he spoke he thrust his whip into the hamper, upon which the dog barked more furiously than ever. " Beggar my limbs if it ain't a rat!" ejaculated the jockey ; " get me a knife to cut the string, so that I may let it out." Suiting the action to the word, he uplifted the lid, and out jumped " Little Peter." " You young rascal!" exclaimed the astonished jockey, " what brings you here ? Get out of my house immediately, or I will lay this whip about your shoulders." The dwarf, thus admonished, proceeded to make tracks with all expedition to the Horse Shoe Inn over the way, at which MrBryant and a knot of expectant friends were eagerly awaiting his arrival.

William Arnull, who was one of the greatest favourites ever known in the jockey-world at Newmarket, or elsewhere, was much afflicted with gout, which caused him to be of a very irritable temper, especially when he was wasting hard. One day, shortly after he had been appointed overseer of the poor, he was riding off the Heath in the company of some gentlemen who were his employers. His temper was in a more than ordinarily crusty condition, and some of the practical jokers, who were his habitual tormentors, saw that he was in a fit state to be experimented upon. Accordingly they assembled opposite " The Rooms," and told a tramp, who had been soliciting alms, to wait there until "that gentleman" (at whom they pointed) " came by, as he was very kind-hearted, and, being overseer, in a position to give jobs to needy men." Thus encouraged, the poor man hobbled up to Arnull's horse's side and pleaded very earnestly for relief, stating that he had had nothing to eat for a long time. " Nothing to eat!" exclaimed Bill; " why, I'll bet a crown you have had something to eat since I have, or you wouldn't look as well as you do."

Despite the practical jokes to which he was continually exposed, no man in New-market was more respected than Bill Arnull. With perfect truth it might have been said of him, as it was

BILL ARNULL. 47

about the same time of Frank Buckle, that " it would have been easier to turn the sun from his course than either of these famous jockeys from the path of duty." Consequently, his services in the saddle were in much request by many distinguished noblemen and gentlemen, whose colours he habitually wore. Whenever he heard of a good horse or became cognisant of the merits of some good performer, he would exclaim, " I wish he were mine ! Wouldn't I turn him into ' Button Park' !" Nevertheless he did not succeed in filling his pockets very full, although, for many years, no man had more riding. In addition to winning countless races, he was continually wanted to ride trials, as he was a capital judge of the noble animal, and always secured a good pace when questions were asked. In 1822, shortly before the Craven Meeting, Lord George Cavendish tried Godolphin to be a good horse. At that time Godolphin had no engagements, and his Lordship was undecided in what race to run him. The Craven Stakes, then a very important event, generally gave rise to some spirited betting. Mr Boyce, who trained for Lord George Cavendish, advised his Lordship to run Godolphin in the Craven Stakes. With his usual caution Lord George interposed with the remark, " Send for Arnull, and let us hear what he says." Upon the great jockey's arrival he was asked whether he thought Godolphin could win the Craven ? " Win, myLord ? " exclaimed Arnull; " of course he will win, and easily enough too, unless a crow flies down his throat as he comes across the flat." Lord George followed his jockey's advice, and Godol- phin was duly entered. His weight was eight stone, and, ridden by Bill Arnull, he won in a canter, as had been prophesied by his pilot. Lord George won a good stake; and to show the difference between then and now, Mr Boyce and Arnull stood a fiver apiece on the horse, which in these days fashionable jockeys would doubtless magnify one-hundredfold. Vast as were the number of races in which " Old Bill" rode, no one ever dreamed of accusing him of riding dishonestly. Such, however, was not always the case at the period of which I am speaking, and the very mention of the word " Escape " recalls an episode as to which I will only add that Colonel Leigh, who had the management of the Prince Regent's stud, accused Sam Chifney of foul riding. Sam Chifney's son William was then a boy, but old enough to feel great indignation at Colonel Leigh's unjust aspersions. Walking up to the Colonel, the high-spirited boy told him to his face that when a little older he would have his revenge. Straightway he set to work to practise boxing, and took every opportunity of learning the pugilistic art. When he had grown into a lanky stripling of eighteen, he waited for Colonel Leigh in the street at Newmarket, as he was going to

BILL CHIFNEY. 49

the Rooms, and exclaimed on approaching him, " I told you I would one day have my revenge for your ill-treatment of my father; and now the time has come." With that he struck the Colonel a violent blow in the face with his fist, knocking him down, and striking him as he lay in the road. But for the intervention of the bystanders it was thought that he would have killed the Colonel, who was then a stout and pursy man. The latter had him up for assault before the magistrates next day. They sent William Chifney to prison for six months, with hard labour; and when he came out at the end of his term he oifered " to make door mats for a pony " against any other inhabitant of Newmarket. Six months of hard labour had indeed made him an expert at picking oakum. Bill Chifney was at the climax of his fortunes when he won the Derby in 1830 with Priam, whom he bought as a yearling for a thousand guineas from Sir John Shelley. In that year the two brothers, Sam and Bill Chifney, lived in adjoining houses at Newmarket, one of which (that occupied by Sam) was greatly improved and enlarged by the eccentric Duke of Cleveland, who was one of Sam's employers. This circumstance caused great jealousy between the two Mrs Chif- neys, and William's wife persuaded her husband to build a new house so as to cut out their sister- in-law. She vowed that not a single old brick should enter into the composition of the new

building. Pride, however, comes before a fall, and scarcely was the house finished before its owner found it unavoidably necessary to sell it at a ruinous sacrifice to Mr J. F. Clark, who afterwards resold it to Count Batthyany. It is now the residence of Mr John Dawson.

It is not generally known that H.R.H. the Prince Regent was not driven away from Newmarket by the " Escape" affair, but by another race in which his horse Sultan was supposed to have been ridden foully. H.R.H. then resolved to sell all his horses and to retire from the Turf. Bill Chifney's house became, as I have just said, the property of Count Batthyany, and his stables and paddocks at Headley (near Epsom) passed into the hands of " Lawyer " Ford, who afterwards disposed of them to my noble master Lord George Bentinck; and there Gaper, Refraction, Surplice, Loadstone, and many other horses from the Goodwood stable, were located before they met their Epsom engagements. The inconveniences then experienced in getting horses from Newmarket to Epsom have often led me to admire the foresight and sagacity of Lord George Bentinck, who predicted that railways would entirely revolutionise horse-racing. The youngest boy at Newmarket can now appreciate the accuracy of Lord George's prophecy.

With one final tale, which about that time caused no slight amusement, let me close a chapter

AXECDOTE OF GOODY LEVY. 51

which is already, I fear, too long. Three gay youths, belonging to a class or type which to-day is far more numerously represented than it was in my youth, chanced one rough morning to enter a little wayside inn near Six Mile Bottom, to get a drop of " something hot" to keep out the cold. At the fireside a harmless-looking old Jew was quietly seated, whose pronounced Hebrew features tempted the three mischievous young sprigs to make him their butt. " Good morning, Father Abraham !" exclaimed the first. " I hope I see you well ?"

" How are you, Father Isaac ?" continued the second, with well-counterfeited civility.

" All hail, Father Jacob !" reiterated the third. " I wonder what brings you out so far from home on this raw day ? "

Rising humbly from his seat, the old Jew lifted his hat with much mock dignity, and replied in quiet tones, " Gentlemen, you do me too much honour by your courteous inquiries and by the names you have been pleased to bestow upon me. My real name is Saul, the son of Kish; and I have been sent forth in search of my father's asses which he has lost. I was about to return despairing of finding them, when, lo and behold! the God of Abraham, of Isaac, and of Jacob has brought them into this very room; and here will I leave them while I go to report to my father."

With these words, and doubtless with many a secret chuckle, the old man tottered feebly along the passage and left the house.

There is a tradition | whether resting on a stable foundation or on none at all, who shall say ? |that the hero of this story was none other than the celebrated " Goody Levy " of " Running Rein" notoriety. He had gone down to Newmarket on a touting expedition, and had disguised himself as an old and infirm Jew to prevent his being recognised, as " The Heath," off which he had been warned, was to him forbidden ground.

3

SECTION 3

CHAPTER III.

EARLY RACING DAYS.

Lord George Bentinck evidently took an interest in racing at an early age, as in 1824, when twenty- two years old, he rode Mr Poyntz's chestnut mare, Olive, for the Cocked-Hat Stakes at Goodwood, beating Lord George Lennox's bay gelding, Swindon, and three others, after running two dead heats with Swindon. In the third heat his Lordship rode without spurs, and to his great delight won, beating Captain Berkeley, an excellent rider, who piloted Swindon. At that time Lord George Bentinck was staying with Mr Poyntz at Cowdray, and some ladies who were also guests in the house kindly undertook the task of making a jacket for him to ride in. How far this gratifying success tended to promote his partiality for Goodwood I cannot say, but after its occurrence he attended Goodwood races without intermission; was a subscriber in 1827 to the Cup, Stakes, and Drawing - Room Stakes; and was Steward in 1837.

As his father, the fourth Duke of Portland, took, as I have already said, the greatest interest and delight in breeding and racing his own horses, Lord George was familiarised from his youth upwards with the noble sport to which he subsequently became so attached. Although his Grace was a great supporter of Newmai'ket, and seldom engaged his horses elsewhere, Lord George, aided by his first cousin, Mr Charles Greville, obtained the Duke's support as a subscriber, in 1827, to the Stakes, Cup, and Drawing-Room Stakes at Goodwood, where H.R.H. the Duke of York was Steward the previous year. At the same time Lord George had an interest in some of the horses running in Mr Greville's name, and was a very heavy speculator. Thus it is well known that he backed Mr Richard Watt's Belzoni and Lord Fitzwilliam's Mulatto for the Doncaster St Leger of 1826 for a considerable amount. The race, however, was run when the ground was very deep, and was won by Lord Scarbrough's Tarrare, so that Lord George lost heavily|it was reported $27,000; but from his Lordship subsequently admitting to me that it was " the most disastrous event of his racing career," I feel sure that his loss must have greatly exceeded that sum; and his mother, and sister, Lady Charlotte Bentinck, afterwards Viscountess Ossington, most kindly and generously assisted him to meet it. It may naturally be supposed

BEGINNING OF THE STUD. 55

that this untoward incident could not be unknown to his father, who was much troubled and grieved about it, and expostulated most earnestly with his son, pointing out the consequences of such reckless speculation. To wean Lord George from such a dangerous pursuit, the Duke purchased an estate in Scotland for his Lordship,1 urging him with affectionate importunity to forswear racing and betting. For a few years Lord George respected his father's wishes; but the natural instinct could not be suppressed, stimulated as it was by his father's stud, and by that of his cousin, Mr Greville (who was his senior by seven years), and by his own great attachment to Goodwood, and to his valued friend, the fifth Duke of Richmond. The latter took the greatest interest in the noble sport of horse-racing, and permitted Lord George to share a few horses with him. This induced Lord George to make several other purchases, running his horses in the name of the Duke of Richmond. These purchases were, in 1832, Kislar Aga and a black yearling colt by Reveller; and in 1833, a chestnut filly, Chanterelle. In 1835 his Lordship bought Pussy, Tiber, and three yearlings|viz., a colt by Sultan out of Gold Pin, a colt by Sir Benjamin Backbite, and Wimple, a filly by The Colonel. In 1836 and 1837 there were added Zipporah, Frontignac, Chateau La- fitte, Hooghly, and Guava. In 1838 the stud was augmented by The Currier, Tamburini, and others, all running in the name of the Duke of Richmond. Lord George also had horses running in the names of Lord Orford, Mr Greville, and Lord Lichfield|Ascot and Bodice, for instance, running in Lord Orford's name ; Preserve, Dacre, and Elis in Mr Greville's; and Elis, Arbaces, Ascot, El Pastor, with others, in Lord Lichfield's. It was not to be expected that so many different interests could be reconciled for any great length of time without some conflict of opinion arising, and accordingly the two keenest speculators, Lord George and Mr Greville, soon came into collision. Their differences became so great that all efforts on the part of their most intimate friends to compose them were of no avail|the result being that the horses in Mr Greville's name were removed to other stables, whilst Elis, with others, was intrusted to John Doe, Lord Lichfield's trainer. Preserve joined Lord George's stud at Doncaster, where his brood mares were under the charge of Mr Bowe, who kept the Turf Tavern, and in whose name his Lordship subsequently ran most of his horses.

1 The estate in question was at Muirkirk, in Ayrshire. On the death of Lord George Bentinck, his brother, Lord Henry, succeeded to it, and sold it some years later to Mr James Baird of Cambusdoon, whose nephew, Mr John Baird, now holds it.

This Mr John Bowe was at that time ostensibly landlord of the Turf Tavern at Doncaster, but the real lessee was Mr Samuel King, whose daughter

BENTINCK STUD AT DANEBURY. 57

Mr Bowe had married. Lord George Bentinck ran some of his horses in the name of Mr King, but the latter was a trainer who, among other horses, prepared Tarrare|the property of the Earl of Scarbrough|for the Doncaster St Leger of 1826, which Tarrare won. Mr King therefore thought it would expose him to invidious comments if he appeared as nominator of mysterious horses of which he was not the trainer, and with which he had no intelligible connection. Under these circumstances he begged Lord George to find some other nominator for his entries, and in this way the services of Mr John Bowe were secured for that purpose. In reality, Lord George would have preferred to use Mr King's name, as he was very energetic and skilful in managing Lord George's paddocks and brood mares at Doncaster, and Lord George knew him well and trusted him thoroughly. The Duke of Richmond did not approve of having any more of his Lordship's horses at Goodwood to run in his Grace's name, although it was his Lordship's wish to have all his stud there. In consequence, therefore, of this objection on the part of his Grace, Lord George established a stud at Danebury, where he expended a large sum in building stables, forming paddocks, making roads and plantations, and double-turfing the gallops ; in fact, it was rumoured that his Lordship expended $1500 for bone-dust alone. At that time John Barbara Day, familiarly known as " Honest John,"

was at the head of the Danebury stables, and he had long been the Duke of Portland's favourite jockey.

As previously stated, his Lordship entertained a great predilection for Goodwood from its privacy, excellent downs, elastic turf, and glorious expanse of ground, affording superb gallops at all seasons of the year and under all vicissitudes of weather, and it was greatly against his will that it became necessary for him to go elsewhere.

Being favourably impressed with my father's training and stable-management, more especially when Mr Kent's (in reality the Earl of Uxbridge's) Rubini won the Goodwood Cup in 1833, beating Mr Greville's (Lord George's) Whale, and again when the Duke of Richmond's Elizondo won the Port Stakes at Newmarket, beating Sylvan and Bodice, Lord George told my father that these horses had won solely by reason of the condition in which he brought them to the post. His Lordship lost heavily upon each race, but he did not omit to tell his friends, including the Duke of Richmond, that it was " all owing to Kent's train- ing."

In 1834 his Lordship bought Venison as a yearling, and as he hoped soon to have all his horses at Goodwood, Venison was entered for the Derby in the Duke of Richmond's name. Owing, however, to his Grace's subsequent objection, Venison was sent to John Day's at Danebury to be trained.

VARIED FOBTUNES. 59

When two years old he ran for the Lavant Stakes at Goodwood in John Day's name, and was beaten. Gondolier, who had been at Goodwood a year or two previously in the Duke of Richmond's name, was sent, after having been in Prince's stable as Mr Greville's property, to John Day's, in whose name he ran in 1835. These two horses were all that ran in John Day's name that year; El Pastor, Preserve, Dacre, Marmalade, and Elis ran in Mr Greville's till that unfortunate difference occurred, when Elis and El Pastor joined Gab, Arbaces, Ethiopian, and Ascot at John Doe's, nominally as Lord Lichfield's property, in whose name they ran for their engagements. Although Lord George lost heavily upon Preserve for the Oaks, he had already been successful with her in winning the One Thousand at Newmarket, to which were subsequently added the Drawing-Room Stakes and the Verulam Stakes at Goodwood. With Elis his Lordship won the Chesterfield, Clearwell, Criterion, and a sweepstakes at Newmarket, and the Molecomb Stakes at Goodwood. Although at that time his Lordship betted heavily and lost considerably upon Preserve when Queen of Trumps beat her for the Oaks, and when Glaucus beat her for the Goodwood Stakes, he won a big stake upon Queen of Trumps when she won the St Leger, owing to the great ease with which she defeated Preserve in the Oaks ; prior to which Mr Greville, in giving Nat his orders, told him to" come away at Tattenham Corner, but not to spread-eagle them too far!" John Blenkhorn, trainer of the Queen, happened to hear this, and instructed Tommy Lye to " spread-eagle the others as far as he could," with the result that such a tailing race has seldom been seen since !

In 1836 his Lordship entered more fully than ever into the spirit of racing, and increased the number of his horses. Elis was beaten for the Two Thousand Guineas by Bay Middleton, much to his Lordship's disappointment, as he backed him for a considerable amount, after trying him with the Duke of Richmond's Pussy (winner of the Oaks in 1834) and with others, whom he beat so easily that we all thought his defeat impossible. Bay Middleton, however, defeated him in such style that Lord George never ceased to back Lord Jersey's splendid colt for the Derby of 1836 ; and after seeing him saddled and cantered, his Lordship rode up to the ring, which was then formed on the hill near the mile-post, and took $2000 to $1000 three times about Bay Middleton, thereby landing a good stake, although he had Venison running, whom he had also backed.

Encouraged by his success in backing Bay Middleton for the Derby and in owning Elis, of whom, although he admitted his inferiority to Bay Middleton, he entertained a very high opinion, and remembering that Venison had evinced good form by winning the Gloucestershire Stakes and

FIRST IDEA OF VANS. 61

Cup at Cheltenham, his Lordship exercised his active and ingenious mind in giving effect to an idea that race-horses might be conveyed in a sort of van which would preserve them from the risk and fatigue, to say nothing of the delays, inseparable from travelling on foot from place to place. This idea he expounded to my father, who thought there would not be much difficulty in accomplishing it, as he remembered a horse called Sovereign, belonging to Mr Terrett, having been conveyed in a bullock-van from Worcestershire to Newmarket. As there was a similar van upon the Goodwood estate, his Lordship inspected it with my father, who was so convinced that the principle could be adopted for the conveyance of race-horses, that he at once used every means in his power to give effect to his master's wishes. My father judged that if a valuable horse could be moved from the south to the north of England so as to run well in the St Leger, the method would at once be established and adopted. Having Elis engaged in the St Leger, Lord George thought it a good opportunity to make trial of this plan. Accordingly he employed Mr Herring, a coachbuilder in Long Acre, to construct a van capable of holding two horses. Mr Herring was kept in the dark as to the object with which the van was being built, and few were allowed to know of its construction. As it progressed, its successful adaptation to the purpose for whichit was built was confidently anticipated, although it was a heavy cumbrous vehicle, with the wheels running under it, an arrangement which elevated the body so high that it was not easy to get the horses inside. This difficulty was surmounted by raising or banking up the surface of the ground into a sloping approach. In order to ensure success, Lord George sent Elis to Goodwood to be prepared upon its splendid gallops, and to run in the interim for his Goodwood engagements, and for another at Lewes. The horse was under the care of John Doe, who was also in charge of Ascot, Arbaces, and Toss Up. Elis won the Drawing-Room Stakes at Goodwood, and in reward for his victory Lord George presented my father with $25 for the following reason. The day previous to the race Elis had a severe attack of gripes, and Lord George thought all chance of his being able to run was at an end. Even after the horse's recovery, thanks to remedies suggested by my father, Lord George feared that the effects of the medicine would weaken Elis and prevent his winning; but my father assured his Lordship to the contrary. After Elis had won the Drawing- Room Stakes, his Lordship's hopes that he would also win the Goodwood Cup began to revive. He had backed the horse heavily for the Cup, which was run two days after the Dra wing-Room Stakes ; but it was hardly to be expected that a three- year - old should beat such a four - year - old as

ELIS. 63

Hornsea at 15 Ib. over a distance of two miles and a half. Nevertheless, Elis ran a great horse, and for a time appeared likely to win; but at last the distance and the disadvantage in weight told upon him, and he finished a good second to Hornsea. Notwithstanding this race, Elis was pulled out for a second time on the same day| to run for the Racing Stakes|which he won easily, beating the Drummer and Taglioni, with odds of 10 to 1 laid on him.

A fortnight later Elis won the Lewes Stakes at Lewes over a mile and a half, giving 21 Ib. to Lord Egremont's Hock, and beating seven others, including Rockingham. This was a great performance, and Lord George's hopes of winning the Doncaster St Leger with him were raised higher than ever. As the horse continued to take his gallops at Goodwood with The Drummer to lead him, assisted by Pussy and Tiber, it was the general impression that after four races (three at Goodwood and one at Lewes) Elis would never see Doncaster. Fortunately he possessed a strong constitution, like his grandsire Selim. Both were ravenous feeders, but Elis differed in one respect from Selim, whom, from his restive and violent behaviour in the box, it was difficult, and even dangerous, to approach with a feed of corn. Elis, on the contrary, was very quiet both in and out of the stable. Some time after the race at Lewes, Venison was sent to Goodwood to try Elis, whogave him 7 Ib. and 21 Ib. to The Drummer, beating both over the St Leger distance. This was most encouraging to Lord George, who was greatly excited, and more than ever anxious to have his wonderful new van completed.

As John Doe was obliged to return home to Newmarket for a short time, my father took temporary charge of the horse, and had many communications made to him by Lord George on the subject of the van. My father's interest in it was naturally as great as that of his Lordship, and he assisted John Doe in every possible way to prepare Elis for the race, and to make him handy for entering the van. At last the day arrived for the machine to reach Goodwood, and preparations were made for packing Elis and The Drummer into it side by side, and despatching them to Doncaster. Lord George, who had been a frequent visitor to Goodwood while Elis was there, and who posted down from London or from Andover to see his favourite, was on the spot when the van arrived. He inspected it inside and out with the greatest care, and was vastly pleased with the result of the examination. Next he proceeded to inquire with characteristic thoroughness what the two horses would require on the road, and gave orders that until the St Leger was over Elis should eat no corn or hay except what was drawn from my father's granary at Goodwood. Even the sieve out of which the horse was fed was to be taken from Goodwood.

FIRST TRIAL OF THE VAX. 65

As I have already stated, the body of the van was lifted high above the ground, on account of the construction of the wheels|being built, in fact, on the same lines as the old gipsy-vans. It therefore became necessary to back it against a bank which formed a boundary of old Goodwood Park, and stood opposite the kennels. In this way entrance into the van was made easy for the two horses ; and the platform or gangway being covered with straw litter, the horses entered without hesitation, especially Elis, who was a very docile and tractable animal. All being prepared, the six post-horses were attached to the vehicle, and Mr John Doe mounted the box. After this fashion was the great tentative experiment initiated, and the start effected, greatly to the delight and astonishment of all who had witnessed the preparations by which the first specially constructed racehorse van on record was brought into active requisition.

Nor were the curiosity and wonder less as it proceeded on its way, the greatest surprise and interest being excited by it in every village and town through which it passed. Some of the spectators asserted that a wild beast of extraordinary ferocity was locked up inside; others that a notorious criminal was being sent from jail to be tried at the assizes. Pedestrians stopped and eyed it with amazement. The coachmen and passengers of the various coaches were astounded at seeing

six post-horses attached to such an uncommon and strange-looking machine. At some of the towns through which it passed three pairs of horses could not be obtained ; at others it was thought advisable to have but two pairs. The distance from Goodwood to Doncaster (about 250 miles) was divided into three sections of aboiit eighty miles *per diem.* At the end of the second day, which was a Saturday, Elis and The Drummer were taken out of the van, and galloped on the following morning on Lich- field race-course ; and on Monday morning they proceeded on their way to Doncaster, where they arrived in the evening (two days before the St Leger), to the undisguised amazement of thousands of beholders.

As it required some time to complete the necessary preparations for unvanning the two horses, a multitude assembled at the Turf Tavern to witness the disembarkation of the mysterious favourite, Elis, who a few days previously was supposed to be still at Goodwood, and not likely to put in an appearance at Doncaster. When Elis was landed upon *terra firma* he shook himself vigorously, and walked unconcernedly into his stable. At the betting-rooms in the evening all sorts of conjectures were rife, and the odds fluctuated a good deal. In the morning Elis was taken out upon the racecourse accompanied by The Drummer, and the two went a good gallop. The rapid strides and healthy appearance of the Goodwood favourite so satisfied

OTHER VANS. 67

all vho saw him that it was generally remarked, " Although he came into Doncaster in the rear of six horses, he will leave twice that number to inspect his tail in the great race."

The van, although cumbrous and heavy, was a commodious vehicle, and completely fitted internally with padded sides. Moreover, the horses stood upon a hard-stuffed mattress, so that their knees might not be broken if they fell down. There was also a manger for each, and every other convenience; so much so, indeed, that the machine resembled a movable stable.

As this enterprise proved beyond expectation successful, Mr Herring was instructed by Lord George to build another van upon an improved principlelin short, a less cumbersome and ponderous conveyance. A hind platform was attached, which could be let down, so that the ascent might be made less steep. A door was also added in front, to obviate the necessity of turning the horses round or backing them when getting them out. This second van was used by me for many years. Mr Hunnybun, a coachbuilder at Newmarket, subsequently built others upon greatly improved principles, with peculiar axles which brought the body of the van much nearer the ground, so that the difficulty often experienced of getting the horses into their travelling carriage was overcome. Mr Hunnybun's vans were beautifully finished and admirably constructed, costingfrom $150 to $160 for a double, and $120 for a single one. At Goodwood we soon had three of the former pattern and two of the latter, in addition to the first constructed by Herring. They were frequently used, his Lordship being so much in favour of their employment that he insisted upon having even the most inferior animals conveyed to their destination in themlsome of which, indeed, were of less value than the horses employed in drawing them. As the average cost of a pair of post-horses was 2s. per mile, the expenses were naturally very heavy; but his Lordship thought it might be the means of avoiding the introduction of disease into the stable, which was often contracted through horses being put into unhealthy quarters at the various inns at which, when travelling on foot, they were compelled to stop. The journey of Elis from Goodwood to Doncaster could not have cost less than from $80 to $100. It was said at the time that the old- fashioned trainers complained in no measured terms of this new mode of conveyance for race-horses, and insisted that it was unnatural, and certain to be injurious to the delicate constitution and organisation of the trained thoroughbred. This they very soon discovered to be an error, as it enabled horses which were heavily engaged to run at many meetings which they never could have reached on foot. To no racing centre was it of greater advantage than Newmarket, as horses trained there could b&

If . .

. . ' I'.-:.. ;

: ., l'. :".: ii" i1.1 . '.'! ' ' : Ilih
' l! ,. . ,
'..,... TV. I- v-v. :-.
. . . . i . 'IS .' I II - ' .. (1 !i:.r- -s
V ' ' -(.; ! t- 1" I :(li..' ' "
' i-v . :,.; i.r.v i" '.-! . l'- '
.. ,-.-i ...). i ;' j.-i,..ii. , ! ; .-r; ,
i , . Ik , .-.i.HAi " piio : ;!"
r. W

ADVANTAGES OF THE VAN. 69

despatched with comparatively little fatigue, and no wear and tear, to run at meetings to which it would have been impossible for them to proceed by road. At that
time there were not more than 250 horses in training at the metropolis of the Turf,
while far larger numbers were prepared for their engagements at various provincial
places. In this manner the van was of immense advantage to racehorses, and also
to their owners and trainers, and, like many other reforms initiated by Lord George
Bentinck, it was of untold benefit to all who took an interest in horse-racing. Indeed
the introduction and universal employment of vans inaugurated a revolution in the
management and engagement of race-horses. When it is remembered that Mr John
Scott's Cyprian walked from Malton to Epsom and won the Oaks on May 20, 1836,
and was immediately despatched on foot to Newcastle- on-Tyne, where on June 22
she won the Northumberland Plate, having taken nearly a month to walk 300 miles
from Epsom to Newcastle, it is easy to understand that, previous to the employment
of vans, young horses were often temporarily worn out, and sometimes lamed for life,
by long journeys on the hard road.

Some two or three weeks before the St Leger of 1836 it became evident that Elis
was being backed for large sums, and that the market was being worked actively by
some persons who, as Lord George had reason to suspect, were betraying him, and
getting on a big sum of money. To test his suspicions, his Lordship made it publicly
known that he would not run the horse unless he could obtain the odds at 12 to 1
to $1000, knowing well that no one, unless he had previously backed Elis heavily,
would be in a position to lay such a bet. The result was that $12,000 to $1000 against
Elis was laid to his Lordship's commissioner. Nothing could have been more to his
Lordship's gratification, as it proved beyond doubt that he was right in his conjectures.
Although Mr W. Scott's Scroggins was a great favourite, having been heavily backed
at 6 to 4, Elis won rather cleverly, and Lord George was rewarded by landing a good
stake. In my opinion he never would have succeeded in getting the odds against Elis
at 12 to 1 to that large amount had it not been that the layers believed it impossible for
the horse to reach Don- caster in time to run for the St Leger. They were well aware
that Elis was still at Goodwood in the middle of the week preceding the Doncaster
meeting, and that it took fifteen or sixteen days for a horse to walk from Goodwood
to Doncaster. Under these circumstances, the Danebury party, who had backed him
heavily, became uneasy, and were not long in making up their minds to " unload."
They were perfectly cognisant of the fact that Venison, who came from Danebury to

Goodwood to be tried with Elis, had been beaten by the latter when in receipt of 7 lb., and accordingly

PURCHASE OF BAY MIDDLETOX. 71

they made haste to " get on," never caring whom they forestalled. They soon found, however, that Lord George was a dangerous customer to take liberties with; and I am perfectly confident that his Lordship would not have allowed Elis to start for the St Leger unless the bet of $12,000 to $1000 had been forthcoming.

In the First October Meeting at Newmarket, Elis again met Bay Middleton for the Grand Duke Michael Stakes; but Lord George, satisfied that although Elis had won the St Leger, Bay Middleton was the better animal, invested merely a trifle on his own horse. In the race Bay Middle- ton, beautifully ridden by Jem Robinson, beat Elis, ridden by J. B. Day, rather easily, and proved to be what Lord George considered him. Determined to acquire possession of this grand horse, Lord George offered Lord Jersey 4000 guineas (the largest sum ever paid for a horse down to that time) for Bay Middleton, which Lord Jersey accepted. Lord George then proposed to make use of Elis's van in order to convey Bay Middleton to Danebury in it. Upon this "Tiny" Edwards, Lord Jersey's trainer, exclaimed, " You may send the van, my Lord, if you like, but all Newmarket will not get Bay Middleton into it 1" As usual, his Lordship was not to be turned from his purpose. The van was sent, and Bay Middleton was easily induced to enter it, and was thus conveyed to Danebury,greatly to the surprise of all who were acquainted with the horse's impetuous temper. An attempt was made to train him, but it failed, as his foreleg had gone before Lord Jersey sold him. He was then sent to join Lord George's stud at the Turf Tavern Paddocks at Doncaster, where Ascot, who ran second to Mundig for the Derby, and from thirty to forty brood mares, were already ibstalled. In addition, his Lordship had a lot more brood mares at Danebury, and others at Bonehill, near Tarn worth, making in all about sixty-five. Next year he had about thirty foals by Bay Middleton, some of which were out of valuable mares; and as his fee was only thirty guineas, Bay Middleton had some very high-bred mares sent to him in addition to those belonging to his owner. Although a most superior racehorse, Bay Middleton was for a long time very unsuccessful at the stud, so many of his stock being unsound and very difficult to train, which was not only a great loss to his Lordship but also a great disappointment. A very remarkable fact was that daughters of Velocipede| of all mares the most unlikely to throw sound stock, as their sire was notoriously infirm in his knees | nicked best with Bay Middleton. On the other hand, the progeny thrown to Bay Middleton by Emilius mares and Whalebone mares were generally unsound, and sometimes cripples. Still Lord Geprge believed that some day BayBay Middleton's Progeny. 73

Middleton would get a good race-horse, and it was only in consequence of continual failures that he was at last induced to send Crucifix, Latitude, and one or two others to Touchstone, with the result that Surplice and Loadstone were foaled in

1845, and sold by Lord George as yearlings in

1846, with the rest of his stud. His Lordship did not live to see the full realisation of his anticipation that one day Bay Middleton would become the sire of a great horse. This happened in 1846, when The Flying Dutchman was born, and in 1851, when Andover, another winner of the Derby, first saw the light. Again, in 1848, Sir

Joseph Hawley's Venus gave birth to Aphrodite", and in 1853 to Kalipyge, both being daughters of Bay Middleton,|the last-named being, in Sir Joseph Hawley's opinion, the best mare that he ever owned. She broke down in 1856, after winning the Craven Stakes at Epsom.

The site selected by the present Duke of Portland for his breeding establishment at Welbeck Abbey, upon which he has erected extensive buildings and formed very complete and well- arranged paddocks, is the very spot which it was Lord George's ambition to employ for the same purpose, if he could have prevailed upon his father to entertain the idea. The extraordinary success attending the valuable stud installed at this moment upon the site in question is another proof of Lord George's foresight; but it is doubtfulwhether a stud owned by Lord George would have attained that excellence, or afforded him as much pleasure as it has to the present Duke, more especially if Bay Middleton had been stationed there. It was Lord George's hope, when he bought Bay Middleton, that the horse might be able to win the Ascot Cup as a four-year-old in 1837; but one of his fore - legs, which had been very suspicious - looking when he ran his last race, failed in training, and though entered for the Cup, to which there were forty subscribers, he could not start. He was then sent, as I have already said, to join his Lordship's stud at Don- caster. Nothing could exceed Lord George's disappointment when Bay Middleton failed as a stallion. The enormous amount of forfeits paid in produce stakes for his stock would have discouraged any one else, while to some it would have been absolutely fatal. But Lord George was too firm of purpose to be daunted or turned aside by any disappointment. The only effect it had was to make him patronise more successful stallions at any cost. However clever and practical a breeder or owner of thoroughbreds may be, the uncertainty attending speculation in racing stock is always likely to upset his calculations. Although Lord George possessed two game and fairly good horses in Elis and Venison, he could not be satisfied without investing 4000 guineas in buying Bay Middleton. Simultaneously he sold

CASUALTY STOCK. 70

the other two, which it would, perhaps, have been wiser in him to have kept, and not to have bought Bay Middleton at all. It cannot be denied that the late Sir Tatton Sykes spoke truly and from long experience when he called thoroughbred stallions, brood mares, and their progeny " casualty stock."

4

SECTION 4

CHAPTER IV.

HORSE-RACING PREVIOUS TO VANS.

The success attending the conveyance of Elis to Doncaster by this novel and expeditious method was a great achievement, as upon few, if upon any, previous occasions was the attempt to win the St Leger with a horse sent from the south of England successful. From Newmarket it occupied nine days to travel to Doncaster on foot, and from Goodwood fifteen or sixteen days, which, with all the vicissitudes of weather, undesirable accommodation, and inferior provender, entailed great risk, expense, and frequent disappointment. To set off with four or five horses in order to make a long journey on foot, with little or no change of clothes for the horses or lads, each horse having his muzzle, containing brush and comb, rubber, sponge, and perhaps a set of extra bandages|the whole secured by one of the stirrup-leathers and laid over the withers|was indeed a serious business. I generally accompanied the horses on my own hack, and sometimes driving

HORSES ON THE EOAD. 77

in my buggy. If the weather proved wet, our difficulties were greatly increased, as it took an infinity of trouble to dry all the clothes at the inns where the horses stopped for the night. Colds and coughs, attended with distemper or strangles, were of frequent occurrence, and it was with a knowledge of all this that Lord George exercised his resourceful ingenuity to devise some plan of carrying his horses on wheels to the scene of action. Previously, the endeavour to win the St Leger with what were termed in those days South Country horses had signally failed, although such superior animals had been sent to Doncaster as Sultan, Plenipotentiary, Shillelagh, Ascot, Revenge, Byzantium, Rubini, Marcus, Priam, Frederick, Exquisite, Mameluke, Translation, Spondee, Redgauntlet, and Preserve. With the exception of Mameluke, who ran second to Matilda, and of Priam, who was placed second to Mr Beardsworth's Birmingham, not one of the above-named starters got a place, although some of them were backed heavily.[1] Those were indeed primitive times, and Lord George seemed to possess a special faculty for revolutionising and galvanising them. Previous to the construction of vans, it was a matter of no slight difficulty and risk to get horses even from Newmarket to Epsom to run for the Derby and Oaks. Many a favourite on arriving at Epsom was unable to start, from being amiss on the day. It was usual for Newmarket horses to reach Epsom or the neighbourhood three weeks or a month prior to the races. Some were located at Epsom, some at Ashstead, Leatherhead, Mickleham, and Headley, the last place, when Mr Ladbroke resided there, being headquarters, as, in addition to being an opulent banker, he was an enthusiastic sportsman and a confederate for many years of the late Earl of Egremont. It was his great delight to entertain as many of the most distinguished patrons of the Turf as possible, and also to accommodate their horses. The Duke of Grafton, the Duke of Cleveland, and the Duke of Rutland were always included among Mr Ladbroke's guests, and their horses were provided with excellent stable accommodation. Mr Ladbroke also took lodgings near his own house for their trainers|Robert Robson, R. D. Boyce, and William Chifney. The Cock Inn hard by was well patronised by other trainers and jockeys, so that Headley, as long as Mr Ladbroke lived, was an important racing centre whenever the Epsom Summer Meeting came round. In addition to entertaining as many distinguished guests as he could find room for, Mr Ladbroke took the greatest pleasure in inviting all the

1 For the following statement I am indebted to Mr W. H. Lang- ley : " This was not surprising in Plenipo's case, as he came to the post as fat as a bullock, from having done little- or no work during the time he was located at Brocklesby Park during the previous month. Such information was volunteered to me by a resident at Limber, who saw the horse daily."|Ed.

ASHSTEAD STABLES. 79

jockeys and trainers who stopped at Headley to a sumptuous repast, over which he presided in person, towards the end of the Epsom week. Needless to say, the Epsom meeting was greatly enjoyed by Robson, Neale, William Chifney, R. D. Boyce, and my father. After the death of Mr Ladbroke, Headley ceased to be so attractive to frequenters of Epsom, and deeply indeed was his loss felt and lamented by the inhabitants. Leatherhead and Ashstead were also favourite resorts 'during the Derby and Oaks week |the former place being frequented by John Scott and James Edwards, and the latter by John Forth and, after Mr Ladbroke's death, by Neale and R. D. Boyce. It was at the " Leg of Mutton and Cauliflower" at Ashstead that Cadland, Frederick, Little Wonder, Merry Monarch, and the notorious Leander were stabled, and also

Gulnare, winner of the Oaks, whom the Duke of Richmond came there to see. With his usual kind and considerate thoughtfulness, his Grace said, " Well, Kent, how is the mare ? I hope she is well, and you too ? You ought to live well, as you have a ' Haunch of Venison' at one end of the village and a ' Leg of Mutton and Cauliflower ' at the other ! "

After Mr Ladbroke's death the Chifneys purchased a meadow and paddock at Headley, not far from the Cock Inn, upon which they built some good stables. Before long the Chifneysexperienced a reverse of fortune, and the land and stables at Headley passed into the hands of " Lawyer" Ford, from whom Lord George Ben- tinck purchased them. It was here that Crucifix and Grey Momus stood, together with other horses, including Gaper and Chatham, all of which belonged to Lord George. In 1845, I passed the Epsom week there with the Duke of Richmond's Refraction (who won the Oaks), and other horses under my charge, and in 1848, full of anxiety about the safety of the favourite, I took Lord Clifden's Surplice and Loadstone to the same spot to run for the Derby, which the former won.

So great was the importance attached by Lord George to having all his horses vanned to Epsom and to other race meetings that, although he had animals running at Epsom on the first day of the races, and again in the Derby on Wednesday, he would insist upon having his mares which were to run in the Oaks conveyed in vans to Headley on the Derby Day. The inevitable result was that he had to pay enormous charges for post- horseslat the rate of fifteen guineas a-pairlto take the vans from Kingston railway station to Headley. This was the price paid in 1842 for Firebrand's van, as his Lordship had backed the mare for the Oaks in consequence of her having won the One Thousand Guineas at Newmarket; but in the Oaks she only finished third to Mr G. Dawson's Our Nell, who was first, and to Mr

LORD GEORGE CAVENDISH. 81

Shackel's Meal (both of them daughters of Bran), who was second. Firebrand was a light-built filly of very delicate constitution, and her noble owner grudged no expense in order to give her every chance. I have known him do the same, however, with animals not worth more than the hire of each pair of post-horses attached to their vans on the Derby Day.

Had Lord George's convenient system of vanning race-horses been available in Lord George Cavendish's time, it is probable that " Royal George," as he was invariably called, would have landed a great stake on the Derby of 1815, which was won by the Duke of Grafton's Whisker. In Boyce's stable at Newmarket, where Lord George Cavendish's horses were trained, there was in 1815 a first-class three-year-old, Sir Joshua, the property of the Hon. Richard Neville, who was afterwards Lord Braybrooke. Sir Joshua had won the Riddles worth at Newmarket, and some other races, and Lord George Cavendish, one of the heaviest speculators that I can remember, backed him for the Derby for an enormous sum. Unfortunately, the horse caught cold while journeying to Epsom on foot, and was unable to start. At the Houghton Meeting of that same year, Sir Joshua was matched to give Whisker, the Derby winner, 5 Ib. across the Flat. The betting was very heavy, and when Sir Joshua won cleverly, Lord George Cavendish got back most of hisEpsom losses. Like Lord George Bentinck, the nobleman of whom I am now speakinglwho, by the way, was great - grandfather to the present Duke of Devonshire I could not be daunted or turned from his purpose. I have often heard my father describe the celebrated match between Filho da Puta and Sir Joshua in 1816, when both were four years old. Filho da Puta had won the St Leger easily in 1815, and was undoubtedly a great horse. He was matched to give Sir Joshua 7 Ib. over the Rowley mile in the Craven meeting of 1816. The winter of 1815-16 was extraordinarily severe in the north of England, and Filho was sent by Croft, his trainer, from Middleham to Newmarket many weeks before the great match. The horse stood at William Chifney's stable at Newmarket, and was under the charge of John Scott, afterwards the famous Whitewall trainer, who was then head-lad to Croft. Not long before the match Sir Joshua was tried with Lord George Cavendish's Bourbon, and won his trial. On the first day of the Craven meeting, Bourbon won the Craven Stakes very handsomely, beating a good field of sixteen horses, which gave Lord George Cavendish and other patrons of Boyce's stable great confidence in Sir Joshua.

During the race meetings at Newmarket Lord George Cavendish always lodged at Mr Boyce's house. When he arrived there shortly before the Craven meeting of 1816, he was met by the Hon."royal George" At Newmarket. 83

George Watson (one of his most intimate friends), and by Mr Boyce and my father, who was then head-lad to Mr Boyce. They told Lord George Cavendish that the Yorkshire gentlemen had mustered in great force at Newmarket to back Filho, whom they thought invincible. " I am glad to hear it," rejoined " Royal George," " as I have brought my strong-box with me." When his Lordship entered the betting-rooms on the night before the match, he was received with three times three by the north-country sportsmen. Not much time was wasted in useless preliminaries. His Lordship was assailed on all sides by offers to bet 500 to 400 on Filho, and, taking out his betting-book with the utmost composure, he wrote down all the bets offered on those terms. Then there was a momentary lull, to which Lord George put an end by offering to bet 500 even that Sir Joshua won. Again he was accommodated to a very large extent, and again he tired out all the backers of Filho at even money. Finally, looking round the room, the indomitable backer of Sir Joshua exclaimed, " As no one will go on backing Filho at evens, I shall be happy, before going, to bet 500 to 400 on the little horse as often as any one will take it." The last voice heard that night was Lord George Cavendish's, as he shouted out, " Five hundred to four on Sir Joshua !" without finding a taker.

How much money Lord George Cavendish stakedthat night will never be known; but it was the opinion of my father, and also that of the late Earl of Stradbroke, whose horses were trained at that time by Mr Boyce, and who managed the trial of Sir Joshua, that it could not have been much less than $50,000. Next day the match came off, and Sir Joshua just won. When the start was effected, Filho, who was very impetuous, reared high in the air, losing two or three lengths, which he could never quite regain. Perhaps " Royal George " was fortunate in getting safely through this desperate encounter between two good horses; but although invited to do so, neither he nor Mi- Neville would consent to make the match over again, although the backers of Filho offered to put down $3000 against Mr Neville's $2000.

It is a little remarkable that mv father should

have served two noble patrons of the Turf who were so much alike in the magnitude of their betting ventures as Lord George Cavendish and Lord George Bentinck. When Bourbon won the Craven Stakes some foreigners wanted Mr Boyce to ask Lord George Cavendish whether he would sell him, and' if so, what price he would take. Mr Boyce replied, " I might as well ask him to sell Burlington House; you had better ask him yourself." And when the question was put to Lord George, the answer he gave was, " When I want to sell him I will let you know." At this time Lord George Cavendish was considered the most85

influential patron of Newmarket; and Lord George Bentinck in his day was regarded by many as " The Rothschild of Tattersall's."

It was always Lord George's opinion that the most satisfactory races are those over a distance of ground, and of his preference evident proof was afforded by his gift of the Waterloo Shield, the largest and most valuable prize ever given to a race by one person, which was run for at the Goodwood meeting of 1837. It may appear to some that the three prizes of $1000 each, so generously given in 1890 by Mr C. D. Rose, were each of them equal to the Waterloo Shield; but the advertised cost of the latter was greatly exceeded by additional embellishments suggested by his Lordship after it was supposed to be completed. This magnificent piece of plate was, in conformity with Lord George's predilections, run for over the King's Plate Course of about three miles and three quarters. There were forty subscribers of $25 each, fifteen forfeit, and eighteen runners, and the shield was won by Colonel Peel's Slane, who claimed a 7 lb, allowance for having been beaten in the Cup. Since 1834 it had been the custom for one of the Stewards of Goodwood races to give a Cup of $100 value. In 1837 the Earl of Albe- marle was Steward with Lord George Bentinck, and being the senior of the two, he did not feel disposed to relinquish his right to give the annual $100 Cup; so that, in order to enhance the popularity of his favourite meeting, Lord George promptly gave the Waterloo Shield.

Lord George's father, the Duke of Portland, was also disposed to encourage long-distance races, and he established the Portland Handicap at Newmarket, to be run for over the last three miles of the B.C., to which race his Grace added $300. The Duke seldom or never ran a two-year-old; and at that time it was considered unwise to encourage three-year-olds to race too much, as is shown by the following extract, which appeared in the 'Sporting Magazine' of 1836: "The tendency of the great three - year - old races is to deteriorate the breed of the English race-horse. Nothing can be done to correct it till the close of the present season. For a true patriotic attempt in this direction we are indebted to the Duke of Portland, who has founded and endowed the Portland Handicap ; and there can be little doubt that we shall find other stakes upon the same plan instituted at all the great race meetings." There is no question that races exceeding a mile in distance afford more opportunity of exhibiting fine horsemanship than the short-course races of the present day. The riding of such artists as Samuel Chifney, Frank Buckle, and James Robinson over some of the long courses at Newmarket was quite an attraction, and far more interesting to good judges than the competition of the horses.

FRANK BUCKLE. 87

My father used to say that Frank Buckle had the finest character of any jockey that he ever knew. His power of riding long distances was unequalled in an age when all jockeys performed their journeys on horseback. In point of fact, Robert Robson, who was called " the Emperor of Trainers," would have nothing to do with any jockey unless he rode long distances almost every day on horseback. For many years of his long life Frank Buckle resided at Peterborough, where he was born, and where he now lies buried. Although Peterborough is about ninety miles distant from Newmarket, Buckle thought nothing of riding from his own home to the Heath and back on the same day. In finishing a race, he had recourse to a circular motion of his arms, which caused him to be often called the " Peterborough screw." His integrity was so well known that, in a corrupt era, no one ever thought of approaching " Old Frank" with dishonest proposals or suggestions, as in one instance he was said to have drawn his whip smartly across the face of a gentleman who, although a member of the Jockey Club, had the audacity to ask Buckle to pull a horse in a match. During the whole of Buckle's career the rivalry between North and South was infinitely greater than it has been during the last twenty or thirty years. Owners and trainers of race-horses, and the jockeys who bestrode them, were greatlyunder the influence of this predominant feeling, which was perhaps at its climax in 1827, when the Honourable Edward Petre's Matilda beat the Derby winner, Mr Gully's Mameluke, for the great St Leger Stakes at Doncaster. At the beginning of this century Frank Buckle was the crack jockey at Newmarket, which was always regarded as being in the south of England, and simultaneously John Shepherd held a similar position among his northern congeners. Buckle and Shepherd were frequently in the habit of meeting in races and matches, and no slight jealousy existed between them, although Buckle was naturally too kind-hearted and easy-going to harbour an unkind thought about anybody. He was sometimes forced, however, to ride with suspicion, because Shepherd was by no means scrupulous, and would take every unfair advantage that came in his way, which indeed was at that time a characteristic of most of the north-country jockeys. Frequently there was a great deal of money betted upon matches in which Buckle and Shepherd met, and in those days it was generally impossible to draw a line, or form an estimate as to the comparative merits of the two opposing horses. As a rule, it was Shepherd's policy to make running, while Buckle waited, following immediately in his antagonist's track. It once occurred that, in a match over the four - mile course at York, Buckle had his enemy dead - beat about a hun-

BUCKLE AND SHEPHERD. 89

dred yards from home, and came up between Shepherd and the rails. Even then the north- country jockey would not allow himself to be beaten ; as he drove Buckle, who would otherwise have won in a canter, upon the rails, and kept his own knee in advance of Buckle's knee, so that the latter found it impossible to extricate himself from the position in which his old antagonist held him as in a vice. In those days there was no such thing as disqualification for foul riding, and Buckle knew full well that no complaint made by him would be listened to for a moment on a Yorkshire course. He contented himself, therefore, by saying to Shepherd: "It will not be long, I reckon, before you and I meet again at Newmarket, where you cannot drive me on the rails; and then I warn you that I will have my revenge."

The words were prophetic, as within a few weeks the two jockeys met in an important match over the Beacon Course at Newmarket for a thousand guineas a side. Shepherd was universally regarded as a wonderful judge of pace, and resorted as usual to his favourite game of making play. Buckle, on the other hand, was one of the finest finishers of a race that ever galloped across the Flat, and his skill and *finesse* in getting the last ounce out of a tired horse at the end of four miles have never been surpassed from that day to this. In the match of which I am now speaking Shepherd made thepace so good, that, glancing repeatedly over his shoulder, he soon satisfied himself that, long before the winning-post was reached, he would succeed in galloping his adversary to a standstill. As the two horses drew near to the judge's chair Buckle kept close to the heels of the other horse, so that Shepherd could not see him without turning right round in the saddle to look. At this critical moment the north-countryman became aware that he had not yet done with his pertinacious opponent, who gave every indication of intending to come up on Shepherd's whip-hand. When they were about a hundred yards from the chair, Shepherd's eye was anxiously fixed upon the winning-post. Observing Shepherd's preoccupation, Buckle pulled his horse to the near side, and before Shepherd had withdrawn his eyes from the judge's box, Buckle had stolen a march upon his enemy, and was leading a couple of lengths on the near side. Loud cries of " Look at Buckle ! look at Buckle ! " arose from the onlookers, who were waiting on horseback at the cords. When it was too late Shepherd perceived his danger, but Buckle had got the first run, and although there was a good effort left in Shepherd's horse, who had been most judiciously ridden, the race was over, and Buckle had won by half a length. Such shouting and cheering as arose upon the Heath had, according to my father, never been heard before that day. As the two rivals rode back to scale, Buckle curtly re-

BUCKLE AS A EIDER. 91

marked, " I told you when you came to Newmarket that I would pay you off, as I have done to-day."

Never was jockey more respected than Frank Buckle during the last thirty years of his honourable and spotless career. He was a most agreeable man, and always glad to give hints about riding to his younger rivals. When it came to a fine point between two horses after a long gallop, it was 6 to 4 on " Old Frank " against any other " knight of the pigskin." No man had a more powerful seat upon a horse, and in the longest race he was never known to tire. Occasionally he had to ride horses which, without his knowledge, had been nobbled or in some way made safe before leaving their stables. My father often told me that in 1811, at the Second Spring Meeting, he saw Mr Christopher Wilson's chestnut horse Wizard beat Lord George Cavendish's Middlethorpe (also a chestnut horse) over the Beacon Course in a 500-guinea match. Wizard was ridden by Buckle, and Middlethorpe by Arnull. In the race, Milddlethorpe, who was the son of Shuttle, and, like all of Shuttle's breed, a bad-tempered horse, stopped so short that Arnull was pitched off, and Buckle galloped home alone. Much to his astonishment, Buckle experienced the greatest difficulty in keeping Wizard upon his legs till the winning- post was passed. The horse reeled and staggered like a drunken man, and seemed to be wholly bereft of sight. " I don't know what you have doneto this horse," exclaimed Buckle to the trainer, " but he is as blind as a bat." No reply was made by the trainer, who, as subsequently became known, lost a heavy stake by backing Middlethorpe for the match, which, in Wizard's condition, it would have been impossible for Middlethorpe to lose had not his jockey fallen off.

In order to get back his losses, Wizard's trainer persuaded Mr Wilson to make another match between Wizard and Middlethorpe, conceding 2 Ib. to the latter. It came off over the Two Middle Miles in the First October Meeting 1811, and again the dishonest trainer had to' put up with a costly defeat. He backed Wizard for enough money to get back all his previous losses. Unfortunately the horse, on whom odds of 7 to 4 were betted at the start, fell lame in the race, and Middlethorpe won by more than a hundred yards.

In 1836, when James Robinson won the Two Thousand Guineas upon Bay Middleton, and the Portland Handicap upon Sheet-Anchor, the following remarks were made by a sporting writer at the time : " A very remarkable display of jockey- ship occurred on the part of Jem Robinson at the First Spring Meeting at Newmarket over the last three miles of the B.C. upon Mr Cooke's Sheet-Anchor, when he beat Lord Chesterfield's Hornsea, ridden by William Scott, and Mr Mos- tyn's Birdlime, ridden by T. Lye, in addition to Revenge, Rioter, Pelops, Tiber, and other starters.

I l' ' I
c o ?
Q
O

X
H

REMARKABLE DISPLAY OF JOCKEYSHIP. 93

Lye upon Birdlime made running to the distance, when Bill Scott, who had been nursing Hornsea, brought him up resolutely, challenged Lye, and raced with him. The pace was good, and the punishment severe, and to all appearances Scott had the race in hand, when, on the lower ground, for the first time his eyes caught sight of Robinson on Sheet-Anchor. A glance was enough, as Robinson was sitting quite still in the saddle, with the race evidently in hand, and close upon home out he came with a rush that sent your heart into your mouth, and won by a length, while half the lookers-on believed Hornsea had caught the judge's eye. When shall we again see two such races as this and the Two Thousand between Bay Middleton and Elis ?" Being an eyewitness of this consummate display of jockeyship, it reminded me of the same two opponents when they met in the Derby of 1828, and Cadland, ridden by Robinson, ran a dead-heat with The Colonel, ridden by William Scott. In the deciding heat, Robinson, after making running to the distance, gammoned Scott that Cadland was tiring, which induced Scott to take the lead, and, as he expected, to go up and win. But Jem had a good effort left in Cadland, for which Scott was quite unprepared, and to his great astonishment Jem beat him on the post by about a neck. To witness Robinson's riding was indeed a treat, for as a specimen of skill and knowledge of the animal it could not be surpassed. I could mention a number of instances of this famous jockey's matchless prowess in the saddle, equal, perhaps, to those above enumerated.

The great secret in his art was, that it was impossible for any one, not even the old jockeys who so frequently rode against him, to know whether his horse was extended or not, or whether he was on the back of a free or a sluggish animal. He sat without any apparent motion; and when it suited his purpose he would appear to be riding as if his horse were tiring, whether he was so or not, a latent effort being nearly always left in him sufficient to win the race. He had a great aversion to short - course races, and as much as possible avoided riding in them, stating that often some stable-boy upon an animal hardly able to carry a saddle got off in front, and was past the winning- post before any riding on the part of real jockeys could be called into requisition.

With the view of promoting long races at Goodwood, Lord George Bentinck, at a great expense, constructed the Maidstone Course, four miles long ; and the King's Plate Course (another of his creations) which was three furlongs short of four miles. The desired length could have been obtained by going twice round the hill, as used to be done for sweating horses in those days; but of this his Lordship did not approve, and preferred to make a course outside the old circle round the hill and the various clumps of trees. This course was

MATCHES. 95

used for a few years; but as the taste for short races increased, the number of courses made by Lord George was found to be confusing, so dolls were put across those which were not used, with a view to guiding and directing the jockeys as to the right track for them to follow. Even with these precautions, mistakes sometimes occurred, as in the case of Ithuriel and Red Deer.

Being always ready to make matches and promote sport, Lord George pitted his Captain Cook against Lord Maidstone's Larry M'Hale over two miles and a half at Goodwood, nominally for $100 but in reality for $1000; as it was customary with Lord George to advertise the amount staked in some of his matches as one-tenth of the actual sum. Hence the match between his Bramble and Lord Maidstone's The Caster the same year in the Craven Meeting at Newmarket, over the B.C., was for 1200 sovereigns, 800 forfeit, although advertised at sixty sovereigns each and forty forfeit. Also at Goodwood the same year, in a match between Olive-Oil and Rose of Cashmere for 500 sovereigns each, the sum was advertised at $50. Although gratifying his partiality for long races, Lord George did not profit by the result of his match against Lord Maidstone's Larry M'Hale, nor by the example of the magnificent riding of Jem Robinson, whose style he so much admired, as there was much more agitation in his Lordship's long arms and legs than wouldhave been visible in Robinson's when his opponent closed with him for the final struggle. Whether the course was too long for Captain Cook, who was a bad roarer, trained by the late Isaac Day, I cannot say ; but it evidently was for his pilot, who was not so fit for the contest as Lord Maidstone. The latter, being in fine condition, rode four winners during the week, beating, upon Lord George's Naworth his own horse, Mechanic, after the two had run a dead-heat over the Maidstone course, Captain Percy Williams riding Mechanic. If Lord Maidstone was able to beat such a jockey as Captain Percy Williams, after running a dead-heat with him, it was not much discredit to Lord George to be beaten only by a neck by such an excellent rider over a course of two miles and a half, when, moreover, Lord George was altogether out of condition and his noble opponent as fit as a fiddle.

5

SECTION 5

CHAPTER V.
REMOVAL FROM DANEBURY.

In the autumn of 1841 Lord George Bentinck resolved to remove all his horses from Danebury to Goodwood, and to sacrifice the enormous outlay he had incurred at the former place. He stated his intention to me as he rode off the course at Newmarket on the Friday of the Hough ton Meeting of 1841, desiring me to send at once and take charge of those horses he had at NewmarketIviz., Tripoli, Topsail, Halfcaste, and Crusadelas "he had made up his mind not to continue at Danebury." I was also instructed to arrange for the removal of the remainder of his stud from Danebury to Goodwood, with everything belonging to him; which I must confess greatly surprised me, and caused me to feel in a somewhat unpleasant position. I was well aware that for a long time his Lordship had been dissatisfied with certain proceedings at Danebury, upon which he enlarged during the Houghton week at New-

market, and especially upon the circumstances connected with Mr Etwall's Melody colt, who was heavily backed for the Cambridgeshire Stakes and ran second, having been trained by John Day, who also trained Lord Palmerston's Ilione, the winner of the Cesarewitch during the Second October Meeting. Rather than submit to what he deemed an injustice, Lord George thought no sum of money too great to sacrifice, and showed his indomitable spirit by leaving Danebury, where, as was often stated at the time, he was " literally walking on gold laid out by himself."

When I went to Danebury I found five or six horses in training, a large number turned out, and several yearlings. It was his Lordship's wish that all of them should be conveyed in vans to Goodwood ; and as the yearlings were unbroken, the carrying out of this plan was attended with no little anxiety, trouble, and risk. From the unusual circumstance of the yearlings not having been broken, I fully believe that Lord George contemplated this great change some months previous to effecting it, as it was his custom to have his yearlings broken early in the year, and to try them before the closing of the Stakes after the Houghton Meeting. He told me he did not desire to have them broken at Danebury, in order to avoid any estimate of their merits being formed there. Four of these yearlings|Farintosh, Gaper, Bramble, and Fore-

TRANSPORT TO GOODWOOD. 99

saillhe considered very promising, and wished them to be conveyed in vans to prevent their incurring any risk in travelling on foot. This arrangement necessitated the employment of four vans (two double and two single ones) for four days, on the journey from Goodwood to Danebury and back, a distance by road of about 106 miles per day. I left home between four and five each morning, and returned at night about ten o'clock. My daily freight consisted of horses in training and of yearlings, as I did not think it advisable to convey all the yearlings by themselves. Under the most favourable circumstances my responsibility was far too great to be pleasant. Before leaving Danebury in the morning, I was occupied for two or three hours in making arrangements for the journey, some of the youngsters being most difficult to get into the vans, and refractory when there, not to mention that during the journey they were sometimes almost unmanageable. What with the fatigue of the four consecutive days' journey and the anxiety attending it, I was glad enough when my task was completed; especially as I was under the impression that the removal could have been effected with considerably less expense, less risk, and inconvenience, had all the horses left Danebury on the same day, and proceeded on foot to Goodwood. So positive and peremptory, however, were his Lordship's instructions, that I came to the conclusion he had morereasons for such arrangements than he cared to express. As we were starting from Danebury on the last day, John Day's lads jeered at my lads, and told them that all Lord George's horses combined were not worth as much as their journey to Goodwood would cost. Before the end of the following year they had to change their tone, especially when Firebrand won the One Thousand Guineas, Flytrap the Column, and Tedworth a One Hundred Sovereign Stake, all at Newmarket; Misdeal the St James's Palace Stakes, at Ascot, value $650; the Racing Stakes, at Goodwood, value $1300; the Grand Duke Michael Stakes, at Newmarket, value $1100. That same year, also, Tripoli won the Somersetshire Stakes, and Topsail the Cup, at Bath ; Mustapha a stake at Goodwood of the value of $1950 ; and finally, Gaper the Criterion, at Newmarket.

Lord George's instructions to me were to take my own lads and servants in the Duke of Richmond's vans, which his Grace lent him. My next instructions were to arrange for the transport of the cart-horses, carts, rollers, &c., from Danebury to Goodwood, and to provide temporary shelter for them near the stables at the latter place, as, naturally, such an addition to the Goodwood establishment made it necessary to provide greater accommodation, which his Lordship, with the consent of the Duke of Richmond, lost no time in doing. He superintended the work at Goodwood personally ?

DIETING KACE-HORSES. 101

and soon forgot the great sacrifices he must have made by leaving Danebury. This did not appear to trouble him in the least, but rather to incite him to find means to replace what he had left behind, and, if possible, to improve upon it. During the winter months much of his time was spent at Goodwood with the Duke of Richmond ; and he took the greatest interest in the work as it proceeded, spending many hours each day with the labourers employed. Often he was accompanied by the Duke, who was also greatly occupied in watching the various works, some of which might have been thought likely to intrude upon the privacy of his Grace's splendid estate. On account, however, of the long personal friendship existing between himself and Lord George, the Duke made concessions to him which he would never have granted to another.

Some of the horses from Danebury being very light in condition, and others infirm, his Lordship was most anxious that every effort should be made to recover them. He therefore suggested to my father that they should be liberally fed upon split beans and white peas. Of this my father did not quite approve, alleging that he had frequently known horses select the beans and peas, and refuse to eat the oats with which they were mixed. He much preferred giving them a certain quantity of flour in their water, as from experience he found great nourishment was afforded by it to suchanimals as were subjected to severe races and strong exercise entailing fatigue, and even distress ; and it did not discourage them from eating their corn. This seemed to impress his Lordship very favourably, and he desired that its effects might be fully tested upon all those horses whose constitutions were not as robust as could be wished. As time advanced the horses so treated improved greatly in appearance. Firebrand and Flytrap, being the most delicate, and most heavily engaged, his Lordship thought their strength and powers might be still further increased by giving them new milk mixed with flour to drink, and a dozen new-laid eggs in each feed of corn. Accordingly, cows were purchased to provide the required milk, and the eggs ordered from the farmers were marked with their initials, to ensure their being fresh, as his Lordship would not buy from a dealer or shopman, for fear of the eggs being musty, so as to give the animals a distaste for their corn. At first there was some difficulty in inducing the horses to partake of this unnatural diet and beverage, but after a time they ate and drank it with avidity, and stood a good preparation, Firebrand winning the One Thousand Guineas and Flytrap the Column.

After these successes Lord George, being so much impressed with the beneficial effects of milk and eggs, wished all the light-fleshed and delicate animals to be fed in the same wav. Some were most

DIETING RACE-HORSES. 103

wretched specimens, especially those got by Bay Middleton, which were not worth keeping in the stable, and still less worth pampering in this manner. One cripple, Crusade, by Ascot, out of Crucifix's dam, was fed some time on this diet. When a yearling he injured his back by falling in the paddock, and if a rehabilitation could be effected, his Lordship thought it would not be difficult to recover the expense of " a little milk and a few eggs." When at Danebury, Crusade had run for small selling races, but without success. His back was so bad that he had entirely lost the natural action of his hind-legs. The case was perfectly hopeless, yet Lord George insisted upon persevering in this treatment till time at length convinced him that it was useless. This milk-and- egg system involved great expense and additional labour with no compensating result, as was observed by the Duke of Richmond, who one day remarked to his noble friend, when looking over the stables with him, " You will soon want my farm and poultry-yard, George, to supply your horses with milk and eggs, in addition to filling all my stables, I think you had better let Kent feed the horses in his own way; he has hitherto been successful for me, and my horses have done very Avell." After a few months the milk and eggs were discontinued ; but the flour, in which my father and I were firm believers, was given to many of the horses|to some to accustom them|to it in case they should ever run down, and need it ; and it was invariably given after a severe race or after running heats|especially after a dead heat|in which we were seldom beaten when it was run off. Whether the result was due to the support afforded by the flour or not, I cannot say; but it was a matter of common remark that deciding heats were almost invariably won by the Goodwood stable. Some of the old horses enjoyed the flour so much that it was with difficulty the pails containing it could be removed from them until the contents were entirely extracted by aid of the tongue, which often amused Lord George greatly.

In 1842 (the first year in which all his Lordship's horses were trained at Goodwood) he ran twenty-one, and was more successful than he expected, many of them being very infirm either in their limbs or wind,-|a great failing in the Bay Middletons, by whom many of them were sired. John Day, indeed, had such an objection to them, that he said, when Lord George's stud left Danebury, he would never train another Bay Middleton. Certainly they were not very desirable animals to have in your stables. The two finest yearlings brought from Danebury|viz., Farintosh by Bay Middleton, out of Camarine's dam, and Gaper by Bay Middleton, out of Flycatcher|were so infirm that it was a great anxiety to a trainer to have to do with them. Farintosh, one of the finest horses ever bred or seen, was a verv bad roarer indeed;

THE HALNAKER GALLOP. 105

and Gaper had such doubtful legs that it appeared almost hopeless to endeavour to train him. John Day, in fact, said he never could be trained; but by the aid of " Kent's charges "|as Lord George subsequently called the application|-and the excellent training-grounds'.at Goodwood, he was kept upon his legs and won the Criteron Stakes at Newmarket in 1842, greatly to his Lordship's delight, as he had a yearling bet of $10,000 to $100 about him for the Derby. His legs being so bad through standing over at the knees like a cab-horse, liberal odds were laid against him for the Derby, after the Criterion, which were taken by and for his Lordship, till he stood to win a very large stake upon him. This unexpected success, enhanced by Gaper's future prospects, stimulated Lord George still further to persist in his endeavours to command success. He determined to extend and improve the exercise - ground, and to form a gallop upon the ascent for a mile and a half upon the most elastic turf that I have ever seen. To attain this object, he devised the famous Hal- naker Park gallop, which, with other

works upon the Molecomb Hill, he was most anxious to complete. After explaining his views and projects to my father and myself, he inquired of me what the cost of such works would amount to, as a large number of immense timber-trees would have to be felled and their roots grubbed up, banks levelled, and turf and mould broughtfrom some distance. I said that it Was a most expensive undertaking, and could not be carried out for much less than $3500 ; to which he replied, "If it enables me to win one race it will pay all that." With his usual ardour, after obtaining permission from the Duke of Richmond, he at once commenced the job, employing over one hundred labourers and twenty-eight cart-horses, the superintendence of the work affording him the greatest pleasure. One day, after riding upon the race-course and the Mole- comb Downs, he pulled up on the summit of the new Halnaker gallop then in progress, and coming suddenly upon the splendid and extensive panoramic view spread before him on emerging from the wood, he remarked, " There's a beautiful sight!" Of course I thought he alluded to the landscape so suddenly brought before his eves. " I did not
/ O /
mean that," he explained, " but the sight of so many men at work, and the means it affords them to provide food for their families during this inclement season." The potato-disease, which prevailed greatly that year, engaged his Lordship's attention. He said the gardener at Welbeck had found that a sprinkling of lime over each layer of potatoes, when storing them, was the best preservative he had tried ; and he added that if any of the Goodwood labourers wished to try the experiment, they were to be supplied with lime for the purpose at his expense. During the progress of these works a labourer metGaper's Career. 107

with an accident by falling from a tree while adjusting a rope to assist in felling it. He sustained a fracture of one of his legs, and was taken to the infirmary at Chichester. When Lord George heard of it he inquired whether the man was married, and on being informed that he had a wife and family, his Lordship directed that the wife should be paid her husband's wages until he was able to resume work.

After the season for laying turf, tan was put upon the various gallops and upon the race-course. The cart-horses were employed upon this work for months, bringing the tan from Chichester, a distance of five or six miles. This was, of course, a heavy expense, but his Lordship believed it to have been of great benefit to the grass at Danebury, where he had caused hundreds of tons to be spread, and he thought it would be of equal service at Goodwood, and repay the cost.

As previously stated, Lord George had backed Gaper heavily for the Derby. During the winter and as the spring advanced he was encouraged in his speculation by the improved prospect of the horse standing a preparation which would enable him to run up to his form. In the Craven meeting at Newmarket Gaper ran on the Tuesday, and won a sweepstakes of 100 sovereigns each, R.M., by eight lengths, beating the Duke of Grafton's Esop, ridden by J. Day, who, although greatly surprised at the easy manner Gaper won, stillthought with his bandaged legs he could not be trained to win a Derby. On the following Thursday Gaper ran and won again, beating New Brighton and Jerry Sneak for a sweepstakes of 200 sovereigns each, D.M. John Day, having laid $20,000 to $250 -against him, examined him very anxiously, and still thought he could have no chance of winning the Derby with such doubtful legs. Cotherstone, whom Gaper had beaten for the Criterion, won the Two Thousand Guineas easily, which increased Lord George's confidence in Gaper, and he continued to back him till he stood to win about $135,000 upon the horse. On account of his legs Gaper was not tried previously to 'running for his engagements at Newmarket; but about a fortnight after the Two Thousand he was stripped and had a roiigh gallop of a mile and a quarter, when he won with ridiculous ease. On the 20th of May, about a week before the Derby, he was again tried a mile and a half with Discord (the Melody colt before alluded to) and others, when he won very easily indeed. This raised his Lordship's hopes and expectations greatly, more especially as Gaper appeared to be perfectly sound, and none the worse for his races and trials. Every precaution was taken to get him safely to Epsom and to the Derby post; and in order to test the form of Discord, he was started for the Craven Stakes on the first day, which he won, to the great surprise of Lord George, beating Knight of

GAPER AT THE DERBY. 109

the Whistle, Alice Hawthorne, and six others. After the race I said to his Lordship, "Where would Gaper have been had he run ?" His reply was, " He would have been in Epsom town before the others reached the winning-post!" Robert Hesseltine, who trained Alice Hawthorne, remarked, "If Gaper can beat Discord at 16 lb.. as stated, the Derby will be won by the Sussex nag by little short of a hundred yards." As I understood that John Day had laid $20,000 to $250 against Gaper, I took an opportunity of advising him in a friendly way not to risk such a sum, and at the eleventh hour he got Mr Gully to take $20,000 to $3000 for him about the horse from Lord George, losing on the balance $2750. The tremendous play made by Gaper cut down more than half the field at once; the hill settled the chance of many more; and as the leading horses neared the turn five only were left in the race. Gaper came gallantly round Tattenham Corner with a lead of a couple of lengths, and had such a winning look about him that shouts of " Gaper wins !" rent the air. " Gaper was fit to run for a man's life, but we apprehend that the course was a trifle too sticky for his action." Such was one report of the race. Another said: " Lord George's horse rattled round the corner at such awful speed, and looked so well, that' Gaper wins !' ' Gaper wins !' was shouted from hundreds of throats; but he ended by being fourth in therace. The greatest winners were Lord George Ben- tinck, who netted nearly ,$8000 by Cotherstone, Lord Chesterfield, Colonel Anson (a handsome stake), Mr Bowes, about $12,000, Mr Gully, Mr O'Brien, the Scotts, and others connected with the Malton establishment." Cotherstone won cleverly by two lengths, Gorhambury being second,|the betting being 13 to 8 against Cotherstone, 5 to 1 against Gaper, 14 to 1 against Newcourt, with a long list of others who were backed at various odds. Such was the termination of Lord George's long- entertained expectations and anxious hopes. I did not feel quite satisfied, and thought if Gaper had been ridden by Abdale, as in the trial, with a snaffle bridle and without spurs, he would have run better, and might probably have won, his health and condition being so good. As it was, he was ridden by Sam Rogers in a severe curb bridle, and was rattled along so mercilessly that the deep ground soon brought him to a standstill. Like his sire, Gaper was very impetuous, and it was difficult to make him submit to any restraint. He was rather a fine and good-looking horse, with much power, but his legs were so unsound that the

Duke of Richmond remarked to his confederate, " I suppose, George, you will have this horse painted some day; when you do, I should advise you to have him taken standing in a quantity of straw to conceal those legs of his." Yet it is very remarkable that Gaper ran fifteen

RACIXG EXPENSES. Ill

times when three years old and won seven races, beating the Duke of Richmond's Lothario by a head for the St Leger at Newmarket (D.I..), ridden for the first time by Flatman, Sam Rogers riding Lothario, whom Lord George and others in the stable backed. The next day Sam Rogers rode Gaper for the Town Plate (D.I.), when 7 to I was betted on him, and he finished last of three starters.

This year his Lordship ran twenty-eight horses in 122 races, and had seventy-three in training, the expenses of which were great. My father's accounts werelJune 30, $3447, 18s. 8d. ; December 31, $3503, 3s. Ild. ; and at the close of the year Lord George said to me, " I never during all my life received such bills as I get from you." Naturally I felt alarmed, and replied, " I am sorry, my Lord, they are not satisfactory. I know they are very heavy, but I really cannot lessen the expenses. My hands are continually in my pocket, travelling so much as I do with so many horses : I am frequently obliged to pay something extra to accomplish the distance in time. I do not think I have charged more than I have actually paid out of pocket. If there is any mistake, it is in not charging some few pounds paid by me which are not accounted for, as it is impossible for me to put down all that I am obliged to disburse." " That is just what I think," was his Lordship's reply; "you do not charge two-thirds, or onehalf, as much for many things as I have paid for the same at Danebury. With all your travelling you must sustain considerable loss by the destruction of your clothes ; therefore for the future charge me $200 a-year for their wear and tear !" That year I travelled 6155 miles, a large portion of it by road. The distances were greatly increased in some years, and for travelling expenses alone I disbursed $3600 in one year. His Lordship would never reduce his expenses by selling a horse. " They will do for the gentlemen to ride," he would say, when advised to dispose of some; and on being told that they were too infirm to carry gentlemen, he would get over the difficulty by saying, " Then they will do to teach the little boys how to ride."

Although he had built a large number of new stables, and converted into stables all available buildings, still the accommodation was insufficient, and Lord George asked the Duke of Richmond to permit him to erect more. " If you had Chichester barracks," replied the Duke, laughing, " you would fill all the stalls. You had better get rid of some of your horses, as Kent recommends." " How am I to get rid of them ?" asked his Lordship. " Sell them, my Lord, if you can," was my reply; " if not, give them away or shoot them," which his Grace thought good sound advice. After much persuasion, Lord George consented that fifteen should go to Tatter-

THE GOODWOOD YEARLINGS. 113

sail's, and made a promise not to attend the sale, but to let them go for what they would fetch. All were sold but one, which, naturally, no one would purchase when offered with its engagements. The highest prices realised were $25 and $30. Some of them were yearlings, and had been tried. Three of the latter became the property of Mr Francis Villiers, who, like his father the Earl of Jersey, had no faith in yearling trials. In the spring Lord George said to me, " You have got me into a pretty mess by your advice to sell those yearlings, as Mr Villiers tells me they can run." I told his Lordship that I was pleased to hear it. " You are pleased when I have sold good horses, are you ?" he rejoined, sharply. I answered that I was glad to hear they could run, for I knew that his Lordship had better in his stables, which I hoped would win some of their engagements. Still he continued to regret having sold them, and in order to try and reassure him, I selected some of our horses which had been tried, and which I thought were better than those sold, although not the best of his lot. I therefore advised his Lordship to make some matches with them against those Mr Villiers had bought. Three or four matches were accordingly made. Lord George won the first very easily, and received forfeit for the others. After this he was satisfied, and no longer regretted the sale of his yearlings.

Counting those belonging to the Duke of Richmond and Lord George, forty or fifty yearlings were broken each year. I found it very advantageous to ascertain their merits as soon as I could, and to select a few of the best for heavy engagements, as was proved by results; for often, when taken from the paddocks, the most promising were put into stakes which closed very early. If possible, all were tried before the end of the Houghton Meeting. In some years many were tried before Doncaster Races, as was the case in 1844, when Ennui (dam of Saunterer, Loiterer, &c.) distinguished herself by winning two trials. At Don- caster John Scott had what was thought a very fine yearling to sell, called Tom Tulloch|by Het- man Platoff, out of Cyprian|which Lord George was anxious to purchase, and desired me to look him over. I did not quite like the colt, as he was heavy-shouldered, and one of his fore-feet rather clubby. Still, his Lordship had a fancy to buy him. I recommended him not to do so, but to let some one else have him, and to match the little filly, Ennui, against him. At the sale Lord George bid 1200 guineas for Tom Tulloch, when I entreated him not to bid more. Eventually the colt became the property of Lord Maidstone for 1500 guineas. The next day Lord Maidstone, the Earl of Glasgow, and others went round Lord George's stud at Doncaster. " So I hear you bought that yearling from John Scott yesterday," said Lord

THE GOODWOOD YEARLINGS. 115

George to Lord Maidstone. " I will run you for $500 at Goodwood next year with a little filly I have got." To which Lord Maidstone replied, " John Scott will not take a two-year-old to Goodwood, but I will run you here." Lord Glasgow wished it to be a sweepstakes, that he might put one in, which was agreed to. "I will bet each of you a thousand I beat you," said Lord George. The bets were taken. When the race came off, 6 to 4 was laid on Tom Tulloch, but Ennui won easily by four lengths. This success encouraged his Lordship to try his yearlings as early as possible, and ultimately some were tried before York Races, with good results. This was one of the many endeavours of Lord George to accomplish what to others appeared impossible. " Nothing is impossible," he would say, " if you will only try." Whenever I told him that I did not think some wish of his could be carried out, he would say immediately, " Will you try ?" and if successful, he would greet me with, " I told you it could be done." If unsuccessful, he would say, " As you could not succeed, I suppose it is not possible. I am much obliged to you for trying all the same." A great and just characteristic of his

Lordship's was, that he always acknowledged a service rendered, and appreciated the effort made. There was no limit to his sanguine self-confidence, or to the resources he suggested and called into play for the purpose of accomplishing some object.To cite expense as a reason for not attempting it was sure to offend him; and he would invariably sign a blank cheque when he deputed me to make any purchase for him, and handed it to me, saying, " There, fill that up for whatever you think it, or they, are worth."

In 1844 Lord George Bentinck ran thirty-eight horses in 175 races, and won fifty-three. He had increased his stud considerably, having about seventy brood mares and two or three stallions, in addition to the large number in training, the forfeits for which alone amounted to $9170. This was rather a successful year. The stable, including his Lordship's and the Duke of Richmond's horses, won sixty-three races, value $19,840, including the Port Stakes at Newmarket, the Somersetshire Stakes at Bath, the Chester Cup, Ham, Drawing- Room, and Nassau at Goodwood, Municipal and Two-year-old Stakes at Doncaster, the Clearwell, a great match with Miss Elis against Oakley and another between Clumsy and Vibration, both at Newmarket. At the First' October Meeting the stable won six races, ten at the Second October and ten at the Houghton Meeting, making twenty- six races in the three weeks. Upon some Lord George won largely, especially on the two matches of Miss Elis and Clumsy. The latter was only a two-year-old, and ran a match over the Two Middle Miles against Vibration, a five-year-old mare belonging to Sir Joseph Hawley. Clumsy carried a

SUCCESSES IN 1844. 117

"feather" and Vibration 8 st. 9 Ib. The betting was very heavy, as it was considered absurd to run a two-year-old over such a long course against a good five-year-old mare; but to win such a race was the height of his Lordship's ambition.

The stable's successes in 1844 commenced with the victory of the Duke of Richmond's Red Deer for the Chester Cup. The betting was heavy, and the race had never been won before by a three- year-old ; in fact, three-year-olds were not entered for it until two years previously, when his Lordship put some in. During the winter Lord George was able to get on a large stake in small sums by backing the three-year-olds, Kent's lot, and Red Deer outright, without directing attention to the horse. As Red Deer was handicapped at 4 st., it appeared to Lord George so great a certainty that he made a book for him, laying against others. In a letter to me dated January 13, 1844, he says : " I am glad to see Red Deer in at 4 st. (as well as Strathspey) for the Chester Cup; for if Kitchener can get Red Deer out, and if he is the horse over a distance of ground that you tried him to be, I don't see how he can be beaten." With his Lordship's love for heavy speculations it may be easily imagined to what extent he would bet upon a race of this description, when entertaining the opinion he expresses in the above letter. In another letter, written from Harcourt House, February 24, 1844, he says: "At present all I havedone is to get 700 to 100 about the lot for the Chester Cup. I wish I had had the luck to get the odds about the three-year-olds. I have desired my commissioners to be on the look-out for any repetition of such offers. I do sincerely hope I may get through in my match with The Caster."

On March 19 his Lordship wrote me: "I am delighted to hear so good a report of Bramble. *If he can vin his match, it iviU pay all my forfeits at the Spring Meetings,* which is as much as I can expect to do. I am very glad to hear Kitchener seems to manage Red Deer so well. I have now got on the odds to $285 about the lot at 7i to 1, and the odds to $75 outright about Red Deer, which averages, I believe, about 24 to 1. It has been very hard work to get on; all in $10 bets. Your father and you shall stand at 25 to 1. Your father wishes to stand $20l viz., 500 to 20 ; let me know what you would like to stand. I am bound to confess that I think Chester the worst course in England for a ' feather'; if it were at Newmarket, Goodwood, or even Bath, I should not be much afraid. If Bramble wins his match against The Caster, he will be first favourite for the Chester Cup; and from what you write me I cannot help being very sanguine." Bramble's match against The Caster was for 1200 guineas (Beacon Course). Although John Scott's party were very confident of winning with The Caster, Bramble made strong

REMOVAL FROM DANEBURY. 119

running and won easily by twelve lengths. As Lord George predicted, Bramble became first favourite for the Chester Cup, being in at 7 st. 9 Ib. and 4 years old, Scott's party backing him stoutly. " Those who like may back Red Deer," said they, " but Bramble will win." John Day's party also backed the latter, remembering how easily he beat Ben-y-ghlo and Vitula at Bath the year before. As Red Deer could beat Bramble at one half the weight he had to give himlviz., 3 st. 9 Ib.lhis Lordship stood a heavy stake against Bramble, and felt much alarmed when he saw him gallop at Chester; but I assured him he had no earthly chance of giving the weight to Red Deer, unless the latter fell down. Few if any other owners would, however, have started Bramble under the circumstances, and allowed the public to have a run for their money, when it would have been so easy to put the pen through the horse's name. As Red Deer belonged to the Duke of Richmond, and Bramble to Lord George, it was impossible to declare to win with the former.

Rumours being rife that some foul play might be attempted, as such reports were frequently circulated in connection with races upon which there had been much heavy speculation, I deemed it advisable to lead Red Deer to the post myself, not feeling disposed to intrust so important and responsible a task to any one else. The fieldbeing so large and the circular course so narrow, the horses were started in two lines. Having Bramble and Best Bower in the race as well as Red Deer, I placed the two former horses immediately in front of Red Deer, and instructed their jockeys to let Red Deer pass between them as soon as the flag fell. It was with no little difficulty that I was able to retain hold of the horse, and avoid being run over or kicked, as Red Deer was of a free and rather nervous temperament. If he had once broken away with such a tiny jockey upon his back, I thought it most improbable that he would ever get to the starting-post again. At last a start was effected, when Red Deer, after making two or three vigorous plunges, passed between Bramble and Best Bower, and took up the running at such a terrific pace that he was soon many lengths in advance of everything in the race, and ultimately won by a dozen lengths, running on to the Dee side before Kitchener could pull him up. So dense was the crowd round him, and so great the enthusiasm, that it was feared an attempt might be made to displace the tiny jockey. With all possible haste, therefore, I made my way to him, and succeeded in getting hold of the bridle and in leading the winner back to the weighing-place, but not till long after all the other jockeys had weighed and the horses had left the course. It will readily be imagined that the announcement

ENTHUSIASM AT GOODWOOD. 121

" All right!" was an inexpressible relief to me. The prevailing opinion that the Chester course was the most unfavourable one in England for such a horse and jockey, in' which opinion Lord George Bentinck fully concurred, proved quite the reverse of the truth, as it was really equivalent to turning the horse loose in a circus from which there was no escape. Instead of a race, it bore more resemblance to a " Red Deer chase," and every arrangement connected with this remarkable event appeared to have been thought out and brought off to perfection.

Upon the return home of Red Deer in his van he was met at the Fareham station by a large number of people amid great rejoicings. At the next stage, Havant, the landlord (Mr Lock), who enjoyed the lucrative privilege of supplying post- horses for all the vans and chaises from Goodwood to Fareham and back, was desirous of adding emphasis to the general jubilations by decorating his horses and the post-boys with a profusion of the victorious colours. At Chichester the van was met by many of the citizens, with flags and banners bearing the well-known yellow and scarlet colours. The enthusiasm and cheering were as great as when the news of the glorious victory of Waterloo was received in 1815. At Goodwood Lodge gates the Chester party found a well - constructed set of rope - harness, with poles, &c., in readiness, and fifty or sixty stablemen and lads waiting to take the place of the post-horses, which were soon detached. The two- legged substitutes made their way with perfect ease to the Goodwood stables, delighted at the good fortune of the Duke of Richmond, the universally popular owner of the horse. If, indeed, I were to say " beloved," I should not exaggerate the prevailing sentiment entertained towards that estimable nobleman.

Lord George Bentinck started the horses at Chester, consisting of a field of twenty-six; and with a view to helping the tiny jockey, Kitchener, who weighed only 3 st. 4 Ib., Red Deer made strong running, and won very easily, much to the gratification of his Lordship, who immediately despatched a messenger to Goodwood to communicate the result to their Graces. The news, however, had been received there many hours earlier, by means of carrier-pigeons sent by me from the course, unknown to any one except my father, so as to avoid disappointment should the pigeons fail to reach home. Upon the race Lord George won a large stake, and stated to me in a letter that he got every farthing due to him, much to his own surprise, as on no previous occasion had he escaped loss from defaulters when betting on the same scale.

6

SECTION 6

CHAPTER VI.

Lord George's Support Of Goodwood Races.

Previous to 1841, when Lord George Bentinck transferred his race-horses from Danebury to Goodwood, he had taken great interest in the Goodwood race-course, and, in conjunction with the Duke of Richmond, had in many ways improved it and its stands. In order to relieve the congestion of traffic flowing through Goodwood Park during the race week, he increased the approaches to the grand stand by making two new roads, one on each side of the park. Subsequently he discovered that the last half- mile of the course was not so elastic as he wished, especially in dry seasons. It was newly made ground, and the soil under the turf had been laid on loose chalk, through which the mould percolated and was carried down after heavy rain, so that the turf subsided in many places. Under these circumstances the Duke of Richmond and Lord George caused four inches of fine mould to be laid upon the old turf, right acrossthe last half-mile of the course. Upon this mould another layer of turf was superimposed, the grassy side being turned downwards, and over it another three-inch layer of friable soil was spread, the whole being crowned by sods, which, together with the mould, were bought from a tenant farmer who lived two or three miles away. Like all Lord George's undertakings, this improvement of the last half-mile of the course was conducted in no half-hearted or perfunctory way. Nothing could be more satisfactory than the results effected by this heavy and well - directed outlay when the season was dry. The mould was held in its place by the double turfing, to which Lord George previously had recourse at Danebury. On the other hand, it was found that in wet weather this portion of the course was very heavy going, as is always the case with newly made ground. In 1848, for instance, Surplice could not raise a gallop when opposed by Distaffina in the Gratwicke Stakes, although Lord Chesterfield was well aware, through his old mare, Lady Wildair, with whom Surplice had been tried, that upon racing-ground the Derby winner could give Distaffina two stone and a good beating. In 1855, again, John Scott, who never was partial to Goodwood, attributed the defeat in the Ham Stakes of Mr Bowes's Fly-by - Night, who was known to be very smart, to the deep ground, through which Mary Copp, the wini.-i

; i t ' , .

'" 1 '

LORD GEORGE AND GOODWOOD.

ner, galloped without sinking, as her feet were very large. The upset of public form which, from the same causes, took place in 1888, will be fresh in the memory of many of my readers.

It is difficult to imagine to what pitch of perfection Lord George would have raised the Goodwood meeting had he been spared to return to the Turf, which, as I shall shortly state, he contemplated at the time of his death. In order to demonstrate what his Lordship actually effected, I have compiled the following comparative tables, showing, on the one hand, what Goodwood races were during the ten years prior to the removal of Lord George's stud from Danebury in 1841, and, on the other, what they were between 1842 and 1851, inclusive :I

TABLE I.

o E*s* !Ec. . *3* Number i Horses running.Number of RacesSubscribe to the Stakes.Acccptanc00Subscribe to the CuStarters,Value of the varioi Stokes. $1832641669281. 10922021104402151422908 1,802TABLE II.

Number of Horses running.Number of Races.Subscribcra to the Stakes.Acceptances.00Su▶ to the Cup.00Value ofthe various Stakes.18421773015150205091 8,417$1843206341614815 1632920,455184920141114412130819,02018501993614043172381 9,0021851193331164 2230359134050317840396198,556The *ttn* prevl-X ous years /10922021104402151... 81,802Increase .113815723610127......116,754Although Lord George ceased to run any horses after August 1846, he had others entered at Goodwood (some of them very heavily engaged) in 1847, 1848, and 1849, which, of course, augmented the value of the stakes. I will venture again to call attention to the extraordinary support given by his Lordship to his favourite meeting; and as specimen years, let me take 1844 and 1845. In 1844 he ran forty-nine horses thereIviz., eleven on the first day, nine on the second, fourteen on the third, and fifteen on the fourth. For the week his stakes and forfeits amounted to $6155Ia sum wholly unparalleled, either before or since, for a single owner of race-horses to put down at one meeting. In 1845 Lord George ran forty-eight

i. . .' - *It'*

I .; i , ' (. , .-
...,;' 1

Lord George's Expenses. 127

horses at Goodwoodlviz., ten on the first day, nine on the second, thirteen on the third, and sixteen on the fourth. This year his stakes and forfeits amounted to $4580.

It was not to be expected that the enormous expenses incurred by Lord George in connection with his stud, including the training of about sixty horses, the maintenance of three stud-farms, the cost of travelling, of stakes and forfeits, and a hundred other charges, could be defrayed, or half defrayed, by the races he won in days when owners ran almost exclusively for each other's money. It was necessary for him to bet, and it must be added that he took the greatest delight in it, so long as he could devote all his energies to watching the running of his own and of other horses, to comparing their respective forms, and to gaining information on all sorts of subjects germane to the Turf, in which respect I never knew his equal. I can well imagine what an effort it must have cost, and what a wrench it must have been to him, to dispose of his stud, and to tear himself away from the Turf, to which his attachment was so unmistakably genuine ; for success in connection with which he was exceptionally adapted ; and which, in addition to affording him great pleasure, contributed materially to the preservation of the robust health which, until he took to politics in earnest, he always enjoyed. It was, indeed, impossible to witness the zest and appetite with which he invariablypartook of breakfast and luncheon at my father's house after walking about the downs, and breathing their elastic and invigorating air, without feeling conscious that his mind and body were at their very best. He repeatedly avowed that he never enjoyed food so much as the simple viands put before him on my father's table, and expressed a wish to know where they were obtained, so that he might procure some of the same sort and send them to Welbeck Abbey. Even the common fruits and vegetables at Goodwood he thought superior to those he tasted elsewhere. He was hardly aware for how much health and enjoyment he was indebted to the fine air he was breathing, to the simple life he was leading, and the entire absorption of his faculties in a pursuit to which he was passionately devoted.

Had it not been that the fifth Duke of Richmond and every member of his family appreciated the enjoyment taken by Lord George in Goodwood and in his race-horses, he would hardly have been permitted by the Duke to keep such an enormous number of horses in training, necessitating the constant employment of a corresponding number of boys and stablemen. It must not be forgotten that the racing stables are close to Goodwood House, and that any lack of order or discipline among the stable-boys might, and probably would, have been extremely disagreeable to the members of the family. My father fre-

EMILIUS'S PKOGEXY. 129

quently inquired whether the noise inseparable from such a large establishment, but which he always endeavoured to keep within bounds, was the cause of any inconvenience, and was repeatedly assured that the Duke and Duchess and their family took pleasure in watching the amusements of the boys, and especially the games of cricket in which they took part. When I mention that, in 1844, Lord George ran thirty-eight different horses in 182 races at places scattered all over England, and in 1845, thirty-six horses in 190 races, I do not think that a similar record can be quoted about any other patron of the Turf. The nearest approach to it that I can find was that made by the Prince of Wales in 1789 and 1790, in each of which years his Royal Highness started thirty - five horses, almost all of which he had purchased, while those belonging to Lord George Bentinck were almost without exception bred by himself.

Lord George was most favourably impressed with the soundness and stoutness of the progeny of Emilius, finding that when to the above-named qualities Emilius's sons and daughters added speed, in which they were generally deficient, they never failed to make their mark. When Priam, Emilius's best son, won the Goodwood Cup, beating Fleur de Lis, his Lordship took the greatest liking to that noble horse, who, in my opinion (and I am never tired of repeating it), was the best and mostperfectly shaped race-horse I ever saw. It was because Crucifix was a daughter of Priam that Lord George purchased her and her dam at Tattersall's, when the latter was twenty-two years old, and Crucifix one of the scraggiest and most unpromising foals ever seen. There can be little doubt that Crucifix, when tried as a yearling in 1838, kept Lord George on the Turf at a moment when he thought of leaving it for ever ; and, again, the victory of Crucifix's son, Surplice, for the Derby and St Leger of 1848, confirmed him in his determination to return to the Turf, which he would most assuredly have done|probably on a greater scale than ever|had his life been spared.

Some time after the death of Mr Thornhill in 1844, Lord George purchased Emilius privately, although the horse was then twenty-four years old, and very weak. Such was the care taken of- him by Lord George, that the old horse regained his strength and was as fresh as a four-year-old when leased, in 1846, to Mr R. M. Jaques, of Easby Abbey, near Richmond-on-Swale, on the sale of Lord George's stud. Emilius died in 1847 at the age of twenty-seven. " He was perfectly well," writes " The Druid," in ' Silk and Scarlet,' " until just before his death, which was caused by some one giving him a feed of whole oats, which he was not able to masticate. They buried him near some loose-boxes in a paddock which the Abbot of the White Canons of Easby surveyed of yore

DEATH OF EMILITJS. 131

from his study window. A stone that had once been the crosiered tomb of a Cardinal, but had gradually mingled with the ruins, and then served as threshold to the box where Weatherbit now stands, is built into the wall to mark the spot; and thus to a certain extent Frank Buckle's last Derby winner is canonised."

In Mr Langley's ' Reminiscences of Easby,' full justice is done to Emilius's extraordinary career at the Stud ; and it is recorded that " Mr Jaques hired him for $100 for the season of 1847, and, owing to his great age, insured his life|the first policy of the kind ever issued by the office|for that amount, which, curiously enough, fell in, owing to the horse dying in the August of that year, aged twenty-seven."

His Lordship's partiality for stayers was not gratified when he purchased Bay Middleton. Nevertheless he managed to win some races over two or three miles of ground with two- year-olds got by that famous son of Sultan. It was one of their characteristics that they stood less in need of severe training than the young sons and daughters of other sires. When Lord George's horses went from Danebury to

Goodwood, he imagined that they would stay better if trained more severely. After experimenting with some of them in this way, I found that long and strong gallops, often repeated, had the effect of making them worse and worse, until at last they lost evensuch form as they possessed, through tiring from weakness. His Lordship soon came to the same opinion as that inculcated after long experience by my father, and now repeated by me after sixty years of familiarity with the Turf in all its departments. If there be any art in training race-horses, it consists in knowing when they are perfectly fit to run the distance for which they are destined by Nature. Such knowledge can only be gained by close observation and practical experience. I could enumerate a vast number of horses which, within my knowledge, have been sacrificed from lack of judgment and skill in ascertaining what was their best distance and what their constitutions required. One instance I will mention which will perhaps be remembered by some who read these remarks, as it happened in 1865.

In that year Mr Padwick had a three-year-old called Kangaroo, who stood at Drewitt's stable at Lewes, but was under my supervision. With Kangaroo I won for Mr Padwick the Abbot Stakes at Chelmsford on March 28, 1865 ; the Craven Handicap at Lewes on March 30 ; and the Newmarket Biennial on April 18. In the last-named race Kangaroo beat a field of nineteen starters, scattering them in such a manner after making strong running that the Marquis of Hastings gave Mr Padwick 12,000 guineas and contingencies for the horse, upon the strength of his having easily defeated the Duke of Beaufort's Koenig, whom

KANGAROO. 133

Lord Hastings and other patrons of the Danebury stable backed very heavily, taking 7 to 4 to thousands of pounds.

Kangaroo was a very powerful muscular horse, and appeared to those who eyed him superficially to be not half-trained when he won at Newmarket. When I delivered the horse to John Day, he told me that he should give him a couple of good sweats, and try him before he ran for the Two Thousand, distant a fortnight from that day. John Day added that by so doing he expected to improve Kangaroo a stone in a fortnight. My reply was that I doubted whether he or any one else could make the horse an ounce better than he was that day. In addition to severe daily gallops, such as Danebury has always been famous for, Kangaroo had two long and distressing sweats, and when tried was a worse horse by two stone than when he beat Koenig and a large field so easily. In point of fact, Kangaroo never won another race, although he ran at last in very inferior company. He was practically ruined by an injudicious attempt to make him better.

Precisely the same thing happened in 1855 with Oulston, a fine upstanding colt, son of Melbourne and Alice Hawthorne. Oulston did not start for the Derby which Wild Dayrell won, and for which, in point of fact, Oulston was not trained. He was brought out by Mr Pad wick, his owner, to run for the Queen's Vase at Ascot in the expectationthat, having done very little work at Findon, where he was trained by old John B. Day, he would not get half-way. To the astonishment of both owner and trainer, Oulston won the Vase in a canter, and before night Mr Padwick sold him to Mr Elwes for 6500 guineas, who sent him to Danebury. At York August Races Oulston was brought out to oppose Wild Dayrell for the Ebor St Leger, the latter carrying G Ib.

extra for winning the Derby. It was notorious that Wild Dayrell pulled up lame after the Derby, and having a bad leg he had done little or no work before meeting Oulston at York. Infirm and untrained, however, as he was, the extra 6 Ib. did not prevent his giving Oulston a stone beating, as in two months the latter had become a confirmed roarer, and almost worthless.

I have no hesitation, as the result of my long experience, in saying that more horses are ruined by over-training than in any other way. To assist Nature is all that a trainer can effect; but to impose a greater strain on a horse than Nature can bear, is to defeat the purpose for which the animal is put into training. When I add that every horse requires to be trained in a different way|the difference being sometimes grave and sometimes infinitesimal|it will be seen what observation, attention, and vigilance a trainer must exercise who has one hundred horses under his care. Another fatal mistake often perpetrated is to get a horse

REVOLUTION IX TRAINING. 135

fit to run, as the phrase has it, " for a man's life," two or three weeks before the day when his race is due. To keep a horse at concert-pitch for twenty, or even for fourteen days, will try the skill of the very ablest trainer. I may add, at the end of a long life, that I could never have gone through what I did at Goodwood, between 1841 and 1848, but for the constant support and encouragement so generously accorded to me by my two noble masters, the fifth Duke of Richmond and Lord George Bentinck.

The construction and wide extension of railways, the facility, rapidity, and safety with which horses are conveyed in boxes to the scene of action and back to their training stables, and lastly, the electric wire, have revolutionised the whole system of racing and of training, early maturity and quick returns being at present the order of the day. Nowadays a vast majority of horses terminate their racing careers at an age at which they commenced it in my youth, the result being that modern trainers are subjected to much less work and much less anxiety than their predecessors underwent. Such, moreover, is the richness of the prizes now within reach of a good horse during the first two years of his racing career, that enormously increased prices are given for thoroughbreds of all ages, although in my opinion these prices cannot and will not be sustained. Lord George Bentinck was one of the first to pay long prices for horses.He gave, for instance, 1500 guineas at the sale of Sir Mark Wood's stud, in 1837, for the famous brood-mare G'amarine, and 1010 guineas for her yearling colt, Glenlivat, by Rowton or Cetus. As a rule, modern purchasers of thoroughbred yearlings have not the same opportunities of looking over the youngsters which they think of buying as were afforded to their predecessors fifty or sixty years since. At that time yearlings were almost invariably purchased by private contract, and auction sales were almost unknown. Formerly Lord George and other purchasers would pay more than one visit to the best-known stud-farms, such as Riddlesworth, the seat of Mr Thornhill; Euston Park, the seat of the Duke of Grafton ; Uiiderley Park, near Barrow-in-Furness, the seat of Mr Nowell; Bishop Burton Hall, near Beverley, the seat of Mr Richard Watt; Sledmere Park, near Malton, the seat of Sir Tatton Sykes; Rock- ingham House, Malton, the home of Mr Allen, who bred Rockingham and Canezou. Before buying a yearling (whom he had probably seen as a foal), Lord George would run round the paddock after him, rattling a stick inside his hat, and closely observing the youngster's action and style of going. In those days, moreover, yearlings were not fattened up like prize oxen before they were sold, and their condition was such that their trainer had not to strip them of fat before they were fit to gallop. I remember

LORD GLASGOW. 137

to have heard Tom Dawson say that Mr Copper- thwaite, an Irish gentleman, sent him a yearling to train who was as fat as a pig. Six months afterwards Mr Copperthwaite went to Middleham to inspect his colt, whom he found to be not half as heavy as when he last saw him. " Good heavens !" he exclaimed to Tom Dawson, " half the horse is gone already, and if I leave him here any longer, the other half will soon follow ! " To prevent such a catastrophe, the colt was taken away next day.

Vast as is the change which racing has undergone since Lord George Bentinck's day, I have no manner of doubt that he would have reaped a rich harvest by following his old system of early training and early trying if he had been living now. It was his uniform practice to find out the form of his yearlings before he engaged them ; and I do not think that many of the fatted youngsters which are now knocked down at prices varying between one thousand and six thousand guineas would have had much chance with Lord George's picked colts and fillies, bred by himself regardless of expense, and brought up with every care so as to fit them to be running machines of the highest quality.

I never remember any wealthy patron of the Turf who was so obstinate or so blind to his own interests as the late Earl of Glasgow. It was his Lordship's custom to make a lot of matches every year with Lord George Bentinck, seldom winningone of them. In 1843, for instance, these two old antagonists ran a lot of matches against each other, all of which resulted in Lord George's favour, with the exception of one which ended in a dead heat. This match, run at Goodwood, was between Lord George's brown filly Alva by Bay Middleton, and Lord Glasgow's brown filly by Retainer|Purity. Immediately afterwards Lord Glasgow characteristically changed his trainer, and in order to test the capacity of the trainer whom he had left, he insisted upon making precisely the same lot of matches over again to be run in the following year. To this Lord George greatly objected, as some of his animals were so bad that he had no desire to keep them in training for another twelvemonth. Lord Glasgow, however, insisted, and to oblige him Lord George gave way. Curious to relate, the result of all the matches in 1844 was the same as in 1843, including that between Alva and the Purity filly, which again ended in a dead heat. The only difference was that Flatman rode the Purity filly in 1843, and Job Marson in 1844, Sam Rogers being on the back of Lord George's filly on each occasion.

There was certainly a fatality attending Lord Glasgow's numerous matches, for however bad the animal of his opponent might be, Lord Glasgow's was sure to be worse. Again, when Lord Glasgow got hold of one that could run a little, his opponent's almost invariably proved to be a littleLord Glasgow's Unfortunate Matches. 139

better. In 1843 Lord Glasgow was beaten in nineteen matches, received forfeit in three, and ran one dead heat. In 1844 he was defeated in twenty matches, won one, received forfeit in two, and ran one dead heat. Notwithstanding his lack of success as a match - maker, Lord Glasgow's constant aim and ambition was to pit his horses against those of Lord George Bentinck, and to make heavy additional bets when the matches were made. Under these circumstances, no sportsman that ever lived, with the exception of Lord Glasgow, would have insisted upon running off the match when it had been made patent that his animal was worthless, and the animal he was about to oppose had shown some form. By paying forfeit, Lord Glasgow would have annulled the unprofitable bets he had made. He was not " built that way," however, as nothing could ever induce him to pay forfeit unless his horse was dead or a hopeless cripple.

Mr Langley adds : " One of the most extraordinary matches ever conceived, for particulars of which I am indebted to a literary friend of long acquaintance, originated as follows. After a heavy and late debate in the House of Commons, Lord George fell sound asleep next day in the drawing- room at White's Club, so that all attempts to rouse him proved unavailing until the usual afternoon visit of Lord Glasgow, who was at once informed of these fruitless efforts. ' Oh, I'll soon wake him !'remarked Lord Glasgow, and walking up to the chair in which the sleeper was ensconced, called out, ' Bentinck, I want to make a bet with you !' The effect was so magical that Lord George instantly opened his eyes, and replied, ' With pleasure, Glasgow ; what is it ?' 'I want to back the produce of Miss Whip against that of any mare you name for the Derby of 1848.' 'Done; I name Crucifix|for how much ?' ' Five thousand !' The bet was made, Crucifix being at that moment in foal with Surplice, and Miss Whip with a brute called Whipstick."

The history of Lord George Bentinck's Farintosh will further show how atrociously bad Lord Glasgow's luck was. Farintosh, by Bay Middleton out of Camarine's dam, was a magnificent yearling, and, contrary to his usual practice, Loi'd George engaged him very heavily before he was broken. Among his engagements was a match for 200 sovereigns, half-forfeit, in which Farintosh undertook to give Colonel Peel's Murat 5 Ib. at the July meeting of 1842. Long before that date Farintosh had turned roarer; indeed I never knew a worse one of his age. Nevertheless, I had instructions to take him to Newmarket, where I arrived the day before his match with Murat, which was also the day upon which the July Stakes was to be run, in which both horses were engaged. When Farintosh was brought out for the match, his appearance was so formidable that at the last

FAEINTOSH. 141

moment Colonel Peel paid forfeit. I then implored Lord George not to run Farintosh for the July Stakes, as no one was aware that the horse was a bad roarer, and I felt persuaded that if the secret was well kept, Farintosh would receive forfeit in some of his other matches, and might even be allowed to walk over for some of his smaller engagements. Lord George, however, was firm, and Farintosh accordingly started for the July Stakes, in which he met Murat at even weights. The race was won by Mr Thornhill's brown filly Extempore, Lord Exeter's Jerry filly being second, and Colonel Peel's Murat third, beating Farintosh (who was last) by twenty lengths.

Unfortunately Farintosh had several engagements and matches for the following year. One of the last (for 300 sovereigns, half-forfeit) was against Lord Glasgow's Sister to Pathfinder (A.F.) I was instructed to keep Farintosh in training for this match, which it would have been impossible for him to win, as he could not have galloped "across the flat" to save his life. Even under these circumstances Lord Glasgow's luck would not permit him to win such a match, as shortly before the appointed day his filly died.

Lord George never forgot the lesson taught him by Farintosh, whom he entered for thirty- three engagements before he left the paddock. The forfeits for these engagements amounted to nearly $3000, which served at any rate to awaken

%

his Lordship to a sense of the impolicy of engaging yearlings before they had been broken and tried. As early as 1833 the Hon. E. M. Lloyd Mostyn was alive to the advantage of trying his yearlings. In that year he discovered that his superlatively good yearling filly Queen of Trumps was a " flyer," although, like all the Velocipedes, she was heavily fleshed and very robust of constitution, with bad knees.

In those days there were few two - year - old stakes, and it was dangerous for a colt or filly of that tender age to travel long distances on foot. Mr Mostyn, therefore, engaged Queen of Trumps in but one two-year-old race|the Champagne at Holywell Hunt Races, which took place close to her training quarters. This race she won without an effort, and her next appearance in public was for the Oaks at Epsom. Here she met and defeated Mr Greville's Preserve, on whom 2 to 1 was betted, as previously recorded. So favourably was Lord George impressed with that performance, that he gave Mr Mostyn very valuable advice, which resulted in the Queen being moved from the sandy gallops at Holywell to the fine downs at Hednesford, to be trained for the St Leger.

The mention of Queen of Trumps reminds me that a more honest, industrious, capable, and trustworthy man than John Blenkhorn, her trainer, never entered a stable. He enjoyed Mr Mostyn's confidence to the full, and it was a pleasure to see

NAT FLATMAN. 143

employer and trainer agreeing and understanding each other so thoroughly. Some-times it happens that all the integrity of an owner, all the skill and devotion of a trainer, are baffled by the dishonesty of a jockey. Many such cases have I known in my time; but I cannot resist going out of my way to put on record what I know of El- nathan Flatman, one of the most honourable and meritorious men of his class that I ever encountered.

Flatman, better known by the abbreviated *sobriquet* of "Nat," was born in 1810 at the village of Holton, or Holton St Mary, in Suffolk. His father (a small yeoman farmer) gave him a good education at a school kept by a clergyman near to the house in which Nat was born; but in a few years the father failed, and the boy, a pigmy, less than 4 stone in weight, gravitated to Newmarket, where in a fortunate moment for himself he obtained employment in the stable of William Cooper, one of the most upright trainers and best men that ever lived. I have often heard Colonel Peel say that when Nat knocked, as a boy, at William Cooper's back-door, he carried all his worldly goods in a bundle slung to a stick, thrown over his right shoulder. In 1825 there were plenty of stables at Newmarket and elsewhere in which the atmosphere was far less pure than that of the establishment into which Nat was inducted, and of which Colonel Peel was for many years the presiding genius. The boy's rise in his profession was rapid and unintermitted. His first mount was on Lord Exeter's Gold Pin in 1829 ; his last, curiously enough, upon the Duke of Bedford's Golden Pippin in 1859. Being able to ride 7 st. 5 lb. and to keep down to that weight, he soon got more mounts than any other jockey, and for seven years (from 1846 to 1852, both inclusive) he headed the list of winning jockeys. When he died in 1860, having been riding for just thirty years, he left behind him the modest sum of $8000, and, in addition, he gave his sons and daughters|two of whom were drowned when the Princess Alice came into collision with, and was sunk by, the By well Castle on the Thames in September 1878|an excellent education.

Never was there a more faithful or honest servant than Flatman proved himself to all his employers. The masters for whom he rode at the commencement of his career may be set down in the following order: First, William Cooper and his stable, including Colonel Peel, General Yates, Captain George Byng (afterwards Earl of Straf- ford), and Captain Gardner; second, Mr Payne and Mr Greville ; third, Lord Chesterfield ; fourth, the Goodwood stable ; and fifth, Lord Glasgow.

From William Cooper no retaining fee was ever accepted by Nat; and from Colonel Peel he would never take more than $20 per annum, and $50 from Mr Payne. His last list of masters, accord-

NAT FLATMAN. 145

ing to ' Bell's Life,' included Mr Cooper, General Peel, Lord Strafford, Mr Payne, Mr Greville, Lord Chesterfield, Lord Wilton, Lord Ailesbury, and Lord Stradbroke. In addition, he was frequently employed by Lord Zetland, General Anson, Lord Derby, Sir Charles Monck, Sir Joseph Hawley, Mr Bowes, Mr A. Nicol, and John Scott.

Nat's chief characteristics were that, more than any other jockey of my acquaintance, he rode scrupulously to orders; and, secondly, that it was at all times difficult to induce him to stand $5 or $10 on his mount, or on a "good thing" from any of the stables for which he rode. One instance I remember of a race which he lost from not understanding the sluggishness of the horse upon which he was mounted. In 1847 he rode Mr Mostyn's Crozier, by Lanercost out of Crucifix, in a Produce Stake at Ascot, over the Old Mile, against Mr Harvey Combe's Trouncer. The betting was 5 to 4 on Crozier, and Flatman's orders were to make strong running, as Crozier was an extremely lazy horse and a good stayer. To my great surprise and disappointment, Trouncer waited upon Crozier, and beat him easily by a couple of lengths. Two days later Crozier and Trouncer were in another sweepstakes at the same weights, and among others they were opposed by a smartish horse called Epirote, who belonged to Colonel Anson. Mr Cynric Lloyd, who acted for Mr Mostyn, thought it quite useless to start Crozier again;

but I persuaded him to do so, as I was not satisfied about the former race, and was prepared to give W. Abdale the mount upon Crozier, and to let Nat ride Epirote for Colonel Anson. When Nat saw that Crozier was being led about the course, he came up to me exclaiming, " Surely you are not going to run Crozier again, are you ? " I replied that such was my intention, but that T would not interfere with his mount on Epirote, as Abdale would ride Crozier, " and," I added laughing, " would win upon him." The little man was obviously stung by my remark, and said to me in a low voice, and with a very serious manner, " Da you mean to imply that I did not try my best to win upon Crozier the day before yesterday?" "I imply nothing of the kind," I replied; " but I think the horse deceived you, and that you did not make as strong running as you might have done." " Then I insist upon riding him again," he- rejoined. " Certainly," I answerd, " and I will' tell you how I want him ridden. When the flag is down take him by the head, touch him with the spurs, and make the pace as strong as you possibly can every inch of the way." Nat looked very serious, but obeyed his instructions to the letter. The betting was 5 to 4 against Trouncer, 6 to 4 against Epirote, 5 to 1 against Buckston; Crozier not mentioned. The latter was never headed, and won cleverly by half a length|Epirote second, Trouncer third, the rest beaten off.

CKOZIEE. 147

After the race I said to Flatman, " Well, what do you think of Crozier now ? " "I think him the hardest horse to ride that I ever sat on. In fact, he requires two men to get him out, and make him show his true form. Henceforward I will ride more strictly than ever to your orders, as I am now quite conscious that I lost the race on Tuesday." I have often heard him say that there was no stable for which he rode with greater pleasure and confidence than the Goodwood stable, as he always found our horses to be just what they were represented to him before the race. One further trait I must mention, which was, in my opinion, greatly to his credit. No jockey ever rode in more trials than Flatman did, but not a word as to the results ever escaped his lips. He would stop, for instance, at Bretby, on his way back from Malton, where he had been riding trials for Colonel Anson and John Scott. Although Colonel Anson and Lord Chesterfield were brothers- in-law, Nat would never consent to say one syllable to Lord Chesterfield, of whom he was very fond, and for whom he had ridden for years, as to the trials in which he had taken part. It is greatly to be regretted that the fidelity, silence, obedience to orders, and general integrity of Flatman are not more closely copied by his modern successors, some of whom amass in ten years ten times as large a fortune as by steady industry and conscientious honesty he acquired in thirty.If ever it were deemed desirable to erect a monument to a jockey, Nat deserves to have a tablet set up in All Saints' Church, Newmarket (under the tower of which he now sleeps), and dedicated to his memory, as he was beyond all doubt one of the most respectable and honourable " knights of the pig-skin " that ever performed upon an English race-course.

7

SECTION 7

CHAPTER VII.

THE GOODWOOD STABLE IN 1844.

With the year 1844 we enter upon a period when Lord George Bentinck became more than ever engrossed in his stud, which now began to realise his expectations, and to compensate him for his previous heavy expenditure. It was most satisfactory to witness his Lordship's delight and the enjoyment that racing, upon which his whole thoughts were centred, afforded him. Much of his time was spent at Goodwood. He stayed with the family when there ; and when the Duke and Duchess of Richmond were absent he slept at the Swan Hotel in Chichester, breakfasting and lunching at my father's house. When the Duke was at Goodwood, nothing gave Lord George more pleasure than to take the house party over the stables, and to show them the horses. He was ever ready to encourage and induce others to take interest in the sport he enjoyed so much ; and it afforded him no slight amusement to elicit from the ladies who accompanied him an expression of their opinion as to the merits of the horses which they inspected. If, as sometimes, but not often, happened, their guesses were correct, he never failed to reward them by putting the successful guessers on some small sum " to nothing," in case the horse of their choice should win an engagement. So extensive, however, was the Goodwood establishment, between 1841 and 1846, that it would have puzzled not only ladies, but also some of the keenest male judges of racing in England, to make a selection among the horses in the stable, or to read his Lordship's intentions aright. One of his most marked characteristics was, that he was always ready to make matches. At and about that time it was most unusual for a large party of noblemen and gentlemen who owned race-horses, to sit down to dinner without matches of all kinds being proposed before the party broke up. It was his Lordship's custom to note down the weights at which the horses of his friends were pitted against each other; and when a match was proposed to him, he rarely agreed to it until he had sent for me, and consulted me upon it. If I thought that his horse would win, he would go back and make the match ; and his first question when I met him next morning would invariably be, " How much of the match money will you stand, John ? " It was his express wish that I should have a money interest in every match made by him under these circumLord George's Matches. 151

stances; but I seldom stood more than $10, and very rarely indeed $25. It was always a disappointment to his Lordship if I refused to stand anything, or reduced my venture to $5 or $10. On these occasions he would inquire of me, " Why will you not stand more on this match which you advised me to make ? Surely, if it is not worth your money it cannot be worth mine ?" To say the truth, I was never fond of betting on my own account, and was always glad to discourage his Lordship, who was apt on all occasions to bet too much rather than too little. No accountant could be more accurate and methodical than he was in recording every bet made by or through him. If I was a winner, a cheque was invariably sent to me on the following Monday. In all other matters his Lordship's attention to detail was equally minute. Nothing escaped his observation. I once had occasion to foment a horse for many days which had met with an accident, and it struck Lord George that the sponges used were not large enough. Upon returning to London, he instructed Gardner, his valet, to buy some big sponges, and have them sent to Harcourt House, Cavendish Square. When they arrived, they did not satisfy his ideas of magnitude. " Go again," he said, " and search London until you can bring me six sponges half as big again as these." Gardner again sallied forth and returned with six enormous sponges, for which he had paid $15 or $16. "There!" exclaimed his Lordship, "I told you you could succeed if you would only try." The sponges were sent down to Goodwood, where they were kept as curiosities, being useless for the purpose contemplated by his Lordship, as their size and the weight of water which they held made it almost impossible to handle them. The story is indicative of his Lordship's determination to get the best of everythinglor what he thought the bestlif his horses required it.

Never was there a man in any class of life less liable to be daunted or intimidated by difficulties than Lord George Bentinck. The word "impossible " mentioned in his hearing served but to intensify his determination not to be beaten ; and I have often thought that, had his lot been cast in stormy times, he would have gained the greatest distinction as the commander of a large army. Nothing could frighten him; nothing could tire him, or exhaust his resources. He delighted in details, and it was hard indeed for anybody to outwit him or take him in. Mr Greville never made a truer remark than when he observed in his ' Diary,' " Lord George did nothing by halves, and was afraid of no man." But for Lord George's indomitable energy and indefatigable perseverance, the notorious Running Rein case would never have been thoroughly investigated, and the fraud exposed. When Running Rein ran, nominally as a two-year-old, at Newmarket, in 1843, for a two-

THE RUNNING REIN CASE. 153

year-old plate which he won, beating the Duke of Rutland's Crinoline and ten others, the Duke objected to him on the ground that he was three instead of two years old. The case was investigated by the Stewards, who dismissed it with the remark that the Duke of Rutland had not proved Running Rein to be three years old. When, however, the same horse started subsequently for the Clearwell Stakes, in which, although backed heavily by the public, he was beaten, Lord George's keen and vigilant suspicions were aroused by something that reached his ears. During the winter, therefore, he quietly obtained information which greatly strengthened his doubts as to Running Rein's real age. Scarcely had the horse been placed first for the Derby of 1844 before Lord George mentioned the facts which he had accumulated to Colonel Peel, the owner of Orlando, who finished second to Running Rein, and advised him strongly to make an objection, Avhich he did at once, and claimed the Derby Stakes. The Stewards of Epsom Races directed Messrs Wea- therby to pay the stakes into the Court of Exchequer, and to leave the law to settle who was then-rightful owner. Under these circumstances an. action was brought by Mr A. Wood, the nominator of Running Rein, against Colonel Peel in the Court of Exchequer, to decide who was entitled to receive the Derby Stakes. It was tried on the 1st and 2d of July 1844, and resulted in a verdictfor Colonel Peel. I am one of the few survivors to whom every detail of the Running Rein Derby is well known, and I affirm, without hesitation, that but for Lord George Bentinck, Colonel Peel would never have objected to Running Rein, and that but for Lord George, Mr Wood would have won the case. The result of this celebrated trial was to make Lord George what Mr Disraeli, in his political biography of that nobleman, calls him, " Lord Paramount of the British Turf."

Such was the sense universally entertained of the value of the services rendered by Lord George Bentinck in this case, that a public subscription was immediately set on foot with a view to presenting his Lordship with a testimonial, expressing the gratitude and admiration of the subscribers. In an incredibly short space of time the sum of $2100 was collected; but the Hercules of the Turf, having cleansed the Augean stable, refused to accept anything, either in the form of plate or money. It was therefore determined by a committee of the Jockey Club, consisting of the Dukes of Bedford, Beaufort, and Rutland, the Earl of Chesterfield, and Viscount Enfield (afterwards Earl of Strafford), " that the amount subscribed should be applied to some public institution, with a view to forming the nucleus of a fund for securing in perpetuity to a certain number of the children of deserving trainers and jockeys enough to support and educate them from infancy until of an

BENTINCK BENEVOLENT FUND. 155

age to earn their own living." Lord George Bentinck ultimately expressed a wish that the money thus subscribed " should be appropriated for the advantage of trainers and riders of good character." His Lordship's wish was respected, and out of it sprang the " Bentinck Benevolent Fund, for the benefit of the widows and children of deserving trainers and jockeys." Furthermore, it was resolved at a general meeting of the Jockey

Club, held on Saturday, July 6, 1844, "That the thanks of the Jockey Club are eminently due, and are heartily offered, to Lord George Bentinck, for the energy, perseverance, and ability which he displayed in detecting, exposing, and defeating the atrocious frauds which have been brought to light during the recent trial respecting the Derby stakes in 1844." 1

That same year his Lordship distinguished himself by the courage with which he confronted what seemed likely to provel and was in factl-a fraud of a not less flagitious kind than the attempt on the part of Mr A. Wood and Goodman Levy to win the Derby with a four-year-old.

In 1843 Mr Crockford had a two-year-old calledRatan, trained by Joe Rogers at Newmarket. Ratan won the New Stakes at Ascot by three lengths, beating a bay filly, Assay, belonging to Alderman Copeland, who, from her previous performances, was backed at evens against the field. Lord George was a heavy backer of Assay, and lost his money. Ratan was an upstanding, good- looking horse, but rather short. Lord George immediately took the odds about him for the Derby. In the Houghton Meeting at Newmarket Ratan won the Criterion Stakes easily by four lengths, and was ridden, as at Ascot, by Sam Rogers. This encouraged Lord George during the winter to increase his investments upon Ratan for the Derby. In the Craven Meeting at Newmarket, 1844, Ratan again won a race easily by two lengths, beating a field of seven. This again encouraged Lord George to continue backing him for the Derby. At the First Spring Meeting, Mr John Day's The Ugly Buck won the Two Thousand Guineas, beating Lord George Bentinck's Devil-to-Pay by a neck, after a good race; which form Lord George did not consider nearly equal to that displayed by Ratan, and he therefore continued to back the latter heavily for the Derby. Still there was such an unmistakable disposition to lay against Ratan in certain dangerous quarters that Lord George began to suspect something was amiss; but as the horse was doing regular work he could not understand the mar-

1 Mr W. H. Langley, who witnessed the Derby of 1844 and its six predecessors, adds : " Before taking leave of the memorable Derby in question, I cannot resist recording the remarkable coincidence of Leander, a German-bred five-year-old, belonging to Herr Lichtwald, and trained by Forth at Michel Grove, being galloped into by the other ' old 'un' in descending the hill, whereby Leander's off hind fetlock was so badly smashed that he ran home on the exposed bony stump !

RATAN AND THE UGLY BUCK. 157

ket, and was determined to find out what was the matter. By some unaccountable means, which he disclosed to no one, he discovered that Sam Rogers had bets with Mr Gully and others, in which he had backed The Ugly Buck upon such favourable terms that his Lordship's misgivings were aroused. He lost no time, therefore, in communicating his information to Sam Rogers, who was much confused upon finding that Lord George had acquired so much knowledge of the matter. Next day Sam Rogers brought his Lordship a book which contained, or purported to contain, all his bets. There were some very suspicious names and bets entered there, which partly confirmed his Lordship's suspicions, and in conformity with the usual custom Lord George then proceeded to call over and compare Sam Rogers's bets, selecting the Spread Eagle Inn at Epsom (" Lumley's " it was commonly called in those days) for that purpose. Lord George, ascending the steps in front of the inn, said: " Gentlemen, I am going to call over my jockey Samuel Rogers's book, and will thank you to answer to your names and bets !" He began by calling out Mr Gully's name. " Here," replied Mr Gully, quietly removing the cigar from his lips. "You have betted Samuel Rogers 350 to 25 against Ratan, I perceive," said Lord George, in an interrogating voice. Mr Gully gave a nod of assent. " I see," continued his Lordship," that Rogers stands $50 with you on The Ugly Buck, no terms or price being named." Again a nod from Mr Gully. " Are these all the bets you have with Rogers, Mr Gully ? " inquired his Lordship. " If you have any more in my name, my Lord, and will specify them, I shall be better able to answer you," replied Mr Gully, cautiously. Lord George then read out the whole of the book, dwelling particularly on some of the bets he was anxious to emphasise, such as those with Messrs Tom Crommelin, "Dollar" Scott, and a number of other heavy betters. He then closed the book and withdrew into the inn, leaving the crowd of listeners by whom he was surrounded no wiser as to his secret thoughts and future intentions.1

The betting at starting for the Derby was 5 to 2 *v.* The Ugly Buck; 3 .to 1 *v.* Ratan; 10 to 1 *v.* Running Rein; 14 to 1 v. Leander; 20 to 1 r. Orlando. The Ugly Buck, ridden by J. Day, jun., and Ratan, ridden by Rogers, were beaten some distance from home, the running of the former confirming Lord George's estimate of him after he had won the Two Thousand; but Ratan's form was altogether inexplicable. An inquiry was

1 For the following valuable note I am again indebted to Mr W. H. Langley : " The particular transaction he was so anxious to have acknowledged was a bet of 10,000 to 1000 *against* Ratan, which Rogers had laid, and which appeared at the top of a page, as my informant, an eyewitness of the proceedings, can testify."

SAM ROGERS PUNISHED. 159

immediately demanded, but for some inscrutable reason it was not gone into by the Stewards of the Jockey Club until the October meetings at Newmarket came round. The result was that Samuel Rogers and John Braham were warned off the course and exercising-grounds at Newmarket; and Samuel Rogers was declared unfit to ride or train for any member of the Jockey Club either at Newmarket or any other place where their rules and regulations were in force. Knowing Sam Rogers's associates and something of his betting proclivities, I had frequently remonstrated with him upon the danger to which he was exposing himself, and the unpleasant consequences which would ensue if he were detected. After his disgrace he wrote me some very penitent letters, expressing the deepest regret that he had not followed my advice, and thus avoided the sad difficulties which he had brought upon himself. Few people were more free from jealousy or suspicion than Lord George; but facts sometimes occurred to which it was impossible for him or any one else to be blind. I have no doubt he received some deprecatory cautions from Mr Harry Hill, his chief commissioner, respecting his heavy and oft - repeated instructions to back Ratan for the Derbylas Mr Hill was a personal friend of Mr Gully, and shared many horses with him at Danebury. Whatever reports might be circulated, I never remember Lord George expressing a desire to guard against anyfraudulent design or practice beforehand. All he wished was, that every endeavour might be used to get the horses to the post well, and fit to run through their races successfully. Naturally there existed a rivalry between the Goodwood and Danebury establishments, which the Ratan affair tended to increase. After that my doubts were strengthened with regard to the running of Gaper for the Derby, and for a Produce Stake at Abing- don, where Gaper was beaten by Mr Isaac Day's Somerset, when the odds were "breast-high" on Gaper. In the ' Racing Calendar's' official report of the race, the following sentence occurred : " Somerset fell within the distance, but recovered himself and won by half a neck." This was a remarkable occurrence, as the following week at Warwick they met again. The distance (1 mile) and weights were the same, and Gaper won easily. Even this did not excite Lord George's suspicion of any foul play, although at Warwick the betting was even on Gaper, when, after the running of Somerset at Abingdon, it ought to have been 2 to 1 on Somerset. When Sam Rogers rode the Duke of Richmond's Red Deer at Liverpool for the Liverpool St Leger, and the Gratwicke Stakes at Goodwood the following year (1844), there were unpleasant rumours about him then. At Liverpool it was remarked that " he rode Red Deer with the greatest severity,|in fact, that he rode his head off." Red Deer was beaten two lengths

SAM ROGERS PARDONED. 161

by Ithuriel, Flatman up, the betting being 6 to 5 on Red Deer. The week afterwards the two horses met again at Goodwood, when Sam Rogers went the wrong course, though he had so frequently ridden over it, and was cautioned by Nat that he was " going wrong." Even then Lord George continued to support him through that week, and through the following one at Brighton.

The punishment inflicted on Sam Rogers was prolonged for three years, on the expiration of which Lord George, being then senior Steward of the Jockey Club, invited the favourable consideration of his brother members to a measure which he brought forward in the July meeting of 1847, by proposing that the sentence passed on Sam Rogers and other jockeys should forthwith be remitted. His Lordship added that Rogers had been represented to him as having conducted himself well and discreetly since the infliction upon him of the severe punishment which he had incurred in 1844. It was resolved, therefore, *nemine contradicente,* that, " upon the recommendation of the Stewards, the sentences passed in 1844 and 1845 upon Samuel Rogers and others, excepting John Braham, shall now be remitted, and that they be allowed to come on the course, and to ride and train at Newmarket as formerly." In addition, the Stewards expressed their sincere hope " that the punishment these delinquents have received may be a warning to them which they will never forget,

and that their conduct hereafter may justify the leniency now extended to them."

When, ridden by Sam Rogers and trained by his father, Mr Stirling Crawfurd's The Cur won the Cesarewitch of 1848, beating Colonel Peel's Dacia, who ought to have won, and affording Sam Rogers an opportunity for displaying a fine bit of jockeyship, all recollection of Ratan's year, and of other transgressions, was obliterated from the public mind.

8

SECTION 8

CHAPTER VIII.

THE GOODWOOD STABLE IN 1845.

The winter of 1844-45 was very severe and protracted, commencing on the 4th of December 1844 with sharp frosts, which continued with little intermission till the 23d of March 1845ltwo days before the Northampton meeting. So severe and wintry was the weather a week before the races that it was thought they would have to be postponed, there being 19 of frost from the 14th to the 17th of March, and 11 on the 21st. In order to utilise to the fullest extent the great advantages afforded by the exercise - grounds at Goodwood, which are completely sheltered by plantations and trees, Lord George caused straw- beds of immense magnitude to be laid down, the outer ring being nearly half a mile in circumference, within which two lesser rings were formed. As these straw-beds were some distance from the stables, it was necessary to make an approach to them by covering a track or path with litter,leaves, and straw. As there were from sixty to seventy horses to be exercised every day, I did not like to trust more than a few of them upon the track leading to the straw-beds at the same time, for fear of one or more lads being pitched off, and the horses getting loose. The straw - beds were surrounded by a high ring-fence, and as soon as one detachment had got safely inside the fence, others were despatched from the stables.

There were outlets provided at many points in the surrounding fence through which riotous horses could be removed, in order not to disturb or demoralise their quieter and better-behaved companions. In this manner the horses engaged at Northampton and other early meetings were able to do enough work to make them far more fit to run than others which had not enjoyed the same advantages. The famous Halnaker gallop, which ran for a long way through a wood in the park, afforded a convenient trial-ground for the Northampton lot: and as the Halnaker gallop was between two and three miles distant from the stables at Goodwood, each horse about to be tried was, by Lord George's instructions, conveyed in a van to the trial-ground. He took great pleasure, and was much interested, in making all these preparations to circumvent " Jack Frost," and was not a little encouraged by the results of the trials in which Cherokee, a two-year- old filly by Redshank ; Discord, aged eight years ; John o' Gaunt, aged seven years, and others, were

CHEROKEE. 165

" put through the mill." Cherokee won her trial so easily by four or five lengths, that his Lordship was afraid some of the old horses in the gallop had not run up to their form by reason of the shortness of their preparation. He therefore desired me, before I left for Northampton, to try My Mary (who was second to Cherokee) over again with the unerring old African, as it was his Lordship's intention to stand a good stake on Cherokee for the Althorp Park Stakes, if I was able to make out that My Mary, aged three years, was in form. The second trial came off all right, as My Mary won it easily, making it pretty evident that Cherokee was very smart, as My Mary had won the Prendergast at Newmarket in the preceding autumn. Accordingly, Lord George, after arriving at Northampton, gave his chief commissioner, Mr Harry Hill, an unlimited commission to back Cherokee for the Althorp Park Stakes. As I was saddling the mare, Mr Hill came up to his Lordship in great tribulation, stating that he was unable to execute the commission, as they only offered 5 to 4 against Cherokee, although there were ten starters, and two or three others heavily backed. " Don't come here to bother me with your fears," exclaimed his Lordship, testily; "go back and get on as much money as you can, and you will find 5 to 4 good enough odds when the race is over." And so it proved, as Cherokee won in a canter by two lengths. Lord George next proceeded to backDiscord with great spirit for the Northamptonshire Stakes, having already made a book for him, as in those days the betting on this race commenced many weeks before it came off. At that time, indeed, the Northamptonshire Stakes was one of the heaviest betting races in the ' Calendar.'

In order to discourage others from backing Discord, Lord George started Clumsy, aged three years, for the Trial Stakes, and backed him for $100. The horse was slightly amiss, and ran second to Mr Osbaldeston's Sorella, who won by three lengths. Everybody supposed that Clumsy was Discord's trial horse, and therefore Discord receded in the betting, much to his Lordship's satisfaction when Clumsy was beaten. I need not add that the two horses had never been together, as Clumsy had not been in condition to be tried for some weeks before Northampton. The race was won by Discord by three lengths, and his Lordship added considerably to his winnings upon Cherokee.

After this second victory, Lord George thought he had a choice rod in pickle for his old antagonist Mr Osbaldeston, with whom he had fought a memorable duel two or three years before, to which reference will be made hereafter. Mr Osbaldeston had his famous mare Sorella engaged in the Queen's Plate at Northampton on the second day, for which Lord Geoi'ge's John o' Gaunt, one of the stoutest horses in training, was also entered.

JOHN O GAUNT. 167

John o' Gaunt had finished second to Discord in the trial at Goodwood, and the approaching contest between him and Sorella appeared to excite his Lordship more than either of the preceding races upon which he won so largely. For the Queen's Plate there were five runners, including Coranna (a good old horse), and the betting opened at 4 to 1 but closed at 2 to 1 on Sorella, and 5 to 1 against John o' Gaunt. Lord George freely confessed to me that there was no man whose money he should more like to win than that of Mr Osbal- deston, unless it were that of Mr Charles Greville, for whom his antipathy was still more pronounced. The Queen's Plate distance was two miles, and the orders given to Flatman, who rode John o' Gaunt, were to make the strongest running possible. Flatman obeyed his orders to perfection, making the pace so desperate that all the starters except Sorella pulled up a long way from home, and did not run the course at all. In the end John o' Gaunt won in a canter by three or four lengths. In general, winning or losing produced no visible effect upon Lord George Bentinck; but on this occasion he did not attempt to conceal his delight. As I led John o' Gaunt back to the weighing - room his Lordship remarked to me, " This is indeed a victory ! The old 'squire will now have to pay me in coin instead of in lead." His Lordship's winnings upon the three races must have been very considerable, and his outlay incausing the three concentric straw-beds to be made was repaid a hundredfold. Undoubtedly he was most fortunate in getting two broken-down horses, like Discord and John o' Gaunt|for such they were considered at the end of the previous year| through a couple of big races of this description by their superior condition. In 1844 Discord had failed in both fore-legs, his back sinews being fearfully bowed. By the aid, however, of the " Gaper charges," Discord was restored during the winter to such an extent that his Lordship resolved to run and to back him at the Epsom Spring Meeting for a selling race|winner to be sold for $250. When the weights for the Northamptonshire Stakes came out in February, I advised him to accept with Discord, who was handicapped at 8 stone. The horse's legs were so improved by the charges that I was able to give him a good deal of work on the straw-beds, and to get him very forward in condition. On February 25, 1845, his Lordship wrote to me as follows:|

" By your advice I will accept with Discord at Northampton, but with such legs I cannot think he has any earthly chance of getting two miles in a strong-run race, unless you have given him a new pair of fore-legs. However, it will only cost $10, and will not prevent my running him in the selling race at Epsom."

It was certainly a wonderful restoration, as

JOHN O' GAUNT. 169

Discord won not only the Northamptonshire Stakes, but also, during the following week, the Granby Handicap at Croxton Park, carrying 11 stone 10 lb., and the Cup next day, carrying 12 stone. Later in the year he ran in many other races, and was repeatedly tried at home, leaving off at last perfectly sound.

After these two experiences of Discord and John o' Gaunt, his Lordship would never believe that any horse was absolutely incurable, however badly broken down he appeared to be. When he bought John o' Gaunt the year before from the Duke of Bedford, Mr William Edwards, then his Grace's trainer, remarked to Lord George : " I suppose, my Lord, you have bought John o' Gaunt for a stallion, as it is useless to attempt to train him again. We have had him fired and otherwise treated, but to no purpose." When the horse arrived at Goodwood, his Lordship said to me : " I wish you would try the effect of your charges on John o' Gaunt's legs, as I could win some money on him if he could be brought sound and well to the post, since he stays so well." Not only did John o' Gaunt win the Queen's Plate at Northampton, but another at Newmarket, and also the Cup at Stockbridge and the Cup at Egham. His Lordship then obtained a good price for him as a stallion. He afterwards became the sire of Bolingbroke|a good horse if he had not been "messed about"; in fact, he was only half trained when a distance from home he|looked like winning the Doncaster St Leger, for which Voltigeur and Russborough ran a dead heat. The " Gaper charges " certainly effected some marvellous cures, especially upon the progeny of Bay Middleton. But I was also greatly assisted by the excellent gallops at Goodwood, which were kept in perfect order at Lord George's expense. I do not believe that it would have been possible to bring Discord or John o' Gaunt sound to the post in 1845 had they been prepared on any other training - ground. Every day the gallops were bush-harrowed and carefully rolled, and a band of women were employed to repair the tracks, remove stones, and fill in the footprints with forks specially made for the purpose. His Lordship walked over the tracks after the women had left, and the slightest imperfection in their work was sure to catch his eye, when he would desire me to point it out to them. Although the kindest and most generous of masters, he would never suffer a servant or employee to scamp his work or shirk his duty.

It must be confessed that the Goodwood stable had a phenomenal year in 1845. Commencing, as I have just stated, at Northampton and Croxton Park, horses belonging to the Duke of Richmond and to Lord George Bentinck won the One Thousand Guineas at Newmarket; the Oaks at Epsom ; the Ascot Stakes; the Liverpool Cup; the Goodwood Stakes and Cup ; the Champagne and Great York-

A PHENOMENAL YEAR. 171

shire Stakes at Doncaster (all of them heavy betting races, and therefore very acceptable to his Lordship), in addition to many less important stakes, such as the Port at Newmarket; the Mostyn Stakes at Chester; the Surrey Cup at Epsom; the Great Produce Stakes and the Fern Hill at Ascot; the Bretby, Prendergast, and Glasgow Stakes at Newmarket; and, finally, a great match between Miss Elis and Oakley, which the mare, ridden by William Abdale, won by a head, although the betting|enormously heavy| was six to five on Oakley, ridden by Robinson. In fact, the Goodwood stable won eighty - two races in 1845, the collective value of which was $31,502|an unparalleled sum for any stable to win in those days when " added money " was an almost " unknown quantity." Lord George as a thorough, uncompromising, unblemished sportsman was always ready to promote sport. At the same time, he steadily kept in view his main design and chief amusement, which was auxiliary betting; and, to this end, it was his custom whenever possible to try, just before the race in which he was engaged, any horse that he intended to back. In those days most of the races for three-year-olds arid upwards were over long distances, and it sometimes happened that horses with delicate constitutions were unfavourably affected and thrown off their feed by a long and severe trial. I therefore begged his Lordship onmany occasions to desist from this practice on the eve of a big race, particularly in the case of Miss Elis, who was always a difficult and delicate mare to train, and who had disappointed us more than once by not running up to her trial. As the Goodwood Stakes drew near in 1845, for which Miss Elis was handicapped at 5 stone 7 lb., Lord George, having already backed her for several hundred pounds, was anxious to have her tried with Discord, John o' Gaunt, Naworth, and others,lall of them capable of getting the distance, and of telling his Lordship to a certainty whether Miss Elis was good enough to win the Stakes. For this purpose his Lordship came to Goodwood, and I lost not a moment in entreating him not to upset her by a trial when I was able to assure him with confidence that she would win in a canter if she came to the post as well as she was then. It was a vast responsibility for me to assume, and great was the difficulty I had in persuading his Lordship to abstain from trying her. At last, however, he consented; and my words, " The Goodwood Stakes will only be an exercise gallop which will not prevent her from winning the Cup next day," were fulfilled to the letter. Never before had I ventured to remonstrate so earnestly with his Lordship ; and although I had little fear of her being beaten for the first race, it was a great relief to me when, as I anticipated, she " made hacks" of all her opponents.

MISS ELIS. 173

After deciding not to try Miss Elis for the Goodwood Stakes, his Lordship was anxious to see her gallop at half speed with John o' Gaunt, Discord, and other old horses. I again ventured to remonstrate, explaining that down to that time Miss Elis had done all her work by herself entirely to my satisfaction, and that, contrary to her wont, after being galloped in company with other horses or tried, she had fed remarkably well, and would go to the post in better condition than ever before. After she had taken her usual gallop by herself, Lord George wished to 'see the rest perform, and was so much impressed by the style in which John o' Gaunt did his work, and the determined way in which he galloped, that he became quite excited, remarking, " I have laid heavily against this horse, and shall be half ruined if he wins." I replied that if he were not mulcted in pocket until John o' Gaunt gave Miss Elis 2 stone 10 Ib. over two miles and a half, no harm would happen to him for a long time to come, as I knew that over that or any other distance he would not give her 7 Ib. and a beating. " But," he rejoined, " that was some time ago ; are you sure that they are in that form now, as I never saw John o' Gaunt go in such style before ?" I lost no time in reassuring his Lordship, and begged him to make strong running with John o' Gaunt (who was nicely handicapped for an old horse at 8 stone 3 Ib.), in order to let the mare settle down to her work, when I promised himthat he would never have another uneasy moment. John o' Gaunt's last appearance in public had been at Stockbridge, where he won the Cup very easily indeed, and was immediately made favourite for the Goodwood Stakes. Not long after Stockbridge Races the Duke of Richmond's Lothario won the

Liverpool Cup, and passed John o' Gaunt in the betting for the Goodwood Stakes. The starters for the latter race‖ quote from the ' Racing Calendar'‖were as follows :‖

" Lord George Bentinck's ch. f. Miss Elis, by Stockport

3 yrs., 5 St. 7 lb. (Kitcheuer), 1. Mr F. Ongley's ch. g. Roderick, 6 yrs., 6 st. 12 lb.

(Crouch), 2. Duke of Richmond's b. h. Lothario, 5 yrs., 8 st. 11 lb.

(Flatman), 3. Lord George Bentinck's ch. h. John o' Gaunt, aged, 8 st. 3 lb.

Lord Eglintou's b. g. Aristides, 5 yrs., 8 st. 2 lb.

Mr H. Robinson's br. c. Morpeth, 4 yrs., 7 st. 11 lb.

Sir J. Hawley's b. m. Venus, 5 yrs., 7 st. 9 lb.

Lord George Bentinck's b. g. Naworth, aged, 7 st. 9 lb.

Mr Clifton's ch. g. Nottingham, 5 yrs., 7 st. 7 lb.

Mr Ramsbottom's br. h. Pineapple, 5 yrs., 7 st. 3 lb.

Mr S. Herbert's ch. h. Ajax, aged, 7 st. 2 lb.

Mr A. W. Hill's br. c. The Libel, 3 yrs., 7 st. 2 lb.

Mr Mostyn's b. c. A-la-mode, 4 yrs., 7 st.

Mr Collin's br. h. Rochester, 6 yrs., 6 st. 10 lb.

Lord Exeter's br. m. Wee Pet, 5 yrs., 6 st. 9 lb.

Lord Stradbroke's b. f. Boarding-school Miss, 4 yrs., 6 st.

Mr Parr's b. m. Europa, 5 yrs., 6 st.

Lord George Bentinck's bl. f. Coal-black Rose, 4 yrs., 5 st.

13 lb.

THE GOODWOOD STAKES. 175

Duke of Richmond's b. c. Laird o' Cockpen, 3 yrs., 5 st. 12 Ib.

Mr W. H. Johnstone's ch. f. Pythia, 3 yrs., 5 st. 13 Ib.

Mr Etwall's ch. f. Egis, 3 yrs., 4 st. 10 Ib.

Sir J. B. Mill's br. f. Giantess, 3 yrs., 4 st 10 Ib.

Mr H. J. Thompson's b. f. by Stumps, dam by Comus 3 yrs., 4 st.

" Betting‖7 to 1 agst. Pythia, 8 to 1 agst. Lothario, 10 to 1 agst. Pineapple, 11 to 1 agst. Wee Pet, 12 to 1 agst. Rochester, 13 to 1 agst. Boarding-school Miss, 14 to 1 each agst The Libel, Egis, and Miss Elis, 20 to 1 each agst. Europa, Aristides, and Morpeth, 25 to 1 each agst. Laird o' Cockpen, Ajax, and Venus, 30 to 1 agst. Roderick, and 50 to 1 agst. Nottingham.

" Aristides led for a short distance, but at the first turn *JEgis* and Miss Elis went in front. In coming round the last turn -Egis, being then second, just behind Miss Elis, ran against a post, which broke between her legs, and fell just before Nottingham and Lothario. At this part of the race Miss Elis increased her lead, and won very easily by six lengths. Lothario was beaten by a length for second place, Pythia and Ajax being close together, just behind Lothario."

It was Lord George's intention that John o' Gaunt should jump off with the lead and make strong running, and orders to that effect were given to his rider. When the flag fell, however, Lord Eglinton's Aristides, a five-year-old gelding by Bay Middleton, outpaced John o' Gaunt and cut out the work at a tremendous pace, until Miss Elis got into her stride and passed Aristides, soon having everything behind her safe. When she went first past the winning-post by six lengths (which she could easily have made ten or twelve),she ran nearly to the top of Trundle Hill before Kitchener could stop her. It will be observed that in this race six of the twenty-three starters were supplied by the Goodwood stable|viz., Lothario, John o' Gaunt, Naworth, Coal-black Rose, Laird o' Cockpen, and Miss Elis, whom Kitchener rode in a 7-lb. saddle. But it is also worthy of remark, in these days when there are no six-year-old and aged horses in training, and when five-year-olds and even four-year-olds are rare, what was the composition of the field that Miss Elis beat so easily. Among the starters there were three aged horses|John o' Gaunt, Naworth, and Ajax ; two six-year-olds | Roderick and Rochester; seven five-year-olds|Lothario, Aristides, Venus, Not tingham, Pineapple, Wee Pet, and Europa; four four - year - olds|Morpeth, A-la-mode, Boarding- school Miss, and Coal-black Rose; and seven three-year-olds|Miss Elis, The Libel, Laird o' Cockpen, Pythia, -Egis, Giantess, and bay filly by Stumps. In estimating the merits of modern three-year-olds like Robert the Devil, St Gatien, Foxhall, and Plaisanterie, which are able to win the Cesarewitch and Cambridgeshire with 9 stone, or nearly 9 stone, on their back, I, for one, should feel more certain that they were better than Faugh-a-ballagh, The Baron, and Alarm, if, like these last-named horses, they were capable of beating large fields of old horses, such as Miss Elis defeated for the Goodwood Stakes in 1845.

THE GOODWOOD CUP. 177

After Miss Elis's victory in the Goodwood Stakes Lord George was naturally much gratified, though not in the least elated. Deeming nothing done while aught remained to accomplish, his thoughts flew forward to the next day, and he remarked to me that he hoped he should be able to win the Cup with her, although well aware that in Weath-erbit he had a formidable opponent. That same night his Lordship sent for me, after dinner, at Goodwood House, and inquired how Miss Elis was, and whether she had fed well. I replied that she did not appear to be in any way the worse for her race, which I regarded as only an exercise-gallop preparatory to her weight-for-age race on the morrow. " In that case," he remarked, " I shall back her to-night, as there is sure to be some betting on the Cup, for which Weatherbit has many friends."

Next day the Goodwood Cup brought twelve starters to the post, and the result was reported as follows in the ' Racing Calendar' :|

"Lord George Bentinck's ch. f. Miss Elis, 3 yrs., 7 st. (Abdale), 1.

Mr Gully's br. c. Weatherbit, 3 yrs., 7 st. 4 Ib. (White- house), 2.

Sir C. Monck's b. g. My Old Hack, aged, 7 st. 5 Ib. (Lye), 3.

Lord George Bentinck's b. h. Discord, aged, 9 st. 12 Ib. (W. Hewlett).

Mr Gully's br. h. St. Lawrence, aged, 9 st. 7 Ib. (J. Day).

Mr Surtlen's b. h. Gorhambury, 5 yrs., 8 st. 13 Ib. (J. Hewlett).

Mr A. Johnstone's ch. f. Eowena, 4 yrs., 8 st. 6 Ib.

(Marson). Sir G. Heathcote's ch. c. Akbar, 4 yrs., 8 st. 5 Ib.

(Chappie).

Mr Vane's ch. c. Valerian, 4 yrs., 8 st. 1 Ib. (F. Butler).

Colonel Anson's b. g. Arundo, 5 yrs., 7 sL 12 Ib. (Flatman).

Baron K de Rothschild's Drummer, 5 yrs., 7 st. 5 Ib.

(E. Flatman).

Duke of Richmond's br. c. The Laird o' Cockpen, 3 yrs.,

6 st. 13 Ib. (Esling).

" 2 to 1 each agst. Miss Elis and Weatherbit, and 6 to 1 agst. Valerian. Discord
made play at a great pace, Miss Elis next; she passed him at the turn round the hill and
was never headed, and won by two lengths. Weatherbit came up to Miss Elis about
the commencement of the rails and ran with her for a short time, but she increased her
lead, and was never approached afterwards. My Old Hack was a bad third."

I have frequently been present upon race-courses when the betting was heavy, but
never have I seen money staked so lavishly as it was by Lord George on the one hand,
and by the Danebury party on the other, just before this event. Weatherbit had been a
great favourite for the Derby of that year, which was won by Mr Gratwicke's Merry
Monarch in a field of thirty-one starters; but in coming round Tattenham Corner, Lord
Chesterfield's Pam fell just in front of Mr John Gully's Old England and Weatherbit,
both of whom jumped over him. Old England finished third, but Weatherbit was the
best, as was proved at Ascot, where Weatherbit

GOODWOOD AND DAXEBURY RIVALRY. 179

beat Old England, and also the Duke of Richmond's Refraction, who, however,
carried 6 Ib. extra for winning the Oaks. Weatherbit's next race was for the Goodwood
Cup, and his owner, trainer, and all the patrons of the Danebury stable, thought he was
the best three-year-old in England. Lord George, however, had won so much money
on the Stakes, that in backing Miss Elis for the Cup the firm front maintained by his
opponents exercised no effect upon him, and was incapable of stalling him off. In
1845 the Goodwood stable and the Daneburv stable were nat-

ural rivals, and Lord George was not the man to forget when he had good reason for
resenting supposed wrong and injustice inflicted upon him. The money, therefore, was
piled upon Miss Elis and Weatherbit with a recklessness which I never saw equalled,
and their respective supporters were both equally determined to have a good pace.
For this purpose Lord George started Discord, and Mr Gully started St Lawrence, but
when the flag fell Discord jumped off with the lead, and St Lawrence was not speedy
enough to take any part in the race. So good was Miss Elis's condition that at the end
of the first mile she passed Discord, and was never again headed. After her victory,
Lord George, although showing no external signs of elation, gave me to understand
how much he was gratified, exclaiming, *sotto voce,* " I think I have at last got the better
of Danebury."

In both races Miss Elis was ridden without spurs. The large sumlabout $30,000lwon
by Lord George 011 the Stakes and Cup would have been much reduced had the mare
been tried before the former race.

To commemorate the double triumph more fully, Lord George presented my father with a picture of Miss Elis, concerning which he wrote the following characteristic letter :|

"harcourt House, *Aug.* 6, 1845.

" Kent,|As a token of my sense of the ability and skill with which you and John trained Miss Elis for the Goodwood Stakes and Goodwood Cup, and as a memorial of the fidelity with which on this occasion in particular my secrets were kept, by which I was enabled to win, and without which I could not have won, the large stake I did win, it is my intention to make you a present of a picture, in which I propose that your portrait and John's as well as hers should be comprehended.

" In presenting you with this memorial of your joint triumph with your son, I must add the wish that the picture I give you shall descend as an heirloom in your family. The way I propose to group the picture is that Abdale should be mounted upon her, John leading her in his left hand| dressed in his Gordon tartan waistcoat|whilst you must be 011 the old grey mare, in your Cluny Macpherson Avaistcoat. The scene should be in the front of the Goodwood stand; a picture of

1 1-. .

u ;

x

w

w o s; o w

PRESENTATION PICTURE. 181

the Goodwood Cup should be introduced, and, if it can be managed, Kitchener walking away in the distance, loaded with a leathern purse, with ' Goodwood Stakes' inscribed upon it.

" I mean to employ Mr Abraham Cooper to paint this picture for me. He has promised to go down on Saturday next. I am anxious to have the picture speedily taken, for many reasons. First, I wish it to be taken whilst she continues in her present blooming condition, fearing, if I put off the day, I may never have her in the same condition, which happened to me when Elis was painted, who in consequence appears with ' a pot belly,' which if he had had it when he ran for the St Leger, he never would have won it. Secondly, I am anxious to have her painted during the bright summer weather, which makes such a difference in the colour and bloom of a horse's coat. Thirdly, whilst this weather continues warm, there will be little fear of the mare catching cold whilst she is stripped. Fourthly, the printsellers are anxious to have the picture done as quickly as possible, in order that the engravings may be made whilst her victories at Goodwood are still fresh in the public mind.

" Under the circumstances, if there is no objection, I will engage Mr Cooper to go to Goodwood on Saturday next.|I am, your obedient servant

"G. Bentinck.

" To Mr Kent, Trainer."

When the picture was completed, and Lord George saw it at my father's house, he was sodelighted with it that he desired Mr Cooper to paint him a facsimile, which now adorns the walls of Welbeck Abbey, together with the cap and jacket the mare carried, enclosed in a glass case suspended above the picture. The Goodwood Cup of 1845 is also at Welbeck, together with others which the present Duke of Portland has won; and although his Grace has not acquired so much money by betting as fell to Lord George's portion at Goodwood in 1845, it is within my knowledge that he views his equine treasures|St Simon, Ayrshire, Donovan, and others|with as keen appreciation as that with which his illustrious ancestor regarded Crucifix and Miss Elis.

Still further to recognise the services done him, Lord George made handsome presents to every one employed in the Goodwood stable. For all his labourers employed upon the gallops and racecourse (there were about eighty of them in all), together with others employed on the Goodwood estate, he desired a dinner to be prepared ; but inasmuch as it was harvest-time, this part of the rejoicing was delayed until the corn was carried ; and then all upon the estate were regaled with a most sumptuous banquet in the tennis-court, to which about two hundred guests sat down.

After dinner there was a general expression of hope that another Miss Elis might be found next year, and the only division of opinion was as to the colours which the said successor should carry.

MISS ELIS AND WEATHEBBIT. 183

Some hoped it might be " yellow, scarlet cap, and gold tassel" ; others inclined to " blue and white cap." At last it was carried unanimously that it was expedient that the two colours be amalgamated, as upon the present occasion. - What was left of the feast was given to the wives and families of the labourers who served the owner of Miss Elis.

Although Miss Elis had won the Stakes and Cup, both races being over a long and severe course, Lord George resolved, much to my regret, to pull her out for the Chesterfield Cup on the last day of the meeting. Her race for the Cup had been a very trying ordeal, as the pace was tremendous, and Weatherbit, whom she beat, was undoubtedly a good horse. Despite the 7 Ib. extra which she carried in the Chesterfield Cup, making her weight 6 stone 13 Ib., Miss Elis started favourite at 3 to 1 in a field of nineteen. She was beaten a long way, and finished almost last, the Cup being won by Mr Etwall's Egis, who was seriously disappointed in the Stakes by coming into collision with a post before referred to. From the effects of the two last races Miss Elis never really recovered, and Weatherbit, after his defeat for the Cup, was never the same animal again. In the Doncaster St Leger, won by The Baron, he was beaten a long way, and next day, with odds of 3 to 1 on him, was defeated for the Three-Year-Old Stakes of 200 sovereigns each by Sir R W. Bulkeley's Chertsey|a very moderate horse.

Before concluding this chapter I wish to put on record a few words about the way in which Miss Elis came into his Lordship's possession. She was bred by Mr S. Reed of York, who sent her to Doncaster to be sold by auction as a yearling. Although very light in flesh and rough in her coat, she struck me as being a sound racing-like filly, who would improve upon good keep. I therefore offered Mr Reed forty guineas for her, and a thousand more if she won the Oaks, for which he had entered her. He was anxious that she should get into a good stable, and let me have her at that moderate price. I told Lord George what I had done, and when he saw her he was only too glad to take her on the same terms. Before the end of the Houghton Meeting I tried her with seven other yearlings, and, although beaten, she showed more form than I expected from her, six weeks after I had bought her, a mere bag of bones. Her trial told me, however, that she was game and looked like staying, so that Lord George engaged her in ten races, most of them over long distances of ground. Stockport, her sire, was own brother to Elis and Epirus, both of them good horses; and her dam, Varia, was by Lottery out of a Blacklock mare. She stood rather more than sixteen hands, and although of a very nervous disposition, was as game as a pebble, and liked to make her own running.

9

SECTION 9

CHAPTER IX.

LOBD GEOBGE AS A LETTEK-WRITER.

In 1864 Lord Beaconsfield remarked to an old friend, who is still living, and has repeated the story to me, that Lord George Bentinck's failure as a Cabinet Minister, or in other words, as a statesman of the first class, would have been inevitable, for the following reasons. " Owing to his incapacity for condensing or compressing what he had to say," added Lord Beaconsfield, " he could not write a letter on any subject without pouring forth at great length all that was in his mind, with the result thatlto quote some well- known lines, the author of which I have forgotten, but which still linger in my memoryl

' Blenheim's field became in his reciting
As long in telling as it took in fighting.'"

It has been stated to me by other friends of Lord George Bentinck that he assisted to break down his own health by the extraordinary length and prolixity of his letters. I remember that old John Day, the rider and trainer of Crucifix, once observed to me " that he had not time to read Lord George's endless yarns about his race-horses at Danebury." It must be remembered, however, that old John Day was not much of a scholar, and that his own letters were of the briefest. I will not deny that my father and I sometimes found it difficult to answer Lord George's letters in full, as they frequently covered six, seven, or eight sheets of note-paper; but, as evidences of his Lordship's astonishing industry, and of the intense interest which he took in the minutest details of a pursuit to which his whole heart and mind were given up, I propose to print a few letters from his pen which were received on various occasions by my father and myself, as I am quite sure that no other owner of race-horses ever wrote to his trainer almost every day of his life, and at such length as Lord George frequently found necessary, in order to express his meaning fully.

I have selected for my purpose a few specimens which will derive interest from the fact that most of them have for their subject what I verily believe to have been one of the three best race-horses ever owned by Lord GeorgeIto wit, Gaper. If this horse had been by a sounder stallion than Bay MiddletonIsay, for instance, Gladiator or TouchstoneII am fully persuaded that he would have won the Derby as easily as in the Criterion Stakes at Newmarket he beat Cotherstone when both were two-year-olds. As matters stood, however,

GAPER. 187

Gaper could never take a strong gallop or win a race without pulling up more or less lame, and, in addition, he was very nervous and excitable, and Sam .Rogers's heavy hand and rough-and-ready style of riding made him more irritable. The first of the following letters was written from Newmarket on the evening of the day when Gaper as a three-year-old had the greatest difficulty in beating a very bad horse called New Brighton, after having won a sweepstakes of 100 sovereigns each, R.M., by three lengths on the previous Tuesday, beating a very moderate horse of the Duke of Grafton's, called Esop, who was ridden by John Day. It will be seen that Lord George was greatly disappointed at this poor performance of a horse whom he had heavily backed for the Derby, and on whom he founded the most sanguine hopes. I should premise that " Philip," to whom Lord George frequently alludes, was Philip Newman, stud groom at the Danebury paddocks, adjoining John Day's stables. To these paddocks considerable additions were made by Lord George when he first went to Danebury ; and on removing his horses from Danebury to Goodwood he retained his paddocks at the former place, thereby turning to account his heavy investments in loose- boxes, hovels, paddocks, tanks, ponds, and fences, together with plantations or belts of trees erected to shelter the thoroughbred stock from the cold winds sweeping over those exposed downs.

"NEWMARKET CRAVEN MEETING, 1843.
Thursday, April 20.

Sweepstakes of 200 sovereigns each, half-forfeit, for three-year-olds. D.M. Nine subscribers.

Lord George Bentinck's b.c. Gaper, 8 st. 4 Ib. (S. Eogers), 1.
Lord Chesterfield's b.c. New Brighton, 8 st. 7 Ib. (Flatman), 2.
Duke of Bedford's br.c. Jerry Sneak, 8 st. 7 Ib. (E.Edwards), 3.
" Betting|9 to 1 on Gaper. Won by a short neck.
Three lengths between second and third."

" Newmarket, *Thursday, April* 20, 1843.

" Kent,|I am sorry to say all our hopes are gone. Gaper, though by the grace of the 3 Ib. allowed him he got in first, ran a very moderate, not to say a very bad. horse to-day. Nat and Sam Rogers being both ordered to make play, they came away as hard as they could, head-to- head together, Gaper with the whip-hand, but never able to get away from New Brighton. He ran, however, very game at last, and, thanks to the 3 Ib., just crawled in a head first at last. Before starting, and during the race, 11 to 1 and 12 to 1 was taken freely about him for the Derby, but after the race 1000 to 10 went a-begging against him !!! Scott turned New Brighton over to Taylor to train, after trying him last year to be good for nothing ; whilst Taylor this year, having tried him with Gamecock, thought him good for nothing also. I am quite beat, and do not pretend to understand it. By the running with Rooksnest it would seem as though St Jean d'Acre were

NEWMARKET CRAVEN MEETING. 189

nearly as good, certainly within 3 Ib. or 4 Ib. as good, as Pompey ; and allowing Cotherstone to be able to give 10 Ib. to Pompey, if, as we imagined, Gaper could give a stone to St Jean d'Acre, he would have been a dead heat with Cotherstone. Cotherstone can give a stone to St Jean d'Acre, but I should say not 21 Ib., and that is just what we thought to be Gaper's form. Reckoning also the Fidelity filly at 16 Ib. worse than Conquest, St Jean d'Acre can give Conquest 7 Ib., and Maccabaeus being said to be able to give 7 Ib. also, St Jean d'Acre could have given 7 Ib. to Conquest, and ought to be as good as Maccabseus at even weights. I presume Peeping Tom is 5 Ib. or 7 Ib. better than Conquest: this would bring Bramble to a par with Peeping Tom, and make him 7 Ib. better than Conquest.

" Colonel Peel tells me Murat can give 17 or 19 Ib. to Rooksnest.

" I am very glad Jerry Sneak started, and thus won your $20 for you, but I am terribly chapfallen at this lamentable exposure of Gaper.|I am, yr. obed. sert., G. Bentinck."

Two days later his Lordship's hopes began to revive:|

" Newmarket, *Saturday Morning,* 8 A.m.

" Kent,|I am quite satisfied now why Gaper ran so badly on Thursday: the fact is, his legs and joints failed. I thought at the time hewalked home dead lame; and though John says he was three times as lame after running for the Criterion, and that he has frequently seen him quite as lame after sweating, I should have said of him that he was as lame as a tree yesterday morning, and but for John's confidence of bringing him round, I should have looked upon him as regularly done up, and given it up as a bad job. We had him out again in the paddock in the afternoon, and he was better, but still trotted very lame. John's confidence rests upon the horse's joints and legs being nowhere sore when handled, and to there being no unusual swelling or inflammation about them. I take it the real truth is that, his legs not being able to carry him, he is anything in the world a better horse with 5 stone 5 Ib. upon him than with 8 stone 4 Ib. ; and above all, I take him to be a stone a better horse against a mountain-side like the hill above Swan's pond than he is upon a flat ; and *down a hill* I daresay he would *never gallop*|certainly not if the ground was hard. I have not seen John or the horse this morning, but last night John was confident that he should be able to bring Gaper round for Bath : a fine gentle rain which has come this morning will be of great service to him. I have kept him on here to the last moment, on account of the ground being in such good order here and so bad at Bath : besides, the accommodation here is so much better than at Bath.

A HANDICAP. 191

" I still think that if the ground were soft, and at light weights, 5 stone 7 Ib. each, tried a mile at Goodwood up that steep hill, Gaper would be an awkward customer for all the horses engaged in the Derby, unless it is 'A British Yeoman.'

" I enclose a handicap I have made, which, if Gaper were in his Goodwood form, and the ground were soft, and he could do with 8 stone 7 Ib. on his back what he can with 5 stone 5 Ib., would not, I think, come off against him.|I am, yr. obed. servt. G. Bentinck.

" *One Mile.*
Years. st. Ib.
St Lawrence . . . 6 9 11
Discord 6 9 7
Cotherstone . . . 3 8 7
Gaper 3 8 7
Aristides . . . 3 8 2
Pompey . . . 3 7 11
Murat 3 7 10
Queen of the Gipsies . . 3 7 9
Bramble . . . 3 7 7
St Jean d'Acre . . 4 7 7
Maccabseus . . . 3 7 6
Testy 3 7 4
Canton 3 7 4
Sirikol 3 7 4
Conquest . . . 3 6 13
Portumnus . . . 3 6 9
The Brewer . . . 3 6 9
Rooksnest . . . 3 6 9
Monimia c. 3 6 6
Elysium . . . 3 6 5
Cowslip . . . 3 6 3
Years. st. Ib.
Extempore . . . 3 6 3
Fidelity f. 3 5 11
Fiddlestring . . . 3 5 11

Fragrance1 . . . 3 56

" In handicapping the above, I have put the D.M. Handicap running out of sight as altogether wrong, my belief being that St Jean d'Acre ought to have been Last instead of *second.* There is no doubt Canton in private is Full 10 Ib. *better than Rooksnest!"*

Gaper's next engagement was at Bath, whence Lord George Bentinck wrote the two following letters to my father. I should observe that when " Kent" is spoken of or addressed by his Lordship, it means my father; and that when " John" is named, it means myself. These two letters from Bath reveal the industry with which, in days when newspaper reports of races were very flimsy, and almost confined to ' Bell's Life in London' and the ' Sunday Times' (both of which were published on Saturday), Lord George communicated by letter with my father, rarely missing a day, and giving a most exhaustive account of what had taken place on the race-course.

. " Bath, *April* 26, 1843.

" Kent,|I had barely time to send you a list

1 According to her running in the Chesterfield Stake with Extempore ; but according to our trials with Elysium last October, Fragrance's weight ought to be 6 stone 5 Ib., and I incline to think that would be nearer the mark. Extempore will have a better day.

BRAMBLE. 193

yesterday. Bramble's running was very satisfactory yesterday, as he not only showed speed but appeared to run on too : the ground was rather heavy also. Young John Day, carrying 9 st. 1 Ib. on a three-year-old, made strong play|such strong play that he began whipping his horse *before he had gone half a mile !.'!* Sam Rogers and young John Day both thought Bramble would have beat Kate Kearney colt, at even weights ; but 8 Ib. and such riding as that of young John Day's would make a mighty difference. However, assuming this to be the fact, and that the Queen of the Gipsies and Pompey are where they were last October|viz., a dead heat at even weights| Bramble would give them a stone, and, if we have made no mistake, Gaper would give them two stone apiece, which would make him beat Cother- stone just as easy as he beat him last year. Would to goodness I could hope that you could again bring him sound and right to the post! I am quite satisfied now that Gaper was lamed in the false starts, and that he ran that race with New Brighton on Three Legs. Discord being such a hard - pulling horse, and William Howlett upon him, it is impossible there can have been any mistake about that gallop between him and Gaper; and having only 7 st. 5 Ib. on his back, there can be no excuse for him against the hill.

" If I could believe you could get his leg right for the Derby, I should fear no horse in it except

' A British Yeoman'; but I cannot flatter myself that you will be able to do so.

" I find that, besides the colt by Slane out of Zoe, belonging to Isaac Day, which John Day has in training, and of which they were fond, there is a colt by Elis out of Rosalie, trained by Montgomery Dilly, which they have tried to be smart, and Mr Greville was backing last Monday for the Derby. I hope, however, that Bramble may prove good enough to pull me through.

" The ground was very heavy, which may account for the trial of the two two-year-olds coming off so very wrong. They both got off well|viz., they were the two first; whilst Charming Kate lost two lengths' start, and appeared to run slow in the early part, but won very easy at last. Pastoral ran faster than anything for 300 yards, and then stood still. She is a mean, little, short, runtish-looking animal, with short quarters, but strong back, good shoulders, good legs, and good feet; looks like a strong hack. To look at the lot, it was 4 to 1 on Pastoral. Mr Wreford's is said to be the worst of all John Day's lot, but Roe was fond of Midnight Star. I should think Abraham never can have got Best Bower out in your trial: I think he ran fast and tired in his race yesterday.

" I have quite decided not to run Gaper to-day.

" I fear Brother to Harold must beat Discord to-day. I suspect he is much about the form of Peeping Tom. Mr Collins, who is rather thick

HINTS TO KENT. 195

with John Day, tells me that, having a dead line of the Queen of the Gipsies, and being quite certain to beat her in a canter, which he did, and never dreaming of my beating him with Bramble, he made sure of winning the Lansdowne with Peeping Tom, whilst he kept the 4 Ib. off Brother to Harold in the Cup.

" I understand that old John Smith, who had all these horses in training, and recommended John Day to buy the three he bought, says that Brother to Perseus was a long way the best, Brother to Harold second, Kate Kearney third, and Pompey the worst of the lot. I suspect, however, that *speed* is the best of the Brother to Harold, and in that case it is just possible he may not stay the distance, but I have no notion that Discord can get the distance either: a mile has always been held to be his best course, and that he gets worse and worse every step he goes beyond a mile.

" I hope when you try you will keep the weights down as much as possible, and I presume you will try up to Gaper's form|viz., a stone under Discord and a stone above St Jean d'Acre. I suppose, too, you will put Sam Rogers on the old one to take care it is no humbug pace. However, I don't wish to interfere. I merely throw out these as hints, leaving it to Lord March to try the horses as he likes, and make what use of any of my horses he thinks proper, except Gaper, who is lame, andBramble, to whom, considering Gaper's leg, I must now look to carry me through all those engagements in which the two horses are engaged together : besides, having run two races here on two following days, he would be in no plight to try Cornopean on Saturday. I I am, yr. obed. servt., G. Bentinck."

In the next letter, as well as in one of its predecessors, it will be noticed that " 8 A.m., Tuesday morning," is prefixed to both. My father and I received scores of letters from his Lordship written at the same early hour, which always found him at work during the whole of his racing career.

" Bath, *Tuesday Morning,* 8 A.m., *April* 27, 1843.

" Kent,|The horses are all here perfectly well,, and the course yesterday was in capital order| quite soft|to add to which it began to rain about half an hour since, and has all the appearance of a wet day. Gaper cantered yesterday, and went quite sound, and John thinks his leg a great deal better. I don't think, however, that I shall venture to run him. John is not much alarmed about his leg for the future, *if I save Mm here;* but I confess I have no great hopes of it. The ailment is about two inches and a half above the fetlock- joint, on the middle tendon of the near fore-leg on the outside ; there is a knot upon the tendon, and

TWO-YEAR-OLDS. 197

I fear this must be considered a bad place. With regard to our two-year-olds, I fear we are altogether in a hole with them. We have no reason to think we have a two - year - old at all who can give 10 Ib. to Pastoral, and I cannot make him much above the form of Rooksnest and the Brewer, weight for age. Gaper would give these two-year-olds the best part *of four stone!!!* Colonel Peel says a real good two-year-old should run with Garryowen at 21 Ib. I can't have this; but John Day says a good two-year-old can just beat St Lawrence at *three stone,* which is more consonant with my notions of a two-year-old at this time of year. If the Wadastra colt and the Ugly Buck can do so, they have 21 Ib. in hand of the best two-year-old we can turn out. I hear from Philip that St Lawrence was John Day's trial horse last year for his yearlings, and the two-year- olds have been following him in their exercise this year. John Day asked Colonel Peel how he should try a good two-year-old with St Lawrence. The Colonel replied, 'An out-and-out good two-year- old should beat him at 21 Ib.' Upon this John Day exclaimed, '21 Ib., Colonel!!! A two-year-old beat St Lawrence at 21 Ib.!!! Why, I will run any three-year-old at Newmarket. I will run Cother- stone to-morrow a mile with St Lawrence, and give him 21 Ib. No, Colonel; I say I am quite satisfied to see a two-year-old beat St Lawrence clever at *three stone.'*

" From this I take it that is about the mark of the Wadastra colt and the Ugly Buck.

" I fear St Lawrence could give four stone or four stone and a half to the best two-year-old we can produce. I enclose a handicap. I have assumed that T.Y C., instead of half a mile, Yorkshire Lady would give the two - year - olds more weight, viz., 28 Ib.|I am, yr. obed. servt.,

"G. Bentinck.

"I consider 21 Ib. about the weight a three- year-old should give a two-year-old, half a mile.

"T.Y.C.

Years. st. Ib.
St Lawrence . . . 6 9 11
Garryowen . . . 6 9 11
Discord 6 9 7
Jeremy Diddler . . . 4 9 4
Gaper 3 8 7
Cotherstone . . . 3 8 7
St Jean d'Acre . . . 4 7 7
Yorkshire Lady . . 4 7 0
Farintosh . . . 3 6 10
Rooksnest . . . 3 6 7
The Brewer . . . 3 6 7
The Devil-to-Pay . . 2 5 10
Prince of Wales . 2 5 6
Pastoral. . . . 2 5 0
Best Bower . . . 2 5 0"

The description of Gaper's Derby was given in an earlier chapter. For myself, I must avow that I have never been able to reconcile myself to his defeat on that day by Cotherstone. Without

CORNOPEAN AND GAPER. 199

entering further, however, into details and devising excuses, which is as useless as " crying over spilt milk," I come next to a letter which was written more than a month after Gaper's defeat for the Derby. It runs as follows, and is very characteristic of his Lordship's painstaking thoroughness, and his practical good sense in always seeing things in their true light:|

" Harcourt House, *My* 1, 1843.

" Kent,|John will have told you, though he won a head after a desperate race, how wretchedly bad Cornopean ran yesterday. Whatever we may have thought before the race yesterday, it is quite clear now that Cornopean can have no chance at Winchester; and the Duke of Richmond and I, after talking the matter over, think the best plan now will be to send Bramble to Winchester to see what he can do *a mile, following* Decisive and Chotornian, and so keep Gaper and Cornopean fresh for Liverpool. I then thought of leaving Gaper to fight out the stakes about the country, and giving up Bramble for the Grand Junction Stake at Liverpool. I think Gaper keeps gradually getting worse and worse, as Flytrap did; whilst I cannot help thinking that Bramble has not yet got over his Ascot cough. You hardly ever heard a horse blow and appear so distressed as he did after his race for the Stockbridge Produce.

" I have left Mus, Naworth, and Lothario in theLiverpool Trade Cup, and struck all the others out, and have made up my mind not to send Discord to Liverpool at all; else had he been well, I know of nothing in the North to beat him for the Croxteth Stake, whilst I fear St Lawrence is cock-sure to beat him both for the Craven Stake and Welter Stake at Goodwood.

" I have left Lothario in the Trade Cup to take the double chance of his being well by that time, or else of starting him to get the 5 Ib. allowance in the Cup at Goodwood, by which time I imagine, if he goes on well, he will be quite up to the mark again.

" There will be a great acceptance for the Trade Cup. I reckon about fifty horses, many of them of a good class. Pompey is first favourite, and they take 6 to 1 about him : his running at Bath must be all wrong; that never can have been the same form as that in which he ran at Newcastle.

" I think it more than probable I may go down to Goodwood by the mail-train to-morrow night, and so spend Monday at Goodwood.

" I have a dreadful prospect before me: my stakes and forfeits at Goodwood amount to $4900, I think, and at Liverpool to $670, and I doubt $2000 will scarcely cover those I shall incur at Doncaster, Liverpool, and Newmarket, besides those all over the country, and I really scarcely see where I have a reasonable chance of getting through a stake.

UGLY BUCK. 201

" Tripoli had better go over to Winchester. I daresay I shall be able to get my stake back to run. He can walk to Fareham the day before the race, and thence go on by the train.|I am, yr. obed. servt., G. Bentinck.

" Lord Chesterfield says the Ugly Buck is the finest horse he ever saw. Colonel Anson says he is a very clever horse, and one that must run, but thinks him rather small in the middle-piece. Lord Maidstone thinks him a clever horse, but not of sufficient scale to please him. Isaac Day says, to his mind he is just the size he would choose for a race-horse—in fact, Venison on a larger scale.

"G. B."

Before quitting the year 1843 I should add a few words about the year which preceded it, as on many occasions horses trained at Goodwood in 1842 beat great pots from Danebury, which John Day, father and son, and their party backed heavily, because Lord George's horses which opposed them had been trained in 1841 at Danebury, and their form was therefore supposed to be well known to the owners and masters of that great racing establishment. Perhaps the most notable instance of this occurred at the Bath Meeting, of which I give the subjoined account, so far as concerns two races in which Lord George defeated the Danebury stable. The following description is from ' The Racing Calendar ' :|

" Bath And Bristol Eaces, 1842.

Tuesday, April 19.

The Somersetshire Stakes Handicap.

Lord George Bentinck's Tripoli, 3 yrs., a feather (Sharp), 1.
Mr Maley's ch.m. Bellissima, aged, 7 st. 13 lb., 2.

" Seven others started. Betting|6 to 4 against Tripoli, 7 to 2 against Bellissima.

" *Thursday, April* 21.

" The City Cup, of 100 sovereigns, added to a Sweepstakes of 20 sovereigns each; half-forfeit; 18 subscribers; 2$ miles.

Lord George Bentinck's b. f. Topsail, 3 yrs., 6 st. 5 lb. (W.
Hewlett), 1.

Mr Bigg's ch. c. Eleus, 3 yrs., 6 st. 6 lb., 2.
Mr Wade's gr. c. Greenharn Boy, 4 yrs., 7 st. 12 lb., 3.

" Betting|3 to 1 on Eleus.- Won easily by two lengths."

I should mention that Lord George sent Topsail to Bath solely for the purpose of meeting Eleus, and that he wrote to me the day before the race, giving me orders not to allow Topsail to run unless Eleus started. His Lordship gave a heavy commission to back Topsail, and was rewarded by winning a very good stake, about which he cared nothing in comparison with triumphing over the Danebury stable.

I now come to a letter written in 1844 from Bonehill, where his Lordship had paddocks, as

IMPROVEMENTS AT BOXEHILL. 203

well as at Doncaster, and addressed to myself. It will serve to show what a fine judge he was of a foal's shape and make, and with what minuteness he entered into a detailed description of what he saw. The first sentences of the following letter refer to the improvements which he was then engaged in making in the race-course at Goodwood :|

"BONEHILL, *NOV.* 21, 1844.

"JoHN Kent,|Upon reconsideration, I think three inches of mould is too little to place under the turf. Having decided to take the field mould, which is to be had at so little expense, and of which there is no limit in amount, I am clearly of opinion we should not be stingy of one depth of mould, and instead of three inches, as was settled, desire Charles Shepherd to put double that quantity, viz., six inches,|*not, hoivever, undoing or disturbing any ivorlc that is already done.*

" I have also bethought myself, as I am going eventually to pick up that old road across the top of Molecomb Hill, and to returf it, if the old materials were to be picked up now they would serve admirably, being so close and handy to mend the road with at the top of Charlton Park between my field and the race-course. With this fine dry weather I hope in the course of next week you will be able to ascertain the real merits of all the rough lot of yearlings.

" I think I have upon the whole rather a good lot of foals here. I annex an account of them on another sheet.|I am, your obdt. servant,

" G. Bentinck.

"1. Bay colt by Bay Middleton | Olive. A slashing fine colt; great size, great length, enormous arms and legs, stands straight and well on his fore-legs, and with his hind-legs well under him. I cannot span his leg below the knee. Shoulders come right into the middle of his back, and his quarters come well into his back likewise ; good loins and good quarters, and pretty good thighs with great hocks; a little flat-sided, and might be a little deeper in the girth, but not much fault to be found ; plenty of body; sour, thick, and rather lop - eared but small head ; rather a small, bad eye, but apparently an idle, easy- tempered animal ; in the paddock a slashing, striding, true galloper, and I have set him down to win the Derby and Leger in 1847.

"2. B. c. by Lanercost | Crucifix. A pretty good colt; immense loins, good quarters and hocks, and deep in the girth ; very thin through the shoulders ; rather flat-sided though deep in the body; ewe-necked; refined head; good knees, but very light below them; very small in the fetlock-joints and pasterns, and small feet; but his bone and sinew flat, clean, and sound-looking ; a good goer in the paddock, with quicker action,

FOALS AT BONEHILL. 205

but nothing like the easy stride of the Bay Middleton colt. Mr Edmund Peel has backed him with me to beat the other in the Derby.

" 3. Ch. c. by Plenipotentiary | Glentilt. A sturdy, sound, muscular, hard-constitutioned-look- ing colt. Looks like plating or winning the 300 sovereigns stake at Goodwood, but a little slack in the loin, and rather short in the body; a good true galloper.

" 4. Ch. c. by Plenipotentiary | Latitude. A long-legged, thin, narrow caricature of Longitude and Binnacle, having all the bad points of both ; won't feed, and looks in the last stage of a consumption ; apparently weak and hardly able to walk. Upon taking him into the paddock, however, with the Glentilt colt and with a filly by Plenipotentiary out of My Dear, he proved able to gallop past either of them, and appears to be the quickest galloper of all the lot. We galloped the three till the filly and Glentilt colt were in a lather all over, but, strange to say, we could not get the consumptive horse to sweat, neither did he blow half so much as either of the others; but they say they can neither get him to eat or drink!! !

"5. B. c. by Plenipotentiary|Vacuna. A fair- sized lengthy colt, but long and weak below the hocks and knees, and not a very good head, but a moderate goer.

"6. B. c. by Plenipotentiary|Lady Emmeline.

A sturdy colt, very like Plenipotentiary in shape, but very *short arms,* and short bad action; no stride, putting down his feet pretty nearly where he takes them up.

" 7. Sister to Pug. Very like Pug, but a finer Gohanna head, with enormous nostrils, and in all respects mending upon Pug ; a very fine galloper, and a very likely mare to win the Oaks.

" 8. Ch. f. by Plenipotentiary | Let-us-stop-a- while-savs-Slow. The favourite Here of All the

Fillies. No favourite of mine. A good galloper certainly, and a fine head, but short in the body, and drooping short Camel quarters ; good shoulders, and muscular-looking.

"9. B. f. by Plenipotentiary | My Dear. A small, smart, racing-looking filly; beautiful head, neck, shoulders, body, loins, and quarters, with fine length, but no legs below the knee ; no bone and no sinew; small fetlocks, and straight; well put on, but nasty fleshy - looking legs | one of the old specimens of Bay Middleton legs; looks like flying half a mile, but no further ; a good- actioned filly, but seemed to have no chance with the consumptive one.

"10. B. f. by Bay Middleton | Chapeau d'Espagne. Very like, but on a still less scale than, the two-year-old out of her; her hock has got right, but she has a ringbone on the other hind-leg; very pretty hack action, but no stride. I have ordered it to be sold for *$5* if no more canLord Chesterfield's Establishment. 207

be got for it. I have eighteen mares here|six of which are certainly in foal to Touchstone, ten certainly in foal to Colwick, Camarine's dam barren to Colwick, and Armida supposed to be barren, but I think in foal. G. B."

The next letter gives an interesting peep into Lord Chesterfield's racing establishment at Bretby Park in Derbyshire, where during the last twenty years of his Lordship's Turf career his horses were trained by old Tom Taylor, the father of the still living Alec Taylor. Colonel Anson was married to a sister of the Countess of Chesterfield and of Colonel Henry Forester, and many of his mares and yearlings were accommodated at Bretby by Lord Chesterfield, his brother-in-law, as will be seen from the following letter:|

" Welbeck, *Nov.* 30, 1844.

" John Kent,|I am afraid we have nothing very clipping. As you say, they are always behind the old ones, and to be Really Good they ought to beat such things as Moonshine and the Estelle filly at even weights, T.Y.C. I reckon that the Real filly, Ennui, and Vacuna would about beat the Estelle filly at 16 lb., for I think we may assume that they can give the Torch filly 16 lb. If I am right in this, I think they will pay their way, but not do any great things, unless we find *one* amongst them to be superior over a distance ofground. We *avefour* much too near together for there to be a real good one in the lot. " This is my handicap :|

"T.Y.C.

Age. st. lb.

African . . .5 97
Cowl . . .2 77
Rose of Cashmere . .2 73
Moonshine . . .2 62
Estellef. . . .2 60
Realf. . . .1 4 12
Ennui . . .1 4 12
Vacunaf. . . .1 4 12
Torch f. . . .1 3 10

" If I am right in this, it will bring them up to be as good weight for age next year as Cowl and Rose of Cashmere,|which may not win the Oaks, but will win a good many things.

" I forgot exactly what was our best trial last year, but I think we were always trying the old horses with their heads From *home,* and that last year we only tried half a mile instead of three- quarters. I think you say, too, that the Torch filly would have won half a mile; if so, Real filly and Ennui would have been about winning, carrying 5 st. 7 Ib. half a mile|*i.e.,* just 4 st. under African. The question, therefore, is, How have our yearlings been with African last year and the year before half a mile ?

" They have taken no taste yet of their yearlings at Bretby, but mean to do so about Christ-

THE BRETBY PARK YEARLINGS. 209

mas. Some of their best|viz., Birkenhead, Mar- text, the mare by Touchstone|Hornsea's dam (a splendid animal), and the sister to Euclid|are still in the paddocks. *Spanish Jack* (Don John over again, but out of a mare that never bred anything to run), Ginger (brother to Mango), the colt by Camel|Gladiator's dam, the colt by Don John|Scandal, Stitch, by Hornsea out of Industry, a colt (a very clever one) by Jereed out of Dirce, (Sir Harry's dam), Turpin (I think, next to Birkenhead, Taylor's favourite), by Hetman Platoff out of Black Bess, and five others, amongst them a great favourite of mine, Shelford, by Colwick out of Marchesina, are all up in the stable, and have had two sweats apiece, but are nothing like so forward or fit as ours. Most of them have been singed all over like my cart-horses, but none of them have been tried in any way. Spanish Jack is the most perfect horse to look at, but the dam has never bred anything that could gallop.

" I think all Col. Anson's were going off the end of this week to Scott's. Lord Chesterfield is going to train almost entirely with Taylor at home, and means to make some great improvements in his training-ground, which at present hardly deserves the name of a training-ground.

Take them altogether, I never saw such a lot of yearlings together, especially when I consider how much good looks and running blood are combined

in them ; and they are all such sound - looking horses, besides plenty of size without lumber. I am glad to say all the mares I sent to Touchstone are heavy in foal, Moss Rose included, and I have ten out of twelve in foal to Colwick.|I am, yr. obedt. servant, G. Bentixck.

" I am very partial to the Colwicks, and wish I had hired him this year.

" I 'am sorry to say I have only got three subscriptions to Sir Hercules : I wanted six, but he is full."

From the above letters it can easily be imagined that such an establishment as ours, and such a correspondent as Loi'd George, involved an immense amount of letter - writing on my father's and my part. In addition to answering his Lordship's letters, three of which sometimes came by the same post, we had to attend to nominations, entries, and declarations of forfeit, and also to making arrangements for travelling to the countless race meetings where horses were engaged. All this could not be accomplished without economising time to the utmost. With this end in view, I found it necessary to write a vast number of letters while travelling by railway, and I often had occasion to rejoice that, thanks to his Lordship's kind consideration, I

HIS EXHAUSTIVENESS. 211

was always instructed to travel in a first-class carriage, wherein I was frequently the only passenger.

I will now bring to a conclusion a chapter which might be indefinitely extended were I to include in it further specimens of the numerous letters which Lord George Bentinck wrote to my father and myself. It was his custom thoroughly and fundamentally to exhaust every subject and every detail upon which he touched; and as a further evidence of his untiring industry, I have now before me ever so many letters which he wrote upon a new system of ventilation which he desired to apply to some stables he was building at Goodwood. The perusal of these and other letters from his active pen recalls to my mind a few words spoken to me not long ago at Newmarket by my old friend the ex-racing Judge, Mr J. F. Clark, who was well acquainted with the Goodwood stable when in its prime. " I do not think," exclaimed Mr Clark, " that any of the present lot of trainers in England would have long kept the situation of trainer to Lord George Bentinck, which would have worn any of them out in less than a year." To prepare a hundred horses for their engagements is under any circumstances a laborious undertaking, but to do so fifty years ago was almost more than one man could long sustain. I am quite sure that I should not be here now to write these words if I had been called upon to look after such a stable of horses as I had under my charge at Goodwood; and to do so continuously for such an indefatigable and exacting master as Lord George Bentinck over a period of twenty years, instead of being in harness only from the end of 1841 to the August of 1848 inclusive.

10

SECTION 10

CHAPTER X.
LATTER HALF OF THE RACING SEASON OF 1845.

Three weeks after her severe exertions at Goodwood, Miss Elis ran at York for the Great Yorkshire Stakes, when Lord George Bentinck backed her again. She was beaten easily by Miss Sarah, a fine slashing filly, who had run third to the Duke of Richmond's Refraction for the Epsom Oaks, and was a daughter of Gladiator (at that time one of the best stallions in England), and of Major Yarburgh's famous mare Easter, by Brutan- dorf. The ground at York was excessively deep, a large portion of the course being under water. I well remember that Mr Ramsay's Malcolm, a very powerful chestnut two-year-old colt, who won the Prince of Wales's Stakes on the first day, sank down into the mud as he was being saddled, and was quite unable to extricate himself until four or five strong men, whose assistance was invoked by Tom Dawson, his trainer, applied their shoulders to his ribs on both sides of his body, and fairlylifted him out of the morass into which he was subsiding. Next morning, when I took my horses out to exeicise, I encountered an old acquaintance on the farther side of the course under the wood, who thrust his walking-stick into the spongy soil up to its handle, remarking that " there was no bottom to be found." A shrewd, hard - headed Yorkshire labourer who was engaged in filling in the holes made by the horses' hoofs on the previous day, overheard my friend's remark and ejaculated, " You be mistaaken, zur; there be a parlous good bottom, nobut goe deep enouf doun to foind it."

Lord George was at all times very sceptical as to the soundness of excuses made for any of his horses which failed to win a particular race. He would not listen, therefore, to the assurances forced upon him by some of his friends, that Miss Elis had been beaten through the deepness of the ground. In addition to Miss Elis, Major Yarburgh's mare had also beaten Mr Bennett's Hope, who was second to Refraction for the Oaks. With his usual practical good sense, Lord George soon convinced himself that Miss Sarah would win the Doncaster St Leger, and immediately commenced to back her heavily for that race. Before long his Lordship's money made Miss Sarah first favourite for the St Leger, and when the flag fell she started with odds of 5 to 2 against her. In the race, for which she was trained by the late Charles Peck, she was beaten rather cleverly by Mr Watts's chestnut

THE BARON. 215

colt, The Baron, who was bred in Ireland, and never came to this country until he put in an appearance at the Liverpool July Meeting, to run for the Liverpool St Leger. It was won by Mr St Paul's Mentor (a bad - tempered brute, who was said to have nearly killed Mat Dawson in his brother Tom's stables at Middleham), with Sir R. Bulkeley's Pantasa second and Lord Eglinton's Vaudeville third I four others not placed. As The Baron was being led off the course, John Scott, after inspecting him long and keenly, said to Mr Watts, his owner, " If you will send that horse to Whitewall without delay, he shall win the Doncaster Leger for you." Mr Watts took the great Yorkshire trainer at his word, the result being known to all. The Liverpool St Leger was run on July 18, and the Doncaster St Leger on September 17, so that John Scott had less than nine weeks in which to effect a transformation in the Irish horse. He certainly worked wonders by his skilful preparation of The Baron for the Don- caster St Leger and Cesarewitch; and it is noteworthy that after the latter race, The Baron, for whom Mr E. R. Clark, familiarly known as " D'Orsay Clark," immediately gave $4000, never won again in the hands of another trainer.

When Lord George came, as usual, to the Turf Tavern to look at his horses in the evening after the St Leger, he remarked to me in a low voice, " I have had rather a bad day, as I backed MissSarah for $3500. I hope you will get it back for me to-morrow with My Mary ? " At that time the Great Yorkshire Handicap was run on the third day of the Doncaster September Meeting. Without hesitation I replied that I had no doubt My Mary would win, as she was so " well in," having only 5 stone to carry, which was equivalent to putting in Miss Elis at 5 st. 7 Ib. and Miss Sarah at 6 st. 2 Ib. When My Mary was tried with Miss Elis for the Goodwood Stakes, the latter won with the greatest difficulty, giving My Mary 7 Ib. I remarked, however, that at the end of a mile and three-quarters (the exact distance of the Great Yorkshire Handicap) My Mary would have won, and this made me feel great confidence that she would get back Lord George's St Leger losses, and probably a little more, on the following day.

It may not be out of place or uninteresting to my readers if I recite here the circumstances under which My Mary came into Lord George's hands. She was bred by Alderman Copeland (a very good and popular sportsman) in 1842, her sire being Bran by Humphrey Clinker, and her dam by Oiseau, a grandson of Harnble- toniau.

Bran ran second to Touchstone for the Doncaster St Leger of 1834, and was the sire of several good horses, among them being Our Nell and Meal, who ran first and second for the Oaks in 1842, as previously recorded. My Mary was own sister to Our Nell, and had run nine times as

MY MARY. 217

a two-year-old, winning thrice, her last victory being for the Prendergast Stakes at Newmarket. After that she was pulled out by Alderman Cope- land to run for a Selling Plate in the Houghton Meeting, winner to be sold for $350. She was beaten by Brother to Chummy, and no one claimed her. I then advised Lord George to buy her from Alderman Copeland, adding that I did not think the Alderman would want much for her. When she started for the Selling Plate in the Houghton Meeting I observed that she was ridden in a tremendously severe curb bridle, and was led to the post by one strong man and followed by another with a cart whip in his hand. She was more like a wild animal than a race-horse in training, and I attributed her fractiousness to a misconception in bitting her, and to want of patience and gentleness in handling her. She was a sound pretty little filly, and I thought that she might be got through a good stake if trained and managed with judgment. Lord George got her with little difficulty for $250, her former owner and trainer being equally glad to get rid of her.

When we got her home to Goodwood, I began at first to fear that I had induced his Lordship to make a bad purchase. She could not be persuaded to accompany the other horses, but would bolt with her rider, running under the trees, or anywhere to get out of the way. Her boy had no power or control over her, and when in the stable she wouldtremble and quiver like an aspen leaf. I could not get her to touch food; and when she went out, I was full of apprehension that she would run against a tree and kill herself or her rider. In despair I resolved at last to put a very steady quiet lad upon her, who weighed nine stone, and had very light hands. I told him to keep her out all day, sometimes riding and sometimes leading her, first with one set of horses and then with another. In the afternoon she accompanied the yearlings; and at last I discovered, to my infinite satisfaction, that she was becoming less fractious,, and regaining her confidence. Soon she began to feed better, and I added a liberal supply of flour to the water which she drank. I then put her into the yearling trials, telling her lad to stop her when she had galloped a couple of furlongs, and to canter in gently after the others.

At last I got her perfectly quiet, so that a friend of mine who had known her at Newmarket exclaimed, " Why, that is not the same animal that I saw win the Prendergast! You have made her as round as an apple and as sleek as a mole." Time, patience, and gentle treatment had worked wonders with her, as they will with all horses which have been maltreated and misunderstoodl a very common occurrence in these days of sprint- races, in which no starter has any chance unless " quick out of the slips," and, as the phrase runs, " always on his tiptoes." As My Mary was a

MY MARY. 219

small filly, and known to possess speed, I got her ready to run early in the spring, and tried her half a mile twice before Northampton Races. On each occasion she won, and it did not upset her in the least. I then tried her three-quarters of a mile, and she won again. Presently I asked her to go a mile, and she proved herself equal to the task by winning easily. It struck me that, being by Bran, she might, if trained for it, " get a distance," and in that case I felt persuaded that she would win a good race. Accordingly I gave her a stronger preparation, which she stood well, feeding capitally all the time, and when ridden in a snaffle going as quietly as a pony. When the Goodwood Stakes trial came off, I put her in it, with the result recorded above. She was struck out of the Goodwood Stakes, which she would easily have won with Miss Elis out of the way. Lord George then made up his mind to put her into the Great Yorkshire Handicap, as it was just the right distance for her, and in those days a very heavy betting race. Six or seven other horses from the Goodwood stable were entered along with My Mary, and when she was handicapped at 5 stone Lord George rubbed his hands, exclaiming, " What a good thing !" On the day when the $5 forfeit was to be declared, nominations had also to be made for some other stakes, and I came up to London to submit a list of entries to his Lordship, whom I accompanied to Messrs Weatherby's office.We did not get back to Harcourt House until 11 P.m. As none of our horses had been struck out of the Great Yorkshire Handicap, Mr Charles Weatherby kindly sent a messenger to Harcourt House with a letter asking me to remind his Lordship that he had several horses engaged in that race, all of which would accept unless he declared forfeit for some of them before midnight. I wrote back hurriedly to Mr Weatherby, thanking him in Lord George's name for his considerate attention; and adding that, as we had not had time to look over the handicap, all his Lordship's horses had better remain in.

When I was saddling My Mary I found that his Lordship was unusually anxious. He said to me, " I suppose we had better wait with the mare, as last year she always showed more speed than stoutness." I assured his Lordship that he would find her a very different animal to-day from what she was last year, when, from what I saw of her condition and excitability, it was impossible to train her. " She will never be fitter," I added, " than she is to-day ; and as she has stood a good preparation, and could not be better in, she ought to be allowed to make the pace good if nothing else does." His Lordship consented, although he did so silently, and without much approving the policy I suggested. I felt confident, however, that, if the pace was good and true, My Mary would win before they got to the Red House,

MY MARY. 221

and my words were literally verified. There were eleven starters, and My Mary made most of the running at a smart pace. As the field approached the Red House, she had them all in difficulties, and won very easily by a length, which Kitchener might have made twenty or thirty had he cared to do so. He rode her very steadily in a snaffle bridle, and without spurs. Before the race, some good judges who had often seen My Mary when she was trained as a two-year-old at Hednesford laughed at the idea that she would get the St Leger course, and lost their money accordingly.

As we walked away from the course following the filly, his Lordship, after pausing for a minute to hear "All right" pronounced when Kitchener got into the scales, thanked me very warmly for winning this race with a mare whom no one else, as he kindly remarked, had ever been able to get to stay a mile. " You have got all my money back for me," he added, " and a little more on the top of it, as I have won rather more than $15,000."

A few days later I received from his Lordship the following kind and considerate letter:l

" Welbkck, Worksop, Notts, *Sept.* 22, 1845.

" John Kent, I Our Commissioner made poor work of it for us on the Great Yorkshire Handicap, averaging only 2 to 1. However, as I consider it a great triumph of training getting My Mary,vho was not in other hands able to get T. Y. C. to run If mile, as well as curing her bad temper, I shall make up the odds you and your father stood with me to $25 to $200, which I send you in my cheque.

" I am obliged to be in London on Thursday for a meeting on Friday. If any trial of interest were to take place on Saturday or Monday, I could be at Goodwood for it. We ought not to try till we can trust Miss Elis to have got over her two races, as she must be considered now the key to all the Cesarewitch horses.

" I cannot estimate her nearer than 9 Ib. under Miss Sarah, and I suppose, as The Baron actually gave Miss Sarah 5 Ib., lost start, and beat her a length, we must estimate him at least 8 Ib. better than Miss Sarah. This makes 17 Ib. We must therefore find something, which I fear we shall not do, that can beat Miss Elis, assuming her to be in the Cesarewitch at 6 stone 8 Ib., and in the Cambridgeshire at 6 stone 4 Ib. Discord and Refraction are the only chances we have in the Cesarewitch of finding one to do it.

" Lothario and Croton Oil are our only chances in the Cambridgeshire, but I cannot help suspecting that Kitchener never got My Mary out the first day we tried her with Croton Oil. We ought to try My Mary, Clumsy, Croton Oil, Miss Elis, Refraction, and Lothario together before the Cambridgeshire Stakes : if the last two are not

BACKING THE BARON. 223

prepared, I think Clumsy, Croton Oil, Miss Elis, and My Mary should be tried over again, to enable me to decide whether or not I should let those foreigners have Croton Oil.II am, your obedient servant, G. Bentinck."

Before I left Doncaster to return to Goodwood, Lord George remarked to me with characteristic foresight, " I think The Baron cannot lose the Cesarewitch, although I am told that Colonel Anson and John Scott think he has no chance at the weight he has to carryl7 stone 9 Ib. Nevertheless, I shall back him and take my chance, as he is as well in as Miss Elis would be at 6 stone 6 Ib. or My Mary at 5 stone 12 Ib. Surely my two fillies would be bad to beat at those weights ? " With his usual courage, and in total disregard of what he knew to be the conviction of John Scott's powerful stable, his Lordship threw a lot of money on the market to back The Baron, which he increased as the day approached, upon learning that in my Cesarewitch trial Miss Elis and My Mary finished first and second, beating the old horses at very little difference of weight. His Lordship's money soon made The Baron first favourite, and he told Colonel Anson what he had done, offering to give up some of his bets to the stable if they liked to share with him. He then added that he had retained Flatman to ride for him in the Cesarewitch, but that having no horse he fancied, hewould surrender Flatman to ride The Baron. Both offers were gladly accepted, and when the flag fell The Baron was a great favourite at 9 to 2 Iodds which could hardly be obtained. The pace was moderate, and at the Bushes Flatman took the lead, winning at last cleverly by a length. About that time Flatman was riding with great nerve and skill, and, above all other jockeys that I ever had to do with, he invariably obeyed the instructions he received to the very letter. In addition to winning the Cesarewitch upon The Baron, he also won the Cambridgeshire upon Mr Greville's Alarm|the best three-year-old of his year, with perhaps the exception of Sweetmeat. In the Cambridgeshire, Alarm, carrying 7 stone 9 lb., beat The Baron carrying 7 stone 8 lb. by several lengths, owing to the latter having been "messed about" in his work: yet, ridden by Bumby, he started at 4 to 1, and Alarm at 9 to 1. The pace in the Cambridgeshire was as good as it had been bad in the Cesarewitch.

11

SECTION 11

CHAPTER XL
Lord George's Gains In 1844 And 1845.

Mr Charles Greville, in his remarks upon the character of Lord George Bentinck and his untimely death, which extend over nearly thirteen closely printed pages of his ' Diary,' employs the following words :|

" I have always thought that his [Lord George's] conduct in selling his stud all at one swoop, and at once giving up the Turf, to which he had just before seemed so devoted, was never sufficiently appreciated and praised. It was a great sacrifice both of pleasure and profit, and it was made to what he had persuaded himself was a great public duty. It is true that he had taken up his new vocation with an ardour and a zeal which absorbed his old one; but still it was a very fine act, and very creditable to him. He never did anything by halves, and having accepted the responsible post of leader of his party, he resolved to devote himself to their service, and did so without stint or
reserve."

That Lord George's determination to sell his stud at one swoop was, as Mr Greville says, "a very fine act," will be denied by none who know what were his Lordship's gains upon the Turf in 1845, and also that in Surplice and Loadstone he possessed, and knew that he possessed, in 1846, the two most promising yearlings that ever called him master. From the details recorded in the last two chapters my readers will not be surprised to learn that, to the best of my belief, Lord George's winnings by betting during the year 1845 must have amounted to close upon $ 100,000. It was seldom his Lordship's habit to speak of money matters, about which, as about all his business transactions, he was one of the most reticent of men. His avowal, for instance, after the Great Yorkshire Handicap, that he won more than $15.000 on that race, was almost the only statement of the kind that he ever vouchsafed to my father or myself. Nevertheless, the amount of his outlay on a race was in every instance approximately disclosed by the statement of the quoted odds when the flag fell; and on such subjects popular rumour, emanating from well-informed racing and betting men, is seldom far from the mark. In this manner I could not help being made aware what were the races upon which his Lordship had staked most

COUP UPON LOTHARIO. 227

money; and in addition to the Goodwood Stakes and Cup won by Miss Elis, and to the Great Yorkshire Handicap won by My Mary, it came to my knowledge that his two best races in 1845 were the Liverpool Cup, won by the Duke of Richmond's Lothario, and the Cesarewitch, won by Mr Watts's The Baron. Upon these five races his Lordship must have landed in bets not less than from $60,000 to ,$70,000, and this large sum was augmented when the Duke of Richmond's Red Deer won the Port Stakes at Newmarket, Picnic won the One Thousand Guineas, and Refraction the Oaks. In the last-named race Lord George had three mares of his ownIMiss Elis, Rose of Cashmere, and Longitudelengaged, all of which started, as they had shown some form. None of them had been tried with the Duke of Richmond's Refraction, and therefore his Lordship confined himself to backing " Kent's lot " for a large sum, whereby he showed more judgment than by taking 8 to 1 about Miss Elis, while Refraction's starting price was 25 to 1.

But, as I have already said, one of his biggest *coups* in connection with that fortunate year was upon the five-year-old Lothario, when he won the Liverpool Cup, for which he started first favourite in a strong field at 4 to 1, to which price he was brought by Lord George's money. Among the eighteen starters were reckoned some fairly good old horses, such as Corinna (who subsequently wonthe Chester Cup), Winesour, and Rowena, and one good three-year-old, the Ironmaster, who belonged to the almost invincible Mr A. W. Hill, the owner of Sweetmeat, the Libel, Salopian, Alonzo, and Burlesque. The previous career of Lothario shows (if that were necessary) what the uncertainty of horse - racing is. At Epsom Summer Meeting Lothario ran for the Surrey Cup, which Lord George's Croton Oil won, although Lothario, who ran very badly, and was beaten a long way, was much better than Croton Oil at the weights. A day or two after Lothario appeared very dull, and was off his feed I the result of a chill which he caught at Epsom. I was therefore obliged to ease him in his work, and between Epsom and Ascot he was limited to an occasional canter. In this condition he ran for the Ascot Stakesla race of which the Duke of Richmond was very fondlalthough I had not the slightest expectation that, over the severest course in England, Lothario would win it, and he was not backed for a shilling by the stable. To my intense astonishment, however, Lothario fairly wore down Mr Meiklam's five - year - old mare, Inheritress, who started first favourite at 3 to 1, and was backed for a heap of money. For this race Lothario's only backer was, so far as I know, the Marquis of Exeter, who trusted him with a " pony," as he had vowed, after Lothario beat

LOTHARIO. 229

his own horse Phlegon for the Port Stakes in 1844, that Lothario should never run again without carrying some of his Lordship's money.

When the weights appeared for the Liverpool July Cup, Lothario was handicapped according to his Ascot Stakes form, which Thomas Dawson, the trainer of Inheritress, made sure that he could beat with Mr A. Johnstone's Rowena, 4 years, 7 st. 2 Ib. All this Lord George, who knew everything that was going on, repeated to me when he came to Goodwood, adding that Mr Meiklam made light of Lothario's chance. I replied that if between the 10th of June and the 17th of July I could not improve Lothario from 7 to 10 Ib., there was no use in exercise, vigilance, and training. The Duke of Richmond was never fond of trying his horses when he believed them to be well and fit, and therefore Lothario was not "put through the mill" before the Liverpool Cup, which he undoubtedly would have been if Lord George's property. The horse gave me entire satisfaction, however, and went through a good preparation, becoming, so far as I could judge without taking off his clothes, as fit as possible. Lord George trusted him with a very big stake, as was proved by his starting first favourite in the teeth of the heavy sums laid out by the northern division on Tom Dawson's lot, as well as on Mr Bell's Winesour and Mr Mostyn's Milton. Therace was run at a capital pace, and Flatman on Lothario won cleverly by a length, with Tommy Lye on Rowena second.

His Lordship also won a good deal of money by backing three of his own two-year-olds, Cherokee, Princess Alice, and Ennui. The first won the Althorp Park at Northampton, the Woodcote at Epsom, the Fern Hill at Ascot, and walked over for the Theatre Stakes at Wolverhampton. The second (Princess Alice) won the Weston Stakes at Bath, the Two-Year-Old Sweepstakes at Chester (beating a large field), the 200 Sovereigns Sweepstakes for fillies at Goodwood, the Champagne at Doncaster, and the Prendergast at Newmarket. The third (Ennui) came out for the first time at Doncaster to again against Lord Maidstone's Tom Tulloch in a match, nominally for 500 sovereigns, but really for 1500 sovereigns each. Upon this match I shall have something further to say presently, when I have related that, after Princess Alice's victory in the Champagne Stakes, I mentioned that it was customary for the winner to give six dozen of that wine to the guests who dined at the Turf Tavern after the races. His Lordship therefore instructed me to give the necessary orders, adding that he hoped in this way to confer some slight benefit upon the hostess, Mrs Bowe, who was the widow of Mr John Bowe, in whose name some of his Lordship's horses had previously run and won, most notably Grey Momus,

DRINKING THE CHAMPAGNE STAKES. 231

when he won the Two Thousand in 1838. "Let the supply of champagne be ample, so that all may enjoy themselves," were his Lordship's concluding words to me, as he left the course to return to Welbeck.

The Turf Tavern was the abode during the Don- caster race week of a jovial crew, including Mr Dawson (himself the most hospitable and generous of men), and his employers, Mr William Hope Johnstone, Mr Meiklam, and Mr O'Brien. In addition, I invited John and Bill Scott to dinner, and any friends whom they might like to bring with them from The Salutation, where John Scott's horses always stood. In point of fact, the Turf Tavern that night was open to all who liked to enter its doors, and champagne flowed like water for many hours. At the dinner-table the mirth was fast and furious, as can easily be imagined when such guests as Mr Orde of Nunnykirk, owner of the famous Beeswing, Mr Pedley, Mr Wyndham Smith, better known as " The Assassin," and many other choice spirits, were also present.

When Lord George drove over next morning from Welbeck to Doncaster|there was no Great Northern Railway in those days|his first question to me was, " How did the dinner at the Turf Tavern go off ?" I replied that everybody had enjoyed himself more than I could describe, but that I feared the expense would exceed his Lordship's anticipations, as the bill for wine, almost entirely champagne, amounted to about $75, showing that the traditional six dozen had been greatly exceeded. " I am very glad to hear it," rejoined his Lordship. " We do not win the Champagne Stakes every day, and I hope it will do Mrs Bowe a little good. I shall be only too glad to pay the same bill for wine over again under similar circumstances." This very liberal expenditure on his Lordship's part was not solely due -to Princess Alice's victory in the Champagne Stakes, but was also prompted by Ennui's match. I have already mentioned that his Lordship was much struck by Tom Tulloch's good looks when John Scott brought him as a yearling to Doncaster to be put up at auction. It was with the greatest difficulty that I dissuaded his Lordship from bidding more for Tom Tulloch than 1200 guineas, seeing that he was a colt with heavy shoulders, roguish eyes, and a clubby foot. Tom Tulloch was knocked down to Lord Maidstone at 1500 guineas, and the match previously alluded to was ratified. John Scott thought so highly of Tom Tulloch that he encouraged Lord Maidstone to back him for the Two Thousand and Derby of 1846 before his form was exposed at Doncaster, where he was expected to show his heels without difficulty to Ennui. Tom Tulloch had been tried greatly superior to Colonel Alison's Iago, who ran second to Princess Alice for the Champagne, and it never occurred to John Scott and Frank Butler that a little scratching filly like Ennui could beat

TOM TULLOCH. 233

that form. As I was saddling Ennui, and giving Flatman orders to come right through with her, he said to me, " Give what orders you may, you are sure to be beaten, as I am told you are going to meet a great horse." Lord George, however, was not in a mood to be daunted, as he knew there was not much between Ennui and Princess Alice, by the latter of whom he had won largely. So freely did his Lordship back his filly, that, despite the great reputation of John Scott on a Yorkshire race-course, and the confidence generally reposed in his judgment, the odds were never more than 6 to 5 on Tom Tulloch. When the signal was given, Flatman made running as hard as his filly could lay legs to ground, and, to the dismay of John Scott and his powerful stable, Tom Tulloch showed the white feather before the distance was reached, and Ennui won in a canter by four lengths. I then ventured to remind his Lordship that making a match against Tom Tulloch was more profitable than buying him, with which he heartily concurred. Another race which brought grist to his Lordship's mill earlier in that same year was the Great Ascot Produce Stakes of 100 sovereigns each, with 200 sovereigns added, for three-year-olds, which was won by Cowl, who beat Mr Wreford's Winchelsea, a great Danebury " pot." The betting was very heavy, but in the end weight of money told, and the odds on Cowl were 3 to 1, which he landed ina canter by two lengths. Upon a number of small races secured by the Goodwood stable in 1845 his Lordship won considerable sums, and, as a rule, he had the market all to himself. I remember a curious race at Goodwood in which Lord George, always fond of novelty, had recourse to an experiment which turned out entirely to his satisfaction, when Farthing Candle, a two-year-old belonging to him, won the Innkeepers' Plate in heats. The conditions of the race were as follows : " The Innkeepers' Plate of 50 sovereigns added to a sweepstakes of 5 sovereigns each, for two-year- olds, a feather; three, 7 stone 4 Ib. ; four, 8 stone ; five, 8 stone 7 Ib. ; six and aged, 8 stone 10 Ib., the winner to be sold for $50; heats, T. Y. C." There were seven starters, and the betting was 6 to 4 against Farthing Candle, 7 to 2 against the Mus Colt, and 4 to 1 against Sister to Pompey. The first heat, in which Farthing Candle cantered almost at the tail of the field without trying for it, was won by Auricula, who immediately became favourite for the second heat, and gave Lord George an opportunity of investing more money at a good price upon Farthing Candle, who won the second and third heats easily, and was then claimed by Mr Shelley. It must be confessed that in this and many other races the light weight, fine judgment, and good horsemanship of Kitchener were of great service to his Lordship, who appreciated the lad's good qualities greatlyIwithout spoilingLord George's Expenses. 235

him, however, as is now the fashion, by extravagant presents and undue familiarity.

It was not without heavy expenditure and strict attention to business that Lord George was able in 1845 to win 58 races, amounting collectively in value to between $17,000 and $18,000. That year his Lordship had sixty horses in training, thirty-six of which started in 195 races. The accounts sent in by my father for the first half of the year were $43 5 8,13s. lljd., and $5586, 5s. 6d. for the second half, making together an aggregate of $9944, 19s. 5id. To this must be added jockey's fees, about $800 ; stakes, $5970 ; forfeits, $4420. Nor must I omit to include his Lordship's breeding-studs at Doncaster, Bonehill, and Danebury, among which three stallions, sixty broodmares, and from forty to fifty yearlings, together with about the same number of foals, were distributed. Taken altogether, his Lordship's expenses could not have been less than $40,000 in 1845 I a large sum to recover before anything could be put to the profit side. His Lordship was well awareIit was, indeed, an accepted axiom in those daysIthat without heavy and successful betting no man could make a large stud pay ; and also, that without the closest attention to details, trials, and the public running of his own and of other horses, it was impossible for any man to win by betting. There can be no question that the increasing demands of his Lordship's parliamentary duties towards the close of 1845 and at the beginning of 1846 made it difficult for him to give as much attention to his stud as he had bestowed upon it during many previous years. Mr Greville truly said of Lord George that " he did nothing by halves," and the necessity of maintaining the position which he had taken up in the

House of Commons and in the country weighed heavily upon his mind. Among the few books written by friends and contemporaries of Lord George Bentinck, there is none, within my limited knowledge, which affords a clearer insight into his Lordship's character than the ' Correspondence and Diaries of the Right Honourable John Wilson Croker,' which appeared in 1884. From it I venture to quote the following letter :|

"Lord George Bentinck to Mr Croker.

" Welbeck, *near* Worksop, Notts, *October* 5, 1847.

" My Dear Mr Croker,|My services, such as they are, shall always be at the command of any one like yourself who can put the facts which I am able to collect with more force and in a more striking light before the world.

" Virtually an uneducated man, never intended or attracted by taste for political life, in the House of Commons only by a pure accident, indeed by an inevitable and undesired chance, I am well aware

LETTER TO MR CROKER. 237

of my own incapacity properly to fill the station into which I have been thrust. My. sole ambition was to rally the broken and dispirited forces of a betrayed and insulted party, and to avenge the country gentlemen and landed aristocracy of England upon the Minister who, presuming upon their weakness, falsely flattered himself that they could be trampled upon with impunity.

" I did deceive myself, I own, with false hopes that the old English spirit would have been roused, and that it was only necessary to keep the dismantled ship floating and fighting under jury- masts till she went through the repairs of a new election, and then that scores of better men than myself would have come to her rescue.

" I own I am bitterly disappointed and brokenhearted that England has proved so degenerate that, in face of an emergency, she has produced, as far as I can see, no new leader to take my place.

" When their rents are not paid, and their mortgages are called in, the country gentlemen will exert themselves, and so will the farmers when wheat falls under 45s. per quarter, but not before.

" Nothing but pinching adversity will bring such men to a proper sense of their duty.

" As regards the gentlemen, the entire fund subscribed for the general election did not, I believe, exceed $8000, and of this King Hudson subscribed $6000.

" Till the landed interest and the colonial andshipping interests all together feel intolerable distress, we shall do no good; but in my conscience I believe if the Navigation Laws are repealed, which I scarcely doubt, this will happen within two years.|Always yours most sincerely,

"G. Bentinck."

It will not seem surprising to those who read this and other letters, addressed about the same time by Lord George to Mr Croker, that his Lordship should have found it impossible to conduct such a correspondence, to work for fifteen or sixteen hours a-day, and simultaneously to manage a stud comprising altogether more than two hundred head of thoroughbred horses. Long before the sale " of everything, from little Kitchener to old Bay Middleton," I saw plainly what was about to happen. For the present, it only remains for me to conclude this chapter by stating that, stimulated by his great success in 1845, his Lordship engaged his brood-mares in Produce Stakes, and his yearlings and foals at the end of that year, to an extent which has, I believe, never been equalled in the history of the Turf by a single individual. He began by entering eighteen colts in the Derby and eight fillies in the Oaks. Five yearlings or foals he entered in Two Hundred Sovereigns and Three Hundred Sovereigns Stakes p. p. ; seventeen brood-mares in Produce Stakes of one hundred sovereigns each. When I ap-

ZENITH OF LORD GEOEGE's CAREER. 239

preached his Lordship with a list of suggested engagements for stakes which closed on the 1st of January 1846, he glanced at it and exclaimed, " Surely I have more animals which ought to be put into these important stakes," meaning the Two Hundred Sovereigns and Three Hundred Sovereigns races at Goodwood, to which there was no forfeit. In the end, his Lordship's stakes for 1846 amounted to $35,115, and his forfeits to $22,110, the total number of engagements being 479.

The point in his Lordship's racing career at which I have now arrived was its zenith. Had he not been called away by the imperious claims upon him made by what he considered a paramount duty to his country, it is impossible to say to what magnitude his stud and his engagements might have ascended. Upon two of his Derby horses since he came to Goodwood in 1841, Gaper and Chatham, I had known him stand in each case to win between $100,000 and $150,000. Who can doubt that if he had kept Surplice and Loadstone in his own hands, he would have won such sums upon the Two Thousand, Derby, and St Leger of 1848 as have never been landed before or since ? I have known other rich men who could not stand to win even a small sum on a horse without betraying the most painful excitement. Lord George, on the contrary, was perfectly calm ; his pulse " made healthful music "when he stood to win more than $100,000 upon a horse like Gaper, whose chance he thought as good if not better than that of Cotherstone, the first favourite and winner. Under every test to which nerve and courage could be put, whether at two o'clock P.m. or two o'clock A.m., Lord George Ben- tinck, who, as Mr Greville said of him, " was afraid of no man," never quailed, and was never found wanting.

12

SECTION 12

CHAPTER XII.

THE SALE OF LOKD GEORGE'S STUD.

In the early part of 1846 Lord George Bentinck often expressed to me his deep regret that, by reason of the severe pressure of his parliamentary duties, he found himself unable to devote as much time as he could wish to managing, engaging, and watching the running of his race-horses in training. The inevitable consequence of this preoccupation was, that the great pleasure which his extraordinary devotion to the Turf had afforded him was now at an end. It so happened that on the evening of the third day's racing at Goodwood in 1846, after the Cup had been won by Mr O'Brien's Grimston, some of the guests assembled round the Duke of Richmond's table fell to discussing the magnitude of Lord George's racing establishments, and the large number of horses that he had in training. Suddenly his Lordship, who appeared to be more than half asleep, struck into the conversation with the question, " Will any of

you give me $10,000 for all my lot, beginning with old Bay Middleton and ending with little Kitchener, and take them with all their engagements and responsibilities off my hands ? " Mr George Payne immediately replied, " If you will give me till to-morrow at noon, Bentinck, to consider the matter, I will either accept your offer or will pay you down $300 if I decline it." " Agreed," said Lord George, quietly; and upon that Mr Payne sat down by his Lordship's side, and they entered into a long *sotto voce* conversation with each other. Mr Payne remarked that his own trainer, Montgomery Dilly, was not equal to the task of training so many horses, and presiding over such a monster establishment, and therefore he asked Lord George to advise him what to do in case a bargain was concluded between them. His Lordship was pleased to advise Mr Payne to engage me to train the horses and to manage the stud; adding that, from my long experience in connection with the Goodwood stable, I knew the horses and their dispositions thoroughly, and was better qualified than any other man to undertake the business. Thereupon Mr Payne sent for me immediately, and from him I learned for the first time that Lord George had resolved to quit the Turf. Knowing his Lordship's inflexibility and the iron firmness of his character, I was well aware that it was useless for me, or for any one else, to attempt to turn him from his purpose.

MR GEORGE PAYNE'S OFFER. 243

The announcement was, however, a great blow to me, although his Lordship's repeated intimations that he could no longer carry on his racing and his political careers simultaneously should have prepared me for his decision. Even at that early date I had come to the conclusion that his Lordship had, in Surplice and Loadstone, the two best yearlings that he ever owned; and none of the friends with whom I was intimate could have failed to understand what inexpressible pleasure it would have given me to win the Derby for my beloved and honoured master, with a horse bred by himselfla son of his old favourite, the peerless Crucifix.

Scarely had I found myself alone with Mr Payne before he announced his intention of leasing Michel Grove, near Worthing (which was then to be let), if I would consent to take charge of all the horses. Mr Payne added that if I would become his private trainer, he would give me $500 a-year beyond what I was in receipt of from the Duke of Richmond and Lord George. Although much distressed at the prospect of losing such a master as Lord George, I thanked Mr Payne as best I could for his flattering and generous offer, and for the confidence which he was pleased to repose in me. I added, however, that it was impossible for me to close with him until I had ascertained the Duke of Richmond's wishes upon the subject, as his Grace was also my master, andhad been so long before Lord George joined the Goodwood Stable. At this moment a note was brought in and handed to me, with a verbal request that I would read it at once. Having obtained Mr Payne's permission, I opened it, and found that it contained a request from the Duchess of Richmond that I would go and see her Grace before I returned to my own house.

Immediately upon leaving Mr Payne, to whom I respectfully refused to bind myself, one way or the other, until the evening of the next day, I was ushered into the Duchess's boudoir, where I found her Grace, accompanied by two or three younger members of her family. I shall never forget the scene. Her Grace's kindness and sympathetic nature were well known to all her friends and dependants, and of these inestimable qualities I had already received from her a thousand proofs. When, therefore, she inquired with unrepressed emotion, " John, is it true that you are about to leave us and to train for Mr Payne ? " I felt as if I was going to break down completely, and it was with no little difficulty that I could find voice to reply, " Your Grace, it appears that Lord George has offered Mr Payne his stud at a ridiculously low figure, and has recommended me to Mr Payne as better able to train and manage them than any one else. I have already told Mr Payne, however, that I can enter into no arrangement with him until I have ascertained the pleasure of his Grace."

. i .-
! t.. M . . '..
..' .. . ... '(-.
.. , i .,-:,,;.. , I...I-. i .
1 i- . t '!: VMii... ', . '!]:', CV l.'il ; ' . :!i'il, -s ; . . .- in;
'i ,' : i.'-r :i . ;! i
I (' . .Ml1 ')! ,
ii- i-..- .. ' ! (:'. - -t
. !' I'tii- T
-t,. I 'm -
I I 'ill C. '
i . . .i. vf1: ' i!i:'1 L'.-ii! i ' .
I I S - ' i .1 I !1 v" i.'1"1 .1..-
;.-. .m [':. i . - . Mr i'. .,'.. ' 11.;'. -n.-c i !. n 1: :!.."
.-.': ;.. !'.'U '!, ! .!.! -. I V.. ...'. ; r- . . . -ir-j,. ,.,., t. s 'i !, K; .l
MR PAYNE PAYS FORFEIT. 245

" John," rejoined her Grace, " if you leave Goodwood, there will be an end to the delight and pride which we have all taken in the horses. As long as his Grace lives he will always keep horses, and so long there will be a comfortable home for you." Without a moment's hesitation I answered, " If it be his Grace's wish and your own that I should continue at Goodwood, I will not leave it until you wish me to do so."

I did not see Mr Payne again that night, but what I had said to her Grace was quickly communicated to him. Next morning at breakfast he pulled out his pocket-book, and without a word handed $300 to Lord George, who, I have no doubt, was sorry under the circumstances to receive the forfeit. Upon reaching the racecourse, I found that every one knew what had transpired on the previous evening, and that morning at Goodwood House, and that the desire to purchase Lord George's magnificent stud for what one gentleman described as "a crust of bread" was almost universal. Among others, a group consisting partly of gentlemen and partly of bookmakers, with Mr Henry Padwick of Horsham I commonly called " The Sussex Lawyer " I at their head, were conspicuously busy in making preparations, until their further negotiations were summarily arrested by Lord George's declaration to me that " nothing would induce him to sell to a set of bookmakers." He added that unless somenobleman, or gentleman of position, or two or three of them in combination, should arrange to purchase the stud, and to accept the grave responsibilities involved in forfeits amounting to about $18,000, he would not sell at all.

It so happened that the Hon. Edward Mostyn Lloyd Mostyn, who was then forty years of age, and who became second Baron Mostyn on the death of his father in 1854, was at that time on intimate terms with Lord George Bentinck, who had taken great interest in his splendid Velocipede mare, Queen of Trumps, after she defeated

Preserve in the Oaks. Lord George's judicious advice had powerfully contributed to Queen of Trumps winning the St Leger, upon which, as before explained, Lord George was a large winner. After conferring with his cousin, Mr Cynric Lloyd, who was an ardent devotee of the Turf, Mr Mostyn resolved to approach Lord George and to make him an offer for the whole stud, on the understanding that the horses then in training at Goodwood might remain there so long as he and Mr Lloyd should desire. The bargain was soon concluded, and in this manner 208 thoroughbreds|viz., 3 stallions, 50 horses in training, 70 brood-mares, 40 yearlings, and 45 foals|passed into Mr Mostyn's hands. The following letter from Lord George apprised me of the unwelcome intelligence that I should probably never see his colours|light-blue jacket

/ W

I , t

XUW, 7 &Q-

/T V

BOUGHT BY THE HOX. MB MOSTYST. 247

with white cap|on a race-course again, although it was destined that Slander should carry them to victory at York for the last time, albeit the Prince of Wales's Stakes, which Slander won in the old jacket, went to Mr Mostyn's credit. Lord George's letter, which Mr Cynric Lloyd brought to me at the York August Meeting in question, was in these words :|

"harcourt House,

Augiiit 18, 1846, 7 P.m.

"JOHN Kent,|Mr Mostyn has purchased my stud. Mr C. Lloyd, his cousin, is the bearer to you of this letter, and from this time Mr Mostyn stands in my shoes. Carts, cart-horses, saddling, and horse-clothes are all included in the sale.

" You will therefore, as regards my horses, from this time receive your instructions from Mr Mostyn or Mr Lloyd, as may be settled between them.'|I am, your obedient servant, G. Bentinck.

" To Mr John Kent, Junr."

Mr Lloyd handed me Lord George's letter just before the races commenced on the first day of the York Meeting. I had prepared his Lordship's two- year-old filly Slander, by Pantaloon out of Pasquinade, to run for the Prince of Wales's Stakes. She was own sister to Mr A. W. Hill's celebrated horse The Libel, and, like him, was bred by the Marquis of Westminster, who was at that time the owner of Touchstone and Pantaloon, probably the two best stallions in the world. Previous to her York engagement, Slander had already won the New Stakes at Ascot.

There was no time to substitute Mr Mostyn's colours, yellow jacket and black cap, for Lord George's, and with a heavy heart I saddled the last animal that I thought would ever run in that familiar jacket, which in the last three years I had so often seen carried to victory. I have ever since taken a pride in reflecting that on the very last appearance of Lord George's colours they occupied their accustomed place in the van. There were twenty-one starters for the Prince of Wales's Stakes |a larger field than is commonly seen at the post in these days. Mr Mostyn had another filly engaged, called Twysoges, by Picaroon out of Her Highness, who could run a little; and in addition, there was Mr Payne's Clementina, by Venison out of Bay Middleton's dam, who was very smart, and started first favourite. The race ended thus :|

Mr Mostyn's b. f. Slander (Abdale), 1.

Mr Payne's b. f. Clementina (Flatinan), 2.

Mr Mostyn's b. f. Twysoges (Bumby), 3.

Mr Mostyn's c. Vice-Consul (H. Bell), 4.

Seventeen others unplaced. Won cleverly by a length.

The fourth horse, Vice-Consul, was Lord George's second string, whom I brought to York in case Slander should go amiss or get disappointed in the race. Thus it will be seen that in the very first race in which Lord George's horses ran as Mr Mostyn'sMr Mostyn's Arrangements. 249

property, the latter gentleman was first, third, and fourth, the winner being one of Lord George's lot. Scarcely was the race over before Mr Payne remarked to me, with his usual *bonhomie, "* So you have beaten me the first time you ran against me after refusing to become my trainer !" Mr Lloyd was much elated at winning such a race the first tune of asking, and all the more so because, by my advice, he backed Slander. Upon the Monday following York Races Mr Mostyn and Mr Lloyd came to Goodwood to inspect the stud they had purchased, and to make the necessary arrangements for the future. Naturally their first and greatest desire was to reduce the number of animals feeding at Mr Mostyn's expense, and to limit the outgoings as soon as possible. Their first design, and that which seemed to be the most prudent plan under the circumstances, was to offer the whole of Lord George Bentinck's stud for sale by auction, and to buy in what they wished to keep ; but this did not appear to me at all the best course. In the first place, I entertained strong doubts whether it would be agreeable to the Duke of Richmond to have a monster sale of this kind at Goodvood. If his Grace objected | and I felt pretty sure that he would|to such a proceeding, I considered that it would be a great risk to send heavily engaged horses by railway to London, to thread their way in large numbers through crowded thoroughfares to Tattersall's. It will|be remembered that in 1846 railways were in their infancy, and that the skill and safety with which race-horses are now boxed and despatched on a long journey were then unknown. Besides, it was certain that bidders would fight shy as soon as they found that the sale was not " without reserve." It therefore seemed to me that by far the best plan would be for Mr Mostyn and Mr Lloyd to select the animals which they wished to retain, and to send the rest by instalments to Tattersall's. The public, I argued, were naturally prepared to learn that Mr Mostyn intended to largely reduce the enormous expenses attaching to such a stud, and were expecting a *bond fide* sale of a considerable portion of it.

To these views Mr Mostyn assented, and on September 7, 1846, a huge draft was sold at Hyde Park Corner, and, as might have been expected, drew a large attendance. Thirty lots were put up|viz., nineteen brood-mares (by no means the cream of the stud), three yearlings, and eight horses in training. All sold well, Princess Alice fetching the top price. This day's sale realised 3195 guineas. On Tuesday the two-year- olds, seventeen in number (Tattered-and-Torn having been presented to one of the Duke of Richmond's daughters and thrown up), which had been inspected at Goodwood by breeders from all quarters, were put up, but to very little purpose, only two being sold|viz., Blackcock (engaged in

SALE AT TATTERS ALL'S. 251

the Champagne at Doncaster, in the Criterion and Clearwell at Newmarket, and the Drawing-room Stakes at Goodwood) for 250 guineas, and Growl (in the Oaks, Gratwicke, and a 50-Guinea Stake at Newmarket) for 70 guineas, with their engagements. Master Butler (engaged in the Drawing- room and St Leger, 1847, and the 300 Sovereigns Stakes at Goodwood, 1848) was privately sold, with his engagements, for $30. Particulars of the first day's sale are subjoined :|

Brood-Mares.

Guineas.

The Maid of Orleans, ch. m., 4 yrs., by Jereed out of

Anchorite's dam, &c.; covered by Slane . . 200 Charlotte, b. m., 5 yrs., by Liverpool out of Brocade;

covered by Slane 100

Charming Kate, sister to Coronation, 5 yrs.; covered

by Slane 90

Mora, 4 yrs., by Bay Middleton out of Malvina;

covered by Slane 70

Souvenance, b. m., 7 yrs., by Bay Middleton out of

Souvenir; covered by Emilius .... 62 Eatifia, b. m., 4 yrs., by Bay Middleton out of Carna-

rine's dam; covered by Emilius .... 60 Papilio, b. m., 5 yrs., by Bay Middleton out of Bob

Peel's dam; covered by Einilius . . . . 56 Yawn, sister to Gaper, 5 yrs.; covered by Emilius . 54 My Dear, b. m., 5 yrs., by Bay Middleton out of Miss

Letty; covered by Emilius 54

Supine, b. m., 4 yrs., by Bay Middleton out of Marrowfat ; covered by Slane 52

All-round-my-Hat, br. m., 5 yrs., by Bay Middleton

out of Chapeau d'Espagne 50

Guineas. Nightcap, 4 yrs., by Bay Middleton out of Chapeau

d'Espagne; covered by Slane .... 49 Pulce, b. m., 4 yrs., by Bay Middleton out of Puce;

covered by Emilius . . . . . 41 Kitten, 4 yrs., by Bay Middleton out of Pussy;

covered by Emilius 40

Skill, br. m., 5 yrs., by Bay Middletoii out of Skilful;

covered by Emilius 39

The Dutch Girl, b. m., 3 yrs., by Bay Middleton out

of Flamaude; covered by Emilius ... 30 Clink, b. 111., 5 yrs., by Glaucus out of Jingle; covered

by Emilius 30

Alva, 5 yrs., sister to Mora; covered by Emilius . 26

Phantasima, by Phantom; covered by Emilius . 15

Horses in Training.

Princess Alice, 3 yrs., by Bay Middleton out of Her

Majesty 600

Blackbird, 3 yrs., by Plenipo out of Volage . . 320

Comrade, 4 yrs., by Bentley; dam by Picton . . 300

Marquis of Conynghaiu, 3 yrs., by Slane out of Volup-
tuary 260

Discord, aged, by Mulatto out of Melody . . . 165

Clumsy, 4 yrs., by Bay Middleton out of Skilful . 150

Pug, 4 yrs., by Bay Middleton out of Barbiche . 110

A bay yearling colt, by Elis out of Miss Petworth . 300

A bay yearling colt, by Col wick out of Skilful . 100 Sombrero, 3 yrs., by Bay Middleton out of Chapeau
d'Espagne 55

A chestnut yearling colt, by Bran out of Katherine . 17

On Tuesday, Dean Swift, The Merry Monarch, and Playful were put up, and the latter sold for 30 guineas. The Merry Monarch was bought in

for 88 guineas. Total produce of the two days'

SALE OF SUKPLUS STOCK. 253

sale, $3720, 15s. What a contrast to the prices realised by blood-stock since ! Princess Alice was bought by Mr B. Green, and went into H. Steb- bing's stable at Hambleton.

Soon after this sale Mr Mostyn was offered $5000 for the two-year-olds Planet and Slander, which he refused. Simultaneously $7000 were offered for Crucifix, and for the two yearlings Surplice and Loadstone, which offer was also refused. It will thus be seen what a phenomenal bargain Mr Mostyn had made in buying 208 thoroughbreds Ito say nothing of cart-horses, clothing, bridles, saddles, buckets, brushes, rubbers, and all other paraphernalia of a racing-stable in full blastlfor $10,000, when he was able in a couple of months to refuse $12,000 for four animals amongst this splendid lot. As it turned out, neither Planet nor Slander were very fortunate as race-horses. At Goodwood, Planet in 1846 won the Molecomb Stakes, value $650. At Doncaster, he ran second to Van Tromp for the Champagne Stakes; but later in the year he won the Glasgow Stakes at Newmarket, value $800. Next year he won as a three-year-old a Sweepstakes, value $800, at the Craven Meeting; ran second for the Two Thousand to Sir Robert Pigot's Conyngham, who was ridden by Jem Robinson; won the Racing Stakes at Goodwood, value 1150 sovereigns, ridden by F. Butler; was beaten for the Derby, won by Mr Pedley's ch. c. Cossack, by HetmanPlatoff (War Eagle being second and Van Tromp third), ridden by Flatman ; was beaten in the Doncaster St Leger by Lord Eglinton's Van Tromp, Cossack being second and Lord Eglinton's Eryx third.

As regards Slander, she was beaten at Doncaster by Mr Pedley's Foreclosure for the Two-year-old Stakes in 1846 : later in the year she won the Rutland Stakes at Newmarket, value $270 ; broke a blood-vessel after passing the Judge's chair, and never won again. She ran second to Mr Payne's Clementina for the One Thousand in 1847, and second to the same filly for the Nassau Stakes at Goodwood. In the Oaks she was ridden by Bartholomew, and started at 11 to 2, but was beaten out of place by Sir Joseph Hawley's Miami, Mr Payne's Clementina being second and Captain Harcourt's Ellerdale third, Slander finishing sixth in a field of twenty-three. In the Park Hill Stakes, Doncaster, she ran second to Ellerdale. At the Stud, Slander, despite her splendid breeding|by Pantaloon from an own sister to Touchstone|was even more unsuccessful than upon the race-course. Between 1850 and 1858 she produced nothing worth training for her then owner, Lord Clifden, at whose sale in 1859 Lord Fal- mouth purchased her; but she produced six very moderate foals, and after being barren for two years was destroyed in 1866, at the age of twenty-two.

SURPLICE AND LOADSTONE. 255

If, however, the later careers of Planet and Slander were destined " to unbeseem the promise of their spring," very different was the case with Surplice and Loadstone. I have already stated that each of them, when tried as yearlings, performed so well that the brightest auguries were formed for their future. As a yearling, Surplice, who was named by Lord George Bentinck, showed considerable speed, which is not always concomitant with great size and an extremely lazy disposition. Moreover, his action appeared to me to be that of a stayer. In addition to all Lord George's other yearlings, Surplice beat some speedy old horses very easily indeed ; and, being the son of Touchstone and of Crucifix, it was natural that great hopes should be built upon him after he had won his trial in such grand style. It was at once determined to reserve him for the Derby, and to make no more two-year-old engagements for him than those in which he was already entered. Loadstone, on the other hand, was a smaller horse; and, being possessed of capital speed, was engaged in a great many two-year-old stakes, including the Champagne, and the Two-year-old Stakes at Doncaster, and the Clearwell, Prender- gast, and Criterion at Newmarket.

Although Lord George had ceased to be the owner of Surplice and Loadstone, his interest in them seemed to revive when he heard from Mr Mostyn that they had been favourably tried asyearlings. He was very anxious that they should not leave Goodwood, for which beautiful domain his affection was undiminished to the last hour of his life. On Christmas Day 1846 he wrote a letter from Welbeck Abbey, which showed that politics had not quenched his ai'dent spirit. It was couched in the following terms:|

" Welbeck, *near* Worksop, Notts, *Dec.* 25, 1846.

" John Kent,|I am very glad to hear Mr Mostyn has a good promise in the yearlings, and trust that between this and next Goodwood Races everything will be made pleasant and right, so that the horses may permanently continue at Goodwood. I hope your father will lose no opportunity of getting the Duke's permission to this effect.

" Let the Duke once take an interest in any of Mr Mostyn's horses as a Derby horse, and he will be as anxious about him as if he were his own, and as unwilling as I should be to see him leave Goodwood.

"I, who stood to win above $100,000 on Gaper, was scarcely more interested in him than the Duke was before the Derby of 1843. I believe Mr Mostyn never bets a shilling.|I am, your obedient servt., G. Bentinck."

No one was more gratified than his Lordship when he heard that Surplice's merit as a yearling

SURPLICE AS A YEARLING. 257

had been ascertained to my entire satisfaction. A commission was given by his Lordship, with Mr Mostyn's consent and approval, to back Surplice for the Derby, and in it the late Duke of Richmond and every member of the Goodwood family pai'ticipated, obtaining liberal odds. When Surplice made his *debut* for the Ham Stakes, at Goodwood, in 1847, he was ridden by Flatman, who received orders to make a good pace, and to keep him going, as he was a very idle horse. I impressed upon Flatman also the necessity of not easing or checking his mount if he found himself (as I expected he would) to be winning easily. He told me after the race that he had won before half the distance was run, but that he let him stride along at three-parts speed, winning in a common canter. The betting was 7 to 4 on Surplice, " who," according to the ' Racing Calendar,' " took the lead, kept it, and won very easily by two lengths."

It was natural that such a fine, upstanding, good - looking colt, the son of Touchstone and Crucifix, should attract very general attention and admiration, with the result that, after his easy victory in the Ham, Surplice was freely backed for the Derby at comparatively short odds. The Ham was run for as usual on the first day; and upon the last day of the meeting Surplice and Loadstone were engaged in a 200 Sovereign Two-year-old Stakes, with eight subscribers. I

advised Mr Mostyn to run them both, and to declare to win with Surplice, whose idleness, I thought, would make him appear to win with some difficulty. Loadstone, on the other hand, was such a free runner that spectators might easily imagine that he could have beaten Surplice but for the declaration to win with the latter. I little anticipated, however, that the rider of Loadstone would be deceived as to the comparative merits of the two. Flatman, who rode Surplice, had orders to make running, and to win after making the best semblance that he could of a race. Loadstone was ridden by Frank Butler, whom I told to wait upon Mr Dixon's Hope (a Danebury filly upon whom her party were rather sweet), and to beat her if he could in the event of her having the foot of Surplice. As the race came off, Surplice made the pace so good that Hope was soon beaten, and the former won in a canter by three lengths. Immediately after the race I asked Frank Butler how Loadstone had carried him. " Very well indeed," he replied, with a broad grin; " I could have won far enough had I been wanted ! "

When he left me Frank Butler joined his first master and great friend, Colonel Anson, and told him that Loadstone would have won easily " had his head been loose." This intimation, coinciding with what the public observed as to the running of the lazy horse and that of his free stable companion, soon had the effect of making Surplice

SURPLICE AS A TWO-YEAR-OLD. 259

recede in the Derby betting. Lord Enfield (afterwards Earl of Strafford) had executed the stable commission about Surplice for the Derby before he won the Ham, and he was requested by the Goodwood party to continue backing him, if the odds increased. The opportunity was not long in coming. That night, after dinner at Goodwood House, Colonel Anson offered $15,000 to $2000 against Surplice for the Derby, which was accepted by Lord Enfield. It subsequently transpired that the Hon. Francis Villiers, youngest son of the fifth Earl of Jersey (the owner of Middleton,

Cobweb, Bay Middleton, Glencoe, and many other great race-horses), stood half of the bet laid by Colonel Anson.

As a two-year-old Surplice ran only once after his two races at Goodwood, in the Municipal Stakes at Doncaster, 200 sovereigns each, where he met Sir Richard Bulkeley's Miss Orbell, whom he beat " hands down," with odds of 10 to 1 laid freely on him. I remember that Admiral (then Captain) Rous laid Mr William Whitfield (who is still living) $100 to $10 on Surplice. The Admiral was fond of laying long odds on a " certainty," and in this case he had no occasion for anxiety. Finally, Surplice walked over at Newmarket for the Buckenham Stakes, 300 sovereigns, half-forfeit, and then went into winter quarters with an unbeaten record.

Simultaneously Loadstone, upon whom ColonelAnson and Mr Francis Villiers built the highest expectations, ran several times. He was beaten by a neck at Doncaster by Mr B. Green's Assault (another Touchstone colt, out of Ghuznee, winner of the Oaks), after meeting with a great disappointment in the race, the general opinion being that Loadstone ought to have won. Next day he won the Produce Stakes in a canter, beating Colonel Anson's Contessa. At Newmarket he ran for the Prendergast, which he won easily by two lengths, beating Lord Albemarle's Kangaroo, Lord Exeter's Tisiphone, Sir J. B. Mill's Deerstalker, and Field-Marshal Grosvenor's Sir Oliver. At the Houghton Meeting he won the Criterion Stakes, cleverly carrying G Ib. extra and beating Lord Exeter's Tisiphone, Mr B. Green's State Anchor, Mr Pedley's Lady Mary, Duke of Rutland's Palamine, and Mr Hargreaves's Sunnyside. Later in the same week he won the Glasgow Stakes, in a canter, by four lengths.

Into the running of these two fine colts I have entered more fully than I should otherwise have done, because of the extraordinary occurrences in connection with them which the coming winter and spring were destined to bring to pass, affecting-Lord George Bentinck, Mr Francis Villiers, Colonel Anson, and the noble family at Goodwood, and in a humbler degree myself, most materially. Here I may add that, disregarding Admiral Rous's opinion expressed before the House of Commons' Select

MR FRANCIS VILLIERS. 261

Committee on Gaming in 1844, Mr Francis Villiers was accustomed to put many questions to the jockeys in whom he reposed confidence, and especially to Jem Robinson and Frank Butler, and to pay the greatest attention to what they told him. Admiral Rous's avowed opinion was, that any one who followed the advice of his jockey would be ruined; and in this case his warning words were prophetically correct. I have already stated what Frank Butler reported about the comparative merits of Surplice and Loadstone, after riding the latter at Goodwood. A few months later Mr Villiers brought Robinson down to Goodwood to ride Surplice and Loadstone in their gallops, and, as will be seen presently, his verdict was the same as that of Frank Butler. Yet it would be impossible to conceive two finer jockeys than Robinson and Butler ; and the latter was, as a rule, a very excellent judge of racing, and especially so, as he himself expressed it, of " a horse which he had once had between his thighs." In what scrapes Mr Villiers, and, in a lesser degree, Colonel Anson (who was more adroit than his obstinate and self-opinionated colleague), were entangled by following the advice of Robinson and Butler will be shown directly.

Colonel Anson and Mr Villiers had (again by Frank Butler's advice) given 3000 guineas|then considered to be a very big figure|for Blaze, a beautiful dark chestnut Irish colt, by Launcelot(brother to Touchstone). With Blaze they won the Hopeful Stakes at Newmarket, but with 3 to 1 betted upon him he was beaten for the Clearwell by Mr Payne's Glendower. During the winter Mr Villiers, who found no difficulty in discovering plenty of excuses for Blaze's defeat in the Clear- well, backed him very heavily for the Two Thousand. Blaze was trained at Whitewall by John Scott, and was thought to be the best colt in his powerful lot. Simultaneously the two confederates backed Loadstone very heavily for the Derby ; and in order to control the latter horse, Mr Villiers prevailed upon the late Lord Clifden to purchase a moiety of Mr Mostyn's stud. When this sale was concluded, on March 28, 1848, I had got Loadstone forward in condition to run for the Two Thousand, and had induced Mr Mostyn to keep Surplice for the Derby. The Two Thousand was to be run on April 25, so that there was only an interval of four weeks before the race took place. When Surplice and Loadstone became the property of Lord Clifden, my plans and arrangements for the future were all upset. It was determined not to pull out either horse for the Two Thousand, but to keep them out of Blaze's way. Never was a young nobleman more glaringly deprived of a good stake, which should have been his legitimate property, than Lord Clifden, when he was induced to strike Loadstone and Surplice out of the Two Thousand, which either of them would have won in a canter.

MR VILLIEES'S TACTICS. 263

Unfortunately all this manoeuvring and wirepulling ended in a terrible fiasco. Blaze was beaten easily for the Two Thousand, finishing a bad third to Flatcatcher and Glendower. This was a sad disappointment and heavy blow to Mr Villiers ; and in the ensuing week he came down to Goodwood, not in a very amiable temper, bringing Jem Robinson with him, to try Surplice and Loadstone. As the former was not fit to be tried, and as Mr Mostyn and the Goodwood family had certain contingent interests in the horses, I objected strenuously to trying Surplice, who, in addition to being a very big horse, went with rather a straight knee, and was by no means a light goer. Mr Villiers was greatly irritated by my opposition to his wishes, but in it I had made up my mind to persist. He then expressed a desire that Robinson might be allowed to ride Surplice a gallop in his clothes, to which I gladly consented. Led by an old horse, Surplice and Loadstone galloped side by side, three - quarters speed, for a mile and a quarter. When they pulled up Robinson shook his head, and curiously eyed Loadstone, who had galloped freely and well by Surplice's side.

In view of coming events " which cast their shadows before," I took the opportunity of pointing out to Mr Villiers and to Robinson what, from sure experience, I knew to be the fact|viz., that they must not take any notice of the way|Surplice went in his clothes, as he was one of the laziest and most deceptive goers that in a long experience I had ever seen. I added that, when stripped and roused, Surplice could give Loadstone a lump of weight and beat him over any distance. Upon this Mr Villiers indulged in a sneering laugh, and ejaculated, " Nonsense! I know much more about these two horses than you do. Loadstone is the best of the two, and so I always thought/' I immediately replied, " If that be your opinion, Mr Villiers, of me and of my judgment, and if these horses were yours, I would not train them for another day. There are others, however, who have an interest in them, whom it is my duty to serve to the best of my ability." " Do you mean to tell me," he rejoined, " that a jockey like Robinson does not know how a horse carries him ?" " He most certainly does not, sir," I answered, " if he believes Loadstone to be better than Surplice." Mr Villiers turned his back upon me with an expression of contempt on his face which I shall never forget.

The Duke and Duchess of Richmond, and other members of the family, were then at Goodwood House, and Mr Villiers lunched with them. He did not fail to relate, in his own way, what had happened that morning, and endeavoured to prejudice my dear old master the Duke, and the rest of the family, against me. He stated that had the horses been under the charge of some trainer more

MB FBANCIS VILLIERS. 265

skilful than myself, the Duke and his family would not have been in the unfortunate position into which I had plunged them by advising them to back Surplice for the Derby. Next morning the Duchess of Richmond sent for me, and told me, with her usual frankness and kind consideration, all that Mr Villiers had said at luncheon on the previous day. Her Grace then added, " Do not heed what Mr Villiers may have said, John, as it will take some one with much more influence than he possesses to prejudice us against you." Her Grace's kind and trusting assurances of her unshaken confidence and support brought balm and healing to my wounded self-respect. Before long the Duke of Richmond came to the stables and remarked to me, " Mr Villiers is still quite a young man, and perhaps does not know quite as much as he thinks he does."

Upon Mr Villiers's return to London, he continued, with his habitual confidence in his own judgment, to back Loadstone" for the Derby, and soon made him first favourite, which caused Lord George Bentinck and Lord Henry Gordon Lennox to feel very uneasy. Lord George wrote to me saying that he had received a remarkable letter from Mr Villiers which he could not understand, and he wanted to know what it meant. His Lordship inquired, further, whether I was still of the same opinion as to the merits of the two horses as when he last saw me. My reply wasthat both horses were going on as well as possible, and that I was more than ever confident as to the correctness of my opinion that Surplice was far and away the better of the two. His Lordship was good enough to write me a most encouraging letter, in which he stated that he was perfectly satisfied with what I had told him, as he had never known me to be mistaken in an opinion which I had formed after deep consideration. Lord Henry Lennox could not support the strain, but brought me his betting-book, which he left in my hands, with the avowal that he was going abroad until the Derby was over, as he was too nervous and agitated to remain in England any longer. He told me to do the best for him that I could, and as I had induced him to back Surplice, to get him out of the difficulty by hedging the money, if it could possibly be done.

Naturally, my position was far from being an enviable one. I knew that if I attempted to save the money Lord Henry had invested on Surplice, those who had laid him the odds would not hedge, in face of the false market established by Mr Villiers, except upon terms very disadvantageous to Lord Henry. At that moment Surplice was very much out of favour, and no wonder, when it is remembered that, not satisfied with backing Loadstone for very large sums, Mr Villiers had several commissioners at work laying against Surplice. In my dilemma I sought the advice of

DIFFICULTY WITH MR VILLIEES. 267

the Duke of Richmond, and unbosomed myself to him. His Grace received me with his usual kindness, and asked me what I myself considered the best course to pursue. " Wait, your Grace, until the two horses have been fairly and regularly tried over the distance, and, my word for it, there will not be much difficulty about deciding what to do then." The Duke assured me that he was entirely satisfied ; and although my anxiety and sense of responsibility were, of course, very great, I continued to train both horses to the best of my' ability, and to await the issue.

About a fortnight before the Derby, Mr Villiers and Colonel Anson prevailed upon the Earl of Chesterfield, with whom they were very intimate, to lend them his five-year-old mare, Lady Wildair, in order to try Loadstone and-Surplice with her. Lady Wildair was known to be a very true runner, and not long before she had won the Northamptonshire Stakes (2 miles), carrying 8 st. 5 lb., giving Mr B. Green's Sylvan (3 years) 2 st. 11 lb. Mr Villiers had ascertained through Mr Harry Hill the relative merits of Sylvan and his stable companion, Flatcatcher, who had won the Two Thousand. He therefore regarded Lady Wildair as a very valuable trial horse, and through her he felt sure that he should be able to ascertain whether Surplice or Loadstone, or either of the two, could have won the Two Thousand. In addition, I put Mr Mostyn's Sagacity, 4 years, in the trial, makingSurplice give her a year and 12 lb., and Loadstone a year and 10 lb. Not long before Sagacity had won a handicap (distance l$ mile) at Northampton. It was my intention that Sagacity, availing herself of her light weight, should make running, but this Surplice never allowed her to do. My first proposal was that Surplice should give Loadstone 10 lb., but at this Mr Villiers jeered, saying that Loadstone would win in a canter, and then it would be impossible to form an idea of the true form of the two horses. Very reluctantly, therefore, I consented to putting Loadstone into the trial at 2 lb. less than Surplice, knowing full well what the result would be.

The trial came off over a mile-and-a-half course, on May 13, 1848, and ended as follows :|

Surplice, 3 yrs.; 8 st. 8 lb. (Robinson), 1.
Sagacity, 4 yrs., 7 st. 10 lb. (Green), 2.
Lady Wildair, 5 yrs., 9 st. 4 lb. (Flatraan), 3.
Loadstone, 3 yrs., 8 st. 6 lb. (Kitchener), 4.

Surplice won with consummate ease by four lengths; Sagacity beat Lady Wildair by half a length; and Loadstone was at least ten lengths behind Lady Wildair.

Then followed a scene which, " while memory holds her seat," I shall never forget. Mr Villiers had witnessed the trial on foot, standing about half a distance from the winning-post. When I rode up to him he threw both his arms into the air, and exclaimed in a frantic state of excitement,

THE TRIAL RACE. 269

and with ghastly pallor upon his countenance, " I am a ruined man ! I am a ruined man ! What on earth am I to do ?" " Whose fault, sir, is it ?" I could not help replying. "

Whom have you to blame but yourself?" Wringing his hands, and in accents of despair which moved me to pity even in the midst of my natural resentment, he kept on talking to himself more than to me : " If I back Surplice for large sums for the Derby, it will be odds on him before I am half-way out of my difficulties." After waiting a little until he had partially recovered from his overpowering agitation, I ventured to say to him, " Mr Villiers, the Derby and St Leger have been won only once by the same horse : if you back Surplice to win them both, the bookmakers will lay you long odds, and before four months have elapsed you can. win as much money as you like."

This advice I have good reason to know that he subsequently followed, and thus avoided the total ruin which otherwise must have befallen him, although he never had the generosity to acknowledge it to me. When Robinson dismounted, he remarked to me that it seemed to him almost impossible to believe that Surplice was the same horse that he had ridden three weeks before. This memorable trial made me aware how much more sensible and practical Lord George was in managing a stud than his friend Mr Francis Villiers. The latter indulged in fancies based upon his own

II!'':.

..-,..- I,

'- -I-', v . , '... '

Q

O

O

H: o o o

j)

a z.

y.

westimate of the way in which horses galloped in their clothes; the former was never carried away by predilections or prepossessions, and nothing could induce him to back a horse until after one or more genuine trials.

It was upon the Saturday before Bath Races that Surplice and Loadstone were tried, and when the betting - ring was formed in front of the Grand Stand on Lansdown, the anxiety to back Surplice was so great that business was altogether impossible, until Davies, " the Leviathan," laid $1000 to $700 against him several times. Most of these bets were taken by Mr Justice, acting for Harry Hill, who was acting for Mr Villiers. As was usually the case about forty or fifty years ago when a horse became a great favourite for the Derby, there were plenty of rumours in circulation that Surplice would be " made safe " : that, in the teeth of the immense sums laid against him, " he would win no Derby "land much more of the same sort. Mr Cynric Lloyd, in particular, Avho had backed Surplice steadily ever since he won the Ham Stakes at two years old, was seriously alarmed, and came to me in great agitation about what he had heard. Of course my anxiety was great, and all the more so because the family at Goodwood House had backed Surplice, and never allowed themselves to be shaken by anything that Mr Villiers said. Under these circumstances I pursued my usual plan when in perplexity, and

-.- . ; . ' '.$ i . . -. ' . 1
i ' 1 1...
a o o
I

fl

PRECAUTIONS ABOUT SURPLICE. 271

consulted rny kind and trusted master, the Duke of Richmond. His Grace observed to me, " You cannot always be watching the horse and his boy, as he stands in the top stable along with seven other horses." I suggested to his Grace that the safest plan would be to move Surplice and Loadstone from the Goodwood racing-stable into that at the Kennels, where two good loose-boxes stood side by side, and a stall by the side of each loose- box, in which my father's and my hacks were accommodated. This stable was close to our house, and into it Surplice and Loadstone were moved, much to Mr Cynric Lloyd's relief. I assured him that unless I myself were laid by the heels, Surplice should not be got at, for I would never let him go out of my sight except when he was under lock and key, with the key in my pocket. I added that every feed of corn, and every bucket of water, should be given to him by my own hands.

13

SECTION 13

272

CHAPTER XIII.

THE DERBY OF 1848.

Notwithstanding the ceaseless vigilance exercised by all to whom the care of watching and guarding Surplice was intrusted after he had been tried, rumours that attempts would be made by fair means or foul to ensure his defeat for the Derby were freely circulated on all sides. Such rumours were naturally to be expected in view of the enormous sums of money laid against him during the winter of 1847-48. Under these circumstances his transportation from Goodwood to Epsom became to me a cause of the deepest anxiety, and endless were the suggestions made as to the best method of effecting it in safety. One of these suggestions was, that I should allow the horse to travel to Epsom under the charge of two of my most trusted men, supervised by a policeman, who was to be specially called in for that purpose. This proposition I met with a decided negative. Having undertaken the responsibility of guarding the horseSurplice's Departure From Goodwood. 273 myself, of feeding and giving him his water with my own hands, of taking care that neither his food nor his drink should be doctored in any way, and, finally, of never allowing him to be out of my sight except when he was locked up and the key was in my pocket, I did not feel inclined to permit a stranger, even though he were a policeman, to take my place. Knowing that many who placed confidence in me had backed Surplice heavily from what I thought of him long before his trial, I felt, as the Derby Day drew nearer and nearer, and the rumours of intended foul practices grew louder and more sustained, that my responsibility was almost more than I could bear.

At last the anxious day|Monday the 22d of May 1848|arrived, upon which Surplice was to take his departure from Goodwood. I placed him, accompanied by his provender, in a single van, which I had carefully prepared for his. reception. Locking the door of this van, and putting the key in my pocket, I proceeded next to ensconce Loadstone and Sagacity safely in a double van. In addition to the vans, three or four horses made their way on foot to the Drayton railway station. The cavalcade was headed by my father, by Lead- better (the detective officer from Bow Street), and by some of the Goodwood stablemen. The vans and horses came to the end of their railway journey at the Reigate and Red Hill station, whence the vans were drawn by post-horses toHeadley, distant about seven miles from Red Hill. The other race-horses followed on foot, and, about four in the afternoon, I had the satisfaction of seeing Surplice, Loadstone, Sagacity, and their companions safely lodged in Lord George Ben- tinck's stables at Headley, which his Lordship retained for the use of the Goodwood stable when he sold his stud, and which were never more useful than on this momentous occasion.

As my father was in charge of the travelling party, I gave myself a little rest in the van with Surplice; but on arriving at Headley, my labours recommenced. I led Surplice out of the van into his loose-box, and gave him a feed of corn which I had brought from Goodwood. Then I locked the stable-door and went with Surplice's lad and our own blacksmith to procure some water at the spring upon " Oyster Hill," from which many a good race-horse has been watered before and since that day. Close to the spring there are some cottages, from one of which I obtained hot wrater to take off the chill of the cold spring. When I returned to the stable, Leadbetter was a little put out, exclaiming, " Surely you could have trusted me for a few minutes with the horse, especially as he would probably be a bit restless in a new box!" " A bit restless, indeed !" I rejoined, laughing ; " he is too docile and quiet to be alarmed at anything." On unlocking the door and entering the box, I found that he had emptied his manger, which was

RUMOURS ABOUT SURPLICE. 275

a great satisfaction to me, although I fully expected it, as there never was a better " doer " than Surplice.

As the Derby approached, everybody, and especially the " sharps," had it that my horse was " a safe un." Out at exercise on Tuesday morning, every acquaintance that I met kept on asking me, " What's the matter with Surplice ? He's up and down in the market in a very queer way." To add to my anxiety, Mr Payne refused to give up Flatman, believing that he had a very good chance of winning with Glendower. It was then arranged that James Robinson should ride Surplice, as there seemed no probability that any of his masters would need his services. At the last moment, however, the Duke of Rutland claimed Robinson to ride The Fiddler, and the difficulty of getting a good jockey for Surplice seemed almost insurmountable. At this critical moment, Mr Harry Hill, whose interest in the horse, for Lord George's sake, remained unabated, and who had backed him heavily, recommended, for private reasons, which he stated to Mr Mostyn and Mr Lloyd, that Sim Templeman should be put on Surplice's back.

It was, of course, a great relief to me when this was settled, although I did not think Templeman the best jockey to do justice to a big lazy horse like Surplice, who would make a race with a donkey, and deceived everybody who rode him for the first time. Sim Templeman formed the sameunfavourable opinion of his mount, after riding Surplice over the course the day before the Derby, that Jem Robinson had conceived when he rode him in a gallop at Goodwood. What increased Templeman's dislike to Surplice was, that the horse refused to cross the tan road when ridden at a foot's-pace down the course, on his way to the starting-post. All these difficulties and gloomy prognostications tended, of course, to increase my anxiety, and made it difficult for me to fulfil my engagement never to let Surplice out of my sight, unless he was locked up in his loose-box. My favourite old pony, with whom Surplice was well acquainted, enabled me, however, to keep close to him when walking at exercise. The curiosity and excitement of the crowd were so great, that it was extremely difficult for Surplice to make his way through them, so closely was he mobbed. I found Leadbetter and the Goodwood stable lads of great assistance in this emergency; but it was fortunate that Surplice was naturally unexcitable and quiet, as he was followed to his stable-door by a large host of gentlemen on horseback, who would have driven a nervous horse of Bay Middleton's type wild with irritability. In those days there was on the Sunday, Monday, and Tuesday preceding the Derby, a vast concourse of people assembled at Epsom to see the Derby horses gallop. Never, however, did I witness such a sensational scene, or such intense curiosity as was manifested to catch a

Surplice's Unpopularity. 277

glimpse of Surplice. In the midst of the crowds by which he was always surrounded he bore himself with an unruffled calmness and tranquillity vhich, despite my intimate acquaintance with his disposition and temperament, fairly surprised and delighted me. I endeavoured to form Leadbetter and a small brigade of boys under his charge into a ring around my horse. These human guards quickly lost their tempers, and became violently agitated, but the horse never turned a hair. The same difficulty and disappointment arose Avhen I placed Surplice in the midst of a group of horses, including Loadstone, 'Sagacity, and other stable companions. Hemmed in by a mob of horsemen, these outposts were always on their hind-legs and dancing about, while Surplice walked sleepily along, as quiet as an old cow. On the night before the Derby a number of roughs surrounded the paddock in the middle of which Lord George's stable stood, and kept watch until midnightlnot from any desire to do mischief, I verily believe, but from simple curiosity. In the morning a fresh lot of touts and runners emerged from the Cock Inn and kept watch until Surplice left his stable and walked on to the course, to start for the Derby.

A great favourite is generally unpopular, but never was there one more so than Surplice. All through the winter he had been regarded as a " dead un," thanks to Mr Francis Villiers's infatuation, and to his reputation for possessing extraordinary talents. Everybody was aware that Mr Villiers had given a never-ceasing commission to lay against Surplice, and, with few exceptions, little backers had staked their money on Loadstone. In an instant Surplice's great trial shattered all their hopes, and he became such a favourite that it was almost impossible to back him. All this tended to make Surplice more disliked than great favourites usually are. This was shown by the hootings and hisses with which I was more than once assailed as I walked or rode by the horse's side, or when, accompanied by boys to cany the bucket, I proceeded to the spring on " Oyster Hill " to bring Surplice his water. I invariably repaired to some cottage for a little hot water to take off the chill, always going to a different cottage. The fee which I gave for any small service rendered to me was more than the poor cottagers expected, and I was pressingly urged by them to come again for anything that I wanted. Although betting men great and small would have rejoiced almost without exception to hear that Surplice had broken his leg, I feel assured that the humble residents in the neighbourhood of Headley sincerely wished him well.

I have entered into all these minute details at the risk of being wearisome, because Surplice's Derby happened at a time when it was more common to poison or lame horses than is now the case, and because the circumstances preceding his attainment of the position of first favourite were of a

SUSPICIONS. 279

most peculiar and exceptional kind. Forty or fifty years ago the sums of money betted upon the Derby were so large, and the excitement so great, that it is difficult for a younger generation of racegoers to understand or realise the anxiety and sense of responsibility of a trainer who was in charge of such a favourite as Surplice was in 1848. I was not unaware that tempting overtures had been made surreptitiously to more than one employee in the Goodwood stable to lame Surplice ; and if he had run badly in the race, suspicion would doubtless have attached to many innocent persons who were as eager to see him win as my father and I were. It will easily be imagined, therefore, with what feelings I saw the dawn of the Derby Day break.

My father and I rode by the horse's side from Headley to the course. I then dismounted and led Surplice, while his regular lad rode him, and two police officers walked immediately in his rear. On nearing the stand, my father went off to see Templeman weighed, and returned to inform me that even at the eleventh hour Mr Francis Villiers had not given up all hope that Loadstone would prove himself the better horse, and, in order to give Loadstone every chance, had made some considerable pecuniary sacrifice in order to secure Job Marson (one of Mr Villiers's favourite jockeys) to ride him. It was not long before Mr Villiers was undeceived. The following seventeen horses cameto the post, with the result given below, which I have taken from the ' Racing Calendar':|

Epsom.
Wednesday, May 24, 1848.

The Derby Stakes of 50 sovs. each, h. ft., for three-year- old colts, 8 st. 7 Ib.; fillies, 8 st. 2 Ib. The new Derby course; a mile and a half.

Lord Clifden's b. c. Surplice, by Touchstone|Crucifix, by
Priam (Templeman), 1. Mr Bowes's b. c. Springy Jack, by Hetman Platoff|Oblivion, by Jerry (F. Butler), 2. Mr B. Green's bl. c. Shylock, by Simoom|The Queen, by

Sir Hercules (S. Mann), 3. Mr Payne's b. c. Glendower, by Slane|Sister to Glencoe, by Sultan (Flatman), 4. Mr J. B. Day's b. c. Nil Desperaudum, by Venison|Grace Darling, by Defence (A. Day). Mr Nunn's b. c. The Fowler, by Irish Bird-catcher|Zillah,

by Blacklock (J. Holmes). Mr Lillie's br. c. Great Western, by Hetman Platoff|Miss Frill, by Action (Hewlett). Lord Clifden's b. c. Loadstone, by Touchstone|Latitude, by Langar (J. Marson).

Mr Baker's br. c. Oscar, by Charles XII.|Morsel, by Mulatto (Bumby). Duke of Eutland's b. c. The Fiddler, by Charles XII.|

Liberty, by Langar (Eobinson). '

Mr E. E. Clark's b. c. Weathercock, by Emilius|Variation,

by Buzzard (Tant). Mr T. Parr's b. c. Sponge, by Ascot|Languid, by Cain (Owner). Sir J. B. Mill's b. c. Deerstalker, by Venison|Virginia, by Figaro (Donaldson).

THE RACE. 281

Mr Eolls's b. c. Comet, by Auckland | Miniature, by

Teniers (Pettit). Lord Eglinton's b. c. Eagle's Plume, by Lanercost|Blue

Bonnet, by Touchstone (Marlow). Major Pitt's b. c. Fern, by Venison|Puce, by Eowtou (E.

Edwards). Mr Osbaldeston's ch. c. Fugleman, by the Saddler|Camp

Follower, by The Colonel (S. Rogers).

Betting|Even on Surplice, 4 to 1 each *v.* Glendower and Nil Desperandum, 14 to *l v.* Shylock, 15 to 1 *v.* Springy Jack, 20 to 1 *v.* Loadstone, 40 to 1 *v.* Great "Western, The Fiddler, and Fugleman; 50 to 1 *v.* The Fowler; 1000 to 15 each *v.* Fern and Eagle's Plume; 1000 to 10 *v.* Deerstalker.

Won by a neck; length between second and third.

The following description of the race appeared in ' Bell's Life.'

" Precisely at the time named on the card the horses were at the starting-post, and we must do the starter, Mr Hibberd, the justice to say that a finer start was never seen on this or any other course. The Fowler jumped off with the lead; but either from not being ambitious, or from inability to keep it, he fell back in half-a-dozen strides, and Great Western went on with the running, followed by Loadstone and Fugleman, Nil Desperandum being fourth on the inside. Behind him came Surplice, Fern, and The Fowler, with The Fiddler and Springy Jack in their wake. The Fowler kept his place till near the Craven post, where he fell astern of The Fiddler. About the same time Nil Desperandum sprained his off knee, and in the next hundred yards from being fourth became the last horse in the race. Great Western maintained his position until close to the top of the hill, when he was passed by Loadstone, and immediately afterwards gave way altogether, leaving Fugleman second to Loadstone, Surplice following Fugleman, with Fern,: i.w u

Pi 53Glendower, Springy Jack, and Shylock running in a group close behind. Half-way between the road and the distance- post Loadstone declined, and Fern also had had enough of it. A new formation ensued, Surplice taking a decided lead, followed by Fugleman with Shylock third and Springy Jack by his side. Just inside the distance Fugleman was beaten and dropped behind Shylock and Springy Jack. The race at this moment was very interesting. To all appearances the ' crack' was going very uncomfortably, and Shylock looked so well that' The favourite's beat!' escaped from a thousand lips. Kor was it until they were half-way up the distance that ' the Jew' was fairly disposed of. Springy Jack now began to look dangerous, as he got to the favourite's quarters, and came with a tremendous rush in the last three or four strides, and almost got up. But it was only ' almost,' as Surplice was never quite reached, and won by a neck."

Sim Templeman assured me after the race that had I not cautioned him so strongly about Surplice's laziness, he might have been beaten, as his horse began to stop directly he steadied him, and would have pulled up altogether had he not kept him going. I had warned him emphatically that directly he ceased to ride him Surplice would cease to run. Had Mr Villiers consented to order Mar- son to jump off with Loadstone, and to make strong running for half or three-quarters of a mile (which Loadstone was well qualified to do), there would have been no danger of Surplice being beaten, or hard run, as he was as fit as he could be made. So obstinate, however, was Mr Villiers in his own opinion, that he would not hear of Loadstone being

. ' : : : t .
ii'in i"
.-.! r
i . i . ; ., ..-'
l t i'. I!' . '(','! I " I l
ii- ..i !o '! M
lit ' ii "-(,' '1l' ' : i .' !
- ". '! ,, ;...., !:. il-. '.-
l ' ' I l ' - I I
.'. .:: t 'i .v.-,... ., .mj v:::i"ft .:
i. !'. t lit- : S : I :i h !' I' i ,." lv: :
Surplice's Victory. 283
sacrificed for Surplice. The result was that, when Loadstone declined, Surplice had to take his own part, and Templeman said that it was all over as soon as Surplice took up the running.

When Loadstone showed a bold front, until the distance-post was almost reached, Mr Villiers, I heard subsequently, was in ecstasies; but when Surplice took up the running Mr Villiers's face darkened and fell. The pace must have been very moderate for Loadstone to have lasted so long, and if Surplice had not possessed good speed as well as stoutness, the Derby might have been thrown away from want of a strong - run race. Many a good horse, in perfect condition, have I seen beaten under similar circumstances, after the administration of severe punishment during the last half-mile, which he would have altogether escaped by winning easily had the race been run from end to end. It is a fatal mistake not to win your race as early as you can, if you have got a good horse fit to run. I can remember sixty-five races for the Epsom Derby, and I have seen it lost in some instances, and very nearly so in others, from failing to make use of a good horse. Three superior horses I can mention|Surplice, The Flying Dutchman, and Cremorne|all of whom narrowly escaped defeat for want of a strong-run race.

One other extract I am tempted to make from 'Bell's Life' of Saturday, May 27, 1848.

" The Derby nags assembled in the paddock in charge of their respective trainers and grooms, Loadstone and Surplice being foremost in the throng, attended by the elder Kent, Leadbetter, and Thackwell I the former having been in charge of the horse for some nights before the race, with a view of defeating any of those sinister intentions which former experience led to a suspicion might again be put into practice: in fact, every possible care had been taken to protect Surplice from being got at, much to the mortification, it was said, of many who would have been far from displeased to hear that he had had a ' bad night.' Both horses looked remarkably well, especially Surplice, of whom it was said by a competent judge of looks that he was sure to win, as an animal in more splendid condition was never witnessed. In the early part of the day as much as 6 to 5 was laid on Surplice, but a perceptible change took place. Nil Desperandum advanced in favour, and was backed at 5 to 1, and by some parties at 3 to 1, while Surplice went back to 5 and even 6 to 4Ithe latter odds being in some instances laid by those who were well on him, and whose confidence was somewhat shaken at the last moment. This change, we have reason to believe, was effected by a *ruse* got up among a party who were opposed to him, and who, by apparently laying odds against him, induced apprehension in the public mind of which they themselves took advantage, thereby getting on at a better price, and saving some $4000 or $5000. The crush to get a position whence a view of the course could be obtained was terrific.

" We have given a description of the race in its usual place, from which it will be seen that it was keenly contested by Surplice, Springy Jack, and Shylock. Surplice was spurred, although the whip was not used ; and it was remarked that had the pace been good he would have won more cleverly, being such a sluggish horse and requiring a good deal of ridingIevidence of which was afforded in his trial, for when he was nearing the winning-post and

CONGRATULATIONS. 285

experienced the effect of the ' persuaders,' he shot out like a dart, and won with consummate ease. These are, however, matters of speculation with which we must leave the *cognoscenti* to deal. The winners had their turn of joyous cheering, and the congratulations offered to the Duke of Richmond and to his family, who, we are glad to hear, are large gainers by the result, were loud and vociferous beyond description, I congratulations which were given with equal goodwill to Lord Clifden and to Mr Lloyd, co- proprietors of the winner; both of whom, we also learn, have realised a good profit independent of the stakes, which are worth $5500.

Thus terminated this ever-memorable DerbyI memorable not only to me, but also to others who are still living, and were vitally interested in it. I perfectly well remember, when I was leading Surplice back to the weighing-place after the race, that a gentleman congratulated me, and added, " You have now given them the lie direct!" At the time I could not understand what he meant; but from what transpired subsequently, I have no doubt that he congratulated me upon defeating the vile efforts to prevent Surplice from winning the Derby, which were deemed likely to be successfully accomplished by some of the knaves who were heavy losers by him.

Lord Enfield, afterwards Earl of Strafford, being a brother-in-law to the Duke of Richmond, executed some of the stable commission about Surplice, and, having backed him very early, obtained good odds, which he was enabled to hedge afterthe trial at great advantage, so that he and all the members of the Goodwood family, together with Mr Lloyd, had the satisfaction of winning good stakes after hedging their money. Lord George Bentinck himself won about $11,000. Had his Lordship not disposed of his stud, it is impossible to conjecture what he might have won upon such a horse. His mind and heart seemed, however, to be entirely concentrated upon politics after he had parted with his race-horses. Racing, to which he was formerly so devoted, passed entirely out of his head, and his betting soon became extremely limited.

I cannot remember a single instance of his endeavouring to obtain information from Mr Lloyd or from myself about any of the animals which lie had sold to Mr Mostyn. Having occasion to write to Lord George about Christmas time, in 1846, I mentioned, with Mr Mostyn's permission, what I thought of Surplice, from the form he displayed in his trials as a yearling, knowing how interested he would be, as Surplice had been thought likely to go wrong in his windlan infirmity which he might have inherited from Camel, his grandsire, who was a bad roarer. Every opportunity was therefore afforded to enable him to be trained for the Derby. His great size and physical conformation required that he should not be hurried, and fortunately he inherited some of the stoutness of Priam, and the good constitution of Emilius. It was averred by

DEPARTURE OF THE STUD FROM GOODWOOD. 287

some influential noblemen and gentlemen, that had not the Duke of Richmond, at the intercession of Lord George, stipulated with Mr Mostyn that the horses in training should remain at Goodwood till after the Derby, Surplice, after Lord Clifden had purchased an interest in the stud, might not have been allowed to run for that race, any more than for the Two Thousand, but have been withdrawn in favour of Loadstone. Such would certainly have been the case had Mr Villiers's baneful influence prevailed with Lord Clifden and Mr Mostyn.

After the Derby the Duke of Richmond gave his consent to the horses remaining under my charge until the Goodwood Races were over. Lord Clifden immediately purchased the remainder of Mr Mostyn's interest in the stud, and everything went well with the horses until the deep ground at Goodwood interfered with Surplice's long stride, and made him quite helpless in the mud. I can scarcely doubt that my old and honoured master the Duke of Richmond was not sorry when the time came for this large stud of horses to leave Goodwood. Although his Grace was on friendly terms with Mr Mostyn and Mr Lloyd, and also with Lord Clifden and Mr Villiers, he was not so much at his ease with any of them as he had been with Lord George Bentinck between 1841 and 1846. The Duke enjoyed beyond measure his almost daily visit to the Goodwood stable, when it was filled with his own and with Lord George'shorses. It was disagreeable to him, however, to go round the stables when the remotest suspicion might arise that he was trying to pry into the secrets of others.

It may be interesting to my readers if I succinctly recount the performances of Surplice after he won the Derby of 1848. First come his two Goodwood defeats. On

July 25th h,e ran for the Gratwicke Stakes of 100 sovereigns each, half-forfeit, one mile and a half, 50 subscribers. The race came off as follows:|

Lord Chesterfield's b. f. Distaffina (Flatrnan), 1. Lord Clifden's b. c. Surplice (Robinson), 2. Duke of Richmond's br. f. Hornpipe (Templeman), 3. Mr Bowes's ch. f. Wiasma (J. Holmes), 4. The betting was 5 to 2 on Surplice, 3 to 1 agst. Wiasma. Won easily by a length; a neck between second and third.

This was a most extraordinary race, and to this day I am quite unable to explain it. Surplice (who was perfectly well) could always give Hornpipe two stone and a beating, and in this race she ran him to a neck at even weights. Lord Chesterfield told me that his mare, Distaffina, was at least two stone worse than Surplice, and yet she beat him at even weights!

Two days later Surplice ran again for the Racing Stakes of 50 sovs. each, New Mile, 17 subscribers. The race ended as follows :|

Mr Payne's b. c. Glendower (Flatman), 1.

Colonel Anson's b. c. Corsican (F. Butler), 2.

Lord Clifden's b. c. Surplice (Robinson), 3.

Surplice's After Career. 289

Betting|13 to 8 on Surplice, 5 to 2 agst. Glendower, 7 to 2 agst. Corsican. Won by a length. From the very commencement Surplice ran a beaten horse, and took no part in the race.

On August 14, 1848 (a fortnight after Goodwood Races), all Lord Clifden's horses left the stable where they had so long been trained, and were transferred to his Lordship's private racing establishment at Newmarket, over which Robert Stephenson presided. The lot included Planet, Projectile, Fallow Deer, King of Morven, Crozier, Tiresome, Czarina, Mustard filly, Slander, Tamarind, Sagacity, Archness, Surplice, Loadstone, Honeycomb, Cucullus, and the Flycatcher filly. It was arranged that Surplice should be kept for the Doncaster St Leger, and should receive a special preparation for that event. The St Leger was fixed for the 13th of September, and in the four and a half weeks which intervened between Surplice's departure from Goodwood and the St Leger day he fluctuated strangely in the betting.

At last the St Leger day arrived, and the following horses started for the race:|

Lord Clifden's b. c. Surplice (Flatman), 1.

Lord Stanley's br. f. Canezou (F. Butler), 2.

Mr B. Green's b. c. Flatcatcher (Robinson), 3.

Duke of Bedford's b. c. Justice to Ireland (Templeman).

Mr B. Green's b. c. Assault (Winteringham).

Mr T. Parr's b. c. Sponge (Whitehouse).

Mr Humphries's b. c. Escape (J. Holmes).

Mr Pedley's br. c. Bessborough (J. Marson).

Lord Stanley's gr. c. Cannibal, (Marlow), also started and were not placed.

Betting|7 to 4 *v.* Canezou, 2 to 1 *v.* Surplice, 7 to 2 *v.* Flatcatcher, 9 to 2 *v.* Justice to Ireland. Won by a neck: Flatcatcher beaten three lengths.

The ' Racing Calendar' adds :|

" There was one false start, and all the riders were fined 5 sovs. each for starting without orders, except Marson, who pulled up his horse immediately, and was fined 3 sovs. only. The fines were subsequently mitigated to 3 sovs. and 1 sov. with an intimation to the jockeys that if they offended again in the same manner, the highest penalty would be enforced,"

"This mishap," says 'Bell's Life,' "was all the more unlucky because the horses got off capitally on the first occasion|better, indeed, than on the second. When the flag fell, they dashed off at full speed, and Flatcatcher, followed by Assault, at once rushed to the front, the former leading by a few strides, and then giving way to Assault who made running at the top of his speed, Surplice and Justice to Ireland following just behind Flatcatcher, Canezou lying up with them, Sponge next, and Cannibal and Escape in the rear. Assault led the van to the rise of the hill, and then resigned *in toto,* his stable companion Flatcatcher taking up the running. At the Red House Surplice took second place, with Canezou at his quarters, Flatcatcher still leading. Just before the distance-post Flatcatcher was passed by Surplice and Canezou. The mare then took the lead by half a length, and up to the stand appeared to have the best of it. At this point, however, Surplice got to her head, and after one of the most exciting races ever witnessed, won in the last two or three strides by a neck, steel and whipcord having been vigorously plied to laud him. Flatcatcher was three lengths behind the pair, and the rest beaten a very long way off.

SURPLICE AT THE ST LEGER. 291

" It was one of the most desperate struggles ever seen| Surplice proving himself as game and honest a horse as ever breathed, to the great discomfiture of those who did not hesitate to proclaim after the Derby that he was a cur. Lord George Bentinck was not a little gratified at witnessing the success of the produce of his favourite mare.

"There was a great deal of private gossip about the substitution of Xat for Robinson on Surplice's back, and it was remotely hinted that suspicions had been excited, first from Eobinson having been seen in conversation with Messrs Green and Stebbings on the race-course on Tuesday morning, and next from his having hedged the bet which Lord Clifden had laid him|$1000 to $50 against Surplice. We are quite satisfied, however, that such circumstances would have no weight with Lord Clifden and his friends, as the first was a mere commonplace occurrence, and the second was a course which any prudent man would adopt, according to the well-known racing principle, ' No bet is a good bet until hedged.'"

Whatever may have been the motive which caused Nat to be substituted for Robinson, I am in a position to state that it was done solely by the advice, and at the instance, of Mr Harry Hill. It is a satisfaction, however, to me to reflect that such an occurrence never took place in the Goodwood establishment during the thirty years of my connection with it.

The chicanery practised over this St Leger with regard to Surplice was strongly commented upon by numerous supporters of the Turf; and had he not been the superior horse he was, possessing great speed with stoutness, he would in all probability have been beaten. Had Robinson, after making such a desperate pace with Flatcatcher, in strict accordance with his orders, been able to steady him when Canezou and Surplice headed him, and to keep an effort left in his horse, the race might have ended as did the second heat for the Derby of 1828, in which Cadland just beat the Colonel. Evidently it was Robinson's hope that he might win by riding. Otherwise he would not have made so much use of Flatcatcher, when he knew the merits of Surplice as well as he did.

It was a fortunate victory for Mr Villiers, as I know from the most unquestionable authority that he won largely, chiefly by some double event bets, one of which, $10,000 to $100, came to my knowledge, as well as others which were reported to me, but not by Mr Villiers. Nor was my advice to him after the Derby trial acknowledged in any way. I received, however, a far greater reward than any Mr Villiers could bestow upon me; to wit, from my old master, Lord George Bentinck, who expressed his desire that I should serve him again. Any acknowledgments which Mr Villiers might have been pleased to make to me could not have produced so much gratification as I felt when I found that the confidence placed in me by Lord George Bentinck was unchanged.

Two days after the St Leger, Surplice walked over for the North of England Produce Stakes. At Newmarket First October Meeting he met his

SURPLICE AT NEWMARKET. 293

old antagonist, Flatcatcher, in the Grand Duke Michael Stakes, A.F., with the following result:|

Lord Clifden's Surplice (Robinson), 1.

Mr B. Green's Flatcatcher (Flatman), 2.

11 to 4 on Surplice. Won by half a length.

In the Second October Meeting, Newmarket, Surplice started for the Cesarewitch Stakes. The race came off as follows :|

Mr W. S. Crawford's ch. g. The Cur, 6 years, 8.3

(S. Rogers), 1.

Colonel Peel's ch. f. Dacia, 3 years, 4.13, (Collins) 2. Captain Harcourt's br. f. Ellerdale, 4 years, 8.5 (J.

Marson), 3. Colonel Peel's b. f. Palma, 4 years, carried 5.3 (G.

Browne), 4. Mr Meiklam's Inheritress, aged, 8.8 (Templeman); Lord

Clifden's Surplice, 3 years, 8.5, including 12 Ib. extra

(Robinson); and 26 others ran.

Betting|3 to 1 *v.* Surplice, 5 to 1 *v.* The Cur, 12 to 1 *v.* Dacia, 12 to 1 *v.* Inheritress. Won by a length. Surplice was beaten a long way.

Next year, in 1849, in the First Spring Meeting at Newmarket, Lord Exeter's b. m. Tophana, G years, received forfeit from Lord Clifden's Surplice, 4 years, T. M. M., 500 sovs. h. ft.

At Goodwood Surplice ran for the Chesterfield Cup (mile and a quarter), which was won by|

Mr F. Xicoll's ch. c. Woolwich, 3 years, 6 st. (Hiett), 1.

Mr Payne's Crucible, 3 years, 5.7 (Charlton), 2.

Lord Exeter's Medea, 3 years, 4.10 (Barker), 3.

Mr Rolfs Collingwood, 6 years, 9.8 (F. Butler); Lord Clifden's Surplice, 4 years, 9 st. (Robinson); and seven others were not placed.

Betting|G to 4 on Surplice, 5 to 1 *v.* Collingwood, 8 to 1 *v.* Crucible. Won by a length; half a length between second and third.

Surplice was beaten a long way, not displaying much improvement upon his 3-year old form when tried with Lady Wildair and Sagacity.

At Newmarket Second October Meeting Surplice, 8 st. 5 lb., walked over for a Sweepstakes of 1000 sovs., each, 400 ft., A.F. (3 subscribers). In the Houghton Meeting, Collingwood, 9 st. 2 lb., was matched against Surplice, 8 st., A.F., 200 h. ft. Collingwood walked over.

In 1850 Surplice ran but once|viz., in the First Spring Meeting at Newmarket in the following match :|

Duke of Bedford's b. f. St Eosalia, 7 st. 5 lb. (Pettit), beat Lord Clifden's Surplice, 8 st, 10 lb. (Pearl), T. Y. C., 300, 50 ft.

Betting|6 to 4 on Surplice, who was beaten easily by two lengths.

Thus terminated the racing career of one of the most sensational horses of the century. After having accomplished the great feat of winning the Derby and St Leger, beating some really good horses, Surplice failed to win any other race of importance, losing his speed and form altogether. It was rather a remarkable coincidence that he should have won the Derby and St Leger each by theEnd Of Surplice's Career. 295

same distance|a neck, and that F. Butler should have ridden the runner-up on each occasion. To show how naturally sluggish Surplice was, I may mention that Springy Jack, who was second to him for the Derby, was believed by John Scott and F. Butler to be a stone worse than Canezou, who was second for the St Leger. Yet he beat each of them by a neck, although most assuredly as good a horse on the Derby Day as he was on that of the St Leger.

14

SECTION 14

CHAPTER XIV.

LORD GEORGE AS A TURF REFORMER.

Lord George Bentinck's name will endure while horse-racing forms the favourite pastime of the British nation, as that of the greatest Turf reformer ever known. By his stringent code of laws, promulgated in 1844, he purged the race-courses of defaulters, established punctuality in starting for each race by fining the clerk of the course 10s. for every minute behind time, and insisted that each horse should be numbered on the card, a corresponding number being exhibited on the telegraph frame. He required also that the names of the jockeys should be recorded on the board and card, and that the jockey should be properly dressed in a silk, velvet, or satin jacket, and in boots and breeches, as it was by no means unusual to see jockeys riding in trousers or gaiters, with jackets and caps of the roughest and most grotesque description. The saddling of the horses at a given place, and their walking and cantering before the

TURF REFORMS. 297

stand, were likewise enforced by him, together with their starting by the aid of flags. More necessary improvements than the latter two there could not possibly be, as it had long been difficult for jockeys to find the horses they were about to ride when saddling-time arrived, and the consequent delay in starting was most vexatious and annoying. At no place were these improvements hailed with greater satisfaction than at Epsom, as the Derby candidates were so surrounded by gentlemen and others on horseback that jockeys could not find their mounts. When Lord George suggested these rules and conditions for Epsom, the late Mr Dorling, the clerk of the course (to whom Lord George lent the sum of $5000, thus proving the stepping-stone to that official's successful career), stated that he thought they could not be enforced. Lord George, who was Steward, replied, " If the conditions are that the horses must be saddled in Epsom town, never fear but I will enforce them." His first attempt to start the horses by the flag system was with one flag upon a very long pole, with which he marshalled the horses to. the post, walking a little in front of them, and soundly rating any jockey who attempted to advance beyond the line pi'escribed by the starter. The objection to the one-flag system was soon shown, as the jockeys watched its gradual lowering and attempted to jump off before it had actually fallen. His Lordship then instituted the advance-flag ; and wasalso very strict about the weighing of the jockeys, as it was notoriously impossible to weigh some of them accurately, so expert and quick were they with their toes and heels, which enabled certain jockeys to ride some pounds over their proper weight. There was one jockey in particular whom Lord George suspected of this imposition. He related his suspicions to me, and desired me to arrange a trial a few hours before a race in which this jockey had to ride 8 stone, though not on one of our horses. I did so, and with a light saddle he scaled nearly seven pounds over that weight. After the race it was discovered that several pounds of lead had been nailed upon the under part of the scale.

In the report given of Doncaster Races in 1843, it was stated that " the Corporation had been brought to a just sense of their duties by the indefatigable Lord George Bentinck, who may with the utmost propriety be styled the greatest reformer of all abuses connected with the Turf. The same admirable rule respecting defaulters, which worked so well at Goodwood, is to be put into force here." In connection with the Second October Meeting of 1843, the following remarks were written : " Honest men have to thank Lord George Bentinck for this valuable reform of the Turf; for if that nobleman had not persevered to the utmost, even his powerful influence would have been blighted, and a host of rotten sheep left

STUDIES THE PUBLIC CONVENIENCE. 299

to infect the constitution of the remaining flock. We are left without sufficient words of praise to the noble Lord for his indefatigable exertions."

Not only for the general interest of the Turf did his Lordship employ his active mind, but also for the safety and pleasure of the publicalleging that if comfort, convenience, and accommodation were provided for them, to enable them to enjoy more fully the pleasures they sought, they would not object to pay for them. Hence his Lordship's proposition to form an enclosure round the Stand at Goodwood, Liverpool, and Epsom, to which the outside public at first raised great objections ; but his Lordship's observation and forethought soon enabled him rightly to estimate the advantage of such a step, and before long he greatly extended the enclosure at Goodwood till it encompassed the beautiful trees, which now afford the greatest enjoyment to those who partake of luxurious luncheons under their shade. Like other reforms and improvements originally established at Goodwood, these enclosures have been adopted at all the fashionable race meetings of the United Kingdom and throughout the world. Goodwood race-course being private property, and owned by a nobleman who delighted in the noble sport, it was always the Duke of Richmond's desire to make the meeting as perfect as possible, which, with Lord George's energetic and judicious assistance, his Grace succeeded in accomplishing. A sportingwriter on " Glorious Goodwood " in 1844 remarked : " His Grace the Duke of Richmond and Lord George Bentinck are unwearied in their efforts to do away with the few faults and imperfections which still remain." The comfort and convenience of the public were always well considered by these generous and considerate noblemen. It was Lord George who discovered that the public would readily pay for value received ; and that in these receipts there existed a large supplementary and potential source of income which should be applied, and revert to, the public convenience and enjoyment. At that time the added money to the various races at Goodwood was almost nominal, amounting to no more than $1050; while the collective value of all the stakes run for was $32,589, for which 242 horses started. In the four days there were forty-three races|viz., thirteen the first day, nine the second, eleven the third, and ten the fourth, of which the Goodwood stable sent seventy-five to the post. As may be imagined, his Lordship and all connected with the stable were thoroughly tired out ; yet after dinner his Lordship was always eager to add interest to the next day's racing, and was never too weary to make matches and bets. Four glasses of wine were all he allowed himself, and the fatigue of the day often caused him to fall asleep after dinner; nevertheless, he would rouse up when any remark was made which interested him, .particularly when

REFORMS IN JUDGING. 301

any one offered to make matches or bets. He never smoked, and appeared to doze when others were smoking. But, asleep or awake, he was always perfectly self-possessed; and sleeping or waking, no one ever heard from him an indiscretion or an unmasking disclosure. " All the world and his wife know full well how quiet Lord George Bentinck is when he has a good thing." Such was the remark of a writer who had watched him closely and knew him well.

The primitive arrangements for conducting most of the provincial race meetings, previous to the time when Lord George's attention was drawn to them, undoubtedly demanded reform, as among other anomalies it was customary for a private gentleman to officiate in the capacity of judge, and also in that of starter. The consequence was that gross errors occurred in the awards of many races; while the disappointments and unsatisfactory scenes witnessed at the starting-post were disgraceful in the extreme. Two very flagrant errors in the decision of races affecting the Goodwood Stable came under my observation,|one in 1824, when the Duke of Bichmond's mare Dandi- zette ran for the Goodwood Stakes, and passed the winning-post first; but the race was given by Mr Greville, who acted as judge, to Lord Veru- lam's Vitellina. At that time the judge's box was perched aloft, considerably above the level of the race-track. Dandizette finished close to the rails,and passed right under the judge's chair without attracting Mr Greville's observation, which was concentrated on Vitellina and The Ghost on the opposite side of the course|the latter hanging so much upon the former that she was in great danger of being forced against the rails. The jostling race between these two animals absorbed Mr Greville's field of vision, and he saw nothing of Dandizette ; but the oversight was so apparent that Lord Verulam offered the stakes to the Duke of Richmond, stating he was quite convinced that Dandizette had won easily enough. His Grace thanked Lord Verulam for his honourable proposal, but declined to receive the stakes, stating that, whatever his own private opinion and that of others might be, the judge's decision was irrevocable, and must be obeyed. The Earl of Burlington was also present on this occasion, it being the only race meeting at Goodwood that his Lordship was ever known to attend. He said to the Duke, " So you have won the race; but it has been given against you by a judge who is above all things a Newmarket man !" Again, in the year 1837, the Duke of Richmond's Skillygolee, three years old, ran for the Gold Cup at Southampton, which he won easily enough the first time; but the judge gave it a dead heat between him and Mr Sidney Herbert's Bulbridge, three years old. It was so glaring an error that I felt compelled to remonstrate with the judge, whose reply was, " I

IMPROVEMENTS IN STARTING. 303

hope you are not offended, but we wanted to make all the sport we could " ! The next heat I told Reeves (the jockey who rode Skillygolee) not to have another dead heat, and he won by four or five lengths. As I rode past the winning-post I asked the judge how far the horse won this time. He replied, " By a length." " No bad length, either," I rejoined.

Occurrences of this sort were by no means uncommon in those days. The starting of the horses was generally performed by the clerk of the course, or some other official quite unused to the work, and the jockeys took every advantage of him. Jockeys then, as now, would use every device in their power to obtain an advantageous start, and to this end some would deliberately cause false starts until they attained their object. Sometimes a favourite would be kept at the starting-post for an hour in a state of frenzy until he was more than half exhausted before the flag fell. As the horses were started by word of command| the single word " Go " being their *nunc dimittis*| the jockeys were often unable to understand what the starter meant, and sometimes ran the race right through when it was no start. The person deputed to start the horses at Goodwood in 1830 had an impediment in his speech, and when he became excited it was with great difficulty that he could articulate a word. For the Duke of Richmond's Plate that year there were a number of false starts, which delayed the actual start for a very long time. After the race, William Arnull, the oldest jockey who took part in it, and one upon whose word full reliance could be placed, was summoned by the stewards to explain the cause of the long delay. He replied, " Some of the horses were no doubt restive, but in my opinion the fault lay chiefly with the starter. He is just like an old firelock which fizzles ever so long in the pan before it goes off, and when he did get the word out, there was no knowing whether he said ' Go' or ' No'! "

One of the most flagrant attempts on the part of jockeys, and of others behind the scenes who bribed them, to defeat a great favourite, was practised at Doncaster in 1827, when Mameluke, who won the Derby, was brought out to run for the St Leger. There were twenty-six starters, some of them having been sent to the post for the express purpose of impeding and delaying the start, and upsetting Mameluke's temper. Repeated false starts followed each other, in some of which three or four horses ran a considerable distance before they could be stopped and brought. back. All these delays and checks had the natural effect of irritating Mameluke greatly, so that he fretted, kicked, and plunged with such violence that Sam Chifney the younger, who was upon his back, had the greatest trouble to induce him to approach the starter at all. After a monstrous

Jockey's Tricks. 305

loss of time a start was at last effected, but in most irregular fashion, as Matilda and Translation got off several lengths ahead of the rest of the field. When the flag fell Mameluke's head was turned the other way, which caused him to lose at least one hundred yards. Although Jem Robinson, on Matilda, made every use that he could of his advantageous start by forcing the pace, Mameluke gradually made up his lost ground, and got on terms with Mr Petre's filly ; but in the end Robinson's splendid riding was not to be denied, as he nursed his mare for a final effort, and won the race by a short half-length. There are many living, besides myself, who remember the race, and the rumours about it, which were on every tongue. Some blamed the starter, who, I believe, was shortly afterwards dismissed from his situation. At that time the jealousies between tho north- country and south-country jockeys were in full blast, and deep were the ill - feeling and malice existing between them. Nor were these evil practices confined to the jockeys. There were speculators on the Turf who were always ready to purchase horses engaged in a great race, with a view of sending them to the post solely to create difficulties at the start, and thus facilitate the victory of an outsider. For instance, when Priam, who was a great favourite, won the Derby in 1830, there were fourteen false starts, all of which took place in a heavy downpour of rain.

Fortunately Priam was a most docile and tractable colt, and nothing could exasperate him or ruffle his perfect temper. In the end he won easily, beating twenty - two opponents, some of which were sent to the post without the remotest possibility of being able to run into a place. I have seen all the best horses that have flourished and had their day for more than sixty years past, and I now repeat my well-considered opinion that Priam was the most perfect race-horse I ever saw. His constitution was magnificently sound ; his temperament and nervous system beautifully attuned ; his shape, make, and action were faultless. No weight known to the ' Racing Calendar' could crush his spirit. All courses came alike to him. I well remember how frequently I rode him at exercise when, in 1831, he came to our stables to run for the Goodwood Cup of that year, which as a four-year-old he won in a canter, carrying 9 st. 5 Ib. two miles and a half. That was sixty-one years ago, and I question whether there is any other man still living who ever crossed the back of that "bright particular star" among horses, the beautiful and incomparable Priam I the peer of Flying Childers and Eclipse*the* " horse of the nineteenth century !"

Lord George Bentinck's connection with Priam is somewhat remarkable, as it was through his Lordship's instrumentality that in 1831 he was sent to Goodwood, after the Ascot Meeting, to be

PRIAM. 307

trained for the Goodwood Cup. He was then the property of the Earl of Chesterfield, whose horses were trained by Richard Prince at Newmarket. Prince also trained for the Duke of Portland and Mr Charles Greville, with each of whom, as son to the first and cousin to the second, Lord George was intimately connected. Being so favourably impressed with the advantages of Goodwood as a training-ground, Lord George persuaded Lord Chesterfield (then a young man of twenty-six) to send Priam there from Ascot, instead of allowing him to travel on foot to Newmarket, and thence to walk to Goodwood. It was Lord George's admiration for Priam which induced him to purchase at Tatter- sail's, as a foal, the most extraordinary animal that he ever possessed. I well remember that when Octaviana and her filly foal by Priam were put up for sale in 1837, the foal was as weak, narrow, and puny a thing as could well be seen. But in her veins there coursed the blood of Priam, Emilius, and Orville on the father's side, and of Octavian, Shuttle, Delpini, and King Fergus on the mother's. Always a firm believer in good blood, Lord George purchased Octaviana when she was twenty-two years old, because by her side there ran a filly foal got by Priam. The price he paid for the pair was 65 guineas. It was in this manner that he became the owner of the celebrated Crucifix.

Let me conclude with two other instances of Lord George's zeal, energy, and acumen as a Turf reformer, to follow which vocation he was additionally impelled by the fact that he was often the victim of abuses which then existed. In the year 1834, when Preserve won the Clearwell at Newmarket, the horses were at the post an hour before the start took place, although there were but nine runners. Preserve was a great favourite at 6 to 4, and there was evidently a concerted endeavour to defeat her by irritating and wearying her as much as possible. This foul design was repeated when Preserve won the Criterion at the Houghton Meeting, the betting being 13 to 8 on her. Although there were fourteen false starts, the Emilius blood, as in the case of her half-brother Priam, was too stout to be exhausted and defeated by manoeuvres of this rascally kind.

Again, when his Lordship brought out his extraordinary filly, Crucifix, he became the target at which the shafts of envy, hatred, and malice were relentlessly aimed. An attempt was made to defeat her for the Chesterfield Stakes at Newmarket, through the usual agency of countless false starts. In one of these all the horses engaged ran the course through, and Lord Albemarle's chestnut filly Iris came in first, defeating Crucifix by half a length. Crucifix was carrying 9 Ib. extra for winning the July Stakes, and lost fifty lengths at the starting-post. It transpired, however, that

ATTEMPT TO DEFEAT CRUCIFIX. 309

the signal had never been given, and it was declared " no start." To run another heat with 9 Ib. extra was undoubtedly a severe tax upon an overgrown, light-framed, leggy, and half-furnished filly of a most irritable and impetuous temperamentl a defect which she inherited from her dam; but such was her superiority that she was equal to the task, and won the actual race in a canter by two lengths, Iris second. It was 7 to 4 on her before the first heat and 2 to 1 against her for the second. When she ran for the Criterion in the Houghton Meeting, it was 3 to 1 on her, although she again had 9 Ib. extra to carry. The usual false starts were resorted to, maddening Crucifix so much that she ran a dead heat with General Yates's Gibraltar. The stakes were then divided, which was to the advantage of both; as Crucifix, although pretty certain to have won the second heat, might have been overtasked, to her own permanent injury.

In the following year (1840), when Crucifix, after winning the Two Thousand and One Thousand Guineas, ran for the Oaks, the betting was 3 to 1 on her. There were fifteen runners, and more than an hour was cut to waste before the horses got off. Although Crucifix won by half a length, it was her ruin, as she had become so fretful that in one of the innumerable false starts she hit her leg and never ran again. She was beyond all question a victim to the rascally policy pursuedby her envious and unscrupulous opponents, after making the utmost possible allowance for her impetuous temper.

Having witnessed and suffered from these unjust and iniquitous efforts to defeat favourites, Lord George resolved that he would introduce reforms to frustrate as far as possible the machinations of the promoters of all this mischief.

15

SECTION 15

CHAPTER XV.

PERSONAL HABITS OF LORD GEORGE BENTINCK.

Lord George Bentinck was the *beau ideal* of an English nobleman. He stood over six feet in height; his figure was, beyond that of any other man of my acquaintance, stately and elegant ; his features were extremely handsome and refined, his hands and feet small and beautifully shaped, and his whole appearance most commanding. He was invariably dressed in a long black frock-coat, a black or very dark blue, double-breasted, velvet waistcoat, and dark trousers, having (in the fashion of that day) straps attached, which passed under his boots. Over his waistcoat he wore a fine, long, gold chain, which went round his neck, and was clasped together on his breast by a gold loop, in which was set a large and very conspicuous turquoise, which I always regarded as symbolising his sky-blue racing jacket. Round his neck he wore a costly cream-coloured satin scarf of great length, knotted under his chin, and with a goldpin stuck in it. This gold pin (he had two or more of them) contained either a big ruby or a pearl. On his head he invariably wore a tall, new, beaver hat. In this costume, including frock-coat and tall hat, Lord George was always dressed when he went round the stables at Goodwood, or proceeded to the exercise-grounds on foot to see his horses gallop. On the race-course he usually wore a green cutaway coat, buckskin breeches, and top- boots. I must revert for a moment to his scarfs, in order to say that, although they cost nearly a pound apiece, nothing would induce him to wear them more than once. They were then put away, and many drawers were full of them when he died. After his death I purchased from Gardner, his valet, the scarf which he had on when his body was found, and half-a-dozen others, which I still keep as mementoes of my honoured master.

Lord George was never known to suffer any of those whom he employed as commissioners to take the slightest liberty with him. In speaking with them he never laughed, and his look, when serious, was somewhat stern. He never sat down, or permitted them to sit down, in his presence, but would stand before the fireplace while talking to them, with the palms of his hands planted just behind his hips. I have heard two of his most trusted commissioners say that, without asking questions or pumping them in any way, Lord George always elicited from them all the racing information that

CORONATION. 313

they knew. In Coronation's year Lord George had a large round book on the Derby, and was at all times prepared to lay $10,000 to $200 against any outsiders, not in John Scott's or John Day's stables, whose name he heard for the first time. One day, at Tattersall's, Isaac Day asked his Lordship to lay him $10,000 to $200 against a Sir Hercules colt, born in 1838, the year of her Majesty's Coronation, from which event he took his name. This colt was trained in a small private stable. Before Lord George could lay the bet he was touched on the elbow by Mr Joseph Bond, whom he often employed to do commissions for him. Mr Bond shook his head, and the bet was not laid. Having thus escaped being caught for the long odds, Lord George never laid against Coronation at all, and won his whole book. The only explanation that he subsequently vouchsafed to his friends was, " I followed Mr Bond," to the great gratification of the latter.

To me his Lordship was always very unreserved and communicative, as he knew from experience that I should never abuse his confidence. My positive instructions were never to come to London without seeing him, let the hour be what it might. Frequently I arrived at Harcourt House very early in the morning by the mail train, and the hall- porter would immediately call his Lordship's valet to announce my advent. Lord George would summon me without a moment's delay to his bedside,and after I had talked to him for one or two hours, would order breakfast to be prepared for me before I left. At that early hour it often took so much time to provide this meal that I was scarcely able to do justice to it, although I felt bound to eat as much as I could, as his Lordship would invariably inquire of me before we parted whether I had enjoyed my breakfast. I often begged him to allow me to get what little I wanted at some refreshment - room, but to this he would never consent.

When I arrived in London late in the evening, Lord George was often at the House of Commons, or at White's Club at dinner. Wherever he might be, it was my duty to find him with the least possible delay; and if not at White's Club, I sometimes remained there, hearing that he was expected at eleven o'clock, as he had ordered dinner then. He would keep me talking till long after midnight; and upon one occasion desired me to meet him next week at the Winchester station, upon the arrival of the first train from London, about 11 A.M., which necessitated my leaving home about 5 A.m. to post to Fareham (a distance of twenty - two miles) to catch the train for Winchester. Thence we posted to Danebury paddocks, to inspect the stud previous to the closing of the stakes on that day (the 1st of January). After minutely inspecting the stud, Lord George found that it had riot occupied as much time as he

PERSONAL KINDNESS. . 315

expected, and said he thought we had better go straight back to London, instead of proceeding to Winchester to dine, as he had arranged, having ordered dinner at the George Hotel. Arriving in London at Nine Elms station about 7.30 P.m., his Lordship, being unable to find his luggage as quickly as he wished, said, " I will drive on to Harcourt House to order you some dinner, if you will get another cab and bring my luggage with you." When I got to Harcourt House about 9 P.M., Mrs Jones, the housekeeper, came to inquire what I would like for dinner, as his Lordship had desired her to provide the best she was able, and to get fish, gamelin fact, whatever I could enjoy. My reply was, " A mutton - chop with some tea, if you please," as I had had nothing since five o'clock that morning. " I must provide more than that, or I feel sure his Lordship will not be satisfied," exclaimed Mrs Jones. Feeling faint and tired, I was not in a mood to wait long, and was therefore allowed to have what I asked for without delay. As I was eating, Gardner, his Lordship's valet, came to me and desired me, when I had dined, to go to White's Club, where I found Lord George at dinner about eleven o'clock. " I hope you enjoyed your meal ? What did Mrs Jones get for you ?" were his first questions. I told him that I had had a mutton-chop and some tea. " Is that all she provided for you !" he answered. I stated that I preferred it to anything else, as itwas so late, and so many hours had elapsed since I had breakfasted. " So long as you have had what you wished, I am satisfied," he rejoined.

As a vast number of stakes closed that day at midnight, the forfeits for which would amount to thousands of pounds, I reminded his Lordship of the time, as he did not appear to consider it. A cab was at once ordered, and we arrived at Weatherby's office about 11.40 P.m. Mr Wea- therby was afraid that something serious had occurred to prevent his Lordship naming for the various stakes to which he was a subscriber. " I am in plenty of time; Kent has all the nominations made out," observed his Lordship, looking over the various stakes to see how they had filled, until two o'clock, when he drove to Harcourt House, and there kept me talking over various matters till nearly five. Then he rang for his servant to order some breakfast at six o'clock for me, as he wished me to see some yearlings Mr Tattersall had for sale at Willesden before I returned home by the coach from Piccadilly at 8.45 A.m. His Lordship never made any allowance for fatigue, either in himself or in others. The exertion and labour he underwent were prodigious, and the strain imposed upon his mind must, indeed, have been great, as it was incessantly at work both night and day. After being upon a race-course all day, he would invariably return to London by a late train, and often desired me to

ENDURANCE OF FATIGUE. 317

return with him. Giving the guard 10s. or a sovereign, according to the distance, he would desire him to keep a *coupee* locked, and he insisted that I should travel with him, when every detail connected with his enormous racing establishment was discussed. After that, he would talk upon various subjects, many of a private and family nature, upon which I could hardly have expected him to speak to me. He would relate anecdotes about his father and brothers, their pursuits, habits, and peculiarities. Of his mother and sisters he always spoke in the most affectionate terms ; and when any question of expense arose he would often remark, " Never mind the money; my mother will let me have any amount."

His prediction as to the great revolution the construction of railways would effect in racing and other interests has been fully realised, and he encouraged railways in every way. He was a considerable shareholder in the London and Birmingham line, as he informed me once when travelling upon it; at the same time expatiating upon the immense advantages that railways had conferred on mankind, and upon the addition to the lives of individuals made by them, in consequence of their having shortened the hours of travel.

When the Chichester Old Bank stopped payment in 1842, my father was a creditor for the amount of $3600, which was not only a veryserious loss to him but also a great inconvenience, as it crippled him in the conduct of his business. A few days after the occurrence Lord George came to Goodwood, and was apprised of it. He sympathised warmly with my father, and immediately placed $2000 to his account at another bank. The consumption of oats in the Goodwood stable was about 1500 quarters per annum, and they were obtained twice a-year in consignments of 700 or 800 quarters at a time. They came generally from Scotland or from Wisbech. A few months after the stoppage of the bank, the usual half-yearly supply of oats had to be ordered, and, with his usual considerate kindness, Lord George said to my father, " Kent, I am sure that you must need a further advance to enable you to meet all your requirements ; here is another cheque for $2500." Neither of these sums would Lord George allow my father to deduct from his account until July 1845, so that he had the use of $4500 for three years without paying a shilling of interest upon it. The July (1845) account amounted to $4704, 16s. Id., which sum appears in my father's ledger with " Deduction of $4500 received on account," written under it. This will be admitted by all to have been a generous and considerate act on Lord George's part.

At Harcourt House Lord George kept about half-a-dozen harness - horses, and a couple of travelling carriages, one of which he made use of

. -i
:i .. . i. i '
...,..- I .. '
: i ',
: i- . i '.:- ." .
; .t .
' ,'t
1 . '- ,': .'i ' i;,- I '. . II . I J ..
i':i - .,1 .- ..-.- ' : -i
y.
c
w I I
HIS HUNTERS. 319

when journeying down to Danebury, or Goodwood, or Welbeck. As railways began to extend over all the kingdom, these travelling carriages were less and less used every year, until discontinued altogether. At Welbeck his Lordship kept some first-class hunters in order to go out with the Ruffbrd hounds; but when in the south he greatly preferred to hunt with Mr Assheton Smith, whose pack brought him more nearly into contact with Danebury and Goodwood. It was one of his favourite fancies to have all his horses (including racers, hunters, and cart-horses) singed, and he always insisted that the hunters and cart-horses should have their manes cut off. Indeed in some cases it was Lord George's wish that a heavy- coated horse should be shaved, although it was by no means easy to get a barber to undertake the job. So much impressed was he with the advantages to condition resulting from depriving all horses of their long coats when employed in any description of hard work, that he gave orders to have all the cart-horses singed, with the exception of a black mare, who had- an unusually thick coat, and was a very free worker. Consequently she was always in a sweat, and very irritable. The carter who attended her thought that, if singed, she would be more irritable than ever, which might bring on some dangerous disease. When Lord George heard the man's objection, he replied, " If she dies, she will die my property, andnot yours. I insist, therefore, that you have her singed without delay." Lord George was quite right in his anticipation ; for instead of becoming more nervous and irritable after losing her coat, she became perfectly quiet in her work, and soon put on a lot of flesh, of which she stood greatly in need.

Although very severe upon his race-horses in training, and resolved to try them constantly, and to run them in as many races as possible, sometimes twice in the same day, he greatly disliked to see them punished and abused by jockeys. In the stable he would go up to them in their stalls, and fondle and caress them as if they were his own children. To show how much he hated to see a horse (however sorry a nag it might be) cruelly treated, I remember being with him very early one morning upon Epsom race-course during the Derby week. In the furze-bushes at the top of the hill a gipsy was ill-using and beating his horse unmercifully, and Lord George called out to him to desist. The gipsy paid no attention to the remonstrance, and Lord George jumped off his horse and threw the rein to me, bidding me to remain there until he had given " that brute" a sound hiding. I implored him not to do so, reminding him that there were a lot of other gipsies and roughs close by, who would be sure to interfere on behalf of their friend and comrade, and might do him some injury. Observing my

HIS HATRED OF DISHONESTY. 321

earnestness, and acknowledging the justice of my remarks, his Lordship remounted his horse, adding, " You have disappointed me in giving that scoundrel a good thrash-ing; but perhaps you are right."

All those in Lord George's service who did their duty with zeal and fidelity were sure to be handsomely rewarded. Although not prone to suspicion, he was indefatigable in his exertions to unmask dishonesty, and to bring those guilty of it to well- merited punishment. In 1844, for instance, when Red Deer and other horses were being prepared for the Chester Cup, my letters to Lord George, addressed to Harcourt House, were opened by some miscreant connected with the Post Office in London. By a clever device the paper was cut just outside of the seallthere were no envelopes in those daysland after the contents had been read, it was again closed by a hot iron applied to the edge of the sealing-wax, which was made to extend over the cut. Occasionally a little additional wax was employed. Upon one occasion the letter had not been effectually reclosed, and Lord George discovered the fraud. He then examined other letters which he had received from me, and had no difficulty in detecting the treachery of which he had been made the object. His first step was to warn me to seal my letters with a wafer, and then to cover the wafer with wax. He remarked that moisture would not act upon thewax or heat upon the wafer, and that between the two no one would be able to tamper with my letters. He then communicated with the Post Office authorities, who soon discovered that the delinquents were two sorters named Saunders and Tapson, who were dismissed the service. It was the opinion of the law officers of the Crown that these men, having opened but not having stolen the letters, could not be further punished. If such an outrage were to be perpetrated now, the offenders would probably find themselves much more severely dealt with than their predecessors were in 1844.

About the same time a well-known pugilist who kept a tavern not far from the Haymarket was found to be implicated in the conspiracy with these rascally Post Office employees. When Red Deer won the Chester Cup the pugilist in question landed a large stake, and gave a sumptuous dinner to his friends, at the close of which he produced some wonderfully fine old port and brandy, which turned out (as he anticipated) to be a capital advertisement, for the same brand of port and of cognac proved to be as inexhaustible as the widow's cruse of oil in Scripture. To prevent treachery among the numerous lads and servants employed in such an immense stable, many of whom were, of course, exposed to all sorts of temptations when attending race meetings, was found to be almost impossible. In one instance I succeeded, however,

A CASE OF TREACHERY. 323

in detecting a culprit. Towards the close of the racing season of 1845 I had reason to believe that the results of our trials were communicated to a party in London. I set to work, therefore, in earnest to discover the traitor, who, I was convinced, must be one of the lads riding in the trials. I therefore arranged some trials with a view to gaining the information that I desired, and at last I succeeded in getting possession of a letter which fully revealed to me who the traitor was. This letter, which gave full particulars of several trials and of other stable secrets, was in the handwriting of a boy who acted as amanuensis to another boy who could not read or write, but who rode in every trial. He therefore employed a quick, intelligent lad to write for him, and to read to him such letters as arrived at Goodwood. Before long I got the amanuensis entirely into my confidence, and by him I was placed in possession of all the rascalities which were going on, and of the names of the parties in London who were implicated in the plot.

Knowing that I had behind me such a master as Lord George Bentinck, who would grudge no expense so long as he was able to find out the villain who was betraying us both, I had at my command all the resources necessary for getting to the bottom of the conspiracy. Upon reporting progress to Lord George, I received from'him the following encouraging letter :l

" Harcourt House, *January* 31, 1846.

" John Kent,|You deserve and I give you the very greatest credit for the zeal, skill, and ability with which you have detected the traitor in our stable.

" Now we have found him, we shall be fools indeed if we cannot ruin him and all his gang.

" Of course we must continue to sham the utmost confidence in him, and then we must take good care to put him wrong in everything of any importance.

"It is too late to put him on the wrong scent as regards Best Bower in connection with the Chester Cup, unless we can manage it by making Miss Elis win the trials a long way. It will be too late, also, to attempt setting him wrong as to Blackbird and the Voluptuary colt; but I think with Nereus and Rose of Cashmere we might have fine game with B. and E. They must both have a ride or two on Nereus when half trained, so that he may be beaten a long way in all his trials. Neither will it be too late to deceive him about Planet. However, I must leave all this to you, as I see you are now quite master of the situation.|I am, your obedient servt., *G. Bentinck.*"

To this letter I replied by suggesting some slight alterations in the programme, and begged his Lordship to let me know what was the amount of the reward which he proposed to give to the lad

DEFEATING TREACHERY. 325

who had been useful and faithful to me as an informant and confidant. I received from his Lordship the accompanying reply by return of post:|

" Harcockt House, *Feb.* 6, 1846.

" John Kent, | Nothing can be more able, clever, and skilful than the manner in which

you have discovered the misdoings of ; but

it is absolutely necessary we should keep him on without allowing him to suspect that we have found him out, and then we will make him the most efficient tool that could be for our own purposes. is the very man of whom I spoke to

you some time ago as having always got the cream

of the betting out of our stable. must not

on any account be discharged, but the boy who tells you must be *well rawarded. I*

therefore authorise you to pay him anything you think

right. must be kept right in All Matters

of Small importance; but where we mean to do great things, such as with Nereus, Rose of Cashmere, and Planet, *he* and B must be put *quite*

in the Hole. I shall have no scruple in dismissing

at any moment, when I find it will best

answer my purpose to do so. Do you think

stands quite clear about the watch ? It seems an odd thing to do|to send a watch to York to be repaired ! Is it quite certain the watch was not a present and a bribe from some betting man at York ? |I am, your obedient servant, G. Bentinck.

" *P.S.*|The way Colonel Anson and John Scott saved first Attila and then Cotherstone from being poisoned was by sending the head lad in the one case and the boy in the other, who were to do the job, suddenly away to fetch a horse from Malton, so that no suspicion that the conspiracy had been discovered was excited. The consequence was that in both cases the whole gang of conspirators were entirely ruined. In like manner we must make excuses for getting out of

the way when occasion requires it. Sometimes we can do so by ordering him to ride some weight we know he cannot ride, and then taking him off at the last moment. G. B."

Liberally as his Lordship paid all his servants, and great as was the trust he reposed in them, it must have been a source of great annoyance to him to find he had been betrayed by one who had in every way been encouraged to do his duty. In addition to his wages the culprit was earning $20 to $25 per annum by riding trials, and frequently was in receipt of presents when a horse won with which he had been in any way connected. It was one of his Lordship's best traits that he dealt with and treated everything and everybody strictly upon their merits. The fidelity and loyalty of my confidant in the above matter were above all praise, as the traitor had not the slightest suspicion that he was mistrusted, but continued to

STABLE PRECAUTIONS. 327

ride trials with the utmost confidence, as I knew by the letters which he persisted iii dictating, some of which were not very correct as to the merits of the animals upon which he gave an opinion. For instance, he made great mistakes as to the weights carried by horses in many of the trials.

I soon found that some change of tactics in weighing the lads was essential. I also had to employ various descriptions of saddles and saddlecloths to attain my object. The traitor considered himself so very clever that in one of his letters he stated, " My master may think he is deep enough to deceive us in the weights, but he cannot deceive me with his loaded saddle-cloths. Such and such a horse must have had a lot of weight to carry, and then won easily." It so happened that he was not within 2$ stones of the right estimate, as the lead in the saddle-cloths had been replaced by pieces of pine-wood of the same shape. All this was very gratifying to Lord George, as it afforded him an opportunity of making a distinction between a faithful servant and a scoundrel. It is needless to add that the traitor, after he had been turned into a dupe and had served his purpose, was summarily dismissed, while those who had bribed him suffered great losses. The faithful servant was liberally rewarded, and eventually had a good situation obtained for him.

Lord George was so frequently at Goodwood,and spent so much of his time there, inspecting his horses and entering into the minutest details, that it was hardly possible for my father or myself to pay him as much attention as we could have wished. We had many other pressing duties to discharge, and were constantly compelled to apologise to him for our frequent absences. He always replied, " Do not mind me ; I can amuse and occupy myself in a dozen ways." Sometimes he would remain a great length of time in the box with some favourite horse, watching every movement, and ending by patting and caressing him or her. If he happened to be present at feeding-time, he would take the greatest interest in their various appetites, and loved to see them enjoying their food. Nothing could exceed the pleasure taken by Lord George in his extensive racing establishment; and although he frequently passed hours in and about the stable unattended by my father or myself, it never came to our knowledge that he applied to a servant or a lad for information on any subject. I cannot say as much for some other professed gentlemen whom I knew too well.

It is impossible that any one could ever have cared less for money than Lord George did. At the same time, he was far too clear-sighted and too practical to allow any one to wrong him long. In these matters Lord George realised the description given of him by Mr Disraeli, when he says : " Lord George valued the acquisition of money on

HIS DISREGARD OF MONEY. 329

the Turf because there it was the test of success. He counted his thousands after a great race as a victorious general counts his cannon and his prisoners." Mr Disraeli adds in another passage of his ' Political Biography of Lord George Ben- tinck,' that if certain letters written by the latter, which Mr Disraeli had seen, were to meet the public eye, they would cause their author to be regarded as a far more amiable and tender character than those who knew him but slightly gave him credit for being. " Not," says Mr Disraeli, " that it must for one moment be supposed that Lord George was blind to what was occurring on all sides. He was the most sensitive as well as the proudest of men."

When Mr Disraeli called at Harcourt House just before the Christmas holidays in 1846, his Lordship remarked to him with great emotion, " In this cause I have greatly shaken my health, shattered my constitution, and shortened my days, but in it I will succeed or die." The words were prophetic, and to me it will ever be a painful thought that my dear and honoured master wore himself out while still in the very prime of life for politicians who were too selfish to bear any portion of the immense burden which he voluntarily took upon his own shoulders. That he was aware of this would, I feel sure, have been made apparent if his political correspondence had been preserved. But in a note appended to Mr Louis J. Jennings's' Correspondence and Diaries of the Right Honourable John Wilson Croker,' I find the following words : " The editor has made diligent inquiry for Lord George Bentinck's political correspondence, and has been informed by Viscountess Ossington, his Lordship's sister, that the whole of it was probably destroyed by the fourth Duke of Portland, his father."

But although all the letters addressed to Lord George by Mr Disraeli, Mr Croker, Lord Stanley (afterwards Earl of Derby), and others, have perished, some of those written by Lord George himself are still extant. Knowing him as well as I did, I can well conceive the feelings with which he must have penned the following passage to Mr Croker from Welbeck on October 8, 1847:|

" When I accepted the lead of what was left of the old Conservative party, I did deceive myself with false hopes that the old English spirit would have been roused, and that it was only necessary to keep the dismantled ship floating, or fighting under jury-masts, till she went through the thorough repair of a new election. I own that I am bitterly disappointed and broken-hearted that England has proved to be so degenerate that, in face of a tremendous emergency, she has produced no new leader to take my place. Nothing but pinching adversity will bring such men to a proper sense of their duty. As regards the gentlemen,

HIS CONFIDENCE. 331

the entire fund subscribed for the election did not exceed $8000, and of this King Hudson subscribed $6000."

When it is remembered that Lord George's own expenditure upon political and parliamentary objects was as unstinted as it had formerly been upon horse-racing, I can well understand his disappointment upon finding that others were not so ready as he was to pay in purse and person. Mi- Disraeli, who speaks of Lord George Bentinck as " the most generous of men," was well aware how much money he spent upon politics, although he never permitted Mr Disraeli nor anybody else to allude to it. This trait it was, I imagine, which made Mr Disraeli term him " the proudest of men." So far as I was myself concerned, Lord George never showed any pride or *hauteur* in dealing with my father or me. Where he gave his confidence, he was not only condescending but confiding; and I was often astonished at the unreserved freedom with which he used to speak to me about matters with which I had no concern. Lord George was a Mason, and in one essential qualification, reticence, was well fitted to belong to a secret society I never heard, however, that he took any step to make himself a distinguished member of the craft.

16

SECTION 16

332

CHAPTER XVI.

THE FIFTH DUKE OF RICHMOND, K..G.

Fifteen chapters of this work have thus far been mainly devoted to the racing career of Lord George Bentinck, and to its bearings upon his social, political, and sporting character. It will now be my duty to offer to readers who have had the patience to follow me thus far, a few reminiscences of Lord George's racing confederate, the fifth Duke of Richmond.

My father and I had the honour to serve his Graceland never was there a better or a kinder master I before Lord George ever entered the Goodwood stable as an owner of race-horses trained therein, and long after he had left it. I have no hesitation in asserting that some of the Duke's most valuable qualities were not without their influence upon Lord George, who never showed himself greater than in 1848, when Surplice, whom he had bred, won the Derby for Lord Clifden. From many things that I have seenII

THE DUKE OF RICHMOND. 333

and heard, I feel persuaded that the Duke of Richmond was not only Lord George's safest guide and most judicious friend, but also that insensibly he was to no slight degree a pattern for his Lordship between 1841 and 1848.

In one of his numerous letters to the ' Times,' Admiral Rous states that during the whole of his long experience of the Turf, he had come across only two owners of horses|the fourth Duke of Portland, and the fifth Earl of Glasgow | who raced solely for honour, without one mercenary thought in their minds. I cannot understand why Admiral Rous excluded the fifth Duke of Richmond from the above-named category. However honourably and unselfishly the Duke of Portland and Lord Glasgow may have conducted their racing operations, it is impossible that in this respect they should have surpassed my old master, the Duke of Richmond. It is because I believe such noblemen as the three just mentioned ought to be held up to the admiration and the possible imitation of their successors in all future ages, that I now take delight in supplying the foDowing details respecting his Grace's racing career and high-souled disposition.

He was born on the 3d August 1791, and succeeded to the title and estates of his ancestors upon the death, in Canada, of his father, the fourth Duke, in August 1819. At an early age his Grace was sent to Mr Howe's school at Chiswick, where he remained until, a few months later, he was moved to Westminster School. I have it on the authority of some of his contemporaries at Westminster, especially the late Lord Stradbroke, that he was most attentive to his studies. In addition, he had all the inherent courage of his race, and it cannot be doubted that had he been sent to either of the Universities, he would have become a fairly good scholar. Quick of perception, and gifted with a retentive memory, he was one of the most assiduous and persevering of men.

Even in boyhood the love of discipline, for which he was celebrated in the Peninsula, was very marked. But his most noticeable and lovable quality was his hatred of oppression, which led him to interpose on behalf of the weak whenever threatened or attacked by a bully or tyrant. At school, for instance, it signified nothing that the aggressor was several inches taller and a stone heavier than himself; for in more than one of the fights in which his Grace, then Mr Lennox, was engaged, he held his own successfully against older and bigger boys than himself. It was a fighting era, as may be seen from Sir Denis Le Marchant's ' Life of Viscount Althorp,' and Mrs Henry Baring's ' Autobiography of the Right Honourable William Windham.' In fact every record of our great public schools between 1780 and 1840 shows that fights between boys were

HIS SERVICES IN THE PENINSULA. 335

much more frequent and determined than they have been since the latter date. Few men throughout life had more disputes referred to them for arbitration than his Grace, and the spirit of fairness which he brought to his task was so well known that his decisions were never appealed against even by those who were losers thereby. The Duke, or rather Mr Lennox, entered the army at a very early age, and was at once gazetted to the 13th Light Dragoons, then in the Peninsula. In the summer of 1810, being then in his nineteenth year, he embarked from Portsmouth for Lisbon, where he met upon his arrival with a most cordial reception from Vice-Admiral Berkeley, whose wife was his aunt, and who invited him to share his quarters until his guest had recovered from the fatigues of his voyage. Neither the Admiral's pressing invitation, however, to regard his house as a home, nor the gaieties of Lisbon, could induce Mr Lennox, who had now become Lord March, to absent himself from his regimental duties for a single day. Without losing a moment he made his way on horseback to the headquarters of the army, and reported himself to Sir Arthur Welles- ley, Commander - in - Chief, who immediately appointed him to his personal staff, which consisted of the first Lord Raglan, then Lord Fitzroy Somerset; of the latter's nephew, the seventh Duke of Beaufort, then Marquis of Worcester; of Lord George Lennox, Lord William Russell, LordCharles Manners, and Lord Clinton; of the Honourable Fitzroy Stanhope, the Honourable Henry Percy, Major the Honourable Sir Alexander Gordon; Captain Colin Campbell, Major Canning, " Jack" Fremantle, and the Prince of Orange. We learn from ' A Memoir of Charles Gordon Lennox, fifth Duke of Richmond,' published anonymously in 1862, that "the hunting- field in England had made many of the above- named officers competent for an important branch of their duty|that of conveying orders to distant posts|a duty which, in a savage, mountainous country, with an ever - vigilant enemy in front, required no slight energy, courage, and quickness of eye."

Scarcely had Lord March attained this proud position before his regiment, the 13th Light Dragoons, was detailed to reconnoitre the enemy's movements. Lord March heard of this order with unfeigned regret, as his position on the headquarters staff forbade his going to the front with his regiment. He soon recovered from his disappointment on learning that a general engagement was imminent,|an anticipation which was speedily verified. On the morning of July 27, 1810, the French, under Massena, made two desperate attacks on the English position (a very strong one) at Busaco. The action lasted the whole day before the enemy was finally repulsed, leaving nearly 3000 killed and wounded on the field. Lord

IN THE PENINSULA. 337

March had taken out with him to the Peninsula three clever chargers; one of them|a chestnut thoroughbred|which carried him at Busaco, was named after the battle. When Lord March retired from active service at the close of the war, he brought Busaco home with him. I have often seen the horse, and he bore about him the marks of many gunshot wounds. In addition, his head and neck were scarred by heavy sabre-cuts, which the noble animal probably diverted from his rider by accidentally raising his head. Upon his return to England Busaco was turned out for life in Hal- naker Park, where he lived some years, until, becoming very old, he was killed, and buried in the home park close to the ice-house, and a tree was planted over his remains, which has now grown into a noble specimen. Between the battles of Busaco and Orthez, at the latter of which he was severely wounded, Lord March suffered greatly from ill health, being unable to stand the excessive exertion and exposure to bad weather which his staff duties necessitated. It is not generally known that all through the Peninsular War the English troops, including officers as well as privates, served without tents, sleeping out by night in the open air. The French had, as usual, their *tentes d'abri.*

Under these circumstances Lord March was sent down by Wellington, in October 1811, to Lisbon, where he fell in with his first cousin, Charles James

Napier, through whose jaw a bullet had passed. After inquiring into the circumstances of Lord March's ill health, Captain Charles Napier wrote to his mother, Lady Sarah Napier (with whom, when Lady Sarah Lennox, George III. was notoriously in love), in the following terms :|

Lisbon, *JTor.* 1, 1811.

Lord March has just been here, and tells me that you have had your eyes done, and can see a little. Oh! my beloved mother, is this blessed news true ? Heaven grant that it may be! March has been very ill, and will require at least two months' rest and care before he can hope to resume his headquarter duties. Charles Napier.

Soon rejoining the Commander-in-Chief, Lord March was present at the siege of Ciudad Rodrigo. " He entered the breach," writes his biographer, "with the storming-party of the 52d, his companions being the Prince of Orange and Lord Fitzroy Somerset. The Commander-in-Chief rebuked them for exposing their lives in a service which, as officers of the staff, they were not called upon to undertake." In this connection Colonel Gurwood tells a good story of Lord March. When the former was about to return the sword of the French governor of Ciudad Rodrigo, Lord March plucked his superior officer by the sleeve, whispering in his ear, " Don't be such a fool as to give him back his weapon" ! In the attack on this fortress Captain George Napier (brother to Charles Napier) was severely wounded, upon which occa-

RETURN FROM SPAIN. 339

sion Lord March addressed the following letter to Lady Sarah, the mother of these two young heroes :

Galleoos, *Jan.* 21, 1812.

I am sorry to tell you that George has had his arm amputated, in consequence of a musket-shot he received at the top of the breach. It has been cut off just above the elbow of the right arm. He suffers very little pain, and is in high spirits. He volunteered to lead 300 as fine fellows as. ever marched, from the Light Division, and with them stormed the small breach. Everybody in the army admires his gallantry, and they cannot refuse, I trust, to make him a Lieut.-Colonel. I will let you know how he is by the next mail, and I am convinced it will be a favourable account. He wanted to write to you, but I told him I would. He is coming to my quarters, and I will take every care of him. |Believe me, dear Lady Sarah, ever yours affectionately,

Makch.

After the battle of Salamanca, Lord March was sent to England with despatches, and started for Corunna, where he embarked for Portsmouth. He had been present at three battles and two sieges, at skirmishes and brushes innumerable; but in those days special war - correspondents were unknown, and few details, except those conveyed in headquarter despatches and in private letters, were sent home.

Lord March returned to Spain just before the Christmas of 1812. At that time his father was Viceroy of Ireland, and Wellington wrote to him that Lord March and his brother George, both of them A.D.C.'s on the headquarter staff, were inexcellent health. Both were present at all the engagements of 1813, including Vittoria. Lord March had been anxious to witness the conduct in battle of the 52d Light Infantry, and to obtain a practical knowledge of regimental duty in the field. He sought permission, therefore, to leave the headquarter staff for a while, and to join the 1st battalion of that gallant regiment as Captain in the 52d. Lord March led his company to attack the enemy's right at the battle of Orthez. On the crest of the hill he was struck in the chest by a musket-ball, which was never extracted, and which, forty-eight years later, he carried with him to the grave. The wound was at first pronounced to be mortal; but Surgeon Hair of the 52d attended him with such fidelity and skill, that Lord Wellington, on coming to see him, found him sleeping tranquilly. In his surgeon's opinion he had already surmounted the dangerous crisis. Youth and a good constitution soon enabled him to recover and to rejoin the Duke of Wellington at the battle of Toulouse. Speaking of Orthez, Sir William Napier, in his ' History of the Peninsular War,' remarks that " the loss of the allied army was 2300 ; among the wounded being the Duke of Wellington, slightly, and the Duke of Richmond (then Lord March), very severely. The latter had served on Wellington's personal staff throughout the war without a hurt ; but being made a captain in the 52d, he joined

ACCIDENT IN THE HUNTING-FIELD. 341

his regiment like a good soldier before the battle. He was shot through the lungs during the battle ; thus learning by experience the difference between the dangers to which staff and regimental officers are exposed, which are generally in an inverse ratio to their promotion."

I have entered into the details of his Grace's military life at a length which to some may seem inconsistent with what I must necessarily say about his racing career, because it was from his Peninsular experiences that he acquired his great love for horses, and especially for thoroughbreds, which, as he had practically ascertained, make the bravest and most enduring chargers in the world. Upon the restoration of peace Lord March returned to Goodwood House, and devoted himself with great ardour to hunting. It is probable indeed that he would have re-established the far-famed " Goodwood Hunt" but for an accident which befell him when out with the Earl of Egremont's hounds. As he was galloping down one of the steep hills near Goodwood, his horse fell and trod upon his chest, injuring him severely. For some days his life was in imminent danger, and the surgeon in charge believed that the bullet which Lord March had received at Orthez was displaced by the fall. Be this as it may, he was advised to give up hunting, and most reluctantly but with sound judgment he accepted the fiat of the doctors.

It is possible that, but for his banishment from the hunting-field, Lord March would never have taken to horse-racing. In 1817, however, we find him running two horses at Goodwoodlto wit, Hermes, aged four years, and Princess, aged three years, by Gohanna, the Earl of Egremont's celebrated stallion. With the former Lord March won his first racela match for fifty sovereigns a side, half a mile, against Lord Apsley's nameless bay gelding (catch weights). In 1818, Lord March ran two horses at Goodwood, Roncesvalles and Gas, winning with the former a sweepstakes of ten guineas each. In 1819, Roncesvalles won a match for fifty guineas at Brighton against Mr Ball's Lustre. Again, on August 17, 1819, Roncesvalles won a sweepstakes at Brighton, which was the last race won by Lord March in that name. Eleven days later his Lordship succeeded to the title as fifth Duke of Richmond, and shortly afterwards his racing careerlthat is to say, the portion of it conducted on a large scalelmay be said to have commenced.

In 1823 his Grace resolved greatly to extend his stud, and engaged my father to assume the duties of his private trainer. My father was recommended to his Grace by the then Lord Dunwich, who subsequently became second Earl of Stradbroke, and was, more or less, a racing confederate of the Duke. Lord Dunwich, like his brother Henry, who afterwards became Admiral Rous, was an excellent

THE GOODWOOD STABLE. 343

judge of racing, and advised his Grace to purchase Hampden from the Duke of Grafton, and Dandi- zette from Mr Walker. Hampden proved to be a bad-tempered horse, and had evidently lost his form prior to the Duke of Grafton's selling him. He turned out a very bad purchase, and Lord Dumvich was greatly annoyed, as he imagined that some misrepresentations had been made to him about the horse, who was five years old when he purchased him for the Duke of Richmond. Hampden was taken out of training, and being a son of Rubens, was put to the stud, where, again, he was very unsuccessful, as he generally imparted his own vicious temper to his progeny. With Dandizette, on the other hand, the Duke was very successful. . In 1825 his Grace purchased a yearling filly, by Smolensko out of Medora, whom he named Gul- nare, and with whom he won the Oaks at Epsom in 1827, together with some other good races. In fact, she won eight times as a three-year-old without ever sustaining defeat. His Grace was greatly encouraged by Gulnare's success, and thenceforward he entered more fully into racing engagements. The Goodwood stable was also reinforced, after 1828, by horses belonging to the Earl of Stradbroke, the Earl of Uxbridge, Colonel Peel, Captain Byng (afterwards Lord Enfield, and finally second Earl of Strafford), Sir James Graham, and others. Among the new supporters of the stable were included Mr Charles Greville, Mr Houldsworth, and Lord George Bentinck. My father has often told me that he never knew a lot of noblemen and gentlemen, all of them owners of horses, who acted together more harmoniously for a considerable time than the above - named group. Their concord and good-fellowship were not a little promoted by the delightful surroundings which they found at Goodwood. Many of them spent a large portion of their time at Goodwood House, and found in his Grace the most cordial and hospitable of hosts. After breakfast the whole party, often accompanied by the ladies, came *en masse* to the stables, round which they were escorted by my father. His Grace had spent a good deal of money in making new paddocks, supplied with excellent hovels, and with everything necessary for a select breeding stud. Among the horses inspected was Moses, winner of the Derby in 1822, whom the Duke of Richmond purchased on the dispersal of the Duke of York's stud, after the death of his Royal Highness in 1827. In the previous year, the Duke of Richmond also purchased three very valuable mares from Mr Lambton lviz., Leopoldine, Loo, and the Duchess, the latter having won the Doncaster St Leger for Sir Belling- ham Graham in 1816.

Upon the return of each successive race meeting at Goodwood, the noble owner of that enchanting domain greeted the advent of " The Races " with the greatest zest and delight. Nothing afforded

THE GOODWOOD MEETING. 345

him greater pleasure than to invite the most distinguished patrons of the Turf to his beautiful home, where they were entertained for many days in princely fashion. The carriages pulling up at the front door for three or four days previous to the races generally numbered forty or more. Many had four horses attached to them, and the amount of luggage that they carried was simply enormous. The landlords of the two great hotels at Godalming and Kingston were brothers named Moon. The landlord of " The King's Arms," Godalming, who was a very keen sportsman, was called " Full Moon," to distinguish him from his brother at Kingston, who was called " Half Moon." Each of these posting-houses habitually kept from ninety to one hundred pair of post-horses for the use of their customers. Despite the vastness of these numbers, the demand for post-horses before the Goodwood Meeting often exceeded the supply. During the meeting the big stable-yard at Goodwood, which was of immense size, was completely blocked up with carriages. To every detail connected with the accommodation of his guests, their servants, and their carriages, the Duke himself paid the minutest attention when the recurrence of each meeting drew near.

In those comparatively primitive times there was, in my opinion, much more genuine enjoyment of pleasures and amusements than exists in these more luxurious and civilised days. I feelcertain that his Grace would not have enjoyed the Goodwood Meeting of to-day half so much as he did those which came to pass between 1830 and 1860. I have already stated that, through the joint exertions of the Duke of Richmond and Lord George Bentinck, Goodwood soon rose to be the best and most fashionable meeting in the world. The training-grounds on which the racehorses of the two noble confederates were prepared for their engagements were as perfect as money and ingenuity could make them. I remember the time when Goodwood Park, in front of the house, and in other parts, was studded with innumerable ant-hills, which were pared down and burnt, producing many hundreds of cart-loads of ashes. The Duke soon became so enthusiastically attached to the Turf that he determined to get hold of a domicile at Newmarket. With this object in view, he purchased, in 1828, a house and stables on " The Terrace " at Newmarket, which had been the property of the Hon. Charles Wyndham, whose death took place in that year. This house his Grace put under the charge of his old and faithful servant, Peter Soar,1 who had been coachman, while his wife had been cook, to the fourth Duke, who was father to the subject of the present memoir. It was the fourth Duke who was residing at Brussels when the battle of Waterloo

1 Peter Soar drove his master, the fourth Duke of Richmond, over the field of Waterloo the morning after the battle.

HIS LETTERS. 347

took place, and his name, together with that of his wife, will live for ever in connection with the famous ball given by them on the night preceding the battle of Quatre Braslan event which afforded Lord Byron a theme for one of his most magnificent passages in verse, and which was also selected by Thackeray as a key to his interesting novel, ' Vanity Fair.' No one had more anecdotes to tell about that " king-making victory" than the fourth Duke and his accomplished wife, the daughter of Alexander, fourth Duke of Gordon. The fourth Duchess of Richmond brought that noble Scottish property, Gordon Castle, together with the deer-forest of Glenfiddich, and many miles of the Spey, a magnificent salmon river, into the possession of the Lennox family. Gordon Castle has for many years been the autumn retreat of the late and the present Dukes of Richmond, who resorted to it every year with increasing delight. It was not until the death in 1836 of his maternal uncle, George, fifth Duke of Gordon, that the fifth Duke of Richmond assumed the additional name of Gordon. From the same uncle he also succeeded to the hereditary constableship of Inverness Castle.

As a racing man, the Duke of Richmond dif- ered in many respects from Lord George Ben- tinck. The former was as concise as the latter was voluminous in his private letters. His Grace regarded five or six lines as a long letter for himto write : I have often received as many closely written sheets of note-paper from Lord George. My father once showed me a letter from the Duke containing the single word " Yes." This letter became the subject of a bet between my father and Mr Rusbridger, the land-agent at Goodwood. The latter received a communication from his Grace which contained two words. On the strength of this he betted my father that he could produce the shortest letter in existence from him. His chagrin may be imagined when, on investigation, he was beaten as it were by a head.

Although the Duke never possessed a very superior animal,|probably Ghillie Callum was his best in point of merit, and Red Hart in point of success,|yet his Grace won the Oaks twice|viz., with Gulnare and Refraction. The One Thousand Guineas Stakes at Newmarket he won with Picnic ; the Goodwood Cup twice|viz., with Linkboy and Miss Craven; the Goodwood Stakes thrice; the Chester Cup once; the Ascot Stakes thrice; and some valuable stakes with the following,|viz., Red Hart, Officious, Cuckoo, Red Hind, Harbinger, Pharos, Homebrewed, Dagobert, and others. During the time his Grace kept race-horses he won in stakes about $112,000.

It is not generally known that William IV. had little taste for the Turf, in connection with which his brother, George IV., had sustained great pecuniary losses. Such, however, was the

KING WILLIAM IV. AND THE DUKE. 349

attachment felt by the "Sailor-King" for the fifth Duke of Richmond, that his Majesty was induced to bestow his patronage upon horse-racing, and to retain the Royal stud at Hampton Court, which is now one of the most successful and best conducted establishments of its kind in the world. King William IV. was often heard to declare that his friend, to whose meritorious career this chapter is dedicated, was, as a nobleman, *sans peur et sans reproche;* that is to say, with no other object in view than the good of his country, the maintenance of his own fair fame, and the education of his family, so that, they might grow up good men and good women. It was at the instance of the fifth Duke that William IV. gave a grand dinner to the Jockey Club on May 28, 1833, of which a full account will be found in Mr Greville's ' Diaries.'

In a book entitled ' Horse-Racing : its History ; with Early Records of Principal and other Race Meetings,' published anonymously by Messrs Saunders & Otley, of Brook Street, London, in 1863, I find the following passage: "There were but two noteworthy events connected with the Turf in the year 1836. The first was the speech of King William IV. at Egham races, to which further allusion will presently be made; the second has reference to a dinner given by the same monarch to the Jockey Club at St James's Palace on June 9. It would appear that at thisdinner a good deal of sport was embarked upon in connection with the ensuing Ascot Meeting, and that in the course of conversation the Marquis of Westminster was boasting of his celebrated horse Touchstone, and offering to back him for a large sum against anything that could be named in the Ascot Cup field. The King immediately caught at the offer, and exclaimed, ' I accept the challenge, and will name one to beat him by a neck.' The wager was at once concluded, and his Majesty, amidst a roar of laughter, named ' The Giraffe'!"

The speech adverted to above, which William IV. delivered at Egham races in August 1836, was in response to an address of thanks presented to him for giving " A Royal Purse of One hundred guineas"|or, in other words, a King's Plate | to be run there annually in future. His Majesty observed in reply, " That he most deeply felt the dutiful attention which led to this acknowledgment of an act, prompted on his part by desire to show that he was sensible of the munificence of a people which had not only enabled him to reside in the ancient and splendid castle at Windsor,| the pride of Englishmen and the envy of foreigners,|but also to follow the dictates of his heart in furthering the happiness of every class of his subjects. He considered horse-racing to be a national sport, becoming to a free and noble people. It was with no slight pride that he found

HIS MARRIAGE. 351

himself in a position to encourage sports and pastimes of a nature to suit the habits and feelings of a free country."

But for the encouragement to patronise horse- racing instilled into his Majesty by my honoured master, the fifth Duke of Richmond, this very seemly speech, which was received with storms of applause, would never have been uttered.

It remains for me to add that, on the signature of the general peace which followed Waterloo, Lord March contracted a marriage, in April 1816, with Lady Caroline Paget, eldest daughter of the famous Marquis of Anglesey. The ' Memoir of the Fifth Duke of Richmond,' from which I have already quoted, comments upon this marriage in the following words : "In every respect the union was a most fortunate one, for the Countess of March possessed every quality that could grace the female character, added to a beauty that could find no compeer. As a tender and devoted mother, as an affectionate wife, and as a kind- hearted and generous friend, her Grace ever shone forth pre-eminently great. It was said by one who enjoyed the privilege of her acquaintance after the death of her husband, that ' the vanities of worldly pleasures nestled not in her heart, as the remembrance of her departed husband, and the care of her home, her children, and her grandchildren, engrossed her whole attention.'"

During his father's lifetime, Lord and LadyMarch occupied Molecomb|a very beautiful villa situated at the head of a delightful valley, and within a few minutes' walk of Goodwood House. Backed by the Southdowns, with a gentle acclivity sloping down on either side, and the woods above it richly clothed with luxuriant evergreens and stately oaks, Molecomb and its pretty garden, from which a distant view of the glistening sea can be obtained, is one of the most attractive spots in the beautiful county of Sussex. Their Serene Highnesses Prince and Princess Edward of Saxe-Weimar,|the latter being well remembered by me, and by many others who now offer her through me the respectful tribute of their gratitude and love for the countless kindnesses they have received at her hands,|were the occupants of Molecomb for many years. It is now the abode of the present Lord March, who is Master of the Goodwood Hunt, and also one of the most popular and respected members of the Jockey Club.

I have said that Ghillie Callum was probably the best horse ever owned by the fifth Duke of Richmond, and he was one of the speediest animals that I ever tried. Being, moreover, a son of that stout sire, Gladiator, I have no doubt that he would greatly have troubled Voltigeurlindeed I think he would have beaten himlin the Derby of 1850, if he had come to the post in as good condition as the winner. What makes me think so highly of Ghillie Callum is, that he was of the same

GHILLIE CALLUM. 353

age as Officious, a flying filly belonging to his Grace, who won eight times as a two-year-old without sustaining defeat. In more than one trial in 1849 Ghillie Callum gave Officious 10 Ib. and an easy beating. He ran twice as a two-year-old,l once at Goodwood, and once for the Rutland Stakes at Newmarket,land won each time without being extended. Next year, when they were both three- year-olds, and when Officious had won twice at Newmarket, I tried them again, making the horse give the mare 12 Ib., and again he won in a canter. A commission was then given to back him for the Derby, but unfortunately his near fore-leg gave way about three weeks before the race. I was compelled to restrict him to walking and cantering exercise. Even in this condition he ran very well in the Derby, and the place occupied in that race by Mr Gratwicke's Nigger, to whom Ghillie could give a lot of weight, makes me think that Voltigeur would have had his work cut out for him had he met the Duke's horse when at his best. Certainly the Nigger got closer to Voltigeur than he ever could get to Ghillie Callum when the last two were fit. It was a great disappointment to us all, but as usual the Duke bore it with the greatest equanimity, and did his utmost to console those who had done their best to bring his representative well to the post. In fact, whenever a horse belonging to his Grace was expected to win and got beaten, he would invariably saylwithout attempting to makeout, as so many do, that the race had been lost by the jockey, or by wrong orders, or because of something wrong in the state of the groundl" I suppose we me.t a better horse."

Red Hart, who was his Grace's most successful race-horse, was a big overgrown yearling, and evidently needed time to develop him, which, by turning him out and letting him run about as a two-year-old until the month of October, his noble owner took care that he should not want. The result was that, in 1847, he won eight races as a three-year-old, including the Welcome Stakes at Ascot, in which he beat Sir Joseph Hawley's Miami, who had won the Oaks; the Gratwicke Stakes at Goodwood; the Grand Duke Michael Stakes at Newmarket, in which he beat Sir Robert Pigot's Conyngham, who had won the Two- Thousand ; and the Royal Stakes at Newmarket. Altogether Red Hart won $6405 in stakes in 1847. The Duke greatly preferred to breed his own racehorses, having a great objection to purchasing (as happened to him more than once) " an orange which," as he phrased it, "some one else had already squeezed." Among the animals that he bred, and took the greatest delight in, were Refraction, Picnic, Red Hart, Red Deer, Officious, Cuckoo, Red Hind, Ghillie Callum, Harbinger, Pharos, and Homebrewed. Most of the above-named horses won races at Goodwood, which meeting his Grace always moved heaven and earth to make more

HIS HEART IN GOODWOOD. 355

attractive. From other race-meetings he was often absent, and it was never much of a disappointment to him if he was prevented from going to Epsom, Newmarket, or Ascot. But his whole heart was enlisted in the support and enjoyment of Goodwood, and I never saw any one more delighted than he was when his favourite old horse, Mus, won the Orleans Cup at Goodwood in 1841, giving 13 Ib. and a beating to Mr Lichtwald's Hyllus, 5 years old, who on the previous day had run second for the Goodwood Cup to Mr A. Johnstone's Charles XII. Before the Orleans Cup they laid 3 to 1 on Hyllus, and his Grace's exultation (which he was too guileless and transparent a character to attempt to conceal) was proportionately great.

When I think on the great and palmy days of the Goodwood Cup, and what it was when such superb animals as Fleur-de-Lis, Priam, Glencoe, Hornsea, Harkaway, Charles XII., Alice Hawthorne, The Hero, Van Tromp, and Canezou carried it off, I cannot resist the impression that there are no such champion thoroughbreds now to be found on the British Turf, or conceal my apprehension that the modern system of ceaseless short races, most of them for two-year-olds, wihl inevitably produce the most pernicious results before many years have passed away. When, in 1838, Mr Ferguson's magnificent chestnut colt, Hark- away, won the Goodwood Cup, there were forty subscribers and eight starters for it. Scarcely hadthat grand representative of Erin's Isle passed the winning-post before his gallant owner, with the warmth and generosity of heart for which his compatriots are renowned, approached the Duke of Richmond, and begged his Grace to permit him to lay the valuable trophy which Harkaway had just won as an oblation at the feet of the Duchess. The latter was much gratified at Mr Ferguson's princely ofier, but, after consultation with the Duke, came to the wise conclusion that it behoved her to decline it, from fear of establishing a precedent which might be found productive of inconvenient consequences.

If, however, the Duke of Richmond was, as a thousand acts well known to me proved, the kindliest and most considerate of men, there were occasions when the manliness and independence of his character stood out in bold relief. It will be remembered by many that for a long time Mr Gratwickelwho was a Sussex neighbour of the Duke's familylhad his horses trained by permission in the Goodwood stable. Mr Gratwicke was rather apt to be suspicious, and too ready to imagine that his horses were managed in the interest of other parties in the stablelthan which nothing could be further from the truth. His complaints, made, not to the Duke of Richmond, but privately to friends of his own, reached his Grace's ears, and drew from him the remark, spoken in the hearing of many independent listeners, " If Mr

MR GRATWICKE. 357

Gratwicke is dissatisfied with the management of the Goodwood stable, and thinks his horses can be better trained and better managed elsewhere, by all means let him make the experiment at once, and take them away. We can do very well without them." It was once remarked to me by a great friend of his Grace, " The Duke of Richmond is always the Duke and never the Duke." The slightest intentional liberty or indignity offered to him was resented at once; but, on the other hand, it was his natural impulse to wound no one, and to abound in considerate and thoughtful kindness to all, and especially to the humblest.

The result of what I have just stated was that Mr Gratwicke soon removed his stud from Goodwood to Newmarket, leasing his horses to the Duke of Bedford, upon terms suggested by Admiral Rous, who managed the Duke of Bedford's stable, and exercised great influence upon Mr Gratwicke's rather weak nature. Next year the Duke of Richmond's Pharos and Mr Gratwicke's Sitting- bourne met as two-year-olds at Goodwood in the Bentinck Memorial Stakes. Admiral Rous backed Sittingbourne for $100ǀthe largest sum that he ever staked upon a horseǀand to his great amazement, and also to that of William Butler the trainer, and of his brother Frank Butler, the famous jockey, Pharos won very cleverly. A few weeks later Sittingbourne won the Convivial Stakes at York, beating fourteen others, and wound up atthe end of the year by carrying off the Prendergast Stakes at Newmarket. Next year Sittingbourne ran second in the Two Thousand, and second in the Derby, both to West Australian, and was one of the best three-year-olds in England. In fact, if he had not met such a paragon as West Australian, he would have been inscribed on the roll of fame as winner of the Two Thousand, Derby, and St Leger. What happened to him in the latter race formed the subject of one of the late Mr F. Swindell's most amusing stories; but I cannot venture to describe what that famous *raconteur* used to unfold, or his admirable mimicry of Mr Gratwicke's look, gestures, and ejaculations when the race ended without Sittingbourne getting a place. It often happens that a couple of two-year-olds meet on a T.Y.C. course, and that the smaller is the better of the two. Twelve additional months reverse their relations of form, and the big colt, having had time to grow and furnish, becomes the superior when both are three years old. This was what happened in the case of Pharos and Sittingbourne.

I have often made mention in this volume and elsewhere of the wisdom, nay the necessity, of making use of a good horse when he is well and fit to run. Never was this truth more forcibly exemplified than when Mr Gratwicke had Landgrave engaged in 1850 in the Four-year-old Triennial (First October Meeting at Newmarket), the Cesare-

LANDGRAVE. 359

witch, and Cambridgeshire. This fine horse, a gelding got by Sir Hercules out of the Landgravine, was handicapped for the Cesarewitch at 6 st. 13 lb., and was rather freely backed by the stable, in whose interest $15,000 to $100 was taken that he won the three eventsǀdespite the fact that in the first he had to meet two good horses, Lord Eglin- ton's Elthiron and Sir Joseph Hawley's Vatican. When I saddled Landgrave for the Triennial, run from the Ditchin, Flatman asked how he should ride him. I said, " Take hold of his head, and come truly through till you reach the Turn of the Lands. Then steady him against the hill, and, take my word for it, your two opponents will have had enough of it before you get to the Duke's stand." My words were literally fulfilled, for Landgrave's tremendous stride (he stood 16 hands 1 inch high) told so effectually that in the end he won hands down, and became instantly a great favourite for the Cesarewitch, for which Fobert, the trainer of Elthiron, asserted that he was as well in as the Flying Dutchman would be at 7 st. 7 lb.

The next difficulty was to find a trustworthy jockey able to ride him at 6 st. 13 lb. At last Lord Enfield secured old Sam Mann, who, by reducing himself to the utmost, promised to get down to the weight. Unfortunately in the process he made himself so weak that before half the distance was run he could hardly keep his seat, and Landgrave, who required holding together, was sprawling allover the course. In the end he was beaten half a length by Chappie upon Mr Payne's Glauca, a mare to whom he could have given a stone, and who gave him five pounds and a beating. Everybody saw that it was Sam Mann, not Landgrave, who lost the race, and the latter was installed first favourite for the Cambridgeshire at 6 st. 11 Ib. Jemmy Chappie was engaged to ride him, and was told to come through; but instead of obeying orders he never got near the front until the last few yards, when he came and won by a head. My firm conviction is that if Flatman had ridden Landgrave in the Cesarewitch and Cambridgeshire at 7 st. 8 Ib. (his lowest weight), he would have won both as easily as he did the Four-year-old Triennial. It was perhaps the best thing that, in my long experience, I ever sent forth from the Goodwood stables, and the result proved how often horse and trainer are undeservedly baffled by the weakness or incom- petency of a jockey.

I cannot conclude this brief memoir without mentioning that the fifth Duke of Richmond was, throughout life, a devoted and enthusiastic patron of agriculture, and took the greatest interest in his farms, cattle, and sheep. Never within my memory has there been a moment at which Goodwood Park and Downs were without a superb flock of Southdown sheep which called the reigning Duke their master. No expense or trouble have been spared in obtaining the best sheep that

HIS CHARACTER. 361

money could buy, and countless were the gold and silver medals at the Smithfield Cattle Shows gained by Goodwood sheep. In the midst of a host of sheep - breeders, including the late Mr Ellman of Glynde, Mr Grantham, and Mr Jonas Webbe, his Grace was always prominent, and his flock was in request, not only among English, but also among French, Prussian, Austrian, Russian, and American connoisseurs.

With a quotation from the same source which has already furnished me with more than one passage, I draw near to the close of this humble tribute of grateful and respectful duty and affec- tion, laid on the tomb of my beloved master: " The Duke of Richmond in domestic life realised truly the character of a Christian parent. He possessed a singleness of purpose which made his home the perfection of happiness; his children looked upon their father as their most sincere and loving friend. Their childish sports were never interrupted, and if they paused in their innocent games when their father entered the room, it was to welcome him with that outpouring of the heart which loving children can alone offer."

The only additional remark which I have to offer is, that his Grace's political career was on a par with his social life at Goodwood and at Gordon Castle, and with the courage, loyalty, and fidelity with which he discharged a soldier's duties in the Peninsular war. It is notorious that the great Duke of Wellington entertained the greatest objection to military medals and decorations, which, in common with many other great captains of the past, he regarded as likely to induce ambitious young officers to indulge in ostentatious exhibitions of daring, which were of little or no benefit to the cause for which they fought, but, as the Iron Duke believed, were often undertaken in order to attract special notice to their perpetrators. Under these circumstances the medals for the Peninsula and Waterloo were not presented to the gallant soldiers who had so richly merited them, for more than thirty years after Waterloo was fought. At last the Duke of Richmond determined to strike in on behalf of those of his humble comrades whom in 1847 time had still spared. Rising in his place in the House of Lords in May 1847, the Duke indignantly replied to a sneering remark made by the Marquis of Londonderry, who deprecated " the prostitution of rewards which had recently been squeezed out of the Government." Nothing could have been more dignified and characteristic than the Duke of Richmond's reply. " After the attack," he commenced, " which has been made by the noble and gallant Marquis, who has the audacity to speak of these medals and rewards as being prostituted, I claim your Lordships' kind indulgence while I attempt to reply to those insulting words. He says that these rewards are prosti-

THE DUKE AND THE PENINSULAR MEDALS. 363

tuted when given to soldiers who fought and won those numerous battles in the Peninsula which are the pride of our country; the men who took part in the forlorn-hopes of Badajoz, Ciudad Rod- rigo, and San Sebastian, and Avho gained for the noble Marquis the Peninsula medals with which he is now decorated."

Continuing in the same vein, the noble Duke produced such an effect upon both Houses of Parliament, and upon the country at large, that the tardy act of justice to some of the noblest soldiers that ever faced wounds and death with indomitable fortitude could no longer be withheld. At last the Peninsula warriors were crowned with their well- earned laurels, and every soldier in the British army knew that but for the Duke of Richmond this debt of gratitude would never have been paid. The much-coveted trophies were served out to the survivors in 1849, and after the Duke's victory in the House of Lords came his own well-merited reward. It was proposed " that his Grace the Duke of Richmond, K.G., be presented with a testimonial for his exertions on behalf of the Peninsular heroes." A committee was instantly formed, with the gallant Lord Saltoun for chairman. It was composed of officers of every grade, and in each of the English, Scotch, and Irish counties, sub-committees were appointed to carry out the desired object. Subscriptions were confined to those who had received the medals,ranging from 5s. to $1 for officers, while id. was all the privates were called on to pay. The testimonial was presented to the Duke of Richmond at a banquet in Willis's Rooms, with Lord Saltoun in the chair. It was of the following description : " On the summit of a quadrangular pedestal stood an allegorical group, representing the Duke of Richmond directing the attention of Britannia to the merits of her military and naval forces. In the centre stands his Grace, robed in the costume of a Peer, holding in his left hand a memorial to her Majesty, while with his right he points to the figures of Mars and Neptune. In the hand of Britannia is the war medal she is about to distribute." A panel at the base contained the following inscription : " Presented on the thirty-eighth anniversary of the battle of Vittoria, to his Grace the Duke of Richmond, K.G., by the recipients of the war medal, in grateful remembrance of his long and unwearied exertions on their behalf."

With this crowning and complimentary tribute to a gallant and most estimable nobleman, I now bring this chapter to a close, briefly adding that, for many years before his death, his Grace was subject to frequent attacks of gout and other maladies, which in time undermined a not very robust constitution, somewhat impaired by privations and hardships endured in the Peninsula, in France, and in Belgium, and most of all by reason of the severe wound received at Orthez. At the

HIS DEATH. 365

Goodwood Meeting in 1860 he was far from well, and unable to attend the races or to welcome his numerous guests with his customary hospitality. On the afternoon of the Cup da"y he was wheeled in his garden-chair to the lawn in front of the conservatory, and received his friends on their return from the course.

From Goodwood he proceeded to Gordon Castle by easy stages, where for a short time the Highland air produced such a favourable effect upon his debilitated frame that the anxiety of his devoted wife was greatly diminished. Soon, however, a change for the worse ensued, and Sir James Clarke advised an immediate return to London. In a state of deplorable weakness his Grace, attended by Dr Hair, arrived at his town house in Portland Place, where, at a quarter before two P.m. on Sunday, 21st October 1860, he breathed his last, in his seventieth year.

" Only the actions of the just
Smell sweet, and blossom in the dust."

SECTION 17

CHAPTER XVII.
RACING CAREER OF THE LATE RIGHT HON.
SIR WILLIAM H. GREGORY.

By the Editor.

This work was about to assume its final " form and pressure," previous to publication, when the death of Sir William H. Gregory, K.C.M.G., on Sunday, March 6, 1892, led me to address myself forthwith to the tasklin this instance it is a labour of lovelof writing down what I know of my old friend's racing career. Sir William was born at Coole Park, County Galway, in 1817, and in 1839 was present at the Epsom Derby for the first time. Although no more than twenty- two years old when he saw his first Derby and bought his first race-horse, he was at once admitted to the best society in the United Kingdom, and soon became a prominent pillar of the English Turf. From about the year 1840 until the autumn of 1846, when Lord George Ben- tiuck sold the whole of his racing stud to Mr

SIR V. H. GEEGORY. 367

Mostyn, Sir William Gregory was on the most intimate terms of friendship with the noble owner of Crucifix, Miss Elis, and Gaper. It seems, therefore, in the highest degree desirable and opportune that I should avail myself of the permission which on many occasions he accorded to me, authorising me, if I outlived him, to make what use I liked (when he had passed away) of the numerous letters which I had received from him, and of our still more numerous conversations on racing and political subjects. During his lifetime Sir William was averse from printed allusion to the Turf career which he had pursued with so much zeal and energy in his stirring youth. He had followed racing|and to a man who carries it on as he did, it seldom fails to become an all-absorbing and engrossing profession|with more courage than discretion. About that time Irish property had begun to decline so rapidly in value, that Sir William Gregory's Galway estates brought him in next to nothing. Nevertheless he remained on the Turf, always sticking to the same trainer | William Treen of Beckhampton, in Wiltshire|in the hope that another Clermont or another Loupgarou might arise to retrieve his shattered fortunes. It was not destined, however, that such a horse should again be vouchsafed to him, and his subsequent career, first as a member of Parliament from 1857 to 1872, and secondly, as Governor of Ceylon from 1872 to 1877, proved beyond all doubt|that when, in 1855, he broke down financially, and quitted the Turf for ever, it was the most fortunate circumstance that ever happened to him in a long and distinguished life.

A few words are all that I need devote to Sir William's parentage and station in life. Those who desire to read his early political experiences, as revealed by his own hand, have but to turn to the April, 1889, number of ' The Nineteenth Century,' where they will find an article from his pen, headed, " A Few more Words on Daniel O'Connell." In the autumn of the previous year there had appeared a work in two volumes entitled ' The Correspondence of Daniel O'Connell, the Liberator: edited, with Notices of his Life and Times, by W. J. Fitzpatrick, F.S.A.' There can be little doubt that the two volumes in question constitute the most remarkable work on Irish politics and history that has seen the light since the publication in 1859 of ' The Correspondence of Charles, First Marquis Cornwallis,' edited by Mr Charles Ross. These two books seem to have had a greater effect than any others upon the sensitive mind of Mr Gladstone, in inducing him to attempt to bestow Home Rule upon Ireland. What Mr Gladstone thought of ' The Correspondence of Daniel O'Connell' may be gathered from his striking article in the January, 1889, number of 'The Nineteenth Century.' One passage from it I will permit myself to quote : " There cannot but be many," writes Mr Glad-

HIS GRANDFATHER. 369

stone, " in whose eyes O'Connell seems the greatest Irishman that ever lived. Neither Swift nor Grattan can be placed in the scale against him. If there were competition among the dead heroes of Irish history, I suppose Burke and the Duke of Wellington would be the two most formidable competitors. But the great Duke is, in mathematical phrase, incommensurable with O'Connell. There are no known terms which will enable us to pit the military faculty against the genius of civil affairs. If we take that genius alone into view, it can hardly be doubted that O'Connell is the greater man. With respect to Burke, it seems safe to say that, if far greater than O'Connell in the world of thought, he was far inferior to him in the world of action."

It is time, however, that I should turn to the article in the same magazine from Sir William Gregory's pen, which appeared three months later than that of Mr Gladstone from which I have just quoted. Sir William begins by telling us that he was brought up from a child in the society of Dublin Castle, in which his grandfather, also named Sir William Gregory, was one of the most prominent and quite the most durable of officials. " He was Under Secretary for Ireland," writes his grandson, "from 1813 to 1831, when he retired with a pension and with the distinction of Privy Councillor." During that long period he enjoyed the confidence of all the Chief Secretaries and LordLieutenants who ruled Ireland in succession; and his great experience of the country gave him unusual influence. " It was said of him, and with truth, that ' Gregory was the dry-nurse of young English statesmen.' Although I was but a small boy at the time to which I now refer, I well remember many of the guests who frequented my grandfather's dinner - table, for his house was hospitable and his Sneyd's claret of the best. I have the liveliest recollection of the style of conversation, of the profound distrust and hatred of the Roman Catholic religion, and of the chorus of invective against O'Connell, whom I was taught to regard as an incarnation of the principle of evil."

In 1842 Mr West, the Conservative member for Dublin, died suddenly, and young Mr William Gregory, whose father, Mr Robert Gregory, was then dead, was invited to stand in opposition to Lord Morpeth, who was vigorously supported by O'Connell. It would have been difficult for a young man not yet twenty-five to encounter a more formidable opponent. Lord Morpeth had recently been Chief Secretary for Ireland, and a more amiable, blameless, and respected statesman it would have been impossible to name. He was travelling in America when Mr West died, and had lost his seat for the West Riding not long before. His absence from the House of Commons was universally regarded as a national loss. More-

HIS CONTEST FOR DUBLIN. 3 "71

over, the seat for Dublin was of no slight importance, and the Whigs were extremely eager to wrest it from the Tories.

The description of the contest is given in Sir William Gregory's best manner. " At last," he writes, " came the nomination day|one of deep apprehension to me; for I had to meet the greatest orator of his time. O'Connell Avas then Lord Mayor of Dublin, and by him Lord Morpeth was seconded. The Liberator's speech, though severe on me as a Protestant, was by no means abusive." Sir William replied in what he calls " the best speech of his life." He indignantly denied that his voice had ever mingled in the cry, "To hell with the Pope !" or that he had any sympathy with that sentiment. When he sat down, O'Connell was so pleased with the plucky way in which his youthful antagonist had stood up to him that he exclaimed, " Young man, may I shake you by the hand ? Your speech has so gratified me that if you will but whisper ' Repeal'|only whisper it, mind you|Daniel O'Connell will be the first man at the polling booth to vote for you to-morrow." The mystic word was not whispered or uttered, but from that time forward O'Connell and Sir William were always the best of friends, though divided in age by forty-two years, as O'Connell was born in 1775 and Sir William in 1817. Sir William was returned by a triumphant majority, and after the close of the first day's poll he received the following letter, addressed to him at Dublin, from Lord George Bentinck, who, even at that early stage, did not hesitate to add " M.P." to his friend's name :|

"To W. H. Gregory, Esq., M.P.

" Welbeck, *nr.* Worksop, Notts, *Jan.* 29, 1842.

" My Dear Sir,|The news of your majority on the first day's poll gave every English Conservative, and me especially, the greatest pleasure. I sincerely congratulate you upon it, but still more upon the distinguished fight you made upon the hustings against the great O'Connell. Even the Whigs here have had to acknowledge their admiration of your speech.

" I need not say that I anticipate no reverse on the poll. I doubt not that you will maintain, and even improve, the strong lead you have taken ; but should it be otherwise, I cannot but congratulate you on the compleat *[sic]* triumph of tallents *[sic]* evinced in your first day's battle on the hustings. Verily if the horse Auckland can do as much with the old ones in private as ' the tipsy boy from the Curragh' has done with the great Agitator in publick, he will win the Derby in a canter.

" With sincerest wishes for your continued success, believe me, always yours very truly,

" G. Bentinck."

FRIENDSHIP WITH LORD GEORGE BENTINCK. 373

Commenting upon this letter, which Sir William sent to me on January 12, 1892, he writes thus:|

"3 St George's Place,

Hyde Park Corner, S.W.

" I was looking over some stray papers here lately, and found the enclosed from Lord George Bentinck. It is one of the earliest of his letters to me, and refers to the Dublin election of 1842. Before long we became intimate and attached friends. In those days I was constantly at Har- court House, and, I may say, enjoyed Lord George's entire confidence, which was of course broken up by the repeal of the Corn Laws, when I followed Sir Robert Peel. Mark the old-fashioned spelling of Lord George's letter|just like that of Dr Johnson and Mr Pittl*e.g.,* ' publick,' ' compleat,' ' tallents,' &c. He used always to speak of ' a dish of tea,' and pronounced Rome ' Room,' wonder ' woonder,' and golden ' goulden.'

" The allusion to ' the tipsy boy from the Curragh' was quoted from a Dublin paper, and referred to a great dinner at which I and my supporters had as much on board as we could carry, but did nothing untoward. At that time I had never seen the Curragh in my life."

It will readily be understood that the political harmony between Lord George and Sir William Gregory was cemented and intensified by theircommon passion for the Turf. Lord George was fifteen years older than his Irish friend, and both had commenced their racing careers at the earliest possible moment. Sir William was not yet twenty- two, as I have already said, when, accompanied by the late Earl of Winchilsea and other undergraduates, he rode, in 1839, on a series of hacks, strewn along the road, from Christ Church to Epsom and back, to see the Derby won by Mi-William Pudsdale's Bloomsbury, an outsider who started at 30 to 1. Sir William's own fancy for the race was in favour of Mr Fulwer Craven's Deception, by Defencela beautiful mare, who started at 12 to 1, and was brought to the post in first-rate condition by William Treen, who rode and trained her. The " tip " to back Deception was given to Sir William by his old friend, the late Mr Jeremiah Robert Ives, whom all who were well acquainted with him agreed in regarding as the cleverest judge of racing and of its human supporters that they had known in their time. For many years Mr Ives wrote the sporting letters which appeared above the name of "Judex" in ' The Morning Post'; and the late Earl of Straf- ford, who knew him intimately, used to aver that, had Mr Ives entered Parliament as a young man, he would inevitably have been selected to fill the post of Chancellor of the Exchequer before he was fifty years old.

The result of Sir William's hurried visit to

HIS FIRST PURCHASES. 375

Epsom in 1839 was that he forthwith gave instructions to Treen to purchase for him some yearlings, one of whichlBarricade, by Defencel started a good favourite for the Oaks, and ran third. It may not be an inappropriate moment to quote the following letter, which I received from Sir William on the death of his old trainer, William Treen, which took place in January 1879 :I

" Coole Park, Gort, Co. Galway, *Jan.* 13, 1879.

" I shall be in London on Thursday next, and will then tell you more about old Treen. He hailed from Devonshire, and was brought up at Danebury. At first he trained a few horses for local races in Devonshire, and then took the Beck- hampton Inn on the road between Marlborough and Devizes, where he trained Fulwer Craven's celebrated mare Deception, who soon brought him into notice. Lord George Bentinck thought that Treen's bad riding on Deception lost her the Derby ; but good as she was, public opinion at the time favoured the belief that Bloomsbury had a year in hand.

" This was the first race I ever saw, having ridden from Oxford by relays of hacks to see it, and I was back long before the closing of ' Tom Gate' at Christ Church. So pleased was I with Treen that I bought the following horses and sent them to him to train I viz., FitzRoy and Fitzambo ; Barricade, the best two - year - old that I ever saw tried, and about the worst three-year- old ; Vitellius, a first - class horse, who won the Northamptonshire Stakes in a canter, and beat St Lawrence next day for the Queen's Plate with equal ease. Soon after came Rhesus, a most unfortunate horse, who resembled General Chasse", seeing that neither of them could be ridden or done justice to by a boy. Rhesus, however, was the best three-year-old ever trained by Treen, and twelve pounds better than Loupgarou. Clermont was pretty good, and, as you know, a lucky horse to me. In 1855 I sold all my horses, and Treen's luck left him. At a later date he won the Cesare- witch with Hartington, and, I think, the Chester Cup for Fred Swindell with that very good horse Leamington, who has done so much good to the American Turf. Being owed a great deal of money by some of his recent masters, poor Treen was ruined, and went out to Bangalore on my recommendation to take charge of the stud of thoroughbreds belonging to Mr Downall, a Devonshire gentleman, who had made a large fortune as a coffee-planter in Ceylon.

" It was a fortunate connection for Treen, although his health suffered not a little from the climate of India, whence he returned to England before his new master, who, however, did not forget him. Upon arriving in England, Treen again took to training, but accomplished nothing

TREEN THE TRAINER. 377

worthy of special notice. When Mr Downall came back from Ceylon, and made his home permanently in England, he kindly provided a harbour of refuge for Treen, where the old man, whose experience had been longer and more diversified than that of most of his training brethren, settled down quietly with sufficient employment to amuse him in looking after Mr Downall's hunting stud. To the last, not unmindful of Vitellius, Clermont, Loupgarou, and Windischgriitz, he did not despair of bringing oft1 another *coup.* Fate, however, decreed otherwise, as he died last week after a few hours' illness. He was a remarkably well - conducted and civil man, who never got drunk, never swore, and never took liberties with his employers. Few of his craft have gone before him to the silent land with a more satisfactory record."

I have often regretted that Sir William Gregory, who knew the Turf and all its intricacies as well as Sir Walter Scott's "William of Deloraine" knew the passes and fords of the Scottish Border, could never be prevailed upon to write a history of the " Sport of Kings," to which he was as attached in theory during his declining years as he had been in practice during his vigorous youth. He was the only man of my acquaintance possessed of the literary ability, and also of the keen insight into character, requisite to enable him to draw correct pen-portraits of heroes of the Turf who to the present generation are mere *nominis umbra.* Such patrons of horse-racing as Lord George Bentinck, John Bowes, Fulwer Craven, Squire Osbaldeston, Sir William Massey-Stanley, the fourth Duke of Grafton, the old Duke of Rutland, Mr Sloane Stanley, and others, who were prominent at Newmarket shortly after her Majesty's accession to the throne, would now be alive and " palpitating with actuality " if Sir William Gregory could have been induced to trace their histories. During the last thirty years of his life, however, politics, literature, and art, engaged his attention to such a degree that, beyond writing a private autobiography for the amusement and instruction of his own family, he had no time or inclination for composing a work *de longue haleine* on the pursuits of his youth. Sir William had also remarked that writers who undertake to recall the past are often accused, and nearly always falsely, of a secret desire to blacken contemporaries and friends who have passed away. Be this, however, as it may, he died and left no sign. All that remains, therefore, is to " put together a thing of shreds and patches " from the letters which he has left behind, and from memories of conversations to which he contributed the larger share. Few men ever lived whose experience was more diversified. Like his Irish compatriots, he was a man of quick and ready sympathies, to whom *quicquid agunt*

HIS REMINISCENCES. 379

homines was full of interest. He had known everybody, both male and female, who was anybody for the last fifty-five or sixty years ; for even as a Harrow boy he was intimate with illustrious Harrovians like Sir Robert Peel, Lord Palmerston, Lord Aberdeen, and Sir James Graham. In the belief that a few extracts from his letters, and from notes of his conversations made at the time of their occurrence, will place him before his contemporaries in a truer position than, from his tendency to shrink modestly into private life, he now occupies, I am tempted, with Sir William's own concurrence, to add these two chapters to a work of which Lord George Bentinck is the hero la work of which Sir William was cognisant, and upon which, so far as he was acquainted with it, he was so good as to bestow his approval. Let me begin by quoting the following description from his pen of the universally popular Earl of Eglinton (the owner of Van Tromp and the Flying Dutchman), whom Sir William and his still living friend and contemporary, Chief-Justice Morris, regarded as the best Irish Viceroy that they had ever known.

THE THIRTEENTH EARL OF EGLINTON.

" When first I visited Eglinton Castle, not long after the celebrated tournament, which was completely marred by incessant torrents of rain, theparties assembled there were more renowned for freedom of manners than for feast of reason and flow of soul. Lord Eglinton never drank any wine except champagne, which he consumed in abundance *ab ovo usque ad mala*lthat is to say, from the beginning of the first course at dinner until the end of dessert. I remember to have been present at dinner one evening at the Jockey Club Rooms at Newmarket, and to have heard Lord Eglinton declare that he could drink more champagne without inconvenience than any other man in the United Kingdom. General Peel, always full of fun and ready for every kind of frolic, avowed that he knew a novice whom he would produce next day at dinner, and would back for a pony to drink more champagne than the Scotch Earl, if the latter would accept the challenge. Nothing loath, Lord Eglinton took up the glove, and next day at 7.30 P.m. in walked General Peel, accompanied by a tall, thin, wiry, long-legged customer, who looked for all the world like a pair of elongated tongs. ' Let me introduce you to my brother-in-law, Sir David Baird,' exclaimed the General. Most of the guests, who were about to dine, did not know Sir David by sight; others had heard of his feats across country, and some two or three were aware of his prowess at the dinner-table. Few, however, anticipated that the owner of the invincible Dutchman would have to lower his colours that night to his brother Scot.

BOTTLE FOE BOTTLE. 381

The match was to be bottle against bottlelthat is to say, when one man's bottle was empty, the other was required to finish his, and then each had to begin a new one. Lord Eglinton took the lead at a tremendous pace, hoping to choke his antagonist before the first three bottles were consumed. Simultaneously he kept on chatting merrily, and laughing, as was his wont, while the novice held his peace, but stuck steadfastly to his task. Soon the ominous silence preserved by the latter, and the perfect ease with which he held his own, ' without turning a hair,' began to tell upon his more loquacious antagonist, who was evidently going in difficulty.

" At last Lord Eglinton turned as pale as death, and rose slowly from his chair, exclaiming, ' I can do no more.' The struggle was at an end, and the defeated champion retired to bed, while the novice played billiards with Osbaldeston, winning two games out of three against that accomplished player. Next morning I had occasion to be out early on horseback in order to see one of my two- year-olds gallop. The first sight that met my eyes on the Heath was Sir David Baird, with a short black pipe full of cavendish between his lips, cantering about the course on a hard-pulling hack, with his face as stolid as usual, and with obviously unclouded brow. Meantime, the unhappy Eglinton was walking about in front of The Rooms without his hat, which he confessed was too heavy for his poor head. Let no one suppose, however, that Lord Eglinton was merely a guzzler of champagne, and an idle man of pleasure. In general, he was a man who gave way to no excesses. Not endowed with brilliant talents, he was gifted with strong natural good sense and good-humour, and was a first-rate man of business; as true as steel to his friends and dependants, and of unimpeachable honour. When he became Lord Lieutenant of Ireland, endless were the sneers of his political opponents that the business of the Emerald Isle would be conducted mainly on the Curragh of Kildare, and that his privy councillors would be horse-trainers. Never was there a greater mistake. Lord Eglinton came to Ireland with heavy odds against him. To begin with, he was a Scotsman ; secondly, he was a Tory, and supposed to entertain the most hostile and uncongenial views about the Roman Catholic religion. In an incredibly short time these erroneous impressions were dispelled. Turning his eyes away from abstract politics, he devoted his attention earnestly to the material improvement of Ireland. Moreover, it soon became known that he was animated by the most generous and kindly feelings towards the distressful country which he had been sent to govern, and towards its warm-hearted inhabitants; and that he would never rest until he could make his views prevail with the masters of the English Treasury. He

RECOLLECTIONS OF NEWMARKET. 383

took up the postal contract between Galway and America, and -used all his influence to make that ill-omened undertaking a success. Unfortunately, it never had a chance, having always been under the control of needy adventurers. Still, Lord Eglinton's action in this and in other matters was never forgotten in Ireland, and he undoubtedly left that country the most popular Lord Lieutenant that any Irishman could remember, while in Galway he was simply worshipped. Had he lived, he would, in my opinion, have risen to no ordinary eminence in the Conservative party."

My next extract is from a letter dated " Athenaeum Club, Pall Mall," bearing the date June 7th 1885. I had asked Sir William for some details of Newmarket in his early days, and he replied in the following terms :I

" If ever you have occasion to deal with Nat, or Captain Tommy Gardner, pray remember that they, General Peel, and I formed a band of devoted rat-hunters, who betook themselves, after the races, to their favourite pastime on a fine evening during the July or First October meetings. Our *champ de bataille* was generally some oat-stacks scattered here and there just outside the little town, on the Cheveley estate, which belonged to the Duke of Rutland. As evening began to fall, Nat, the famous jockey, would ride up to Peel, and touching his cap, would remark, ' We shall have a sure find to-night, Colonel, if convenient to you to come.' Not much difficulty was generally experienced about getting ' the Colonel' and all of us to acquiesce. Accompanied by a professional ratcatcher, plentifully supplied with ferrets, and with several terriers at his heels, Nat led the way. Scarcely were the ferrets turned into the ricks before the rats came tumbling out, and men and dogs were soon engaged in hot pursuit. One afternoon Tommy Gardnor was standing underneath the rick with his mouth wide open, when a huge rat jumped down, and fell upon the gaping orifice. ' Bless my soul, Captain,' exclaimed Nat, ' I thought it was old Squire Thornhill jumping down your throat!' After dinner we used to recount our exploits to the old Duke of Rutland, whom Colonel Peel treated with a mock gravity which it was impossible to witness without a painful effort to repress one's own laughter. His Grace took much interest in our sport, exclaiming, ' I am deeply indebted to you, gentlemen, and to Flatman, your fugleman, for extirpating the rats, which were destroying my ricks.' He would not, probably, have been so grateful had he been aware that one day I asked Nat how he found out the stacks which were most infested with vermin. ' Between you and me, sir,' he replied, ' there is not much difficulty about it. After the Second Spring Meeting I turn down a few rats to stockLord Howth's Horses. 385 a rick with, and by the First October, if not by the July Meeting, they are quite ready to be drawn.'"

When Sir William Gregory was in his prime, one of the most successful racing men of the day, and certainly one of the finest judges of the noble animal, was his compatriot the late Earl of Howth. The latter trained with the Days at Danebury, and was always on the look-out for Irish horses, which he bought for, or shared with, his trusted advisers in racing matters, Messrs Gully and Harry Hill. In this way Danebury became possessed of St Lawrence, Peep-o'-Day Boy, and Mincepie, who won the Oaks. Speaking of Lord Howth's race-horses, Sir William remarks :|

" I cannot remember anything of much importance except the stupor and surprise of Danebury when my horse, Vitellius bought by me as a three- year-old for $250, ran away as a four-year-old from St Lawrence, then one of the best horses in England, for the Queen's Plate at Northampton. The betting opened at 4 to 1 on St Lawrence, and ended by my taking 2 to I to all the money that I could get on. This was the great performance of ' Treen's ugly customer,' as Vitellius was called, because of his fiddle-head, lop ears, and ewe-neck. Well do I remember the caricature of old Drinkald .riding St Lawrence for the Chester Cup againstGully on the back of Mendicant. The latter exclaims, with his arms and legs hard at work|' It's all over, mend I can't!' As he speaks, Drinky's horse forges ahead, and keeps sturdily in front. In connection with Howth, and his beautiful home, Howth Castle, I shall never forget the delightful dinners there, at which I met the pleasantest men in Ireland : Sir Philip Crampton, Chief-Justice Doherty, Corry Connellan, Lord Clanricarde, and his son, Lord Dunkellin. The dining-room was quite unique, and I do not hesitate to say, the most charming in the world. It was lined with polished oak, quite black with age, while the vast fireplace yawned like Virgil's gateway of Erebus; and the brazen dogs, across which logs of Irish bog-wood were stretched, would have wrung tears of joy from Sir Walter Scott. The claret, for which, ever since the days of Mary Queen of Scots, Ireland and her sister realm of Scotland have been famous, was unparalleled in smoothness and flavour. You have doubtless heard the legend which connects the celebrated Grana Uile, or Grannwail, better known as ' Grace O'Malley,' with Howth Castle. This Irish queen lived at a castle near Renvyle, in Co. Galway, the ruins of which are still tolerably well preserved. She invited her sister queen, Elizabeth of England, to pay her a visit at her Irish home. The proud daughter of Henry VIII. and Anne Boleyn was, however, an extremely bad sailor, and had the greatest dread

TUEF ROBBERIES. 387

of physical pain. She declined to cross the ocean, and Grana Uile was constrained to visit England, and repair to Windsor. On her return to Ireland, she landed at the base of Howth Castle, and proceeded to the gates thereof, which she found closed, as was the family custom at dinner-time. Indignant at the want of hospitality, she seized the young heir of the St Lawrence family, who was playing outside the castle gates, and embarking on board her ship, carried him prisoner to her castle in Galway. He was not released until after long negotiation, and only on condition that, for all future time, the castle gates at Howth should be kept open when the family went to dinner, and that a cover should be laid for any stranger who might chance to arrive. The custom was still observed when I was last at Howth."

Sir William Gregory's early recollections of the Turf ran back to the days when most of the heavy betting races were settled beforehand, as it was called, " by arrangement." Never, except perhaps in the case of General Peel, was there an owner of horses who could recount more stories of Turf robberies, by some of which he had himself suffered, than Sir William Gregory. One of the most famous he had received from Mr George Payne. It is well known that, at the instance of Mr John Gully, Mr Payne laid heavily against Mr Gascoigne's Jerry, who won the Doncaster StLeger in 1824. The horse was trained at Middle- ham by Croft, the most famous trainer of that day, from whom John and Bill Scott learnt the rudiments of what they knew (and no men knew more) about the management of thoroughbreds. Jerry had been tried so highly that Croft thought it impossible for him to be defeated for the St Leger. Nevertheless, the market showed clearly that there was a screw loose somewhere. Despite the thousands upon thousands of pounds for which he was backed, he kept continually receding in the betting. In those days the St Leger favourites arrived at Doncaster three or four weeks before the greatest of Yorkshire races came off; and Croft was distracted with anxiety to account for the hostility to his horse which prevailed universally. As the race drew near his anxiety increased, and one night he found himself unable to sleep, and walked out shortly before midnight along the Great North Road in the direction of York. As he approached the turnpike-gate which lies a short distance to the north of Doncaster, a post-chaise drawn by four horses drew near from the other side. Ensconcing himself within the shadow of a stable doorway, Croft awaited the chaise, taking stock eagerly of its occupants. Two men were seated inside, the first being Bob Rids- dale, then the confederate of John Gully, and the second Harry Edwards, the jockey who was engaged to ride Jerry. " I have it now," ejacu-

Jerry's St Leger. 389

lated Croft with intense satisfaction, as he returned home, and slept the sleep of the just. In the morning he communicated his discovery to Mr Gascoigne, bidding him keep the secret to himself. The result is well known. At the last moment a fresh jockey, Ben Smith, was substituted for Harry Edwards, and in his new pilot's hands Jerry won in a canter.

The second heat of the above story must now be told in Sir William Gregory's own words :|

" After Jerry had won the St Leger, Gully took George Payne behind the stand next day, and said, ' I am very sorry, Mr Payne, for what has occurred ; but we were entirely deceived. I heard from what I thought the best authority that Jerry was infirm, and doing no work whatever.' ' But,' rejoined Mr Payne, ' Jerry's owner, and his owner's friends, never ceased backing him, and his trainer gave them the most encouraging reports.' ' That is true,' replied Gully; ' but I had the fullest reason to believe that

Croft was having a race for himself. It was a trap laid for me, into which I fell, and unfortunately led you to follow me. But now mark my words; if you will be guided by my advice, you will get all your money back this time next year. You saw Mr Watt's Memnon win The Champagne the day before yesterday. He is quite certain to win the next St Leger, if well on the day.' ' That was nice consolation,' addedPayne, ' for a young fellow who had to pay $24,000 next day; but I took his advice all the same, and got back $12,000 when Memnon won the St Leger in 1825.' ' But how did you get the money for the settling day after Jerry's easy victory ?' ' Oh ! that was all right,' he exclaimed. ' In those days I always posted down to Doncaster with a money- lending fellow of the name of Hitchcock. Until the St Leger was over nothing was good enough for him. ' Hitchcock, let me give you some more venison - fat ;' ' Waiter, bring a bottle of that champagne which Mr Hitchcock liked last year;' ' Hitchcock, I have kept a fine fat partridge specially for you ; let me give you the breast!' It was lovely to watch him writing cheques, like a lamb, when things went wrong. But if the St Leger came off all right, and no money was wanted, the devil a bit of venison-fat did he get, or anything else, except the partridge drumsticks.'

" I could tell you dozens of stories of which Payne was the hero. Nothing was more droll than his management of Charles Greville, his life-long confederate. Do you remember our. old friend Drumlanrig executing a heavy commission for Greville on Adine for the Goodwood Stakes, which she won very easily ? Next day Greville had a great pot, in Muscovite, for the Goodwood Cup, and thought, after Adine's victory on Wednesday, that Muscovite could not be beaten

LORD DRUMLAXRIG AND CHARLES GREVILLE. 391

on Thursday. The Muscovite commission, however, he kept secret from Drumlanrig, denying to him, when questioned, that he himself was backing that horse. Upon discovering the truth, Drumlanrig went up to Greville in great dudgeon, and told him his mind. He ended by throwing down the list of bets which he had taken for Greville about Adine, and told him to collect them for himself. Greville was in great perturbation about the affair, partly from consciousness that he had acted shabbily, and partly because he knew Drumlanrig to be one of the most courageous and impetuous of men. Several messengers were sent by Greville to Drumlanrig, but nothing would soften him ; and so Payne took him in hand.1 Approaching him with a *bonhomie* peculiarly his own, he said, ' Well, Drum, I hear that old Charles Greville has been doing by you what he sometimes does even by me, who am his confederate. At times I feel inclined to kick him round the course; especially so at this moment, when I have a bone to pick with him about a matter with which I need not trouble you.' Having thus spoken, away he went, and returned to the charge after a coupleof races had been run, exclaiming, ' Well, after all, Greville is very contrite for his misconduct to us both, and I have consented to forgive him. It all comes of illness: he has a terrible fit of gout coming on, which makes him miserable. Indeed I think it is through grizzling about you that the gout is sent to punish him. There he stands, dying to speak to you, but afraid to do so, knowing what kind of man you are. After all, there is not a warmer-hearted fellow in existence, but when his gout is coming on, he is not accountable for what he does.' At this explanation Drumlanrig was mollified; and Greville, having been beckoned to by Payne, hobbled up, shook hands, and was duly forgiven. How it would have ended had Muscovite won the Cup, instead of being almost last for it, I will not undertake to say."

1 Sir W. Gregory was not aware that Lord Drumlaiirig's resolve to horsewhip Mr Greville was abandoned, not in consequence of anything done or said by Mr George Payne, but at the earnest entreaty of two of Lord Drumlanrig's younger friends, who represented to him that it would be regarded as a cowardly act on his part were he, an accomplished " bruiser," to strike a man of Mr Greville's age, crippled by gout, and not of a very masculine type.

The letter upon which my eye happens next to fall bears the date of "Milan, October 15, 1885," and has reference to one of the most successful and least generally known patrons of the Turf that has existed in my time. I allude to Mr John Bowes, of Streatlam Castle, near Barnard Castle, in Durham, who won the Derby four times, and owned, in West Australian|the last of his four Derby winners|perhaps the best three-year-old ever known upon the English Turf. Such, at least, was the opinion of John Scott who trained, and of Frank Butler who rode, that wonderful son

JOHN BOWES. 393

of Melbourne and Mowerina, who was herself the daughter of Emma, the dam of Cotherstone. Sir William's letter was couched in the following terms:|

" I have just seen in the English and French papers an account of the death of my old friend John Bowes, with whom I was very intimate forty years ago. He was tall, slight, dark-haired, very refined, but very shy and very reserved. Most of his life was spent in Paris, where he devoted himself to a second - rate actress whom he married, and for whom he hired the Variety's Theatre, whereby he lost a lot of money. When Mundig won the Derby in 1835, Bowes, who won nearly $20,000 on the race, returned from Epsom quite unmoved. A friend of mine, long ago dead, happened to dine that same evening at Crock- ford's, and asked the waiter who that dark pale young man might be who was dining very quietly by himself in a corner of Crockford's superb *salle-a-manger.* ' Oh, sir,' replied the waiter, ' that is Mr Bowes who won the Derby this afternoon.' The same imperturbability was displayed by him at Doncaster, where, from the top of the Jockey Club Stand, he saw his fine colt, Epirus, driven on to the top of the bank on the other side of the course, where he fell, extinguishing his chance of winning a race which, with his fine speed and in very moderate company,it would have been impossible for him to lose. Bowes had a long telescope through which he watched the race, and was surrounded by people eager to know all that was going on. When the catastrophe occurred he shut up his telescope, merely remarking, ' My horse has fallen, and I think Bill Scott is killed.' As matters fell out, the famous White wall jockey got off with a broken collar-bone. I well remember Bowes calling to ask me to do a big commission for him about Cother- stone, another of his Derby winners. One morning, when I was still in my bedroom, my servant came in, announcing that Mr Bowes was below, and wanted to see me. The occurrence was so unusual that I made all haste to join him. As I entered the room, he apologised for troubling me at that unreasonably early hour, adding that he had come upon business, and that his colt, Cotherstone, had been highly tried, and would win the Derby, for which he was then at long odds|to wit, 40 to 1. He asked me to back the horse for $1000, and to put on something for myself. I made one stipulation|that there should be no other commission in the market|to which he promised faithfully to adhere. I returned him next day the odds of $23,000 to $1000. Some of the money was shaky in consequence of the liberties taken with the horse by a gang of nobblers, who thought they had the means of making him safe. When they failed in their nefarious efforts, through the preCotherstone's Derby. 395

cautions taken by John and Bill Scott under Colonel Anson's advice, there was a rush to hedge, and I obtained permission from Bowes to lay them back liberal odds; and, by taking good money instead at a lower price, I was enabled to hand Bowes $21,600 on the evening of the day of settlement. I shall not readily forget the tremendous excitement I experienced when Tom Dawson brought Lord Eglinton's fine colt, Pompey, to run for the Riddlesworth Stakes at Newmarket, full of confidence that he would beat Cotherstone. Many Yorkshiremen, and all the racing Scotsmen, piled their money upon Pompey. The race, however, never was in doubt, as Cotherstone pulled his way to the front, and won as he pleased. From that moment forward the Derby was a foregone conclusion, unless ill-health, accident, or foul play, got rid of Cotherstone. Nevertheless, there were many who could not get over his round hunting action, and vowed that unless the Derby were run up a staircase he would have no chance. George Bentinck was thoroughly convinced that Gaper, who had beaten Cotherstone for the Criterion Stakes at Newmarket when both were two-year-olds, would show his heels to the north-country crack in the Derby. Maidstone was also of the same opinion, and paid dearly for his mistake. I never saw a finer sight than Cotherstone presented as he mounted the hill, which exactly suited his high round action. Upon reaching Tattenham Corner, round which Gaper led, Cotber- stone seemed equally able to come down hill, and ended by winning without an effort."

Upon February 1, 1884, Sir William set forth in happy phrase his views as to Mr Charles Greville's capabilities to fill the *rdle* of a leading statesman, to which he always aspired. The opinion given below by Sir William Gregory was shared in a still higher degree by the late Sir Francis Doyle, who was in the habit of meeting Mr Greville annually for many years at Nun- appleton, the seat of Sir William Milner, from which they all repaired to York August Races. Here are Sir William's words :|

" Charles Greville could never have taken a prominent part as a political warrior. He had good sense, and sound views upon many subjects| witness his book on Ireland, which is very remarkable, considering how far advanced his opinions were beyond those in fashion at the time. I do not think he would ever have been a good speaker; certainly never a leader of men, even if he had enjoyed many years of parliamentary training. He was the worst adjuster of quarrels and what the Americans call " diffi-culties " that I ever came in contact with. In fact, paradoxical as it may seem, I never could regard him as what he most desired to be thought|a man of the world. This

FEED SWINDELL. 397

was also George Anson's opinion. The messes and mistakes in which he got himself entangled when trying his own horses were too comical, and used to elicit roars of laughter from Nat, his favourite jockey. I do not know which was the worse judge of racing | he or his confederate, George Payne."

The next two letters have reference to personal matters in which " The Pope," as he was universally called by his friends and contemporaries, took deep interest. Writing from Coole Park, Gort, on May 30, 1885, Sir William says:|

" The first that I heard as to the death of my old friend Fred Swindell, was from your article. A young lady whose father lives close to this place, and takes in the , told me there was something in that paper about myself and a very rich betting-man who had just died. Fred Swindell was the most remarkable man of his class that I ever met. He was, of course, remarkable for ability, but still more so for kindness of heart. Speaking from much experience, I can say unhesitatingly that he was as true as steel to those who trusted him in their racing transactions. As for his drollery, wit, and power of graphic description, they rendered an evening passed in his company something never to be forgotten. His stories of Palmer the poisoner were droll to a degree, but occasionally terrifying ; nor shall I forget his lookwhen he asked me at Egham Races whether that was not the place where the field beat King John. You dwell rightly upon one remarkable trait in his character|to wit, that all his sympathies were with the gentlemen. Nothing pleased him more than when they had a good race. His reflections on the use of the Turf to British society, as a safety-valve for the lower orders, were excellent, and full of wisdom."

The second letter to which I have alluded above has reference to the authorship of ' The Chaunt of Achilles,' which was published anonymously in 'The Sporting Magazine' in 1838, shortly after her Majesty's Coronation.

" I have in my possession," writes Sir William, "a copy of 'The Chaunt of Achilles,' with the inscription, ' By Bernal Osborne, Jun.,' written on its back. Below are the words, ' Got fifteen guineas from Editor for this.' I am convinced from internal evidence that no one but a member of West-End society could have written it. It is impossible that Surtees, a north-country attorney, could have known all the gossip to which it refers. The style, moreover, in which it is written affords another proof of its authorship, for the versification is exactly similar to that of ' The Voice from Palace Yard,' which is admittedly Bernal Osborne's composition."

GENERAL PEEL. 399

With one final extract from a letter bearing the date of " 3 St George's Place, Hyde Park Corner, S.W., November 25, 1889," I will conclude a chapter which is, I fear, already too long. Speaking of General Peel's boundless store of amusing anecdotes, Sir William remarks :|

" Well do I remember the dear old General's stories; and I ought to remember them, for I heard them often, and they were as good the twentieth time of hearing as the first, because of the undisguised enjoyment with which he brought them out. I shall never forget driving down with him and Lord Eglinton to Gorhambury Races, and to what extent the Colonel's programme (he was then Colonel Peel) was flavoured by Eglinton's *faceticB*, and by the irrepressible peals of laughter with which we made the lanes of Hertfordshire echo again and again."

18

SECTION 18

400

CHAPTER XVIII.

RACING CAREER OF THE LATE RIGHT HOX.

Sir w. H. Gregory|*continued.*

I NOW approach that portion of my task which brings Sir William Gregory into closer communication than ever with Lord George Bentinck. The two famous passages of Lord George's history which it becomes my duty to treat are, in the first place, his duel with Squire Osbaldeston ; and secondly, his hurried journey to the Curragh of Kildare to ascertain from Mr Thomas Ferguson, the owner of the celebrated horse Harkaway, some details about the animal purchased in Ireland by Goodman Levy, and substituted for Running Rein. Other letters of Lord George to Sir William will find a place in this chapter, some of which go far to confirm Mr John Kent's view of his noble master's character. The light thus shed upon Lord George's life will be welcomed by all who recognise in him the strongest and most conspicuous Patron of the Turf that these islands have produced during the present century.

LORD GEORGE BENTINCK AND COLONEL ANSON. 401

I shall begin with Sir William Gregory's narrative, partly taken down from his own lips, and partly confirmed by letters now in my possession touching the famous duel between Lord George and Squire Osbaldeston in 1836. It should be premised that the account usually given of the encounter in question differs in many particulars from the more veracious record supplied by Sir William Gregory. It was well known to their contemporaries and friends that the greatest possible intimacy subsisted between Lord George Bentinck and Colonel Anson. Their friendship was doubtless increased by the fact that, in Lord George's opinion, Colonel Anson had saved his life when subjected to the fire of one of the finest pistol- shots in the world. Some years later, Colonel Anson did his utmost to heal the differences which had long existed between those two masterful first cousins, Lord George and Mr Charles Greville, who, after being racing confederates in youth, became bitterly estranged when they quarrelled about Preserve, whose running has been described in a previous chapter. Colonel Anson obtained from Lord George Bentinck a promise that he would meet and shake hands with Mr Greville after a certain race at Goodwood in 1843. Mr Greville had long been eager for a reconciliation, and when the race in question was over, he lost not a moment in repairing to the tryst named by Colonel Anson, who had addressed himself to the far more difficulttask of bringing Lord George to the same spot. Unfortunately, all his well-meant efforts proved to be futile. Accompanied by Colonel Anson, Lord George drew near, when, catching sight of Mr Greville, his old antipathy to his cousin burst out with renewed vigour. He declined to advance another step, exclaiming to his companion, "After all, I would rather have nothing to do with the fellow!" Against this decision all Colonel Anson's entreaties and arguments were powerless to prevail.

The remarkable duel between Lord George and " the Squire" created the greatest sensation at the time of its occurrence. The popular account is that Lord George fired first and missed. Upon that he is represented to have called out to Mr Osbaldeston in a loud voice, " Now, Squire, the odds are ten to one upon you." No one acquainted with Lord George's aristocratic pride, of which he speaks in a letter to Sir W. Gregory,1 will be likely to believe it possible that under such circumstances he would use language of this kind to an adversary whom he profoundly despised. I am indebted to Sir William for the version which now follows, and its authenticity is confirmed in other quarters. It agrees substantially with an account of the duel which I contributed seven years ago to ' The Sporting Times/ and whicn was read by Sir William Gregory with much satisfaction.

1 See p. 412.

HISTORY OF A FAMOUS DUEL. 403

The Heaton Park Meeting of September 1835, took place, as usual, immediately after the Doncas- ter St Leger. The riders were mostly gentlemen jockeys, who, however, were divided into two classes, of which the first and most aristocratic were Lord Wilton's guests, and the second found quarters at Manchester, within four miles of Lord Wilton's seat. To the latter section Mr Osbaldeston belonged. In common with many others, he had long harboured a shrewd suspicion that the handicaps were generally framed upon terms exceptionally favourable to Lord Wilton and his friends. Resolved to be revenged, and to strike a blow at the aristocratic monopolists, the Squire looked about for a horse likely to suit his purpose. He found one in a four- year-old Irish colt named Rush, by Humphrey Clinker, whom he purchased at Doncaster from his breeder, Mr Watts, for 400 guineas. The Squire tried his new purchase with a mare belonging to old Job Marson over the St Leger course at Don- caster, riding Rush himself. As they rounded the Red House Turn the Squire found that he could do what he liked with his antagonist, and promptly checking Rush, allowed the mare to gallop in first by many lengths. The result of the trial got noised abroad, and, in consequence of his supposed defeat, Rush was very favourably handicapped for the Trial Stakes and Cup at Heaton Park. In the first of these two races he started, ridden by his owner, and finished nowhere. Nextday he was again pulled out for the Cup, and a heavy commission to back him was issued by Mr Osbaldeston. All the money betted against Rush at Lord Wilton's dinner-table upon the previous evening was secured by an agent of the Squire, and when the horses came to the post for the Cup, Rush, who had been backed for large sums, from 10 down to 2 to 1, started at the latter price. As Mr Osbaldeston, seated upon his horse's back, walked by the stand to go down to the starting- post, Lord George Bentinck cried out in a loud voice/'Two hundred to one against Rush." "Done," exclaimed Mr Osbaldeston; " put it down to me." Waiting upon Lord Wilton, who rode Bill Scott's mare, Lady le Gros (also a great pot), the Squire overhauled her at the distance, and coming away, won in a canter. Great was the hubbub that ensued, and Rush's sudden change of form was commented upon in very outspoken language, which was not a little increased and aggravated by his winning again upon the following day. Immediately after the latter race the Squire set off to go cub-hunting, and had no opportunity of asking Lord George for two hundred pounds until they both met at the Craven Meeting next year. The fact that his Lordship, who was usually the most punctual of settlers, had not discharged his debt for many months, gave some presage of the scene which was to follow.

Lord George was standing in front of the Jockey

HISTORY OF A FAMOUS DUEL. 405

Club rooms (arrayed in the green cutaway coat, doeskin breeches, and top-boots which he habitually wore at Newmarket), when Mr Osbaldeston saw and approached him. " My Lord," he exclaimed, somewhat curtly, " you have had plenty of time to digest your loss. May I ask you for the $200 which I won from you at Heaton Park ? " Drawing himself up to his full height, and towering over his puny interpellator, Lord George retorted " that he was astonished to be asked for the money, as the whole affair was a robbery, and so the Jockey Club considered it." Nothing daunted, Mr Osbaldeston answered firmly, " I won the money fairly, and I insist upon its payment." " Can you count ?" sneeringly asked Lord George, as he dived into the inside pocket of his coat, and pulled out a long black-leather case, which he always carried stuffed with bank-notes. " I could at Eton," sharply replied the Squire ; and the specified sum was slowly told out into his hand in small notes. " The matter will not end here, my Lord," exclaimed the Squire, as he marched off with his bristles set. Within a few minutes Mr Humphrey approached Lord George, and, lifting his hat, demanded, on the Squire's behalf, an ample apology, or that Lord George should at once give satisfaction to the man whom he had so grossly insulted. Lord George loftily declined to meet Mr Osbaldeston in the field; and upon receiving this disdainful answer, the latter said, " Tell Lord George thatI will pull his nose the first time we meet." Acting on the advice of Colonel Anson, who officiated as his second, the haughty patrician then resolved to swallow his pride, and to go out with his aggrieved foe. Wormwood

Scrubbs was named as the tryst; and at six o'clock, upon a lovely spring morning, the two combatants were drawn up, pistol in hand, at twelve paces from each other. It was a serious moment. Lord George had never had a pistol in his hand before, while his small and wiry antagonist had often killed birds on the wing with a pistol-ball. When shooting with Sir Richard Button, the Squire, moreover, had, not long before, killed ninety- eight pheasants out of one hundred shots, and at pigeons he had few superiors. Lord George was arrayed from top to toe in black, and not a speck of white was visible about him for his formidable enemy to aim at. The Squire had openly declared that he would kill him; and but for Colonel Anson's adroit management of the duel, it is but too probable that Lord George's mortal career would have ended that day upon Wormwood Scrubbs.

Approaching the two belligerents, Colonel Anson addressed them in a few emphatic words. " He told them that if the affair drifted into a law court, the verdict of the jury would turn chiefly upon his evidence, and that if either combatant disobeyed instructions, and chanced to kill his ad-

HISTORY OF A FAMOUS DUEL. 407

versary, the law would regard him as a murderer." The Colonel added, that he should give the word to fire by exclaiming, " One, two, three!" that each man was to fire directly " Three ! " was pronounced ; that until then they were to keep their eyes fixed upon him. If either man failed to fire instantly when " Three!" was said, the Colonel warned him solemnly to beware of the consequences.

Withdrawing for a few paces, Colonel Anson called out in a loud voice, " Gentlemen, are you ready ?" A couple of nods of the head indicated assent, and the word " One !" rang out with startling clearness. A long pause followed, and then, almost in the same breath, the Colonel vociferated, " Two, three ! " At the sound of the last word Lord George fired in the air, and Mr Osbaldeston was so hurried in his aim that his bullet went through his noble adversary's hat within a couple of inches of its wearer's hair. " I did not think you were so bad a shot, Squire," laughingly remarked the Colonel, overjoyed at the bloodless conclusion of an affair which had augured so ill for his principal. " It might have come off differently next time," growled out the Squire, who was well aware that Colonel Anson had saved his friend's life. For some years Lord George and Mr Osbaldeston never spoke. Then there came a time when Lord George, whose horses were trained at Danebury, wished to become a member of the Bibury Club, and old John Day tried his diplomacy upon the Squire to ascertain whether he would interfere with his former antagonist's election. All animosity, however, had long died away in the Squire's breast; and after Lord George's admission to the club, he invited the Squire to come and see the Danebury horses, and treated him with marked politeness.

The next episode in Lord George's career has reference to the most sensational trial ever yet embarked upon in connection with an English race. There has never been any dearth of floating rumours among old *habitues* of the Turf as regards the frequent occurrence of three-year-old races which have been fraudulently won without detection, though certainly not without suspicion, by four - year - olds and upwards. It is more than probable that in two or three instances, besides that of Running Rein, there is truth in these allegations or surmises. Into them, however, I have no intention to enter, as there is nothing to be gained by chronicling suspicions which cannot be substantiated. The "memorable Derby of 1844" possesses this rare peculiarity|that two horses started for it, each trained in a different stable, which were admittedly four-year-olds, and that one of them broke the other's leg in rounding Tattenham Corner, and ended by catching the Judge's eye as seeming winner of the race.

THE DEEBY OF 1844. 409

Scarcely had he done so before Lord George Bentinck advised Colonel Peel, the owner of Orlando, the second horse, to make an objection against the winner. In order to gain the evidence necessary to prove the fraud, of which Lord George felt sure that Mr A. Wood and his accomplice were guilty, he set out from London to interview Mr Thomas Ferguson at Rossmore Lodge, Curragh of Kildare. The following letter, written by a friend of Mr Ferguson, will speak for itself:|

" At the time when the Derby of 1844 was run I was on terms of the warmest friendship with ' Tom Ferguson,' of Rossmore Lodge, Curragh, who had no secrets from me. This fact was well known to one of Lord George Bentinck's most trusted commissioners, who upon the evening of the day on which Running Rein ran first for the Derby, came post-haste from Epsom to my house in London, and induced me to write to Ferguson, so as to obtain from him information with which he was acquainted as to the substitution for the Maccabeus colt of an Irish horse who, under the name of Running Rein, won the Derby in 1844. The commissioner in question stood to win a very large stake on Colonel Peel's Orlando, and promised me faithfully that he would put me on a large sum to nothing if I assisted in unveiling the fraud. In addition, he pledged me his most solemnword that Tom Ferguson's reply to my letter should be kept secret, and shown to no one.

" When Ferguson's letter reached me three or four days later, Lord George's commissioner was at my house expecting it. I, little knowing what sort of a man I was dealing with, was persuaded by him to let him have the letter, which he solemnly pledged himself to return to me the same evening. From that day forward I never again was in the same room with him, and never spoke to him again. His promises proved to be as faithless as he was himself, and whenever we were near each other on a race-course after the occurrence I am now reciting, he took very good care to get out of my way. Immediately upon leaving my house, the individual of whom I am now writing carried Ferguson's letter to Lord George Bentinck, who saw that the information contained in it would inevitably give the Derby stakes to Orlando. With characteristic energy Lord George started off without a moment's delay to Ireland, and on arriving at the Curragh found Tom Ferguson ill in bed with the gout. At first he refused to see his Lordship, but the latter sent up word that he had in his possession a letter written by Ferguson to myself. Seeing what a fix he was in, Ferguson determined to receive Lord George in his bedroom, and gave him all the information of which he was himself possessed."

The following letter from Lord George Bentinck

TE ABA WAY. 411

to Sir William Gregory shows that his Lordship had made other visits to Ireland previous to that of 1844. The letter is dated " Waterloo Hotel, Liverpool, August 6, 1841," and runs as follows :|

" In my vain and futile hurry last night to save a packet, whose inert captain had not vigour or energy enough to save the London train, which we lost by five minutes, I had not time to thank you sufficiently for the trouble you took for me, or the kindness you showed me. Nor had I time to give you more than half a report of what I saw and did at Rossmore Lodge. I found in Tearaway a fine, lengthy, racing-like animal, about fifteen three highlfine shoulders, fine length of body, good loins, good girth, and as fine hind-legs and hocks as could be put upon a horse ; but also a regular Blacklock head, Roman nose, and a small and soft rather than cowardly eye. His fore-legs are badly put on, with small and somewhat twisted fetlock-joints, and small narrow feet. I should add that he is wanting in bone and power as regards his legs, knees, and arms. Altogether I was disappointed with the horse; but Ferguson assures me that he can give the year and seven pounds to Johnny, which, if true, makes him a race-horse, in spite of his fore-legs. I went to the Curragh prepared to offer Ferguson a handsome moneyed rent for the horse, in addition to thewhole stake if he won the St Leger; but I was so far disappointed in the animal that I restricted myself to a single offer to take and train him, paying his stakes and forfeits, and giving Ferguson the St Leger if he won it, and twenty per cent of any other stakes he won.

" I left my terms in writing, and my impression is they will be accepted; but I could clearly see that Messrs Ferguson and Lea's object in wishing me to have the horse is to get him up to an eight to one favourite, so that they might make a good thing of their fifty to one bets; which made me less keen to have him.

" With regard to the two-year-olds, both are fine animalslFireaway bearing no resemblance to his half-brother Tearaway, but, on the contrary, with a beautiful head and fore-hand, and capital fore-legs. Goneaway is bigger than Fireaway, but looks heavy and slow.

" Harkaway is in training, and appears sound, but has the most frightful leg to look at you ever saw. After seeing the horses, Mr Ferguson showed me into his dining-room, where I beheld one of the finest Liffey salmon ever seen smoking on the table, besides various other good things, composing a dinner for three. But my aristocratick [sic] pride prevailed over the cravings of my belly, and I went hungry away, and sought refuge in the humbler and meaner fare at Harrington's of Naas.lAlways very sincerely yours, G. Bentinck."

s –' I

r?M

"A MANLY SPORTS BILL." 413

The above letter, of which I have quoted less than two-thirds, is so characteristic of Lord George that it will be read with interest by the few survivors who knew him in the flesh. Unfortunately the letter to Sir William about Running Rein's Derby, which the latter has often described to me as the most humorous that ever received from Lord George, cannot be found. It recorded, however, that after some little difficulty Lord George obtained from Mr Ferguson all the information that he needed to disqualify Running Rein for the Derby. The other details of the famous trial and of its result are too well known for repetition here.

Lord George's correspondence with Sir William throws a flood of light on the " Qui tarn " actions of 1843, and upon the extraordinary vigour with which the former combated the " common informers " by whom writs were served upon the Earl of Eglinton, Lord George Bentinck, John Bowes, George Anson, Jonathan Peel, Charles Greville, W. H. Gregory, John Gully, and others, under an old statute of Queen Anne, which was- construed into a legal prohibition of betting. These writs were met by " A Manly Sports Bill," introduced into the House of Lords on February 1, 1844, by the Duke of Richmond, and passed that session by both Houses. At a numerous meeting of the Jockey Club, held at Newmarket, on Tuesday, in the Second October Meeting 1845,it was resolved|" That the unanimous thanks of the Jockey Club be rendered to his Grace the Duke of Richmond, K.G., for his Grace's indefatigable exertions and eminent services in the House of Lords, whereby many obsolete statutes which threatened destruction to the best interests of the Turf have been repealed, and the remaining laws in regard to horse-racing put upon a safe and satisfactory footing." Of this salutary Bill Lord George was the principal instigator, and his letters to Sir William Gregory, from which I shall make two extracts, are full of interesting information. They show in the clearest light Lord George's masculine and fearless character, and also his profound sympathy with the sports of the people.

The first ran as follows :|

"harcourt House, Cavendish Square, *A7ov.* 17, 1843.

" Though I have no apprehension that these rascally informers will succeed in their suits, I cannot consider them otherwise than as serious. Construed as the Judges have heretofore construed the 9th of Queen Anne, there is no doubt but that betting on horse - races comes within the meaning of the Act. It is vain, therefore, to disguise from ourselves that these vagabonds have *primd facie* the law on their side. On ours we have the difficulty of proof, and the indisposition

TRIALS FOR BETTIXG. 415

of juries to give them a verdict. Even if the verdict went against us, such a decision would, I feel sure, be reversed on appeal to the House of Lords; for I defy any man, whose judgment has not been mystified by studying musty law, to rise from a perusal of the 9th of Queen Anne without being satisfied that betting on horse-races was not contemplated by the framers of that Act. . . . For all practical purposes you are as safe in coming over from Ireland now as you would be if you postponed their serving you with a writ until Parliament meets. The suit for the money you won on Cotherstone must be tried in Surrey, and cannot, therefore, come on till the end of March. The only thing I recommend you to do is to give Sir William Follett a general retainer, so as to keep him out of their hands. Thesiger, being leading counsel on the Surrey Circuit, should have a general retainer too. I have given retainers to the leading counsel on all the Circuits where the trials may come on. Eglinton, Bowes, and Jonathan Peel have done the same. From the heavy commission you executed for Bowes you stand in greater hazard than anybody, unless it be Eglinton, for his winnings on Blue Bonnet.

" Peel and Charles Greville are in no slight jeopardy from their notable trial about Canadian at Guildford, where Peel proved half the informer's case against himself and Charles Greville.|Yours very sincerely, G. Bentinck."

The second extract is from a letter dated|

" Harcourt House, *Jan.* 8, 1844.

" Our Bill is to be bold, manly, and straightforward, staying proceedings under the Queen Anne statute without costs, and legalising betting on horse - races, foot - races, sailing matches, cricket matches, coursing, and all other manly and wholesome sports. I cannot, therefore, see the necessity of you and Bowes skulking, you in Ireland and Bowes in Paris. You would both be of much more use here canvassing for support to our Bill, which, thus far, but for me, would have been left to its fate. As yet no satisfactory arrangement has been made as to the great expense already incurred, and as to how it is to be met.IYours very sincerely, G. Bentinck."

In these letters Lord George confirms the repeated views of his ardent and intense character given by Mr John Kent in the earlier chapters of this work. It remains for me to add a few further words about Sir William Gregory himself, and I will begin with the following brief account of the way in which he got possession of Clermont, perhaps his luckiest purchase. His version is as follows:I

"On the day following the Cesarewitch of 1845 I chanced to walk from my lodgings at Newmarket

CLEEMOXT. 417

to the Jockey Club Rooms, to breakfast there, 'as was my invariable habit. It was a wretched morning, and as I approached the Rooms I observed that old Richard Tattersall looked unusually 'downcast and damp,' as he stood in a sort of open box in the High Street, Newmarket, endeavouring to sell some blood stock. My eye caught sight of a scraggy-looking chestnut yearling, by Euclid, a horse of whom I was always fond. Turning to Tattersall as I passed, I exclaimed, pointing at the Euclid colt, ' If that lot goes cheap, buy him for me.' When I came out from breakfast I found that he had bought me the colt in question for the moderate sum of fifteen guineas. You know the rest of Clermont's history. He was a slow, moderate two-year-old, and the only man that ever tried to buy him at that age was your friend John Kent, who would have given a smart sum for him at Goodwood in 1846, had Treen, my trainer, been willing to accept his terms. In the winter I tried the horse to be a good fair stayer, and if the spring had been dry I fully believe that Clermont, as I subsequently called him, would have won four out of the five great handicaps in which I entered him. But he was a ten-pound worse horse in dirt than on the top of the ground, his weak twisted ankles disqualifying him from getting through mud. Fred Swindell won me a good stake on the Newmarket Handicap, and still moreon the Great Metropolitan; but I knocked down some of my winnings on the Somersetshire Stakes, at Bath, where the mud beat me. Moreover, Frank Butler's fine riding on Wolf Dog for the Northamptonshire Stakes was more than my little boy Treen could tackle, although with a little more experience he got the best of the great jockey at Epsom."

Fortunately for himself, as it has often been to many another ruined gambler, Sir William Gregory's active connection with the Turf as an owner of race-horses ceased for ever in the spring of 1855. His first step was to take a long cruise in the Mediterranean, with Sir Sandford Graham for his companion. At that time it appeared little probable that the most useful and blameless part of his life lay still before him. Financial disaster had, however, overtaken him when he was still young and full of energy. Under all circumstances and all conditions he never ceased to be an industrious worker; and his catholic taste for the classics, for literature of all kinds, and for art in particular, was well known to his many friends. None of them anticipated, however, that in the face of recent disasters his rehabilitation was so near at hand. The disruption of the Conservative party, consequent upon Sir Robert Peel's introduction of free trade in 1846, had emancipated Sir William Gregory from the ties of party;

. '-. .' V, ,;
' ' 1 r ...'... ..,,;' . I .- ?
. i . !('.! . !i - i-
'. ' it ;i ,c." !:';'
n-,..' ..' ! ! '..: .- . ; ... ; :
i:' .,:'.. i . ! i- -..-.::' .;. :- ,- .
(.', i i , '- , 'i . H'H i i' v.i- i . '
-.'. : .1 ".i I' 1!" '!.-
..::- I : : ;' 'n-.:i
1 " '.' ' . t '!iv i ' '- i ! ' – V'
„ ; (!' ,.' I i j.i,.i ;-l" , . i
! , 'i')l c.f '. (tii'il j" I: "!. Iii'.'I
l ii " ;11; : ': i.- ... .' ,

LORD GEORGE UEXTINCK.
APPOINTED GOVERNOR OF CEYLON. 419

but the dissolution of 1857, when Lord Palmerston went to the country about the Chinese lorcha, The Arrow, gave him an opportunity of returning to Parliament as Liberal member for his native county of Galway. His parliamentary career (or, at least, its second heat) continued until 1872, when, chiefly at the instance of Frances, Countess Waldegrave, then the wife of the still living Lord Carlingford, he was appointed Governor of the Crown Colony of Ceylon. Before dismissing his House of Commons " record," I should mention that during the Civil War between the Northern and Southern States of the American Union, Sir William Gregory, who had travelled in the winter of 1859-60 through the slave States, and had passed some weeks at Washington on his return from " Dixie," became a strong and able supporter of the Southern cause in Parliament.

Upon domestic subjects, especially upon those connected with Ireland, with the British Museum, the National Gallery, and matters of art and taste, he was a frequent speaker, and with such success that he was appointed a Trustee of the National Gallery by Mr Disraeli, and sworn as a member of the Privy Council for Ireland in 1871 under Mr Gladstone's First Administration. The culminating point of his career was, however, attained when, in 1872, Lord Kimberley, then Secretary of State for the Colonies, appointed him Governor of Ceylon. At last " the hour and the man had both come."It has often been remarked that the best Colonial Governors come from the Emerald Isle; and of those who have served her Majesty within my recollection, none was ever more successful than Sir William Gregory. A Crown Colony like Ceylon gives many chances to its Governor, if he has tact, capacity, and originality enough to seize and work them aright. It would be easy to write a volume on Sir William's five years in Ceylon. At this moment I have before me printed materials from which pages upon pages in approbation of his energy, foresight, breadth of view, and sagacity as an imperial administrator might be compiled. Upon one point I wish for a moment to dwell. No one who studies Sir William's policy in Ceylon can doubt that his nice discrimination of character, displayed both in England and in the East, was due to his long, critical, and painful experience upon the British Turf. Perhaps the most instructive book on Sir William's administration between 1872 and 1877, is Mr John Ferguson's 'Ceylon in the Jubilee Year,' published in 1887. From it I extract the following passages :|

" To Sir William Gregory belongs the distinction of having spent more revenue on reproductive public works than any other Governor of Ceylon. The roads in the north and east of the island, which were chiefly sand-tracks, were completed by him in a permanent form, and nearly every river was

HIS JUDICIOUS ADMINISTRATION. 421

bridged. The North-Central Province, a purely Sinhalese rice-growing division, was called into existence, and large amounts were invested in tanks and roads. About fifty miles were added to the railway system, and arrangements made for a further extension. When Governor Gregory left in 1877, a large extent of previously unoccupied country had been opened up, and an impetus given to natives and European colonists in the cultivation of new products, which alone saved the island from a serious collapse in the years of commercial depression and of coffee blight which followed. Measures were adopted for the conservation of forests, and for preventing the extinction of elk, deer, and elephants; the registration of titles was provided for; Colombo, Kandy, and Galle were much improved ; arrangements were made for a good water-supply to each town.

" Very early in his administration, Sir William Gregory, to his special credit be it said, saw the necessity for new products, and he used all his personal and official influence to secure their development, introducing a new feature into the Governor's annual speech to the Legislative Council in special notices of the progress of tea, cinchona, cacao, Liberian coffee, and rubber cultivation."

With one more passage from Mr Ferguson's book I will conclude these remarks.

" Ceylon wants a Governor like Sir H. Ward orSir William Gregory, who has his whole heart in his work; is ready to sympathise with all classes and races, to see provinces, districts, and public works for himselflby journeys on horseback, if necessary ; is open to receive counsel as to proposed legislation from the most diverse quarters, while deciding for himself after giving due consideration to such advice."

The result of all these beneficent operations was, that when the Prince of Wales visited Ceylon, Sir William Gregory received the honour of knighthood from his Royal Highness's hands ; and finally, a statue of the right honourable gentleman, from which the photograph opposite this page has been taken, testifies, as it stands in the market-place of Colombo, to the high regard and esteem of the population which he governed so well. Upon the pedestal the following inscription is carved :|

The Right Hosble.

SIR WILLIAM GREGORY, K.C.M.G.,

Governor Of Cetlox.

Erected by the inhabitants of this Island to commemorate the benefits conferred by him upon the Colony during his administration of the Government from 1872 to 1877.

After his return to England, Sir William married in 1880 Miss Augusta Persse, a young and much- esteemed lady who lived in the neighbourhood of Coole Park, Sir William's ancestral seat in Gal- way. Never was there a happier marriage. Lady

HIS DECLINING YEARS. 423

Gregory, who was Sir William's second wife, became at once a great favourite in London society, and her little *salon* at 3 St George's Place, Hyde Park Corner, soon became one of the most agreeable in London. During the concluding years of his life, offers from diverse constituencies, both English and Irish, poured in upon Sir William, but in vain. He was equally deaf to overtures made to him by Secretaries for the Colonies that he would accept another Governorship. Fond of society, an admirable diner-out, and blessed with an Irishman's high spirits, Sir William's declining years were undoubtedly the happiest that he ever passed. In 1884 he revisited Ceylon, accompanied by Lady Gregory, and the crowning honour of his life was the erection of the statue, from Sir Edgar Boehm's hand, to which I have above alluded. " Life to the last enjoyed," with memory, hearing, and eyesight unimpaired, full of years and honours, Sir William went to his well - earned rest without leaving an enemy behind him. During his last two winters, the cold of London tried him severely, and it was his intention to escape to a warmer climate, when death overtook him. The last letter that I ever received from him was couched in the following pathetic terms :|

" 3 St George's Place, Hyde Park Corser, S.W., *14th Feb.* 1892.

" I have to thank you for your review of Lord Rosebery's ' Pitt,' which is a fine biography, andthe style admirable. There are phrases and touches in it which are quite *sui generis,* and which send you on your way rejoicing. Among others, there is one which you notice and which struck me much : ' The instinct of self- preservation guides the European Powers with the same certainty as weather moves sheep on the hill.' Another remarkable expression is, ' Buckingham was his brother Grenville's hair-shirt.'

" On the whole, despite the delightful style, it is one of the saddest books I ever read. It is the struggle of the most noble-minded patriotic Englishman that ever lived to establish a wise fiscal policy, to abandon the old insane foreign entanglements, to pacify Ireland by wise and feasible measures, which would have rendered her a glory to England and no longer a shame to humanity. In all these aims he was arrested, thwarted, and beaten back by the powers of evil You should not have concluded your critique without quoting Rosebery's noble final sentence : ' From the dead eighteenth century Pitt's figure still faces us with a majesty of loneliness and courage. There may have been men abler and greater than helthough it is not easy to cite them. But in all history there is no more patriotic spirit, none more intrepid, none more pure.'

" I am as ill as a man can well be. I went to Bournemouth for ten days, but came back much as I went. The doctors are quite ' au bout de

HIS DEATH. 425

leur latin'; but one of them says there is a chance of heat bringing me round. We start, therefore, on Thursday next at 3 P.m., and arrive at Marseilles next day at 2.30.

Is not that wonderful? I remember travelling five days and nights from Marseilles to Paris, to be present at Coronation's Derby.|Yours ever sincerely,

"W. H. Gregory."

That journey to Marseilles he was not permitted to make. At the close of February and during the opening days of March the cold became daily more intense, and told with fatal severity upon his enfeebled frame. For many days before his death he lay unconscious of the tender solicitude lavished upon him by his devoted wife, who never left his bedside by night or day. Upon Sunday, March 6, 1892, the end came. No man ever retrieved more honourably the errors of his youth ; and to him more than to any other man of my acquaintance might be applied the well-known French proverb, " On ne revient pas de si loin pour peu de chose."

19

SECTION 19

426

CHAPTER XIX.

POLITICAL CAREER OF LORD GEORGE BENTIXCK.

Although it was my original intention to confine myself in these pages solely to the " Racing Life of Lord George Bentinck," I cannot, with justice to him or to myself, omit to point out that his political career was very closely associated with, and in some sense sprang out of, his love for the Turf. There can be little doubt that he was warmly encouraged by his intimate friend, the Right Honourable Benjamin Disraeli, to take a more active part in politics than he had ever attempted between 1826, when he first entered the House of Commons, and 1846, when Sir Robert Peel, then the acknowledged head of the Conservative party, rent it in twain by abolishing the import duty upon foreign corn. It is evident, from Lord George's letter to Mr Croker, from which I have already quoted, that he would never have given himself up body and soul to politics if it had not been his rooted and conscientious conviction that the Conservative

LORD GEORGE AND MR DISRAELI. 427

party, of which he had long been a silent member, was being misguided and wrecked by the " man at the helm,"|the great statesman who had until then been its most trusted pilot. To this conviction he was mainly brought by the influence and arguments of Mr Disraeli, who well knew Lord George's character, and appraised his abilities more accurately than any other member of Parliament did. I shall

J

always think that Mr Disraeli allowed himself, as early as the year 1842, to appear to be drawn by Lord George into the vortex of racing, with a view to drawing Lord George, when the right moment came, into the vortex of politics.

In 1842 Lord George owned a very highly bred filly called Kitten, who was the daughter of Bay Middleton, winner of the Derby, and of Pussy, winner of the Oaks. Lord George insisted that in this filly Mr Disraeli should take an interest, by accepting a half share in her, of which I have no doubt that his Loi'dship made him a present. Kitten was engaged in several two-year-old and three-year-old stakes, but unfortunately she was, like many of the Bay Middletons, very light in the fore-legs, and was therefore unable to stand training even to the extent of being prepared for a two- year-old stake over a half-mile course. Worthless as she was, she afforded Mr Disraeli an opportunity to call more frequently upon Lord George, although I do not believe that the former ever took any genuine interest in horses or in racing. Aboutthat time, however, no oue was so constantly found by me in Lord George's room at Harcourt House as Mr Disraeli, and he listened with the greatest semblance of attention to all I had to say about Lord George's horses, and would often accompany Lord George to the stables behind Harcourt House in order to inspect them. In other respects Mr Disraeli seemed to me at this epoch to be greatly inferior to Lord George Bentinck in tact, ability, and address. The subjects of conversation between xis were, of course, perfectly familiar to Lord George, and quite the reverse to Mr Disraeli; but I cannot help adding that to me the contrast between them was very striking. In fact, from what I saw of Mr Disraeli between 1842 and 1848, I should never have thought it possible that he was possessed of the remarkable sagacity and ability which he subsequently displayed, and Avith which he was from the first credited by Lord George, as the following letter shows:|

" Harcocrt House, *2d March* 1848.

" My Dear Mr Croker,|I have been so busy, sitting long days and six days a week on two committees, that I forgot to write to you.

" You ask me of Disraeli's manner of speaking and effectiveness in debate. I will answer you by giving my brother Henry's observation on the various speakers in the House. Henry is rather a cynical critic. He expressed himself as greatly

HIS OPINION OF MR DISRAELI's ABILITIES. 429

disappointed with Sir Robert Peel and Lord John Russell, and concluded by saying that Disraeli is the only man he had heard who at all came up to his ideas of an orator.

" Disraeli's speeches this session have been first- rate. His last speech, altogether burked in the ' Times,' but pretty well given in the ' Post,' was admirable. He cuts Cobden to ribbons; and Cob- den writhes and quails under him just as Peel did in 1846. And mark my words|spite of Lord Stanley, Major Beresford, Mr Phillips, and the ' Herald,' it will end before two sessions are out in Disraeli being the chosen leader of the party, but not, I think, under Lord Stanley's banner, whether the latter turns his coat on the Jew Bill or not.| Always most sincerely yours, G. Bentinck."

This was the last letter, so far as I know, that Lord George ever wrote to Mr Croker, and to the latter it must have been gall and wormwood, as Mr Croker's detestation of Mr Disraeli, who had ridiculed him in conversation and caricatured him in his novel of ' Coningsby' under the name of " Mr Rigby," was well known. Referring to this letter, the editor of Mr Croker's ' Correspondence and Diaries' remarks that it was written in the midst of a great pressure of business, as, in addition to his usual parliamentary duties, Lord George Bentinck was serving on two important committees lfirst, on that to inquire into the state of thesugar and coffee interests ; and secondly, on that which was seeking to ascertain the causes of the prevailing commercial distress. We learn from the same source that the energy, application, and zeal which he brought to his new avocations were never exceeded by any man in Parliament. " This was the period of his life," says Mr Disraeli, " when he was frequently in the habit of working eighteen hours in the day, and when he made great progress towards acquiring the habit of living without food, for he breakfasted on dry toast, and took no sustenance all day or all night, until Parliament was up, when he dined at White's Club at half-past two o'clock in the morning."

I have read all the books within my reach which deal with my dear and honoured master's political career ; but neither Mr Disraeli's ' Political Biography ' nor Mr Greville's ' Diaries,' nor any of the many Lives of the Fourteenth Earl of Derby, give such insight into Lord George Ben- tinck's character as the last volume of' The Croker Papers,' published in 1884. The letters from Lord George to Mr Croker are seventeen in number, the first being dated on June 30, 1847, and the last on March 2, 1848, so that they cover a space of little more than eight months. Within them, however, may be found the germs of what Lord George was, and I venture to think that they explain the extraordinary ascendancy gained in less than two years by a statesmanlfor as such I shall always

CHAEACTER-SKETCH OF LORD GEORGE. 431

regard himlof the purest and most disinterested character, of dauntless courage, and with an entire absence of personal vanity and conceit. Before quoting from two or three of these letters, I must permit myself the pleasure of citing the following passage from the pen of the editor of the ' Croker Papers':l

" Lord George Bentinck is a unique figure in our history. No one before or since has ever entered political life under circumstances so remarkable, or made such rapid strides towards distinction in an equal period of time. All his parliamentary reputation was achieved in about two years. It is true that he had been a long time in the House, but most people supposed that he cared for nothing in the world except horses; and for some years undoubtedly he did not. That a power of mastering facts and accumulating information was among his natural gifts, his letters amply testify. But the Turf engrossed his whole being, and he pursued it, in Mr Disraeli's words, ' on a scale that has never been equalled.' When he went to the House he seldom remained long, and appeared to take very little interest in the debates. He spoke unwillingly and with difficulty. Such was the man to whom the Protectionists looked for guidance when they found themselves cast off by Sir Eobert Peel.

" In 1847 Lord George Bentinck was prevailedupon to take his seat on the front Opposition bench. It required some management to get him into that position. Repeatedly he had told his followers that they must not look to him as their head|that he would do what he could for a time, but it would only be for a time. Apparently, however, Mr Disraeli persuaded him to take the usual place assigned to the Opposition leader. Throughout that session he worked on with great steadfastness and courage. As an orator he might never have made a brilliant reputation; but if no dazzling flights of eloquence marked his brief career, he greatly stirred curiosity, delivered many effective speeches, and sometimes roused his supporters to genuine enthusiasm."

Perhaps the most remarkable letters of those written by Lord George Bentinck to Mr Croker are, first, the one bearing the date of " Welbeck, 27th September 1847," on the export and import trade of this country; secondly, that written two days later, on the question of Jewish disabilities, for the removal of which Lord George had always voted; thirdly, that from Welbeck on October 5, 1847, in which he dilated upon his own disqualifications for the post of leader of the Opposition ; and, fourthly, that from Harcourt House, London, November 3, 1847, on the Bank Charter Act of 1844.

These four letters, showing, I venture to think,

LORD GEORGE AND THE FARMING INTEREST. 433

the modesty and also the indomitable perseverance of my noble master, justify me in believing that *if* his invaluable life had been spared, and he had continued to give his strenuous attention to politics, he would have played a very prominent and distinguished part in public life. Such was, however, his inflexibility, that I question whether he would have remained in Parliament after the complete triumph of Free Trade. The one individual who gained most by Lord George's death was undoubtedly Mr Disraeli, in whom there was a pliancy and a disposition to make the best of the inevitable which were wholly absent from Lord George's composition. The latter would never have given up his advocacy of Protection ; and, moreover, he never would have forgiven Mr Disraeli and others who had stood by his side as Protectionists for abandoning the contest and making terms with the enemy.

It was Lord George's conviction, often expressed by him in my hearing, that 45s. a quarter for English wheat spelt ruin to the farmer. His predictions as to the decay of the agricultural interest in these islands, consequent upon the repeal of the Corn Laws in 1846, were truly prophetic, and have been verified to the letter. Whether it is to the advantage of the British race that the great urban populations should get a so-called cheap loaf at the cost of ruining the landlords, farmers, and farm labourers, it is for the future, and for wiser heads than mine, to determine.

In the July of 1847 came the long-expected dissolution, Parliament having all but lived out its full period. When the contest was over, it was found that the relative strength of both parties remained pretty much what it had been before. Among the members elected to the new Parliament was included Baron Lionel Rothschild, who was returned for the City of London. This circumstance revived the question of the removal of Jewish disabilities, which had been long and frequently discussed. From 1830 to 1840 a Jew was a sort of pariah in the body politic. He was not allowed to vote if he refused to take the elector's oath; he could not practise at the bar, or be an attorney, or keep a school, or be employed as an usher or tutor in public. Gradually concessions were made until, in 1847, the only civic privilege from which a Jew was excluded was the right to sit in Parliament. When Baron Rothschild was returned in that year, Lord John Russell, then Prime Minister, brought in a Bill to enable the Baron to take his seat. It was opposed by the Conservative party generally, but, as on previous occasions, Lord George Ben- tinck voted for it, giving great dissatisfaction to many of his followers. They conveyed to him " their keen sense of disapprobation," and his haughty spirit immediately took fire at the rebuke. Towards the close of the year he resigned the leadership of the Oppositionla post which he had never sought, and was beginning to find

JLETTER TO MR CROKER. 435

very distasteful. At the opening of the session of 1848 he walked up to the head of the second bench below the gangway on the Opposition side, and thus significantly announced that he was no longer the head of the Protectionist party. His place was taken with apparent reluctance by Mr Disraeli, who from that moment forward, until he went to the Upper House, never ceased to be the leader of the Conservative party in the Commons.

It was under these circumstances that Lord George wrote from Welbeck, on October 5, 1847, the following letter :l

" My Dear Mr Croker,lMy services, such as they are, shall always be at the command of any one who, like yourself, can put the facts which I am able to collect with more force and in a more striking light before the world.

" Virtually an uneducated man, never intended or attracted by taste for a political life, in the House of Commons only by a pure accidentlindeed by an undesired and inevitable chancell am well aware of my own incapacity properly to fill the station I have been thrust into. My sole ambition was to rally the broken and dispirited forces of a betrayed and insulted party, and to avenge the country gentlemen and landed aristocracy of England upon the minister who, presuming upon their weakness, falsely flattered himself that they couldbe trampled upon with impunity.lAlways yours most sincerely, G. Bentekck."

In this letter the spirit and character of my noble master are conspicuously portrayed. I have reason to know that he felt his fall from the prominent place of leader of the Protectionist party, in which he had achieved such wonders, more keenly than he allowed outsiders to perceive. One effect of the slight suspension of the pressure of his parliamentary duties resulting from his resignation of the leadership of the Opposition was that he occasionally attended a race meeting. and was present at Newmarket in 1848 to see the Two Thousand Guineas run for, which race was won by Mr B. Green's Flatcatcher, in the absence. as I have stated in a previous chapter, of Lord Clifden's Surplice and Loadstone, both of them bred by Lord George Bentinck, and both engaged in the Two Thousand, which either could have won. Upon the day of the race Lord George was, as usual, upon horseback, and in the afternoon he rode up to the carriage in which those two beautiful sisters, the Countess of Chesterfield and the Honourable Mrs Anson (the latter being the wife of Lord George's intimate friend, Colonel Anson) were seated. Mrs Anson looked at Lord George long and wistfully, and rising in her seat, and throwing her whole heart into her voice, exclaimed, " George, come back to us, and leave those dreadful politics

SIGNS OF ILL HEALTH. 437

alone, or, take my word for it, they will kill you before another year has passed away."a

Her words were, indeed, prophetic, and they have often reminded me of the last interview I ever had with his Lordship at Harcourt House, on which occasion Mr Disraeli was present. I had been much distressed on perceiving the deteriorating effect upon Lord George's health produced by his long-sustained and close application, by his confinement to his own room, hour after hour, without getting a breath of fresh air, and by his neglecting to take necessary nourishment. His countenance was no longer animated, cheerful, and suffused with the glow of health, as when he spent long hours in exercise on the invigorating Goodwood Downs. Furthermore, his piercing, interrogating eye, which looked you through and through, had lost its lustre. On the occasion above referred to I entered the room at Harcourt House, and found his Lordship seated on one side of the fireplace and Mr Disraeli on the other. The floor was literally covered with papers, letters, and documents, and a kind of rampart built up with blue books ran between me and his Lordship. As I hesitated to approach for fear of displacing some of these barriers, he said to me in a reassuring tone, " Come up nearer, John; don't be afraid of stepping over the piles of books or

,l For information as to this incident I owe my best thanks to Mr Edmund Tattersall, who witnessed it, and repeated it to me.

treading on the papers, although I have forbidden Mrs Jones, the housekeeper, ever to touch them, for in putting them to rights, as she sometimes presumes to do, I find that she puts them very much to wrongs."

Presently Lord George left the room, and Mi- Disraeli took the opportunity of accosting me: " What do you think, Kent," he asked, " of all these papers ?" My reply was, " I should much prefer, sir, to see ' Racing Calendars' substituted for them ; and this I say, not for my own interest, but for the sake of his Lordship's health, which is being undermined by long confinement in London, and by the total stoppage of that open-air exercise to which he has been all his life accustomed." " You are quite right," rejoined Mr Disraeli, " but you know his Lordship as well as I do. When he takes anything up in earnest, it is useless to attempt to dissuade him from persisting in it." I could but shake my head mournfully; and when I took my departure that day, a sad presentiment flashed across my mind that never again should I meet and converse with Lord George Bentinck in Harcourt House.

I well remember the surprise and astonishment with which Lord George's unsurpassed power of mastering details and laying his conclusions before the House was received by many of his friends, who had known him for years, as well as by the general public. His fundamental policy was to

HIS SYMPATHETIC DISPOSITION. 439

encourage domestic trade, and stimulate home labour. One of his favourite illustrations was that a $5 note spent at home was turned over a dozen times or more in a year, whereas if sent abroad it did not return in twelve months, if at all. That British labour should find constant, well- paid employment from British capital, was the main aspiration of Lord George's life. An earnest desire to amend the unsatisfactory condition of the labourers in 1846 had much to do with inducing him to take an active part in politics. The misery to which Ireland was reduced by the failure of the potato crop was felt also in England and Scotland; and, if Lord George could have had his way, he would have sent all the available ships of her Majesty's navy to New York, to bring back bread-stuffs for the starving masses at home. His idea of Protection was as generous as his own disposition. He had no desire rigidly to exclude foreign corn by building up a Chinese wall forbidding its introduction until British wheat was fetching prohibitive prices|say, 100s. a quarter, at which it had often been quoted at the beginning of the present century. Be it recorded to his credit that, in view of famine in Ireland, he offered no obstruction to the free importation of corn ; on the contrary, what he did object to was that, in September, October, and November 1846, seventeen of her Majesty's war-ships were lying in the Tagus " taking care," as he expressed

- . r . . ',

(0

as

it in a letter to Mr Croker, " of the Queen's cousin," which, if sent at once to New York, might have brought back 100,000 quarters of grain, and saved a large proportion of a million Irish lives, sacrificed through the *laches* of the Government. .

Undoubtedly Lord George, if he had ever held high office, would have been a favourite with the Irish. It Avas his earnest desire, following the lead of Mr Pitt and Mr Canning, to provide stipends for the Roman Catholic clergy in Ireland; and, as I have already stated, he proposed to advance .$16,000,000 to be expended in Ireland on railways and other public works.

In 1848 the parliamentary session opened with a motion, brought forward by Lord George, asking for a Select Committee to " inquire into the present condition and prospects of the interests connected with and dependent on sugar and coffee planting in her Majesty's East and West Indian possessions, and in Mauritius ; and to consider whether any, and what, measures can be adopted by Parliament for their relief." The Committee was granted, and witnesses of every class connected with the subject |merchants, planters, distillers, brokers, members of Parliament, Secretaries of State, and East India directors|gave evidence before it, with the result that Lord George, who was Chairman, carried his report, and greatly enhanced his reputation as a laborious and able leader.

" He did so," writes the anonymous author of

,::.–, i

! I v ' .

: ' .1

: l-i-l- "

. . - i v I.- !.. t, :,,.-.. ....

! 11. : - i,"' . , il ' ' '

P !. ,;-' ' ii.i : ": .1" ! r ' il ,

..I'/- I"., ' ..: ' .- . ! : - -

". : i. (' M.llii i–i- IIS ;' . :

:'1 ,-.-..., =.-,- . . ,- , :-.,' . : ;-l !..
.ii" ;..! ! I'i . .'. ', .('1
:-;t J ,1" :.'.'.. .' .. -.. '. '. ' M .

:;.". .1." ;.i tlv ; . .-i"i !;1- i -.i,'-'- .: -.:-:, ,1 i.'-1,- !-:. 1—,
'!! I'i'1 M)." V. 1' ?'" .I'.u'. .1 ': S i
pa u W
"THE KNELL OF FREE TRADE." 441
' Memoirs of Charles Gordon Lennox, Fifth Duke of Richmond,' "at a heavy
sacrifice. For years his ambition had been to win the Derby ; but in order to devote
the whole of his energies to the political career which he embraced so suddenly, he
had parted with his racing stud, and a few months later his home-bred horse Surplice
won the Derby. He recovered, however, from his disappointment next day, when his
casting vote carried Sir Thomas Birch's resolution for a ten - shilling differential duty,
and he exclaimed enthusiastically, " We have saved the colonies ; it is the knell of free
trade!"

We all know now that, instead of repealing free trade, the parliamentary session
of 1848 (which, thanks chiefly to the extraordinary energy and zeal brought to bear
upon it by Lord George, lasted for ten months, and was not prorogued until the 5th
of September) confirmed and established free trade on so firm a basis, that to-day,
nearly half a century later, it seems altogether unassailable. Meanwhile, there still
remain some few admirers of Lord George Bentinck who remember the earnestness
with which he exclaimed, " Wait until North and South America are cultivated, and
see what free trade without reciprocity will make of this country 1" and who are
sometimes tempted to ask themselves whether, after all, he was not right. When I read
that, according to the late Sir James Caird, the landed interest in the UnitedKingdom
is poorer by four hundred millions of pounds than it was twenty years ago, and that
thousands upon thousands of acres upon the wheat-growing farms in these islands
cannot be tilled so long as wheat remains at 30s. a quarter, I cannot but reflect what
my two honoured masters, the fifth Duke of Richmond and Lord George Bentinck,
foretold, and what they would have thought of the present condition of affairs. These
illustrious and enlightened men advocated protection, not for British agriculturists
alone, but also for British manufacturers. I am assured by those better informed than
myself that if ever free trade is overthrown in this country, the change will be effected,
not by the agriculturists, but by the commercial classes.

It was during this memorable session, and less than a month before his death, that
Lord George addressed the following letter to Mr Disraeli:|

"harcourt House, *Wednesday, Aug.* 30, 1848, 4.30 A.m.

" I have just come home from the House of Commons, after a sitting of fifteen hours
and a halflthe longest but one, I believe, on record. Late as it is, I send you the report
of the self- constituted Committee on Savings Banks in Ireland. The Bill was only
printed yesterday, and the Chancellor of the Exchequer forces us into a consideration
of it at eleven o'clock at night,

A VOLUMINOUS CORRESPONDENT. 443

after Lord John Russell has gone to bed, and we are kept at it after all the reporters have gone to bed too. I think it a most scandalous proceeding on the part of Government."

It will be observed that at the head of nearly all the letters from Lord George to Mr Croker which are included in the ' Croker Papers,' the word " Extract" is printed. This leads me to observe that a more voluminous correspondent than Lord George was probably never known. As I have already mentioned, I have frequently received letters from him on racing subjects which covered seven or eight sheets of note-paper, and some of those sent to Mr Croker must have been still longer. Not less remarkable is the wide range of subjects treated in his letters to the latter, and the fulness and accuracy of the information which he contrived to accumulate. I had long been aware that his Lordship's financial ability was of a very high order, but I was not prepared for the research and knowledge displayed in his letters and speeches on such subjects as the Bank Charter Act.

I have heard it stated by some of those who were among Lord George's audience that his speeches, though enhanced by no rhetorical arts, commanded as much attention as those of any of the great oi'ators of the day. Even Mr Charles Greville admits that, although Lord George's Irishspeech was " very tiresome," and lasted nearly three hours, " it was listened to with profound and respectful interest from first to last." The 'Annual Register' for 1847 devotes ten columns to summarising it, and its report concludes as follows :|

" The noble Lord then returned to his panegyric on the character of the Irish people, eulogising their patience under the most direful sufferings, and saying that if by his measure he could fill them with good beef and mutton, and their cottages with fine wheat-flour and sound beer, and their pockets with English gold to purchase the blankets of Wiltshire, the fustians of Bradford, and the cotton prints of Manchester, he, though a Saxon, would answer with his head for their loyalty, and would lead them, through their warm hearts and sympathies, not to sever but to cement the union of Ireland with England. The noble Lord concluded a speech which had lasted more than two and a half hours amid cheers from all sides of the House." l

It must also be remembered that all the questions with which Lord George dealt were of colossal magnitude, and that he handled them with the grasp

1 The speech referred to in this extract from the ' Annual Register ' was heard from the gallery of the House of Commons by that universal favourite, Dr William H. Russell, who was then a parliamentary reporter. After listening to it with rapt attention, Dr Russell repaired to the 'Times' office, and told Mr Delane, his editor, that if ever Lord George Bentinck became Prime Minister, the woes of Ireland (Dr Russell's native country) would soon be redressed.|Ed.

LABOEIOUS LIFE WHILE IN PARLIAMENT. 445

of a master, and on the same scale as his operations on the Turf.

I do not believe that any member of Parliament ever went for so long a period through such laborious days and nights as Lord George Bentinck did. At whatever hour he went to bed|and it was usually 4 A.m. before he laid his head upon the pillow|his breakfast, consisting of one boiled egg and a couple of slices of dry toast, was on the table at 8 A.M. precisely. After reading his enormous correspondence, he began to receive visitors at 9.30 A.M. They called to give him information on all kinds of subjects, and his purse was always open to them. When they left, he plunged into the elaborate correspondence which each day brought, conducting it entirely with his own hand, in a writing so clear and legible as to put to shame the scrawl which nowadays is affected by so many public men. At twelve o'clock (noon) he went down to sit on some Committee, and he only left the Committee-room to take his seat, without touching food, in the House of Commons, which he never quitted until it was adjourned. In the House he never missed an opportunity of enforcing or vindicating his own opinions, and of watching with lynx-like vigilance the conduct by Government of public business. Nothing daunted him|nothing exhausted his resources; once convinced that he was in the right, no show of authority, no parade of official experience, no dread of superior ability, knowledge, or eloquence possessed by an opponent, could make him afraid. In common with some old friends who think with me and are of the same opinion|to one of whom I am indebted for much valuable information in writing this chapter|I have formed my estimate of the nobility and magnanimity of Lord George's character in consonance with what I have here stated. Personal ambition, conceit, and vanity he had none; but, as he often showed in the racing world, his self- reliance and fearlessness were unbounded, and he would never trust any other man to do what he could do himself. He brought the same self-sacrificing spirit to bear upon politics, and his life was the forfeit. In his opinions he may, or may not, have been mistaken ; but that he held them with perfect disinterestedness, and without a thought of self, will be denied by none who knew him as I was privileged to do.

CHAPTER XX.

DEATH OF LOED GEORGE BENTINCK.

It is with a lively sense of pain and grief, which the lapse of more than forty years has not yet extinguished, that I approach the closing scene of a life so prematurely ended at a moment when it was fullest of promise. Mr Disraeli remarks that the labours of Lord George Bentinck had been so superhuman from the day when, in 1845, he had been trying to find a lawyer to compose a speech for him to deliver in Parliament, until the end of the session of 1848, that every one ought to have prognosticated at the latter period that it was impossible for them to be continued much longer upon such an exhausting scale. " No friend," adds the future Prime Minister, " could, however, control his eager spirit. He obeyed the law of his fiery and vehement nature, being one of those men who, in whatever they undertake, know no medium, but will succeed or die, come what may." The two friends parted for the last time on the steps of Harcourt House|the last of|the great hotels of an age of stately manners, with its wings, courtyard, carriage-portal, and huge outward walls. " Lord George," adds Mr Disraeli, "put forth his hand to bid me farewell, and his last words were characteristic of the man, of his warm feelings and ruling passion : ' God bless you ! we must work, and the country will come round to us yet.'"

It is evident that some foreboding of the coming tragedy must have crossed Mr Disraeli's mind at that final interview, for he immediately proceeds to say : " But why talk or think of death ? He goes to his native county and his father's proud domain to breathe the air of his boyhood, and move amid the parks and scenes of his youth.

Every breeze will bear health on its wings, and the sight of every hallowed haunt will stimulate his pulse. He is scarcely older than Julius Caesar when he commenced his public career ; he looks as high and as brave, and he springs from a long-lived race." Yet if any gloomy presentiment suggested itself on this occasion to Mr Disraeli's thoughts, it can be shown beyond doubt by many irrefutable evidences that Lord George went down to Welbeck full of energy and hope. On arriving at the home of his childhood, he was thought by some of his attached relativesland never was son or brother more belovedlto be looking worn and pale. Nothing, however, appears to have been said to him on the subject in a family always noted for reticence and

DONCASTER RACES. 449

undemonstrativeness. Lord George seemed to all who came in contact with him, between his arrival at Wei beck on Monday, the llth of September 1848, and the day of his death, September 21, to regard himself as in the best of health. It is certain that he was in excellent spirits, and also that he greatly enjoyed the change of scene and the freshness of the country air after his long incarceration in London.

On Tuesday, September 12, 1848, the first day of Doncaster Races came round. Lord George attended the meeting as usual from Welbeck Abbey, which is twenty-five miles distant from Doncaster, and was greatly interested in the success of Lord Eglinton's magnificent colt, the Flying Dutchman, for the Champagne -Stakes, which he won in a canter against four competitors. Lord George watched the Flying Dutchman's grand action with the closest attention, because he was the son of his old stallion Bay Middleton (then the property of Lord Clifden), and the best animal that ever .sprang from Bay Middleton's loins. In the Municipal Stakes, of 300 sovereigns each, he witnessed the triumph of another son of Bay Middle- ton, Tiresome by name, whom he had himself bred and sold as a foal to Mr Mostyn in 1846. The Doncaster meeting was, indeed, full of attractiveness to Lord George, who had not gone down to Epsom on the Derby day to see Surplice, the son of his old favourite Crucifix, win the " blue ribbonof the Turf." It had always been Lord George's custom to back any good horse that called him master for a very large sum, and it is difficult to say what he would not have won in 1848 upon Surplice, who in his hands would have carried off the Two Thousand, the Derby, and the St Leger. In those days it was easy to back horses for treble events, and the odds laid against Surplice winning the three great classic races would doubtless have been enormous. The feat of winning the Two Thousand, Derby, and St Leger had, in 1848, never been accomplished by the same horse. The only winner of the Derby and St Leger down to that year was Mr Christopher Wilson's Champion, who, in 1800, won the Derby in a field of thirteen starters, and the St Leger in a field of ten. But, in 1800, the Two Thousand Guineas did not exist, as the race was not established until 1809, and was won, oddly enough, by Mr Wilson's Wizard.

That, in 1848, it was deemed to be in the highest degree improbable that the same horse would win the Derby and St Leger, is shown by the facility with which Mr Francis Villiers and his friends succeeded in getting large bets at 100 to 1 against Surplice landing the double event, after he had been tried to be a great horse a few days before the Derby. I remember that the present Earl of Bradford, who was not in the habit either then or now of making heavy bets, was tempted to lay the late Earl of Winchilsea (then Lord Maidstone)

SURPLICE WINS THE ST LEGER. 451

$10,000 to $100 against Surplice winning the Derby and St Leger. It is impossible to conceive what extreme odds Lord George Bentinck would have obtained against Surplice winning what is now called " the triple crown," had the colt been his property in 1848. Lord George was often reported to be extremely anxious to accomplish a feat in which no one has ever been successfullthe feat of "breaking the ring." Never would he have had a better chance than if Surplice had been in his hands and trained at Goodwood, over the finest and most private downs in the world, at the time when that great horse was put through the mill in 1848.

It will readily be understood, therefore, that Lord George's interest in the St Leger of 1848 was extremely great. He had backed Surplice for it before the Derby, and although the stake which he landed at Doncaster|$11,000|was small in comparison with what he would doubtless have netted before he sold his stud, it was enough to make him watch the race with keen attention. The political relations between the fourteenth Earl of Derby (then Lord Stanley) and Lord George were at that time somewhat strained, and although Lord George made no remark on the subject, I think it was a gratification to him to see Surplice beat Lord Stanley's fine mare Canezou, upon whom, although beaten, Frank Butler rode a magnificent race.

I remember that, when the St Leger was over, Lord George's eye and countenance were radiant with some of the old fire which I had seen reflected by them on many previous occasions. That he must have inwardly regretted to have allowed such a horse as Surplice to pass out of his hands it is impossible to doubt. I have lately seen a letter addressed to a friend of his by the late Sir William Gregory, who, as my readers are already aware, was intimately acquainted with, and a great admirer of, Lord George Bentinck. I should premise that, in 1838, Lord Chesterfield's Don John won the St Leger in a canter against a small but good field. As Lord George was walking off the course he fell in with Sir William Gregory, and addressed him as follows :|

" I am now on my way home to discharge the weary task of making out my betting-book, in which I have not one winning bet. But I declare I would rather be in this position than in that occupied by my Lord Chesterfield, who has won a paltry $1500 on such a horse! If Don John had been mine I would not have left a card- seller in Doncaster with a shirt to his back."

It is probable that some such thoughts as these must have passed through Lord George's mind when he saw Surplice wear Lord Stanley's Canezou down in the Doncaster St Leger of 1848, and win by indomitable pluck and stoutness. There can

POLITICS MORE EXPENSIVE THAN RACING. 453

be no doubt that about that time Lord George was beginning to tire of politics, which thus far had brought him nothing but disappointment, while imposing heavy demands upon his pocket. In this impression I am confirmed by the letter which he wrote to me from Welbeck on the day following the St Leger of 1848, bidding me meet him on the following Saturday at the Turf Tavern, Doncaster, behind which his Lordship's old paddocks were situated, which, on his withdrawal from the Turf, passed into the Earl of Glasgow's hands. When I met Lord George on the appointed day, he immediately remarked to me : " I found racing expensive when I was mixed up with it, but nothing like so expensive as politics, for I never saw such a hungry lot of fellows as these politicians; they are never satisfied ! I want you, therefore, to pick out eight or ten horses for me, and I will have another try at the Turf. You and I got on very well together before, and I have no doubt that we shall do so again."

Of course I was overjoyed to hear that my dear old master had resolved to return to the arena in which he had once been so conspicuous, and I can truly say that my satisfaction was greater on his account than on my own. I then ventured to ask him what kind of horses he wished me to purchase for him, and of what age. He replied at once, and with unusual cordiality, " I leave it entirely toyou. You may buy anything that you consider likely to do us all good." These were almost the last words I ever heard issue from Lord George Bentinck's lips, and the emotion with which I now write them down will be fully appreciated and understood by those (they are now few in number) who remember the pride and affection with which I endeavoured to do my duty towards a beloved and honoured employer, whose equal, I am persuaded, has not been seen among patrons of the Turf in my time.

On Saturday afternoon the 16th of September 1848, Lord George returned, on the conclusion, of the Doncaster meeting, to Welbeck Abbey, where the usual family party were assembled. Lord George's mother had died on April 28, 1844, and after her much-lamented decease there was little company entertained at the Abbey. It might have been imagined that at Welbeck Lord George would have eaten more food than it was his custom to partake of in London, where he had to attend the House of Commons, and possibly to make a speech, or at any rate to be prepared to make one. Much as he needed rest, he continued to work as hard in the country as in town, and it was his fixed belief that he could never do himself justice unless he had eaten next to nothing. It was the opinion of many of his friends, as it certainly was my own, that if he had taken as much nourishment as most brain-workers are in the habit of doing,

HIS LAST LETTERS. 455

he would with his splendid constitution, and with physical powers upon which, until 1846, no severe draught had been made, have sustained for many years the stupendous labour which he imposed upon himself in 1847 and 1848, until the "golden bowl" yielded to the strain and was prematurely broken. When I remember that Lord Winmar- leigh, who has only just died, was born in the same year as Lord George, it reopens the old wounds inflicted upon me long ago by the latter's premature death.

On Thursday, the 21st of September 1848, Lord George came down to breakfast at Welbeck Abbey at the usual time. Never did he appear to be in better health or spirits than on that day. He occupied himself during the greater part of the morning in writing three letters in his dressing-room, and studying several printed papers. Of these three letters, the first was addressed to the Duke of Richmond, intimating that it was its writer's intention to return to the Turf; the second to Mr Disraeli; and the third to the then Lord Enfield, who subsequently became the second Earl of Straffbrd. To the last named of the three it was a matter of no ordinary satisfaction, and so remained until his death, that " the ultimate words traced by his old friend George Bentinck's hand were addressed to him." Of these letters each was of very considerable length, and Mr Disraeli mentions that the onereceived by him "consisted of seven sheets of note-paper, full of interesting details of men and things, and written not only in a cheerful, but even in a merry mood." When these letters were concluded and sealed, it is morally certain that not a thought of the impending calamity had entered their writer's mind. He had so much to think of, so much to do, that no time remained for him to consider his health, or to take heed of the many warnings which others under similar circumstances could not have failed to recognise. " He that saveth his life shall lose it," was often on his Lordship's lips, when any one in his employ seemed over-anxious about his own health, and disposed to shirk work. One member of the family who sat down to breakfast that memorable morning at Welbeck told a friend of mine subsequently that he noticed the unusual pallor of Lord George's countenance when he entered the breakfast-room. There can be no doubt, however, as I have already said, that his Lordship's spirits were more than ordinarily bright and gay. I come now to details which, even after a long lapse of years, are too sad for me to attempt to clothe in language. The best and simplest account is that given in the ' Annual Register,' from which I quote the following words:|

" The announcement of the sudden death of Lord George Bentinck on September 21, under

THE INQUEST. 457

the melancholy circumstances detailed in the evidence given at the inquest, caused universal astonishment and sorrow; but was nowhere received with such sorrow as at Goodwood, except, of course, in the neighbourhood of Welbeck Abbey. The inquest was held at Welbeck Abbey on the day following his Lordship's death, by Mr Falkner, Coroner of Newark, and a jury of gentlemen farmers. The jury inspected the corpse. ' Death,' says the report, ' had left no painful trace on the features of the departed nobleman ; a cheerful smile was diffused over the face.'

" William Parks, a footman who waited at the breakfast - table on Thursday morning, deposed that Lord George never seemed in better health or spirits than at breakfast. He took no luncheon, and for the greater part of the morning was occupied in his dressing-room. He remained at home till twenty minutes past four P.m., and then set out for Thoresby Park, where he was going to spend a couple of days with Lord Manvers. Two witnesses, Lenthall a stableman, and Evans a woodman, then deposed to having seen Lord George on his walk towards Thoresby. Richard Evans said: ' On Thursday afternoon I was returning home with my father, and with John Mee, a fellow - labourer, when we saw a gentleman, whom I did not know, standing against the gate on the road to the water-meadows. We thought at the time that it was the Marquis of Titchfield.My father and Mee continued along the road, and I stood for a minute or two looking at the gentleman. While I was standing he turned round and looked towards the kennels. I thought he was reading, as, before he turned round, he held his head down. He was still standing at the gate when I walked on. I was about two hundred yards from the gate ; it was about half-past four o'clock.'

" Lenthall the stable-helper, who drove Gardner, Lord George Bentinck's valet, to Thoresby, related the finding of the body. ' I was called out of bed at night and asked if I had seen Lord George on my wTay home, as he had not reached Thoresby. I got up, and along with Gardner the valet, and George Wilson, went to search for his Lordship. We took lanterns and followed on the foot-road I had seen him taking. We found the body of his Lordship lying close to the gate which separates the kennel water-meadow. He was quite dead, and lying on his face. His hat was a yard or two before him, having evidently been thrown off in falling. He was lying flat on his face, and one of his arms was under him. I left the men with the body, and immediately started off for Mr Hase, the Worksop surgeon. A few minutes before we found the body Mr Hase had passed on horseback, and asked what we were searching for. We declined telling him, as we had no idea that any harm had come to his Lordship, and did not wish to set rumour floating.'

THE INQUEST. 459

" George Wilson, a groom, who accompanied Lenthall, deposed : ' A little after ten on Thursday night, I, along with Richard Evans and William Gardner, followed the path leading to the corner of the deer park. We found his Lordship lying near a gate through which he had passed. He was lying on his belly and face. His hat was about a yard and a half before him. His hands were under his body, and in one of them he grasped a walking-stick.1 The stick was partly underneath him. I felt his leg, and it was quite stiff and cold. A brake was sent for from Welbeck, and in that he was removed to the Abbey. I had not seen him that morning. There was a little blood upon his face. It appeared to have flowed from his Lordship's nose. Besides that on his face, there was some on the grass. The body was not moved until Dr Hase came. Gardner and I carried lights with us.'

"Gardner, the valet, being absent in London on the day of the inquest, the Coroner decided that his presence was not necessary.

" Mr Ward, Lord George's regular medical attendant, gave evidence as to the *post mortem* examination. He said : ' I have this day openedthe body, and am of opinion that he died of spasm of the heart. There was very little food in his stomach, but there was no morbid appearance beyond congestion, which prevailed over the whole system. There was emphysema of the lungs, and old adhesions from former diseases. The heart was large and muscular, and covered with fat. It contained no blood, and bore the appearance of irregular contraction.'

1 This walking-stick was presented to Lord George by myself one day when he came to Goodwood without his favourite companion, which went with him everywhere. After his death, I bought from Gardner, his Lordship's valet, the same stick which I had given him, and which he grasped in his hand. It was the stick alluded to in George Wilson's evidence. It is now at Welbeck Abbey, and is much valued by the Duke and Duchess of Portland.lJ. K.

" A juror inquired as to the state of the brain.

" *Mr Ward.* ' It was perfectly healthy, with the exception of a little venous congestion in about the same ratio as the other organs.'

" Another juror asked if Mr Ward supposed the blood found on his Lordship's face and on the grass to have been produced by the rupture of a blood-vessel in the head. Mr Ward said ' No;' his opinion being that blood flowed from the nose in consequence of the deceased falling on his face.

" The jury immediately returned a verdict of, ' Died by the visitation of Godlto wit, by a spasm of the heart.'"

Such is the cold and simple record of the official chronicler. Mr Disraeli adds that the attack, supposed to be spasm of the heart, was not instantaneous in its effects, and with proper remedies might have been baffled. He says, " Terrible to think of him in his death-struggle, and so near a

WIDESPREAD GRIEF AT HIS DEATH. 461

devoted hearth !" To me, however, it appears more probable that Lord George died, as he had preferred to live, a lonely and inaccessible man. It would have been easy for him, by lifting his hand, to have summoned to his aid the woodman Evans, and the latter's companion. He could hardly have been unconscious of the near approach of death while leaning against the gate, close to which his body was found. From my intimate acquaintance with his Lordship's character and iron courage, I am convinced that he preferred to die alone.

It is seldom that the death of a statesman provokes such general consternation, such widespread grief. On the morrow of the announcement of Lord George's death, all the British ships in the docks and the river, from London Bridge to Gravesend, hoisted their flags half-mast high. Every neighbouring poi't on the Continent, such as Antwerp, Havre, Cherbourg, Bordeaux, and Rotterdam, followed the example set on the Thames. Most of all, however, was his Lordship's death bewailed with their customary warmheartedness and sympathy by Irishmen all over the world. His lofty independence of party ties, exemplified by his support of Catholic emancipation, of justice to Ireland, of a reformed Parliament, and of the removal of Jewish disabilities, gave him a higher place in the public estimation than that won by any of his contemporaries.Cold, proud, and reserved as he often appeared, never was there a warmer and more sympathetic heart than beat in his breast.

The body was moved from Welbeck to Harcourt House, Cavendish Square, and, a week after Lord George's death, was laid in the family vault of the Bentincks, under the communion table of what is now a Chapel of Ease to the Parish Church of St Marylebone. The building in question, which looks like an old brick barn, is situated in High Street, Marylebone, just behind the house in which Charles Dickens and his wife parted company for ever. Scores of pedestrians since that day have passed to and fro under the east window of that dingy little chapel in utter unconsciousness that under their feet there lies all that was mortal of the greatest racing man that ever lived. For many years no monument was raised to the memory of Lord George. Seven years ago, however, his sister, the late Viscountess Ossington, caused two slabs of marble to be fixed inside the east wall of the chapel in which the remains of her ancestors mingle with those of her favourite brother in one common repose. On a dark and drizzling day Lord George's two brothers, the Marquis of Titchfield and Lord Henry Cavendish Bentinck, followed their brother's honoured body to the tomb. Their father, the venerable Duke of Portland, then in his eighty-first year, was too feeble to attend the sad ceremony. One, however, was present who has himself long sinceLines By "the Druid." 463

passed awaylthe late Mr Henry Dixon, better known as " The Druid," who in a few simple but deeply pathetic lines has left his record of a, by him, never-to-be-forgotten scene. The following lines will be found at the end of his ' Post and Paddock' (first edition). They are from the opening stanzas of his " Lay of Doncaster Town Moor":l

"The bells of ancient Marylebone within their towers
swing,

But 'tis not to hail a victory, or greet an infant king;
They usher in no festival, they honour not a bride,
But deep death - notes from their iron throats along the

breezes ride.
" Within yon ducal portals, so shadowy and grim, A gallant heart lies pulseless, a gallant eye is dim; Lo! through those portals issuing, in inky-black array, Bearing its shrouded passenger, a hearse moves forth today.
"E'en hard men's eyes were glistening as the vault that
coffin hid, And the dark earth rattled dismally on its gilded velvet
lid: Methinks the world's cold sophistry some hearts not wholly
sears, When I viewed the bitter Disraeli in an agony of tears."No more shall he at Doncaster each foal and yearling
" Those tears are worthy of thee; thou wast with him in
the van, As his cause became more hopeless and his cheek became
more wan:
When Cobden overcame him, No Truce was still his call, And like another Pericles he denied he'd had a fall.
" Throw wide his chamber window, let the noontide light
rush in; 'Twill wake not one who erst has slept his wakeful sleep
within: That chair and desk will recognise their toil-worn lord no
more, As in winter night or grey twilight he worked till the clock
told four.
" Stern in the path of duty, in his heyday of renown, 'Mid all his proud imaginings the loyal George goes down; As England's tars with Kempenfeldt died 'neath their
native surf, So the death-sweat gathered o'er him as he trod the springy
turf.
pat, Nor ride up Goodwood's leafy slopes to the trial-ground
with Nat; No more with Kent and Marson shall he scan each pet in
form, Nor view their place as in the race they sweep past like the
storm.
LINES BY LOUD WINCHILSEA. 465
"Welbeck's fair park is desolate; the rippling waters
moan, For the grave's dark mystery has claimed their scion for its
own; No more within St Stephen's shall he ground his flag on
truth; No jovial sound of horn and hound shall conjure up his
youth."
Finally, I have to add that the following lines were written by the late Earl of Winchilsea and Nottingham not long after his illustrious friend, Lord George, had passed away. I promised Lord Winchilsea, if ever I wrote a book on my dear and honoured master's racing career, that I would not forget to reproduce the following tribute to the latter's memory, as Lord Winchilsea, who has inserted it in the preface to his longest poem, " Abd el Kader," expressed a strong desire that I should do so :I
"En JHetnartam.
GEORGE BENTINCK.

His form how glorious, his eye how clear,
How cowered a rogue beneath his withering sneer!
Before his stern rebuke bronzed lawyers quailed,
And thieves detected trembled as they railed.
Within, the guileless spirit of a child,
Mailed in the proof of honour undefiled;
Slow to believe malicious slander's breath.
But to a culprit pitiless as death;
A friend's misfortune ever prompt to feel,
He passed not unconcerned, but stopped to heal:
A good Samaritan too oft repaid
With injuries and wrong for timely aid.
Others might boast more questionable arts
In twisting facts, more sleight in juggling hearts.
Rough truths he published, in frieze jerkins dight;
His was no gift of tickling ears polite.
An honest man, with noblest zeal inspired,
Xo threats appalled him, and no labours tired.
Bent to repress the licence of the times,
He tore their silken draperies from crimes.
Straight to the point he went, abrupt and dry;
Tricks he called knavery, and a lie a lie.
Within the portals of that gloomy gate
Where Harcourt House maintains Batavian state,
On the right hand the modest chamber lies;
No scarlet boxes greeting curious eyes.
Yet there he toiled with more results to show
Than well-paid Minister in State bureau.
Health failing, food neglected, rest foregone,
But like the mettled steed, still struggling on,
Oblivious of the paltry bounds assigned
To strongest frame and most capacious mind.
Alas, my friend! had all been such as thou,
Honest and true, I had not mourned thee now!
The springy turf of Goodwood's wide domain,
The stirring contests of Newmarket's plain,
Thou hadst not left, for scenes where parties rave,
A worn-out spirit and an early grave.

Grey morning saw thee full of kindly cheer;
Dark evening brooded pall-wise o'er thy bier;

THE BKNT1NCK MEMORIAL, MAXSFIKI.l).
MEMORIAL AT MANSFIELD. 467

A voice of mourning chilled the autumn blast,
Along mute wires the electric tidings passed;
Palace and castle, hall and peasant's cot,
In grief agreeing, all but grief forgot.
Friends wept, foes pitied, Envy ceased to chide;
All felt the loss of merit undenied.
Others may dedicate to soothe their grief
Historic brass in honour of their chief.
I have it not to give, but what is mine
Verse and a tear shall mingle at thy shrine !
Accept the best a sorrowing heart can give,
And with thy virtues may our friendship live !"

Three years after Lord George Bentinck's untimely death, a Memorial was erected in his honour at Mansfield, of which an engraving is given. The money necessary for its construction was contributed anonymously by public subscription. Upon its base the following words were inscribed:|
" Co tfje JStanorg of LORD GEORGE FREDERICK CAVENDISH BENTINCK,
SECOND SURVIVING SON OF
WILLIAM HENRY CAVENDISH SCOTT,
FOURTH DUKE OF PORTLAND.
HE DIED THE 21ST DAY OF SEPTEMBER AN. DOM. MDCCCXLVIII.,
IN THE FORTY-SEVENTH YEAR OF HIS AGE.

His ardent patriotism and uncompromising honesty were only equalled by the persevering zeal and extraordinary talents which called forth the grateful homage of those who, in erecting this Memorial, pay a heartfelt tribute to exertions which prematurely brought to the grave one who might long have lived the pride of ihis, his native country."

When the present Duke of Portland succeeded to Welbeck Abbey, he found that the Memorial to Lord George Bentinck, standing in the marketplace at Mansfield, Notts, had been damaged by time and damp, and not a little defaced by iconoclastic hands. His Grace immediately gave orders that the monument, in which he naturally took great pride, should be thoroughly restored, and surrounded by a neat iron railing, to protect it from future injury.

I cannot conclude this work (the writing of which has, as I remarked at its commencement, been to me a veritable labour of love) without adding a few valedictory words in grateful acknowledgment of the great and unwearied kindness and encouragement extended to me during its composition by their Graces the present Duke and Duchess of Portland. His Grace began by giving instructions to have several pictures at Welbeck Abbey photographed of which I stood in need for the illustration of this volume; and when, at the last moment, I solicited permission to include the Duchess's portrait in this attempted tribute to the memory of one of the most illustrious members of the Bentinck family, her Grace was pleased to send me a photograph of herself, executed by Miss Alice Hughes, of Gower Street, W.C., which has been faithfully reproduced in the accompanying engraving. Not satisfied, however,

HER GRACE THE DUCHESS OF PORTLAND.

ili.. OF

HIS GRACE THE DUKE OF PORTLAND.

CONCLUSION. 469

with this considerate act of kindness, her Grace was likewise good enough to provide me with a second portrait of the Duke, which is also given here.

It is often my habit to read at night during the long hours of sleeplessness which it is occasionally my lot to endure. Among the books which have lately passed through my hands was included Northcote's ' Life of Sir Joshua Reynolds,' in which it is stated that the last lecture to the students of the Royal Academy ever delivered by that great painter ended with the words " Michael Angelo," the name of the most consummate artist that, in Sir Joshua's opinion, the world had ever seen. In my poor judgment, the noble hero of this imperfect biography was the greatest and most epoch-making patron of the Turf that I have known in my time. Following at an infinite distance the loving and appreciative example set by Sir Joshua Reynolds, I will now conclude by gratefully associating the honoured name of Lord George Cavendish Bentinck with those of his equally generous and large-hearted relatives, the sixth Duke and Duchess of Portland.

20

SECTION 20

473

INDEX.

Ccelebs, attempted poisoning of, 36.

Colombo, statue to Sir W. H. Gregory at, 422.

Conservative party, Lord George Bentinck assumes leadership of the, 225, 432|resigns leadership of the, 236, 330, 434.

Cooper, Abraham, pictures of Mies Elis painted by, 180 *et xeq.*

Cornopean, running of, 199.

Coronation, notice of, 313.

Cotherstone, winner of the Two Thousand, 108|of the Derby, 110, 198, 394.

Cowl, winner at Ascot, 233.

Craven Meeting, Newmarket Biennial Stakes, Kangaroo winner of, in 18B5, 132.

Crockford, Mr, owner of Ratan, 155.

'Croker Papers,'the, 430|quoted, 431 *ft seq.*

Croker, Right Hon. John Wilson, letters from Lord George Bentinck to, 236, 330, 428, 430 *et* passim.

Crozier, Flatman's jockeyship of, at Ascot, 145.

477

IXDEX.

PRlNTKD BY V[LLfAM BLACKWOOD AND SONS

CATALOGUE
MESSRS BLACKWOOD & SONS'
PUBLICATIONS.
PHILOSOPHICAL CLASSICS FOR ENGLISH READERS.

Edited By WILLIAM KNIGHT, LL.D.,
Professor of Moral Philosophy In the University of at Andrews.
In crown 8vo Volumes, with Portraits, price 38. 6d.

No 10 ready|
Descartes, by Professor Mahafly, Dub- |Vico, by Professor Flint, Edinburgh |
lin. | Butler, by Rev. W. Lucas Collins, i Hohber, by Professor Groom Robertson,
M.A.|Bkrkeley, by Professor Campbell London.|Home, by the Editor.|Spinoza, Fraser,
Edinburgh.|Ficute, by Professor by the Very Rev. Principal Caird. Glasgow. Adam-
son, Owens College, Manchester.| |bacon : Part I. The Life by Professor Ka.vt, by
Professor Wallace, Oxford. | Nichol, Glasgow.|Bacon : Part II. Fhilo- Hamilton, by
Professor Veitoh, Glasgow, sophy, by the same Author.|Locke, by | Heoel, by Pro-
fessor Edward Caird, Professor Campbell Fraser, Edinburgh. Glasgow.|Leibniz, by J.
Theodore Merz.
Mill, . . . /preparation.
by Walter Beaant, II.A.|Caldkron, by by E. J. Hasell.|Rousseau, by Henry E. J.
Hasell.|Saint Simon, by Clifton Grey Graham|Alfred De Musset' by W. Collini, M.
A.|cervantes, by the C. F. Oliphant.
In preparation.
Leopardi. By the Editor.

FOREIGN CLASSICS FOR ENGLISH READERS.
Edited By Mrs OLIPHANT.
In crown 8vo, 28. 6d.
Contents of the Seriet.

Dante, by the Editor.|Voltaire, by Editor. | Corneille sn Racine, by General Sir E. B.
Hamley, K.C.|f. Henry M. Trollope. | Madame Dc | Pascal, by Principal Tulloch.|Pet-
Sevione, by Miss Thackeray.|La Foji- Rarch, by Henry Reeve, C.B.|Goethe, Taine,
And Other French FABtruera, By A. Hayward, Q.C.|Moliere, by the ' Editor and F.
Tarver, M.A.|Montaione, by Rev. W. L.Collins, M.A |rabelais,
by Rev. W. Lucas Collins, M.
Ler, by James Sime, M.A., Author of
'Leasing, hit Life and Writing!.'|Tasso,
Theoonis, by the Rev. J. Davies, M.A.|
Greek Anthology, by Lord Neaves.|
Vihoil, by the Editor|Horace, by Sir
Theodore Martin, K.O.B.|Juvenal, by
Edward Walford, M.A. | Plautus And

Brodribb, M. A.|Aristotle, by Sir Alexander Grant, Bart., LL.D.|TnucvDioia, by
the Editor.| Locretics , by W. H Mallock. M. A.|Pindar, by the Ber. F D. Morlce, M.A.
Saturday *Review.*|"It is difficult to estimate too highly the value of such a aerie as
this in giving ' English readers' an insight, exact as far as It goes. Into thos olden
times which are so remote, and yet to many of us o close."

Now COMPLETK.

ANCIENT CLASSICS FOR ENGLISH READERS.

Edited By The Rev. W. LUCAS COLLINS, M.A.

Complete in 28 Vols. crown Svo, cloth, price *as.* 6d. each. And may also be bad In 14 Volumes, strongly and neatly bound, with calf or vellum back, $3,106.

Contents of the Seriu.

Homer: The Iliad, by the Editor.| ; Terence, by the Editor.|The Commek- Homer : The Odyssey, by the Editor.| ! Taries or Cxbar, by Anthony Trollope. Herodotus, byGeorge C. Swayne, M.A.| |tacitus, by W. B. Donne.|Cicero, by Xenophon, by Sir Alexander Grant, Bart, the Editor.|Flint's Letters, by the LL.D.|Euripides, by W. B. Donne.| Rev. Alfred Church, M. A., and the Rev. Aristophanes, by the Editor.|Plato, by j W. J. Brodribb, M.A.|Livy, by the Clifton W. Collins, M. A.|Lucian, by the | Editor. |Ovid, by the Rev. A. Church, Editor.| fiscHVLtrs, by the Right Rev. i M.A.|catullus, Tibullus, And Pro! the Bishop of Colombo.|Sophocles, by Pertius, by the Rev. Ja. Daviei, M.A. Clifton W. Collins, M.A.|Hesiod And |demosthenes, by the Rev. W. J.

CATALOGUE

MESSRS BLACKWOOD & SONS'

PUBLICATIONS.

ALISON. History of Europe. By Sir Archibald Alison, Bart., D. C. L.

1. From the Commencement of the French Revolution to the Battle of Waterloo.

Library Edition, 14 Tola., with Portraits. Demy Svo, j$io, ics.

Another Edition, in 20 vols. crown Svo, *$6.*

People's Edition, 13 vols. crown Svo, *$2, us.*

2. Continuation to the Accession of Louis Napoleon.

Library Edition, 8 vols. Svo, *$6,* 78. 6d.

People's Edition, 8 vols. crown Svo, 348.

3. Epitome of Alison's History of Europe. Twenty-ninth Thousand, 78. 6d.

4. Atlas to Alison's History of Europe. By A. Keith Johnston, Library Edition, demy 4to, *$3,* 38.

Pkople's Edition, 318. 6d.

Life of John Duke of Marlborough. With some Account of his Contemporaries, and of the War of the Succession. Third Edition. 2 vela. Svo. Portraits and Maps, 308.

Essays: Historical, Political, and Miscellaneous. 3 voh.

ACTA 'SANCTORUM Hibernle ; Ex Codice Salmanticensi.

Nunc primum integre edita opera Caroli De Smedt et Josephi De Backer, e Soc. Jesu, Hagiographorum Bollandianorum ; Auctore etSumptus Largiente Joanne Patricio

Marchione Bothae. In Ouo handsome 4to Volume, bound in half roxburghe, $2, 28.;
in paper wrapper, 318. 6d.

AIKMAN. Manures and the Principles of Manuring. .By C. M. Aikman, B.Sc.,
&c., Lecturer on Agricultural Chemistry, West of Scotland Technical College. Cr.
8vo.

Farmyard Manure : Its Nature, Composition, and Treatment.
Crown Svo", is. 6d.

AIRD. Poetical Works of Thomas Aird. Fifth Edition, with Memoir of the Author
by the Rev. Jardini Wallace, and Portrait. Crown Svo, 78. 6d.

ALLARDYCE. The City of Sunshine. By Alexander Allar-
Dtce. Three vols. post Svo, $i, 58. 6d.

Memoir of the Honourable George Keith Elphinstone,
K.B., Viscount Keith of Stonehaven, Mariscbal, Admiral of the Red. Svo, with
Portrait, Illustrations, and Haps, us.

ALMOND. Sermons by a Lay Head-master. By Kelt Hdtchin-
Son Almond, M.A. Oxon.. Head-master of Loretto School. Crown Svo, 58.

ANCIENT CLASSICS FOR ENGLISH READERS. Edited by
Rev. W. Lucas Collins, M.A. Price 28. fid. each. *For IM of Vols., seepage n*

AYTOUN. Lays of the Scottish Cavaliers, and other Poems. By
W. Edmondstoiink Aytoun, D.C.L., Professor of Rhetoric and Belles-Lettres in the
University of Edinburgh. New Edition. Fcap. Svo, 38. 6d. Another Edition. Fcap.
8vo, 78. 6d. Cheap Edition, is. Cloth, is. 3d.

An Illustrated Edition of the Lays of the Scottish Cavaliers.
From designs by Sir Noel Paton. Small *ito,* In gilt cloth, 218.

Bothwell : a Poem. Third Edition. Fcap. 7$. 6d.

Poems and Ballads of Goethe. Translated by Professor
Aytoun and Sir Theodohb Martin, K.C.B. Third Edition. Fcap., *6s.*

-

4 LIST OF BOOKS PUBLISHED BY

AYTOUN. Bon Gaultier's Book of Ballads. By the Same. Fifteenth j
Edition. With Illustrations by Doyle, Leech, and Crowquill. Fcap. 8vo, $.

The Ballads of Scotland. Edited by Professor Aytoch.
Fourth Edition. 2 vols. fcap. Svo, 128.

Memoir of William E. Aytoun, D.C.L. By Sir Theodobi
Martin, K.C.B. With Portrait Post Svo. us.

BACH. On Musical Education and Vocal Culture. By Albert
B. Bach. Fourth Edition. Svo, 78. 6d.

The Principles of Singing. A Practical Guide for Vocalists
and Teachers. With Course of Vocal Exercises. Crown Svo, 68.

The Art of Singing. With Musical Exercises for Young
People. Crown Svo, 33.

The Art Ballad : Locwe and Schubert. With Music Illustrations. With a Portrait
of Loewe. Third Edition. Small 4to. 53.

BALLADS AND POEMS. By Members Of The Glasgow
Billad Club. Crown Svo, 78. 6d

BELLAIRS. The Transvaal War, 1880-81. Edited by Lady Bkl
Lairs. With a Frontispiece and Map. Svo, 158.
Gossips with Girls and Maidens, Betrothed and Free.
New Edition. Crown Svo, 38. 6il. Cloth, extra gilt edges, 38
BESANT. The Revolt of Man. By Walter Besant. Ninth
Edition. Crown Svo, 38. 6d.
Readings in Rabelais. Crown Svo, 73. 6d.
BEVER1DGE. Culrossand Tulliallan; or Perthshire on Forth. It? ,
History and Antiquities. With Elucidations of Scottish Life and Chancttr from the
Burgh and Kirk-Session Records of that District. By David Bkvkripqe. 2 vols. Svo,
with Illustrations, 428.
Between the Ochils and the Forth ; or, From Stirling
Bridge to Aberdour. Crown Svo, 6s.
BIRCH. Examples of Stables, Hunting-Boxes, Kennels, Racing
Establishments, &: By John Bihcii, Architect, Author of ' Country Architecture,'
' Picturesque Lodges,' &c. With ;o Plates. Royal Svo, 7.
Examples of Labourers' Cottages, &c. With Plans for Improving the Dwellings of
the Poor in Large Towns. With 34 Plates. Royal 6vo, 7.
BLACK. Heligoland and the Islands of the North Sea. By William Georoe Black.
Crown Svo, 48.
BLACKIE. Lays and Legends of Ancient Greece. By John Stuart Blackie, Emeritus
Professor of Oreek in the University of Edinburgh. Second Edition. Fcap. Svo. 5s.
The Wisdom of Goethe. Fcap. Svo. Cloth, extra gilt, 6s.
Scottish Song : Its Wealth, Wisdom, and Social Significance. Crown 8vo. With
Music. 78. 6d.
A Song of Heroes. Crown Svo, 6s.
BLACKWOOD'S MAGAZINE, from Commencement in 1817 to
July 1892. Nos. i to 921, forming 151 Volumes.
Index to Blackwood's Magazine. Vols. I to 50. Svo, 158.
BLACKWOOD. Tales from Blackwood. Price One Shilling each,
in Paper Cover. Sold separately at all Railway Bookstalls.
They may also bo had bound in cloth, i8s., and in half calf, richly gilt, 304.
Or 12 volumes in 6, roxburghe, 218., and half red morocco. 288.

Tales from Blackwood. New Series. Complete in Twenty- four Shilling Parts.
Handsomely bound in 12 vols., cloth, 308. Tn leather back, roxburghe style. 378.6d.
In half calf, ullt. 528.6d. In half morocco, 55
Tales from Blackwood. Third Series. Complete in 6
vols. Handsomely bound in cloth, 158. : or in 12 vols. i8s. Bound in roxburgne,
2is. Half calf, 25. Half morocco, 283. Also in 12 parts, price ia. each.
Travel, Adventure, and Sport. From ' Blackwood's
Magazine.' Uniform with "Tales from Blackwood.' In Twelve Paits,eart price Ts.
Or handsomely bound in 6 vols.. 158. Half calf, 25".
WILLIAM BLACKWOOD AND SONS.
BLACKWOOD. New Uniform Series of Three-and-Sixpenny Novels

(Copyright). Crown 8vo, cloth. Now ready :| Reata. By E. D.Gerard. Hurrish. By the Hon. Emily Lawless.

Beouah My Neighbour. By the Same.
The Waters Ok Hercules. By the Same.
Sons And Daughters. By Mrs Oliphant.
Fair To See. By L. W. M. Loekhart.
The Revolt Of Man. By Walter Besant.
Mine is Thine. By L. W. M. Locklmrt.
Altiora Peto. By Laurence Oliphnnt
Doubles And Quits. By L.W. M. Loekhart.
Lady Baby. By *D.* Gerard.

The Blacksmith Ok Voe. By Paul
Cashing.
The Dilemma. By the Author of 'The

Battle of Dorking.'
My Trivial Like And Misfortune. By

A Plain Woman.
Poor Nellie. By thc Same.
Piccadilly. By Laurence Oliphant. With
Illustrations.

Others in preparation.
Standard Novels. Uniform in size and legibly Printed.
Each Novel complete in one volume.
FLORIN SERIES, Illustrated Boards. Or in New Cloth Binding, 28. 6d. Tom Cringle's Loo. By Michael Scott, j Pen Owen. By Dean Hook. The Cruise Of The Midoe. By the Same. Adam Blair. By J. G. Loekhart. Cyril Thornton. By Captain Hamilton, j Lady Lee's Widowhood. By General Aknals Of The Parish. By John Gait. Sir E. B. Hamley. The Provost, &c. By John Gait. Salem Chapel. By Mrs Oliphant.

Hiu Andrew Wylik. By John Gait. j The Perpktoal Curate. By Mrs Oil- The Entail. By John Gait. pliant.

Miss Molly. By Beatrice May Butt. Miss Marjoribanks. By Mrs Oliphant.

Reginald Dalton. By J. G. Loekhart. John : A Love Story. By Mrs Oliphant.
SHILLING SERIES, Illustrated Cover. Or in New Cloth Binding, is. 64.

The Rector, and The Doctor's Family.
By Mrs Oliphant.
The Life Of Mansie Wauch. By D. M.

Sir Frizzle Pumpkin, Nights At Muse.

&c.

The Subaltern.

Moir. , Life In The Far West. By Q. F. Rnxton.

Peninsular Scenes Ant/sketches. By Valerius : A Roman Story. By J. G. F. Hardman.

Loekhart.

BLACKMORE. The Maid of Sker. By R. D. Blackmore, Author of'Lorna Doone,'&c. New Edition. Crown 8vo, 6s.

BLAIR. History of the Catholic Church of Scotland. From the Introduction of Christianity to the Present Day. By Alphons Bellesheim, D.D., Canon of Aix-la-Chapelle. Translated, with Notes and Additions, by D. Oswald Hunter Blair, O.S.B., Honk of Fort Augustus. Complete in 4 vols. demy 8vo, with Maps. Price 128. 6d. each.

BONN A R. Biographical Sketch of George Meilde Kemp, Architect of the Scott Monument. Edinburgh. By Thomas Bonnar, F.S.A. Scot., Author of ' The Present Art Revival,' 'The Past of Art in Scotland,' 'Suggestions for the Picturesque of Interiors,' &c. With Three Portraits and numerous Illustrations. Post 8vo, 73. 6d.

BOSCOBEL TRACTS. Relating to the Escape of Charles the Second after the Battle of Worcester, and his subsequent Adventures. Edited by J. Hughes, Esq., A.M. A New Edition, with additional Notes and Illustrations, including Communications from the Rev. R. H. Barham, Author oi the ' Ingoldsby Legends.' 8vo, with Engravings, i6s.

BROUGHAM. Memoirs of the Life and Times of Henry Lord Brougham. Written by Himself. 3 vols. Bvo, (,?, 8a. The Volumes are sold separately, price i6s. each.

BROWN. The Forester: A Practical Treatise on the Planting, Rearing, and General Management of Forest-trees. By James Brown, LL.D., Inspector of and Reporter on Woods and Forests. Fifth Edition, revised and enlarged. Royal 8vo, with Engravings, 363.

BROWN. A Manual of Botany, Anatomical and Physiological. For the Use of Students. By Robert Brown, M. A., Ph.D. Crown 8vo, with numerous Illustrations, las. 6d.

BRUCE. In Clover and Heather. Poems by Wallace Bruce. New and Enlarged Edition. Crown 8vo, 43. 6d. *A limited number of Copies ofTie Firtt Edition, on large hand-made paper,* 123. 6d.

BRYDALL. Art in Scotland ; its Origin and Progress. By Robert Brydall, Master of St George's Art School of Glasgow. 8vo, 128. 6d.

LIST OF BOOKS PUBLISHED BY

BUCHAN. Introductory Text-Book of Meteorology. By Alex-Ander Bucuan, M.A., F.R.S.E., Secretary of the Scottish Meteorological i Society, &c. Crown 8vo, with 8 Coloured Charts and Engravings, *a. 6d-*

BUCHANAN. The Shire Highlands (East Central Africa). By John Buchanan, Planter at Zomba. Crown 8vo, 58.

BURBIDOE. Dorriestic Floriculture, Window Gardening, and I Flopol Decorations. Being practical directions for the Propagation, Culture, and Arrangement of Plants and Flowers as Domestic Ornaments. By F. W. Burbidoe. Second Edition. Crown 8vo. with numerous Illustrations, 78. 6d. !

Cultivated Plants: Their Propagation and Improvement. ,i

Including Natural and Artificial Hybridisation, Raising from Seed, Cutting, and Layers, Grafting and Budding, as applied to the Families and Genera in Cultivation. Crown Svo. with numerous Illustrations ias 6d

BURTON. The History of Scotland : From Agricola's Invasion to I the Extinction of the last Jacobite Insurrection. By Jobs Hill Bchtoh D.C.L., Historiographer-Royal for Scotland. New and Enlarged Edition 8 vols., and Index. Crown 8vo, $3, 33.

History of the British Empire during the Reign of Queen I

Anne. In 3 voli. Svo. 368.

The Scot Abroad. Third Edition. Crown Svo, los. 6d.

The Book-Hunter. New Edition. With Portrait. Crown ‖

The Roman Breviary : Reformed by Order of the Holy cumenlcal Council of Trent; Published by Order of Pope 8t Pins V.; and

Svo, Ts. 6d.

BUTE.

QScun

Revised by Clement VIII. and Urban VIII.;" together with the Offices since granted. Translated out of Latin into English by Johh, Marquess of Bute K.T. In *t* vols. crown Svo, cloth boards, edges uncut *$2, is.*

The Altus of St Colnmba. With a Prose Paraphrase and '

Notes. In paper cover, 28. 6d.

BUTLER. Pompeii : Descriptive and Picturesque. By W. Butler. Post Svo, 58.

BUTT. Miss Molly. By Beatrice Mat Bott. Cheap Edition, 2.

Ingelheim. A Novel. 3 vols. crown Svo, 255. 6d.

Eugenie. Crown Svo, 6s. 6d.

Elizabeth, and Other Sketches. Crown Svo, 6s.

Novels. New and Uniform Edition. Crown Svo, each 2s. 6d. |

Delicia. *Now ready.* CAIRO. Sermons. By John Caird, D.D., Principal of the Uni-

I

verslty of Glasgow. Sixteenth Thousand. Fcap. 8vo, 58.

Religion in Common Life. A Sermon preached in Crathie

Church, October 14, 1855, before Her Majesty the Queen and Prince Albert Published by Her Majesty's Command. Cheap Edition, 3d.

CALDER. Chaucer's Canterbury Pilgrimage. Epitomised by

William Calder. With Photogravure of the Pilgrimage Company, and other Illustrations, Glossary, &c. Crown Svo, 43.

CAMPBELL. Critical Studies in St Luke's Gospel: Its Demonologv and Ebionitism. By Colin Camppkll, B D., Minister of the Parish of Dan- dee, formerly Scholar and Fellow of Glasgow University. Author of the ' Three First Gospels in Greek, arranged in parallel columns. Post Svo, 78. 6d.

CAMPBELL. Sermons Preached before the Queen at Balmoral.
By the Rev. A. A. Campbell, Minister of Crathie. Published by Command I of Her Majesty. Crown Svo. 48. 6d.

CAMPBELL. Records of Argyll. Legends, Traditions, and Recollections of Ar- gyllshire Highlanders, collected chiefly from the Gaelic With Notes on the Antiquity of the Dress, Clan Colours or Tartans of the i Highlanders. By Lord Archibald Camp- bell. Illustrated with Xineteet full-page Etchings. 4to, printed on hand-made paper, $3, 33.

CANTON. A Lost Epic, and other Poems. By William Canton. !
Crown 8vo, 5.
WILLIAM BLACKWOOD AND SONS.

CARRICK. Koumiss; or, Fermented Mare's Milk: and its Uses
in the Treatment and Cure of Pulmonary Consumption, and other Wasting Diseases. With an Appendix on the best Methods of Fermenting Cow's Milk. By Geohoe L. Carrick, M.D., L.R.C.S.E. and L.R.C.P.E., Physician to the British Embassy. St Petersburg, &o. Crown 8vo, Ids. 6d.

CARSTAIRS. British Work in India. By R. Carstairs. Or. 8vo, 6s.

OAUVIN. A Treasury of the English and German Languages. Compiled from the best Authors and Lexicographers in both Languages. By Joseph Cauvin, LL.D. and Ph.D., or the University of GBttlngen, &c. Crown 8vo. js. 6d.

CAVE-BROWN. Lambeth Palace and its Associations. By J. Cave-brown, H.A., Ticar of Detling, Kent, and (or many years Curate of Lambeth Parish Church. With an Introduction by the Archbishop of Canterbury. Second Edition, containing an additional Chapter on Medieval Life In the Old Palaces. Svo, with Illustrations, ais.

CHARTERIS. Canonicity; or, Early Testimonies to the Existence and Dae of the Books of the New Testament. Based on Kirchhoffer's ' Quel- lensammlung.' Edited by A. H. Chartkrib, D.D., Professor of Biblical Criticism in the University of Edinburgh. Svo, i8s.

CHRISTISON. Life of Sir Robert Christison, Bart., M.D., D.C.L.
Oxon., Professor of Medical Jurisprudence in the University of Edinburgh. Edited by his Sons. In two vols. Svo. Vol. I.lAutobiography. 6s. Vol.11.

Chronicles' Of Westerly: A Provincial sketch. By the
Author of ' Culmshirc Folk,' ' John Orlebar/ Ac. 3 vols. crown Svo, 250. 6d.

CHURCH SERVICE SOCIETY. A Book of Common Order : Being Forms of Worship issued by the Church Service Society. Sixth Edition. Crown, Svo, 6s. Also in a vols, crown Svo, 6s. 6d.

CLOUSTON. Popular Tales and Fictions : their Migrations and Transformations. By W. A. Clouston, Editor of ' Arabian Poetry for English Readers,' &c. 3 vols. post Svo, roxburghe binding, 258.

COCHRAN. A Handy Text-Book of Military Law. Compiled

chiefly to assist Officers preparing for Examination; also for all Officers of the Regular and Auxiliary Forces. Comprising also a Synopsis of part of the Army Act. By Major F. Cochran, Hampshire Regiment Garrison Instructor, North British District. Crown Svo. 78. 6d.

COLQUHOUN. The Moor and the Loch. Containing Minute
Instructions in all Highland Sports, with Wanderings over Crag and Corrle, Flood and Fell. By John Coujuhoux. Seventh Edition. With Illustrations. SVO, 318.

COTTERILL. Suggested Reforms in Public Schools. By C. C.
Cottkrill, M.A. Crown Svo, s. 6d.

CRANSTOUN. The Elegies of Albius Tibullus. Translated into
English Verse, with Life of the Poet, and Illustrative Notes. By James Cran-Stoun. LL.D.. Author of a Translation of Catullus.' Crown Svo, 6s. 6d.

The Elegies of Sextus Propertius. Translated into English
Verse, with Life of the Poet, and Illustrative Notes. Crown Svo. 78. 6d.

CRAWFORD. Saracinesca. By F. Marion Crawford, Author of
' Mr Isaacs," Dr Claudius,' Zoroaster,' &c. &c. Sixth Ed. Crown Svo, 6s.

CRAWFORD. The Doctrine of Holy Scripture respecting the Atonement. By the late Thomas J. Crawford, D.D., Professor of Divinity In the University of Edinburgh. Fifth Edition. Svo, us.

The Fatherhood of God, Considered in its General
and Special Aspects. Third Edition, Revised and Enlarged. Svo, 98.

The Preaching of the Cross, and other Sermons. 8vo, 73. 6d.

The Mysteries of Christianity. Crown Svo, 78. 6d.

CRAWFORD. An Atonement of East London, and other Poems.
By Howard Crawford, M.A. Crown Svo, s.

GUSHING. The Blacksmith of Voe. By Paul Gushing, Author
of ' The Bull i' th' Thorn.' Cheap Edition. Crown Svo, 38. 6d.

Cut with his own Diamond. A Novel. 3 vols. cr. Svo, 253. 6d.

LIST OF BOOKS PUBLISHED BY

D AVIES. Norfolk Broads and Rivers; or, The Waterways, Lagoons,
and Decoys of East Anglia. By G Christopher Davies. Illustrated with Seven full-page Plates. New and Cheaper Edition. Crown 8vo, 6s.

Our Home in Aveyron. Sketches of Peasant Life in
Aveyron and the Lot. By G. Christopher Davim and Mrs Brovouall. Illustrated with full-page Illustrations. 8vo, us. Cheap Edition, 75. 6d.

DAYNE. Tribute to Satan. A Novel. By J. Belford Dayne,
Author of' In the Name of the Tzar.' Crown 8vo, as. 6d.

DE LA WARR. An Eastern Cruise in the 'Edeline.' By the
Countess De La Warr. In Illustrated Cover. 28.

DESCARTES. The Method, Meditations, and Principles of Philosophy of Descartes. Translated from the Original French and Latin. With a New Introductory Essay, Historical and Critical, on the Cartesian Philosophy. By Professor Veitch, LL.D., Glasgow University. Ninth Edition. 6s. 6d.

DICKSON. Gleanings from Japan. By W. G. Dickson, Author
of ' Japan : Being a Sketch of Its History, Government, and Officers of the Empire.'
With Illustrations. 8vo, i6s.

DOGS, OUR DOMESTICATED : Their Treatment in reference
to Food, Diseases, Habits, Punishment. Accomplishments. By ' Maoenta.' Crown
8vo. as. 6d.

DOMESTIC EXPERIMENT, A. By the Author of'Ideala: A
Study from Life.' Crown 8vo, 6s.

DR HERMIONE. By the Author of 'Lady Bluebeard,' 'Zit and
Xoe.' Crown 8vo, 6s.

DU CANE. The Odyssey of Homer, Books I.-XII. Translated into
English Verse. By Sir (jic Aki.k.h Dc Cane, K.C.M.G. 8vo, .08. 6d.

DUDGEON. History of the Edinburgh or Queen's Regiment
Light Infantry Militia, now 3rd Battalion The Royal Scots; with an
Account of the Origin and Progress of the Militia, and a Brief Sketch of the
old Royal Scots. By Major R. C. Dddobon, Adjutant 3rd Battalion The Royal
Scots. Post 8vo, with Illustrations, ios. 6d.

DUNCAN. Manual of the General Acts of Parliament relating to the Salmon
Fisheries of Scotland from 1898 to 1889. By J. Barker Dckcas Crown 8vo, 58.

DUNSMORE. Manual of the Law of Scotland as to the Relations
between Agricultural Tenants and their Landlords, Servants, Merchants, and Bow-
ers. By W. Dunsmorc. 8vo, 78. 6d.

DUPRE. Thoughts on Art, and Autobiographical Memoirs of
Giovanni Dupre. Translated from the Italian by E. M. Peruzzi, with tbe permission
of the Author. New Edition. With an Introdnction by W. W. Story. Crown 8vo, tos.
6d.

ELIOT. George Eliot's Life, Related in her Letters and JournalB.
Arranged and Edited by her husband, J. W. Cross. With Portrait and other
Illustrations. Third Edition. 3 vols. post 8vo, 478.

George Eliot's Life. (Cabinet Edition.) With Portrait
and other Illustrations. 3 vols. crown 8vo, 158.
George Eliot's Life. With Portrait and other Illustration e.
New Edition, in one volume. Crown 8vo, 78. 6d.
Works of George Eliot (Cabinet Edition). Handsomely
printed In a new type, ai volumes, crown 8vo, price $5, 58. The Volumes are also
sold separately, price 58. each, viz. :I
Romola. a vols.ISilas Marner, The Lifted Veil, Brother Jacob, i vol.I Adam Bede.
9 vols.IScenes of Clerical Life. 9 vols.IThe Mill on the Flosa. 9 vols.IFelix Holt 9
vols.IMiddlemarch. 3 vols.IDaniel Deromla. 3 vols.IThe Spanish Gypsy, i vol.IJubal,
and other Poems, Old and New. i vol.ITheophrastus Such, i vol.IEssays, i vol.
Novels by George Eliot. Cheap Edition. Adam Bede. Illustrated. 3S.6d.,
cloth.IThe Mill on the Floss. Illustrated. 35. 6d., cloth. IScenes of Clericnl Life.
Illustrated. 38., cloth.ISilas Mamer: the Wearer of Raveloe. Illustrated, zs. 6d.,

cloth.|Felix Holt, the Radical. Illustrated. 35. 6d., cloth.|Romola. With Vignette. 35. 6d.. cloth. || Middlemarch. Crown 8vo. 7s. 6d.

WILLIAM BLACKWOOD AND SONS. 9

ELIOT. Daniel Deronda. Crown 8vo, ;s. 6d.

Essays. New Edition. Crown 8vo, 58.

Impressions of Theophrastus Such. New Ed. Cr. 8vo, 58.

The Spanish Gypsy. New Edition. Crown 8vo, 58.

The Legend ol Jubal, and other Poems, Old and New. New Edition. Crown 8vo, 58.

Wise, Witty, and Tender Sayings, in Prose and Verse, Selected from the Works of George Eliot. Eighth Edition. Fcap. 8vo, 6s.

The George Eliot Birthday Book. Printed on fine paper. with red border, and handsomely bound in cloth, gilt. Fcap. 8vo, cloth, 38. 6d. And in French morocco or Russia, 58.

ESSAYS ON SOCIAL SUBJECTS. Originally published in the ' Saturday Review.' New Ed. First & Second Series. 2 vols. cr. 8vo, 6s. each.

EWALD. The Crown and its Advisers ; or, Queen, Ministers, Lords and Commons. By Alexander Charles Ewald, F.S. A. CrownSvo.ss.

FAITHS OF THE WORLD, The. A Concise History of the Great Religious Systems of the World. By various Authors. CrownSvo.ss.

FARRER. A Tour in Greece in 1880. By Richard Ridley Farrer. With Twenty-seven full-page Illustrations by Lord Windsor. Royal 8vo, with a Hap, 218.

FERRIER. Philosophical Works of the late James F. Ferrier, B. A. Oxon., Professor of Moral Philosophy and Political Economy, St Andrews. New Edition. Edited by Sir Alex. Grant, Bart., D.C.L., and Professor Ldshinoton. *3* vols. crown 8vo, 348. 6d.

Institutes of Metaphysic. Third Edition. ios. 6d.

Lectures on the Early Greek Philosophy. 30! Ed. ios. 6d.

Philosophical Remains, including the Lectures on Early Greek Philosophy, a vols., 248.

FITZROY. Dogma and the Church of England. By A. I. FlTzRoY. Post 8vo, 78. 6d.

FLINT. The Philosophy of History in Europe. By Robert Flint, D.D., LL.D., Professor of Divinity, University of Edinburgh. 3 voln. 8vo. *[Hew' Edition in preparation.*

Theism. Being the Baird Lecture for 1876. Eighth Edition. Crown 8vo, 78. 6d.

Anti-Theistic Theories. Being the Baird Lecture for 1877. Fourth Edition. Crown 8vo, ios. 6d.

Agnosticism. Being the Croall Lectures for 1887-88. *[In the press.*

FORBES. Insulinde : Experiences of a Naturalist's Wife in the Eastern Archipelago. By Mrs H. O. Forbes. Crown 8vo, with a Map. 48. 6d.

FOREIGN CLASSICS FOR ENGLISH READERS. Edited
by Mrs Oliprant. Price as. 6d. *For Lift of Volumes published, tee page* a.
FOSTER. The Fallen City, and Other Poems. By Will Foster.
Crown 8vo, 6s.
FRANCILLON. Gods and Heroes ; or, The Kingdom of Jupiter.
By H. E. Frascillos. With 8 Illustrations. Crown 8vo. 58.
FULLARTON. Merlin : A Dramatic Poem. By Ralph Macleod
Fullarton. Crown 8vo, 58.
GALT. Novels by John Galt. Fcap. 8vo, boards, 2s.; cloth, 2s. 6d.
Annals of the Parish.|The Provost.|Sir Andrew Wylie.|
The Entail.
GENERAL ASSEMBLY OF THE CHURCH OF SCOTLAND.

Prayers for Social and Family Worship. Prepared by a
Special Committee of the General Assembly of the Church of Scotland. "Entirely
New Edition, Revised and Enlarged. Fcap. 8vo, red edges, 38.
Prayers for Family Worship. A Selection from the complete book. Fcap. 8vo, red
edgea. price is.
LIST OF BOOKS PUBLISHED BY
GENERAL ASSEMBLY OF THE CHURCH OF SCOTLAND.
Scottish Hymnal, with Appendix Incorporated. Pub- i
llshed for Use In Churches by Authority of the General Assembly, i. Large ' type,
cloth, red edges, zs. 6d.; French morocco, 48. . Bourgeois type, limp cloth, is.;
French morocco, 28. 3. Nonpareil type, cloth, red edges, 6d. ; French morocco, is.
4d. 4. Paper covers, 3d. 5. Sunday - Schoo. Edition, j paper covers, id. No. i, bound
with the Psalms and Paraphrases, French morocco, 8s. No. 2, bound with the Psalms
and Paraphrases, cloth, Ib. : French morocco, 38.
GERARD. Reata: What's in a Name. By E. D. Gerard. I
Cheap Edition. Crown 8vo, 38. 6d.
Beggar my Neighbour. Cheap Edition. Crown 8vo,38. 6d.
The Watersof Hercules. Cheap Edition. Crown 8vo, 33.6d. I
GERARD. The Land beyond the Forest. Facts, Figures, and
Fancies from Transylvania. By E.gerard. In Two Volumes. With Mmps and
Illustrations 255.
Bis : Some Tales Retold. Crown 8vo, 6s.
A Secret Mission. 2 vols. crownvo, 179.
GERARD. Lady Baby. By Dorothea Gerard. Cr. 8vo, 35. 6d.
Recha. Second Edition. Crown 8vo, 6s.
GERARD. Stonyhurst Latin Grammar. By Rev. John Gerard.
Second Edition, fcap. 8vo, 38.
GILL. Free Trade : an inquiry into the Nature of its Operation. By Richard Gill.
Crown 8vo, 78. 6d.
Free Trade under Protection. Crown 8vo, 78. 6d.

GOETHE'S FAUST. Translated into English Verse by Sir TheoDore Martin, K.C.B. Fart I. Second Edition, post 8vo. 6s. Ninth Edl- tion, fcap., 38. 6d. Part II. Second Edition, revised. Fcap. 8vo, 6s.

GOETHE. Poems and Ballads of Goethe. Translated by Professor Avtoun and Sir Throdore Martin, K.C.B. Third Edition, fcap. 8vo, 6.

GOODALL. Juxta Crucem. Studies of the Love that is over us. By the late Rev. Charles Goodall, B.D., Minister of Barr. With a Memoir by Rev. Dr Strong, Glasgow, and Portrait. Crown 8vo, 6a.

GORDON GUMMING. Two Happy Years in Ceylon. By C. F. Gordon Cummino. With 19 full-page Illustrations' and a'Map. Fourth Edition. 3 vols. 8vo, 303.

At Home in Fiji. Fourth Edition, post 8vo. With Illustrations and Map. 78. 6d.

A Lady's Cruise in a French Man-of-War. New and Cheaper Edition. 8vo. With Illustrations and Map. tas. fid.

Fire-Fountains. The Kingdom of Hawaii: Its Volcanoes, and the History of its Missions. With Map and Illustrations, a vols.Svo.ass. Wanderings in China. New and Cheaper Edition. 8vo, with Illustrations, Ids.

Granite Crags: The Yo-semitd Region of California. Illustrated with 8 Engravings. New and Cheaper Edition. 8vo, So. 6d

GRAHAM. The Life and Work of Syed Ahmed Khan, C.S.I. By Lieut.-Colonel G. F. I. Graham, B.8.C. 8vo, 148

GRAHAM. Manual of the Elections (Scot.) (Corrupt and Illegal Practices) Act, issio. With Analysis, Relative Act of Sederunt, Appendix containing the Corrupt Practices Acts of 1883 and 1885, and Copious Index. By J. Edward Graham, Advocate. 8vo, 48. 6d.

GRANT. Bush-Life in Queensland. By A. C. Grant. New Edition. Crown 8vo. 6s.

GUTHRIE-SMITH. Crispus : A Drama. By H. Guthrie-smith. In one volume. Fcap. 4to, 58.

HAINES. Unless ! A Romance. By Randolph Haixes. Cro-vm 8vo, 6fl.

HALDANE. Subtropical Cultivations and Climates. A Handy Book for Planters. Colonists. and Settlers. By R. C. Haldane. PostBvo, cji. WILLIAM BLACKWOOD AND SONS.

HALLETT. A Thousand Miles on an Elephant in the Shan States. By Holt 8. Hallett, M. Inst. C.E., F. B.O.S., M.R.A.S., Hon. Member Man- cheater and Tyneside Geographical Societies, bvo, with Maps and numerous Illustrations, 213.

HAMERTON. Wenderholme : A Story of Lancashire and Yorkshire Life. By Philip Gilbert Hamerton, Author of 'A Painter's Camp.' A New Edition. Crown 8vo, 6s.

HAMILTON. Lectures on Metaphysics. By Sir William HamilTon, Bart, Professor of Logic and Metaphysics in the University of Edinburgh. Edited by the Rev. H. L. Mansel, B.D., LL.D., Dean of St Paul's ; and Joan Veitch, M.A., LL.D., Professor of Logic and Rhetoric, Glasgow. Seventh Edition. a vol. 8vo, 941.

Lectures on Logic. Edited by the Same. Third Edition.

i vols., 248.

Discussions on Philosophy and Literature, Education and
University Reform. Third Edition, 8vo, ais.

Memoir of Sir William Hamilton, Bart., Professor of Logic
and Metaphysics in the University of Edinburgh. By Professor Veitch, of the
University of Glasgow. 8vo, with Portrait, i8s.

III Sir William Hamilton : The Man and his Philosophy. Two Lectures delivered
before the Edinburgh Philosophical Institution, January and February 1883. By the
Same. Crown 8vo, as.

HAMLEY. The Operations of War Explained and Illustrated. By General Sir
Edward Brcce Hamley, K.C.B., K.C.M.G.,M.P. Fifth Edition, revised throughout.
4to, with numerous Illustrations, 308.

National Defence ; Articles and Speeches. Post 8vo, 6s.

Shakespeare's Funeral, and other Papers. Post 8vo, ;s. 6d.

Thomas Carlyle : An Essay. Second Ed. Cr. gvo, *2s.* 6d.

On Outposts. Second Edition. 8vo, zs.

Wellington's Career ; A Military and Political Summary.
Crown 8vo, as.

Lady Lee's Widowhood. Crown 8vo, 26. 6d.

Our Poor Relations. A Philozoic Essay. With Illustrations, chiefly by Ernest Griset
Crown 8vo. cloth gilt, 38. 6d.

HAMLEY. Guilty, or Not Guilty ? A Tale. By Major-General W. G. Hamlet, late
of the Royal Engineers. New Edition. Crown 8vo, 38. 6d.

HARRISON. The Scot in Ulster. The Story of the Scottish
Settlement In Ulster. By John Harbison, Author.of ' Oure Tonnis Col- ledge.'
Crown 8vo, 28. 6d.

HASELL. Bible Partings. By E. J. Hasell. Crown 8vo, 6s.

Short Family Prayers. Cloth, is.

HAY. The Works of the Right Rev. Dr George Hay, Bishop of
Edinburgh. Edited under the Supervision of the Right Rev. Bishop Strain.
With Memoir and Portrait of the Author. 5 vols. crown 8vo, bound In extra
cloth, $i, is. The following Volumes may be had separately|viz.: The Devout
Christian Instructed in the Law of Christ from the Written Word, *a* vols., 8.|The Pious
Christian Instructed in the Nature and Practice of the Principal Exercises of Piety, i
vol.. 38. HEATLEY. The Horse-Owner's Safeguard. A Handy Medical
Guide for every Man who owns a Horse. By G. S. Heatlet, M.R.C.V.8.
Crown 8vo, 58.

The Stock-Owner's Guide. A Handy Medical Treatise for
every Man who owns an Ox or a Cow. Crown 8vo, 48. 6d.

HEDDERWICK. Lays of Middle Age ; and other Poems. By James Hedderwick,
LL.D. Price s. 6d.

Backward Glances; or, Some Personal Recollections.
With a Portrait. Post 8vo, 75. 6d.

HEMANS. The Poetical Works of Mrs Hemans. Copyright Editions.l Royal 8vo, js.lWith Engravings, gilt edges, 78. 6d.lSix Vols. in Three, fcap., ias. 6d.
Select Poems. Fcap.. !.. irilt edges, j.

12 LIST OF BOOKS PUBLISHED BY
HERKLESS. Cardinal Beaton : Priest and Politician. By John
Herkless, Minister of Tannadice. With a Portrait. *Post* Svo, 78. 6d. HOME
PRAYERS. By Ministers of the Church of Scotland and
Members of the Church Service Society. Second Edition. Fcap. 8vo, 38. HOMER.
The Odyssey. Translated into English Verse in the
Spenserian Stanza. By Philip Stanhope Wimsi.pv. Third Edition, *i* vol.-.
fcap., las.
The Iliad. Translated by P. S. Worslet and Professor
Conington. 2 vols. crown 8vo, 218.
HUTCHINSON. Hints on the Game of Golf. By Horace G.
Hutchihsoh. Seventh Edition, Enlarged. Fcap. Svo, cloth, is.
IDDESLEIGH. Lectures and Essays. By the late Earl Op
IDDF.8LEIOH, G.C.B., D.C.L , &C. 8VO, 168.
Life, Letters, and Diaries of Sir Stafford Northcote, First
Earl of Iddesleigh. By Andrew La No. With Three Portraits and a View of
Pynes. Third Edition, z vols. Post Svo. 313. 6d.
Popular Edition. In one volume. With two Plates. Post Svo, 73. 6d.

[NDEX GEOGRAPHICUS : Being a List, alphabetically arranged, of the Principal Places on the Globe, with the Countries and Subdivisions of the Countries in which they are situated, and their Latitudes and Longitudes. Imperial Svo, pp. 676, 2TS.

JEAN J AMBON. Our Trip to Blunderland ; or, Grand Excursion to Bluiidertown and Back. By Jean Jamboh. With Sixty Illustrations designed by Charles Doyle, engraved by Dalziel. Fourth Thousand. Cloth, giltedges, 6s. 6d. Cheap Edition, cloth, 38. 6d. Boards, is. 6d.

JENNINGS. Mr Gladstone : A Study. By Louis J. Jennings,
M.P., Author of 'Republican Government in the United States,' "The Croker Memoirs,'&c. Popular Edition. Crown Svo, is.

JERNINGHAM. Reminiscences of an Attache". By Hubert
E. H. Jerninqham. Second Edition. Crown Svo, js.
Diane de Breteuille. A Love Story. Crown Svo, 28. 6d.
JOHNSTON. The Chemistry of Common Life. By Professor
J. F. W. Johnston. New Edition, Revised, and brought down to date. By
Ahthcr Hkkbkrt Chdrch, M,A. Oxon.; Author ot 'Food: Its Sources,
Constituents, and Uses,' Ac. With Maps and 102 Engravings. Cr. Svo, 73.6d.

Elements of Agricultural Chemistry and Geology. An

entirely new Edition from the Edition by Sir C. A. Cameron. M.D.. F.R.C.S.I., &c. Revised and brought do'wn to date by C. M. Aikmin, M.A., H.Sc , F.U.S.E , Lecturer on Agricultural Chemistry, West of Scotland Technical College. Fcap. Svo. *[In preparation.*

Catechism of Agricultural Chemistry and Geology. An

entirely new Edition from the Edition bv Sir C. A. Cameron. Rcvisl and Enlarged by C. M. Aikman, M. A. *[In preparation.*

JOHNSTON. Patrick Hamilton : a Tragedy of the Reformation

in Scotland, 1528. By T. P. Johnston. Crown Svo, with Two Etchings. 58,

KEBBEL. The Old and the New : English Country Life. By T. E Kkbbel, M A , Author of 'Agricultural Labourers,' 'Essays in History and Politics,' 'Life of Lord Beaconslield.' Crown Svo, 53.

KING. The Metamorphoses of Ovid. Translated in English Blank Verse. By Henry Kino, M.A., Fellow of Wadham College, Oxford, and of the Inner Temple, Barrister-at-Law. Crown Svo, ios. 6d.

KtNGLAKE. History of the Invasion of the Crimea. By A. W.

Kinolake. Cabinet Edition, revised. With an Index to the Complete Work. Illustrated with Maps and Plans. Complete in ., Vols., crown Svo, at 6s. each.

History of the Invasion of the Crimea. Demy Svo.

Vol. VI. Winter Troubles. With a Map, i6s. Vol. VII. and VIII. From the Morrow of Inkerman to the Death of Lord Rnglnn. With an Index to the Whole Work. With Maps and Plans. 28s.

Eothen. A New Edition, uniform with the Cabinet Edition

of the ' History of the Invasion of the Crimea,' price 6a.

WILLIAM BLACKWOOD AND SONS.

KNEIPP. My Water-Cure. As Tested through more than Thirty Years, and De-scribed for the Healing of Diseases and the Preservation of Health. By Sebastian Kneipp, Pariah Priest of Worishofen (Bavaria). With a Portrait and other Illustrations. Authorised English Translation from the Thirtieth German Edition, by A. de K. Crown 8vo, 58.

KNOLLYS. The Elements of Field-Artillery. Designed for the Use of Infantry and Cavalry Officers. By Henry Knollys, Captain Royal Artillery; Author of ' From Sedan to SnarlirUck,' Editor of ' Incidents In the Sepoy War,' &c. With Engravings. Crown 8vo, 78. 6d.

LAMINGTON. In the Days of the Dandies. By the late Lord Laminoton. Crown 8vo. Illustrated cover, is.; cloth, is. 6d.

LAWLESS. Hurrish : a Study. By the Hon. Emily Lawless,

Author of 'A Chelsea Householder,' &e. Fourth Edition, crown 8vo, 38. 6d.

LAWSON. Spain of To-day : A Descriptive, Industrial, and Financial Survey of the Peninsula, with a full account of the Rio Tinto Mines. By W. R. Lawson. Crown 8vo, 38 6d.

LEES. A Handbook of the Sheriff and Justice of Peace Small Debt Courts. Bvo, 78. 6d.

LIGHTFOOT. Studies in Philosophy. By the Rev. J. Liqhtfoot,

M.A., D.Sc., Vicar of Cross Stone, Todmorden. Crown 8vo, 48. 6d. LINDSAY. The Progressiveness of Modern Christian Thought.

By Jamcs Lindsav, M A.. B.D., B.Sc., F.R S.E., F.G S. Crown 8vo, 6s. LLOYD. Ireland under the Land League. A Narrative of Personal

Experiences. By Clifford LLovn, Special Resident Magistrate. PostSvo, *6s.*

LOCKHART. Novels by Laurence W. M. Lockhart. *See* Blackwoods' New Series of Three-and-Sixpenny Novels on page 5.

LORIMER. The Institutes of Law : A Treatise of the Principles of Jurisprudence as determined by Nature. By the late James Lorimer, Professor of Public Law and of the Law of Nature and Nations in the University of Edinburgh. New Edition, revised and much enlarged. 8vo, iSs.

The Institutes of the Law of Nations. A Treatise of the Jural Relation of Separate Political Communities. In vols. 8vo. Volume I., price i6s. Volume II., price 208.

LOVE. Scottish Church Music. Its Composers and Sources. With Musical Illustrations. By James Love. Post 8vo, 78. 6d.

M'COMBIE. Cattle and Cattle-Breeders. By William M'CoMBIE, Tillyfour. New Edition, enlarged, with Memoir of the Author. By James Macdonald, of the ' Fanning World.' Crown 8vo, 38. 6d.

MACRAE. A Handbook of Deer-Stalking. By Alexander Macrae, late Forester to Lord Henry Bentinck. With Introduction by Horatio Ross, Esq. Fcap. 8vo, with two Photographs from Life. 38. 6d.

M'CRIE. Works of the Rev. Thomas M'Crie, D.D. Uniform Edition. Fonr vols. crown 8vo, 348.

Life of John Knox. Containing Illustrations of the History of the Reformation in Scotland. Crown 8vo. 6s. Another Edition, 38. 6d.

|| Life of Andrew Melville. Containing Illustrations of the Ecclesiastical and Literary History of Scotland in the Sixteenth and Seventeenth Centnrien. Crown 8vo. 6s.

History of the Progress and Suppression of the Reformation in Italy In the Sixteenth Century. Crown 8vo, 48.

History of the Progress and Suppression of the Reforma tion In Spain in the Sixteenth Century. Crown 8vo. 38. Oil.

Lectures on the Book of Esther. Fcap. 8vo, 58.

MACDONALD. A Manual of the Criminal Law (Scotland) Procedure Act, 1887. By Norman Doran Macdonald. Revised by the Lord Justice-clerk. 8vo, cloth, ios. fid.

MACGREGOR. Life and Opinions of Major-General Sir Charles MacOregor, K.C.B., C.S.I., C.I.E , Quartermaster-General of India. From his Letters and Diaries. Edited by Lady Mac-grkoor, With Portraits and Maps to Illustrate Campaigns in which he was engaged, *i* vols. 8vo, 35.1.

LIST OF BOOKS PUBLISHED BY

M'INTOSH. The Book of the Garden. By Charles M'INTOSB,
formerly Curator of the Royal Gardens of his Majesty the King of the Belgians,
and lately of those of his Grace the Duke of Buccleuch, K.O., at Dalkeith Palace. 2
vols. royal 8vo, with 1350 Engravings. $4, 78, fid. Vol. 1. On the Formation of
Gardens and Construction of Garden Edinces. j$a, xos. Vol. II. Practical Gardening.
$1, 178. 6d.

MACINTYRE. Hindu-Koh: Wanderings and Wild Sports on and beyond the Hi-
malayas. By Major-General Donald Macintyre, Y.C., latr Prince of Wales' Own
Goorkhas. F.R.G.S. *Dedicated to H.R.H. Tlu Prince oj Wulti.* New and Cheaper
Edition, revised, with numerous Illustrations, post 8vo, 78. 6d.

MAC KAY. A Sketch of the History of Fife and Kinross. A
Study of Scottish History and Character. By *$.. 3.* G. Mackay, Sheriff ol these
Counties. Crown Svo, 6s.

MACKAY. A Manual of Modern Geography; Mathematical, Physical, and Political.
By the Rev. Alexander Mackat, LL.D., P.R.G.8. ntb Thousand, revised to the present
time. Crown Svo, pp. 688. 78. 6d.

Elements of Modern Geography. 551!! Thousand, revised to the present time.
Crown Svo, pp. 300, 35.

The Intermediate Geography. Intended as an Intermediate
Book between the Author's ' Outlines of Geography' and ' Elements of Geography.'
Seventeenth Edition, revised. Crown Svo. pp. 238. 21.

Outlines of Modern Geography. i88th Thousand, revised
to the present time. iSmo, pp. 118, is.

First Steps in Geography. ic5th Thousand. i8mo, pp.
56. Sewed, d.; cloth, 6d.

Elements of Physiography and Physical Geography.
With Express Reference to the Instructions issued by the Science and Art
Department, soth Thousand, revised. Crown Svo, is. 6d.

Facts and Dates ; or, the Leading Events in Sacred and
Profane History, and the Principal Facts In the various Physical Sciences.
For Schools and Private Reference. New Edition. Crown Svo, 38. 6d.

M AC KAY. An Old Scots Brigade. Being the History of Mackay't
Regiment, now incorporated with the Royal Scots. With an Appendix containing
many Original Documents connected with the History of the Regiment. By John
Mackay (late) or Herriesdale. Crown Svo, 58. MACKENZIE. Studies in Roman Law.
With Comparative Views of the Laws of France, England, and Scotland. By Lord
Mackenzie, one of the Judges of the Court of Session in Scotland. Sixth Edition,
Edited by John KiiiKi'ATiticK, Esq.. M.A., LL.B., Advocate, Professor of History In
the University of Edinburgh. Svo, latt.

M'KERLIE. Galloway : Ancient and Modern. An Account of the
Historic Celtic District. By P. H. M'KERLIE, F.8.A. Scot., F.R.G.S., 4c.
Author of ' Lands and their Owners ill Galloway.' Crown 8vo, 75. *6i.*

M'PHERSON. Golf and Golfers. Past and Present. By J. Q.
M'piikrson, Ph.D., &c. With an Introduction by the Right Hon. A. J.
Balfour, and a Portrait of the Author. Fcap. Svo, m. 6d.

MAIN. Three Hundred English Sonnets. Chosen and Edited bv David M. Mais.
Fcap. Svo, 6s.

V. A I K . A Digest of Laws and Decisions, Ecclesiastical and Civil. relating to the
Constitution, Practice, and Affairs of the Church of Scotland With Notei and Forms
of Procedure. By the Rev. William Mair, D.D , Minister of the Parish of Earlston.
Crown Svo. With Supplements, 8s.

MARMORNE. The Story is told by Adolphdb Segrave, the
youngest of three Brothers. Third Edition. Crown Svo, 6s.

MARSHALL. French Home Life. By Frederic Marshall,
Author of ' Claire Brandon.' Second Edition. 58.

It Happened Yesterday. A Novel. Crown Svo, 6s.

M.ARSHMAN. History of India. From the Earliest Period to the Close of the India
Company's Government; with an Epitome of Subsequent Events. By John Clark
Marshiiam, C.S.I. Abridged from the Ant nor arger work. Second Edition, revised.
Crown Svo. with Map, 6s. 6d.

WILLIAM BLACKWOOD AND SONS.

MARTIN. Goethe's Faust. Parti. Translated by Sir Theodoke
Martin, K.C.B. Second Ed., crown 8vo, 6s. Ninth Ed., fcap. 8vo, 38. 6d.

Goethe's Faust. Part II. Translated into English Verse.
Second Edition, revised. Fcap. 8vo, 6s.

The Works of Horace. Translated into English Verse,
with Life and Notes, z vols. New Edition, crown 8vo, Jib.

Poems and Ballads of Heinrich Heine. Done into English Verse. Second Edition.
Printed on *papier vergl,* crown 8vo, 8s. || The Song of the Bell, and other Translations
from Schiller, Goethe, Uhland, and Others. Crown Svo, *js.* 6d.

Catullus. With Life and Notes. Second Ed., post 8vo, 78.6d.

Aladdin : A Dramatic Poem. By Adam Oehlenschlae-
Oer. Fcap. Smi, 5S.

Correggio : A Tragedy. By Oehlenschlaeger. With
Notes. Fcap. Svo, 31.

King Rene's Daughter: A Danish Lyrical Drama. By
Hknrik Hertz. Second Edition, fcap., as. 6d.

MARTIN. On some of Shakespeare's Female Characters. In a Series of Letters. By
Helena Fadcit, Lady Martin. Dedicated by permission to Her Most Gracious Majesty
the Queen. New Edition, enlarged. Svo, with Portrait by Lane, 78. 6d.

MATHESON. Can the Old Faith Live with the New ? or the Problem of Evolution
and Revelation. By the Rev. Georoe Matheson, D.I). Third Edition. Crown Svo, 78.
6d.

The Psalmist and the Scientist; or, Modern Value of the
Religious Sentiment. New and Cheaper Edition. Crown Svo, 58.

Spiritual Development ol'St Paul. 3d Edition. Cr. 8vo, 53.

Sacred Songs. New and Cheaper Edition. Cr. Svo, 2s. 6d.

MAURICE. The Balance of Military Power in Europe. An Examination of the War Resources of Great Britain and the Continental States. By Colonel Maurice, R. A., Professor of Military Art and History at the Royal Staff College. Crown Svo. with a Map. 6s.

MAXWELL. Meridiana : Noontide Essays. By Sir Herbert E.

Maxwell, Bart., M.P., F.S.A., &c., Author "of 'Passages in the Life of Sir Lucian Elphin,' &c. Post Svo, 73. 6d.

MEREDYTH. The Brief for the Government, 1886-92. A Handbook for Conservative and Unionist Writers, Speakers, &c. Second Edition. By W. H. Meredyth. Crown Svo, 28. 6d.

MICHEL. A Critical Inquiry into the Scottish Language. With the view of Illustrating the Rise and Progress of Civilisation in Scotland. By Francisque-michel, F.8. A. Lond. and Scot., Correspondant de l'Institut de France, &c. to. printed on hand-made paper, and bound in Roxburghe, 66s.

MICHIE. The Larch : Being a Practical Treatise on its Culture and General Management. By Christopher Y. Michie, Forester,Cullen House. Crown Svo, with Illustrations. New and Cheaper Edition, enlarged, 53.

The Practice of Forestry. Cr. Svo, with Illustrations. 6s.

MIDDLETON. The Story of Alastair Bhan Comyn ; or, The Tragedy of Dnnphail. A Tale of Tradition and Romance. By the Lady Middlkton. Square Svo Ids. Cheaper Edition, 58.

MILLER. Landscape Geology. A Plea for the Study of Geology by Landscape Painters. By Hugh Miller, of H.M. Geological Survey. Cr.Svo, 38. Cheap Edition, paper cover, is.

MILNE-HOME. Mamma's Black Nurse Stories. West Indian Folk-lore. By Mary Pamela Milne-home. With six full-page tinted Illustrations. Small 4to, 58.

MINTO. A Manual of English Prose Literature, Biographical and Critical: designed mainly to show Characteristics of Style. By W. Minto M.A., Professor of Logic in the University of Aberdeen. Third Edition, revised. Crown Svo, 78. 6d.

16 LIST OF BOOKS PUBLISHED BY

MINTO. Characteristics of English Poets, from Chaucer to Shirley. New Edition.revised. Crown 8vo, 78. 6d. I,

MOIR. Lifa of Mansie Wauch, Tailor in Dalkeith. By D. M. Il Moir. With 8 Illustrations on Steel, by the late Geokoi Cbdikbbakk. Crown 8vo, 3. 6d. Another Edition, fcap. 8vo, is. 6d.

MOMERIE. Defects of Modern Christianity, and other Sermon. I By Alfred Williams Momerie, M.A., D.Sc., LL.D. 4th Edition. Cr.Svo.s. il

The Basis of Religion. Being an Examination of Natural Religion. Third Edition. Crown 8vo, as. 6d.

The Origin of Evil, and other Sermons. Seventh Edition, enlarged. Crown 8vo, 55.

Personality. The Beginning and End of Metaphysics, and :
a Necessary Assumption in all Positive Philosophy. Fourth Ed. Cr. 8vo, 3. ||
Agnosticism. Fourth Edition, Revised. Crown 8vo, 53.
Preaching and Hearing ; and other Sermons. Third ||
Edition, Enlarged. Crown 8vo, 58.
Belief in God. Third Edition. Crown 8vo, 38.
Inspiration; and other Sermons. Second Ed. Cr. Svo, 58. M
Church and Creed. Second Edition. Crown Svo, 48. 6d.
MONTAGUE. Campaigning in South Africa. Reminiscences of II
an Officer in 1879. By Captain W. E. Montague, 94th Regiment, Author of ' '
Claude Meadowleigh,' &c. Svo, Ids. 6d.
MONT ALEM BERT. Memoir of Count de Montalembert. A 11
Chapter of Recent French History. By Mrs Oliphakt, Author of the 'Lift of Edward
Irviug,' &c. a vols. crown Svo, $1, 48.
MORISON. Bordello. An Outline Analysis of Mr Browning's ,, Poem. By Jeaxie
Mobison, Author of 'The Purpose of the Ages,' 'Ane Booke of Ballades,' &c. Crown
Svo, 38.
Selections from Poems. Crown Svo, 43. 6d.
There as Here. Crown Svo, 38.
% A limited impression on handmade paper, bound in vellum. 78. 6d.
. "Of Fitine at the Fair," "Christmas Eve and Easter Day,"
and other of Mr Browning's Poems. Crown Svo, 38. MOZLEY. Essays from '
Blackwood.' By the late Anne Mozlet, ,
Author of ' Essays on Social Subjects'; Editor of ' The Letters and Correspond- '
ence of Cardinal Newman,' 'Letters of the Rev. J. B. Mozley,' &e. Vilh a ,i Memoir
by her Sister, Fanny Mozley. Post 8vo,7S. 6d.
MUNRO. On Valuation of Property. By William Mdnro, M.A.,
Her Majesty's Assessor of Railways and Canals for Scotland. Second Edition.
Revised and enlarged. Svo, 38. 6d.

MURDOCH. Manual of the Law of Insolvency and Bankruptcy :
Comprehending a Summary of the Law of Insolvency, Notour Bankruptcy, Com-
position - contracts, Trust-deeds, Cessios, and Sequestrations: and th e Winding-up
of Joint-Stock Companies in Scotland ; with Annotations on th various Insolvency
and Bankruptcy Statutes; and with Forms of Procedure applicable to these Subjects.
By James Murdoch, Member of the Faculty of Procurators in Glasgow. Fifth Edition,
Revised and Enlarged, Svo, $i. ios
MY TRIVIAL LIFE AND MISFORTUNE : A Gossip with
no Plot in Particular. By A Plain Woman. Cheap Ed., crown Svo, 3. 6d.
By the Same Author.
POOR NELLIE. Cheap Edition. Crown 8vo, 35. 6d.

NAPIER. The Construction of the Wonderful Canon of Logar-
ithms. By John Napier of Merchiston. Translated, with Notes, and a
Catalogue of Napier's Works, by William Rae Macdonalp. Small 4to, 158.
A few large-paper copies on Whatman paper, 308.

NEAVES. Songs and Verses, Social and Scientific. By an Old
Contributor to 'Maga.' By the Hon. Lord Neaves. Fifth Ed., fcap. Svo 4.
The Greek Anthology. Being Vol. XX. of 'Ancient
Classics for English Readers.' Crown Svo, *is.* (A.
WILLIAM BLACKWOOD AND SONS. 17
NICHOLSON. A Manual of Zoology, for the Use of Students.
With a General Introduction on the Principles of Zoology. By Henry Al-
l.kvxk Nicholson, M.D., D.Sc., F.L.S., F.G.S., Regius Professor of Natural
History In the University of Aberdeen. Seventh Edition, rewritten and
enlarged. Post 8vo, pp. 956, with 555 Engravings on Wood, i8s.

Text-Book of Zoology, for the Use of Schools. Fourth Edition, enlarged. Crown
8vo. with 188 Engravings on Wond, 78. 6d.
Introductory Text-Book of Zoology, for the Use of Junioi
Classes. Sixth Edition, revised and enlarged, with 166 Engravings, Ik.
Outlines of Natural History, for Beginners ; being Descriptions of a Progressive
Series of Zoological Types. Third Edition, with Engravings, is. fid.
A Manual of Palaeontology, for the Use of Students.
With a General Introduction on the Principles of Paleontology. By Professor H.
Alleyne Nicholson and Richard Lydekker, B.A. Third Edition. Rewritten and greatly
enlarged 2 vols. 8vo, with Engravings,*$3,* 35.
The Ancient Life-History of the Earth. An Outline of
che Principles and Leading Facts of Paleeontological Science. Crown 8vo, with
276 Engravings, ics. 6d.
On the "Tabulate Corals "of the Palaeozoic Period, with
Critical Descriptions of Illustrative Species. Illustrated with 15 Lithograph Plates
and numerous Engravings. Super-royal Svo.zis.
Synopsis of the Classification of the Animal Kingdom. Svo, with 106 Illustrations,
6s.
On the Structure and Affinities of the Genus Monticuli-
pora and its Sub-Genera, with Critical Descriptions of Illustrative Species. Illustrated with numerous Engravings on wood and lithographed Plntcs. Super-royal 8vo,
i8s.
NICHOLSON. Communion with Heaven, and other Sermons.
By the late Maxwell Nicholson. D.D. Crown 8vo, 55. fid. || Rest in Jesus. Sixth
Edition. Fcap. 8vo, 48. 6d. NICHOLSON. A Treatise on Money, and Essays on
Present
Monetary Problems. By Joseph Shield Nicholson, *It.* A., D.Sc., Professor of Commercial and Political Economy and Mercantile Law in the University of Edinburgh.
8vo, 108. 6d.

. Thoth. A Romance. Third Edition. Crown 8vo, *4.8.* 6d.

A Dreamer of Dreams. A Modern Romance. Second
Edition. Crown 8Vo, 6s.

NICOLSON And MURE. A Handbook to the Local Government (Scotland) Act,
1889. With Introduction, Explanatory Notes, and Index. By J. Badenacii Nicolson,
Advocate, Counsel to the Scotch Education Department, and W. J. Mure, Advocate,
Legal Secretary to the Lord Advocate for Scotland. Ninth Reprint. 8vo, is.

OLIPHANT. Masollam : a Problem of the Period. A Novel.

By Lawrence Oliphant. 3 vols. post 8vo, 253. 6d Scientific Religion ; or, Higher
Possibilities of Life and

Practice through the Operation of Natural Forces. Second Edition. 8vo, t6s.

Altiora Peto. Cheap Edition. Crown 8vo, boards, 2s. 6d.;

cloth, 38. 6d. Illustrated Edition. Crown Svo. cloth, 6s.

Piccadilly. With Illustrations by Richard Doyle. New

Edition. 33. 6d. Cheap Edition, boards. 28. fid.

Episodes in a Life of Adventure ; or, Moss from a Rolling

Stone. Fifth Edition. Post Svo. 6s.

Haifa : Life in Modern Palestine. 2d Edition. Svo, 73. 6d.

The Land of Qilead. With Excursions in the Lebanon.

With Illustrations and Maps. Demy Svo, 21?

Memoir of the Life of Laurence Oliphant, and of Alice

Oliphant, hia Wife. By Mrs M. O. W. Oliphant. Seventh Edition. In 2 vols. post
Svo, with Portraits, am.

Popular Edition. With a New Preface. Post Bvo. With Portraits, *75.* 6d.

Lightning Source UK Ltd.
Milton Keynes UK
17 May 2010

154288UK00003B/19/P